D0868343

STAINS ON MY NAME,
WAR IN MY VEINS

STAINS ON MY NAME, WAR IN MY VEINS

Guyana and the Politics of Cultural Struggle

BRACKETTE F. WILLIAMS

DUKE UNIVERSITY PRESS

Durham and London 1991

© 1991 Duke University Press
All rights reserved
Printed in the United States of America
on acid-free paper ∞
Library of Congress Cataloging-in-Publication Data
appear on the last page of this book.

To my mother,
Learoa Williams, and
to the memory of my father,
Jodie Williams

Contents

II *Ideology, Ethnicity, and Anglo-European Hegemony*

III *Ethnicity, Class, and Cultural Production*

List of Tables
and Figures

Tables

Figures

Preface

In 1980, when last I saw the Guyanese whose everyday struggles provide the ethnographic grounding for this analysis of processes of cultural production in the intersection of territorial and cultural nationalism, they were nation building. They were attempting to get their categories in order, their hyphens in place. For all of them, as for all of us, it is a full-time job that must be done in spare time. For them, as for some of us, the difficulties involved in getting the job done are made more painful and costly by the criteria against which success and failure are evaluated. For all the Guyanese the pains, the costs, and the benefits, I shall argue, must be understood as consequences of their efforts to produce a culture and a nation within the constraints and against the grain of the particular form of Anglo-European hegemonic dominance that developed during the colonial era.

As part of their nation-building task, they are trying to relate the past to the present in order to decide how best to mete out material and moral justice in the future. In this undertaking at times they continue to compete with the metropole by upholding "British" standards. Through this process they not only construct themselves as citizens of a new state seeking a place in the international order of nation-states, they also construct themselves variously as members of races, classes, and ethnic groups. Their membership in these subnational, culturally constituted categories differentially links them to a series of what I will argue are disjunctive and conjunctive historical experiences that simultaneously (1) divide them into bounded groups, (2) tie these groups to one another, and (3) link their contemporary cultural struggles to become Guyanese to the struggles through which they and their ancestors became British during the colonial era of conquest, slavery, and indentureship.

Under these conditions history becomes a siren that simultaneously calls them, on the one hand, to construct and maintain distinctive group identities, while, on the other, it encourages them to engage in a nation-building process through which to dissolve those same identities into a homogeneous national identity. Consequently, many of the difficulties faced by the Guyanese, like those faced by others in new and old nations who would build or rebuild a national culture, are traceable to the constraints imposed by their previous political and economic status, though further shaped by those within which they must try to dismantle these past impositions.

Nonetheless, other aspects of the problems confronted in nation building result from the nature of human cultural production in general. All cultural production is to some extent a homogenizing process which is intrinsically incomplete and noncompletable. However stabilized a hegemonic moment in the homogenizing process might appear, it does not and cannot eradicate the heterogeneity consequent to the fact that humans produce arbitrary symbolic systems that they must then make appear natural while allowing sufficient pragmatic flexibility to permit adaptations to changing political and economic circumstances. Controlling the relation between arbitrariness and its naturalization is simply made more difficult under conditions where those who produce the symbolic system lack sufficient power to naturalize it. Thus the Guyanese, like others who would build new cultures on old foundations under conditions of national and international political and economic inequality, find it difficult to legitimate and, hence, to authenticate the culture that they of necessity produce.

Thus, on the basis of field data gathered in a rural East Coast Demerara community, I consider the implications of past and current ideological, political, and economic factors on the ways residents of this community, composed predominantly of Africans and of East Indians, produce and reinterpret the range of criteria they use to explain and to evaluate one another's behavior. Using secondary sources and oral historical accounts, I provide a diachronic view of patterns of identity production and social interaction in order to explore the actual character of the ideological field on which residents are simultaneously concerned with producing and institutionalizing a moral code to evaluate one another's everyday conduct as individuals, kinspersons, neighbors, and as members of class, racial, ethnic, and religious groupings competing for position and power in and over the broader process of cultural production in nation building.

Pathways, Coordinates, and Perspectives

Although social life is a totality in which a range of problems, and a variety of factors associated with them, are simultaneously significant in all social action, the description of this totality requires breaking it into manageable divisions. In making these divisions, I follow a path and a procedure that somewhat mirrors how residents explained, and how I came to understand, particular issues. So, in large measure, the presentation takes the reader through my informants' and my own thinking on these issues. It is a movement, first, through the spatial, material, and moral coordinates of status reckoning (Part I), then, to the ideologically constructed statuses of group identity and ranking (Part II), and, finally, on to the problem of cultural inauthenticity (Part III). This problem is treated as both a legacy of past hegemony and a consequence of contemporary Guyanese responses to the ideological and material constraints of an international politicoeconomic arena that further delineates the standards for civilized conduct against which they must evaluate themselves, their cultural productions, and their state's progress toward the coveted status of respected nation-state.

My aim throughout the book is to provide an analytic description of social reality, making specific the perspective, the person, the time, and the place from which it is described, and then to reexamine my reifications of this reality again and again—each time considering factors that were left out of the previous examination. The intent is to expose, by minimizing obfuscations, the multidimensionalities of the processes, the precepts, and the criteria out of which residents of this community construct personal and group identities, and evaluate the worth and purpose of these identities.[1]

The ethnographic account of the research community, pseudonym Cockalorum, is thus built up through a continual shift in perspective from which I analyze the same issue—the social organization of interaction in relation to the past hegemonic homogenization of culture and its implications for contemporary identities and solidarities in nation building. At times I primarily investigate individuals and their self-identification; at other times my attention is directed to ethnic groups and their competitive positions, to how persons and groups fit into the local community, or to the relation between the local community and the broader society. By moving back and forth between these and other perspectives and the different degrees of inclusiveness they entail, I aim to give the reader a sense of the interrelatedness of a range of problems associated with identity formation in the intersection of territorial and cultural nationalism in a "post"colonial order. Through an analysis of how residents conceptualize and respond to historical conjunctures and disjunctures, I aim to expose the constraints of the ideological field on which they construct identities, evaluate statuses, and most importantly, make decisions about the pragmatic worth of those with whom they must interact daily.

The ethnographic struggle is to accomplish this goal without wrapping the world in a seamless web of totally congruent and integrated ideas and actions, at the same time managing to keep tightly woven into the fabric of the analysis the fact that Cockalorum is situated in a state whose territory was initially conquered by "ethnically" diverse explorers in search of the mythical cities of Manoa and El Dorado, by traders from different nations seeking to make a handsome profit on cheaply acquired goods, and by "nationally" diverse planters, all, nonetheless, intent on becoming wealthy gentlemen at the expense of slave and other bound laborers. Hence, it was—and, unfortunately, in the eyes of many remains—a land of Cockalorums (necessarily self-important small men) in search of Cockaigne: for today, the insistence by impoverished Guyanese on their rights to dignity and to the benefits of the modern world are too often interpreted by many of their own countrymen and by foreigners as apparent continuations of searches for personal aggrandizement and luxury without effort—as a Guyanese lady of mixed race put it—"buying prosperity."

Theoretically, my struggle is to make this microsociological treatment of the particulars of the Cockalorums' cultural struggles speak, first, to broader issues of nation building in Guyana, and second, to a delineation of the character of nation building in the longer history of Western-style nationalism which has served as one of the roots of colonialism and of the so-called colonial mentality that sprouts from this root. In keeping with these goals, Chapter 1, focused on the historical development, spread, and general nature of nationalism and its attendant processes of cultural production in Western and Eastern Europe, provides the framework and theoretical background for my treatment of the politics of cultural struggle in postcolonial societies.

Placing the process of nation building in this historical context sets forth the intellectual issues and theoretical assumptions that underlie and motivate my effort to understand, in microsociological terms, how the distribution of power in a society structures, and is structured by, the processes of cultural production and identity formation in contemporary nation-states defined by their past and present ideological, political, and of course, material links to earlier, parallel, processes in Europe. The issues put forth in this chapter aim to place this microsociological ethnography of a small community, in a small country, at the center of anthropological discourses on the relations among material inequalities, cultural productions, and the distribution of power in the formation of nation-states. It argues for an ethnographically grounded theory of culture as the politics of struggles intended to fix the relations between identity, power, and meaning in defined political units.

Chapter 1 and the concluding Chapter 10 are therefore concerned with what an ethnographic understanding (such as that provided in Chapters 2–9) of the impact of the precepts of Western nationalism on the production of colonialism and its "new peoples" has for general anthropological analyses of the struggles over meaning and status out of which the symbolic systems we call cultures are produced, their particular symbols ordered through local interpretations, and their meanings contested within and across the boundaries of group solidarities and national territories. By treating the relations between dimensions of identity formation such as race, class, and ethnicity as aspects of a single hegemonic process that links meaning, as naturalized conventional understandings and modes of conduct in public and private arenas, to the distributions of material goods and services and of political rights and obligations in nation-states, my ultimate theoretical goal is to suggest how, methodologically and analytically, anthropology can consider symbols, interpretations, and meaning in social life without losing sight of the material and political realities of the contexts in which these processes occur. In conjunction with this quest for improved method and theory, my political goal (or bias, if you prefer) is simple and direct: to suggest the futility and unnecessary pain consequent to ethnic chauvinism as the over-valorization of tradition, even when such is the outcome of an antihegemonic quest for the political freedom and dignity that all deserve and that few, in nation-states, have ever experienced.

Acknowledgments

Any project that takes a long time to complete amasses debts to many people. Sometimes, it is many years after the project is finished before one comes to realize how a brief conversation on a seemingly tangential point influenced one's thinking on what later became a crucial issue. All of which is to say that the following acknowledgments are chronically hierarchicalized representations of my memories of intellectual assistance, interaction, and of my borrowings of others' creativity. To Ms. Mary Mosley, who first allowed me the opportunity and voice to begin formalizing my thinking on issues of race, class, and culture as an undergraduate at Cornell University: thanks for the many lessons on how simultaneously to maintain a number of perspectives without losing my own. To Drexel Woodson, who has been friend, teacher, and formidable devil's advocate for more years than I want to count: I hope you will see your contributions represented here in a nonappropriated form even as I aim to provide you space to deny any culpability for the form I have given them. Thanks, too, are due my graduate colleagues and thesis advisers at Johns Hopkins, especially Scott Guggenheim, Emily Martin, Kathleen Ryan, Patricia Torres, and Jacqueline Yu.

For their tolerance, multidimensional explanations, and challenges, I also reiterate thanks offered to the people of Cockalorum, especially Mr. and Mrs. B., and Mr. and Mrs. M., and their families, whose struggle is, I think, also a dimension of my own struggle. So, if I have have put matters inaccurately here, I hope they will recall what we all understood as I collected the data for this project: It's very hard to see clearly the shape and motion of the boot pressed on your neck as you wriggle on the ground beneath it.

I also thank John and Angela Rickford, Elizabeth and Joe Charette, and their families for assistance and friendship during my stay in Guyana, and the staff at the University of Guyana Library and the National Archives for their assistance. Although it is easier to thank those who have been kind and friendly than those who have been hostile and unyielding, few anthropological projects fail to produce adversaries in the field whose actions are instructive. Thus, I also offer thanks to those in Cockalorum and elsewhere in Guyana who insisted that both my presence and project were unwelcome intrusions. I am especially grateful to them because it was from them that I learned some lessons that, I believe, could have been taught no other way.

I thank Queens College of the City University of New York for the special leave that made it possible for me to spend a year at the Center for Advanced Study in the Behavioral Sciences. I thank the center and its staff for the support without which the timely completion of this manuscript would not have been possible. I offer special thanks to the Spencer Foundation for the financial support that made the year at the center possible, and to Margaret Amara, Muriel Bell, Anna Tower, and, above all, to Denna Knickerbocker, who first processed the manuscript and its graphics.

Although I take responsibility for the final product, it is by no means my creation alone. To Jane Collier, Don Donham, Joseph Emonds, Stanley Engerman, Richard Fox, J. Lee Greene, Joseph Gusfield, Alice Ingerson, Barbara Herrnstein Smith, Carol Smith, Carol Stack, Aihwa Ong, Helan Page, Renato Rosaldo, Eric Wolf, Margery Wolf, Pamela Wright, and members of the Cultural Studies Group at Stanford, who read and commented on all or part of the manuscript at different stages, despite my inability to incorporate all of your suggestions, I thank you for very valuable assistance. I also gratefully acknowledge permission granted by Viking Penguin Books to reprint the Valetta and Constantine dialogue, excerpted from Rebecca West's *Black Lamb and Grey Falcon*. During the final stages of preparation, I thank Helena Acosta and Yvonne Lassalle for editorial assistance. My greatest thanks, however, must be reserved for my assistant and editor, Ulrike Bode, and for Muriel Devack, Sylvia Abramovitz, Marge Mahon, Rosemary Matens, and Grayce Romeo of the Queens College Word Processing Center, without whose patience and consideration this manuscript would never have been completed.

B. F. WILLIAMS   1989

I

Country
and
Community

1

On the Politics
of Cultural
Struggle

We do not face the world in doctrinaire fashion, declaring, "Here is the truth, kneel here!" . . . We do not tell the world, "Cease your struggles, they are stupid; we want to give you the true watchword of the struggle." We merely show the world why it actually struggles; and consciousness is something that the world *must* acquire even if it does not want to.
— Karl Marx in a letter to Arnold Ruge, September 1843
(quoted in Luxemburg 1971: 6)

    Our familiar expression of *melting-pot*—better yet, *stewing-pot*—illustrates the process very well. Put into the pot of physical proximity, covered by the lid of a common political system, exposed to the heat of cultural and social interchange, the various elements will change after a fairly long time—it took a few centuries in the past, but may take less in the future—into a brew. The brew will not be quite homogeneous. You can still point to a grain of rice, to a leaf of onion, to a chunk of meat, to a splinter of bone. But it will manifestly be *one* brew, with its distinct flavor and taste.
— Benjamin Akzin, *State and Nation* (p. 84)

What, after more than a century of structural-functional, structuralist, semiotic, symbolic, Marxist, neo-Marxist, and other forms of analysis, do we know of how people struggle toward the consciousness that Marx, in the first epigram, insists the world must attain? If we intend "merely [to] show the world why it actually struggles," what have we discovered through our presentations, and our quibbles and squabbles over their accuracy, about the nature of these struggles? In characterizing these struggles, what significance can we justifiably attribute to the interrelations between what Akzin, in the second assimilationist epigram, labels "the lid of a common political system" and "the heat of cultural and social interchange," in our representations of the processes (that is, specific struggles) out of which the "not

3

quite homogeneous brew" develops? What can we tell ourselves and others who struggle deep within these brews about how the "distinct flavor and taste" of their particular brew compares with other brews?

Ethnographically, this book focuses on the politics of cultural struggle taking place in the state of Guyana during a period just short of twenty years into its citizens' efforts to refashion its colonial brew into a national brew. Titular independence in 1966 established their right and need to redefine the meaning of being in a pot of physical proximity long capped by the lid of a common political system held down tight by the heat of a transformist hegemony that set the terms of cultural and social interchange among "ethnic" groups, themselves largely the products of this process of transformist hegemony. We enter a situation which is both new and old; a struggle with no assurance of a successful outcome, if success be read as a stable, putatively homogeneous brew. What can we tell ourselves, the Guyanese, and others who struggle deep within these brews about the "distinct flavor and taste" of their particular brew compared with other brews?

In 1940 Rebecca West presented a fictional dialogue between a Croat, Valetta, and a Serbian, Constantine, in which they confront the difficulties of the painful struggle to form a nation of South Slavs. Like the Guyanese and other contemporary participants in nation building, they raise their voices to and against one another as they try to imagine just representations and strategies for the distribution of rights and obligation in a nation of "brothers." Like participants in all putative nation-states, past and present, the passionate debate in which they engage is about how to make these representations and distributions take account of the historically produced heterogeneity of national brews. They lay out the internal contradictions confronted by those who would build a putatively homogeneous state-as-nation in the face of a heterogeneous reality. Their recognition of such heterogeneity, itself partly the product of their previous and ongoing, sometimes joint, sometimes divided, struggles to eliminate external forms of domination, now threatens to provide the grounds for new forms of internal domination. They are angered and frustrated with one another as Serb and Croat, and with the stalemate that occurs each time as Yugoslavians they try to envision strategies that diminish the possibility of valorizing new patterns of domination.

Thus, while they speak of commonalities generated out of their struggles, they also make clear that these commonalities neither inevitably imply strategies for institutionalizing just relations between meaning and power nor between the distribution of material opportunities and the status evaluation criteria on the basis of which such a distribution might be morally justified. Valetta and Constantine's dialogue alerts us to some of the reason why, in nation building, with its attendant processes of cultural authentication, these commonalities are not enough, in and of themselves, to guarantee the formulation of a vision, of the nation-state and its civil society, that transcends the new contradictions that arise when strategies are evaluated in terms of their meaning for the status of categorically distinguishable members of an otherwise "biologically"-defined homogeneous nation; or, and, no less important, for assessments of the relative status of the new nation (as biological groupings and political entity) in the international order of nations-as-states.

Though they are fictional characters—men ironically created by a woman and hung out on the horns of a self-reproducing dilemma—Valetta and Constantine present well the reality scholars must address if we are to describe for people how they struggle and if we are to be able to suggest to them how they might become "conscious" in, and of, the modes of domination that are prior to, as well as those consequent to, nationalist ideologies and their contemporary international economic, political, and cultural linkages. Listen carefully then as they spell out for us the complexities of these problems.

[T]here is no end to political disputation in Croatia. None. . . . Constantine had exploded: "I did not like her. She is not a true Slav. Did you hear what she told you when you were at the Health Co-operative Society Clinic? She said that all such things were very well looked after in the Austrian times. Yes, and she said it regretfully." "Well, it was so," said Valetta. "Yes, it was so," said Constantine, "but we must not regret it. No true Slav would regret it. That is to say no true human being would say it, for a true human being is a Slav, he knows that to be a Slav is what is important, for that is the shape which God has given him, and he should keep it. The Austrians sometimes pampered you, and sometimes the Hungarians, so that each should play you off against the others. Benefits you get so are filth, and they spoil your shape as a Slav. It is better to have nearly nothing at all, and be a freeman with your brother Slavs." . . . "Do you not think it is better?" Constantine asked him. He nodded slightly. "Well, if you do not feel that strongly you can feel nothing at all!" said Constantine a little louder. "Oh, yes, I feel it strongly," said Valetta, quite softly, and then, more softly still, "It would be much better for us to be freem[e]n with our brother Slavs."

For a moment Constantine was satisfied and went on eating. Then he threw down his knife and fork. "What is it that you are saying? It *would* be better. . . . You mean it is not so?" "I mean it is not quite so," said Valetta. "How is it not so?" asked Constantine, lowering his head like a bull. Valetta shrugged his shoulders. Constantine collapsed quite suddenly, and asked pathetically, "But we are not brothers, we Croats and Serbs?" "Yes," said Valetta. . . . "But in Yugoslavia . . . it is not so. Or, rather it is as if the Serbs were the elder brother and we Croats the younger brother, under some law . . . which gives the older everything and the younger nothing." "Oh, I know what you think!" groaned Constantine. "You think that all your money goes to Belgrade, and you get hardly anything of it back, and we flood your country with Serb officials, and keep Croats out of all positions of real power. I know it all!"

"You may know it all!" said Valetta, "but so do we: and it is not a thing we can be expected to overlook." "I do not ask you to overlook it," said Constantine, beginning to roar like a bull, "I ask you to look at it. You did not have the spending of your money before, when you were under Hungary. All your money was sent to Budapest to landlords or to tax-collectors, and you got some railways, yes, and some hospitals, yes, and some roads, yes, but not costing one-half of your money, and you got also Germanization and Magyarization, you got the violation of your soul. But now you are part of Yugoslavia, you are a part of the kingdom of the South Slavs, which exists to let you keep your soul, and to guard that kingdom we must have an army and a navy . . . and we must give Serbia many things she did not have because Serbia was fighting the Turk when you were standing safe behind us, and we must do much for Bosnia, because the Hungarians did nothing there, and we must do everything for Macedonia, because the Turks were there 'til 1912, and we must drain marshes and build schools and make military roads, and it is all for you as well as for us, but you will not see it."

"Yes, I see it," said Valetta, "but if you want to found a strong and civilized Yugoslavia you should have brought the Serb schools up to the Croat level instead of bringing the Croat schools down to Serb level." "But now you should see nothing at all," wailed Constantine; "it is a question of money. It is more important that one should have good schools everywhere than that part of the country should have very good schools. A chain is as strong as its weakest link. What good is it to you in Croatia that your boys and girls can read the Hindustani and paint like Raphael if the young men in Macedonia go bang-bang all night at whoever because they do not know anything else to do?" "We might feel more confidence that our money went to build schools in Macedonia if it did not go through Belgrade. . . . You must forgive us for fearing that a great deal of it sticks in Belgrade." "Of course it sticks in Belgrade!" said Constantine. . . . "We must make a capital. We must make a capital for your sake, because you are a South Slav! All Western Europeans despise us because we have a little capital that is not chic. They are wrong, for there is no reason why we should have a big capital, for we are a peasant state. But you must give these people what they want . . . it is a big shining thing that impresses them. Do you not remember how before the war the Austrian Ministers treated us like dirt, because Vienna is a place of baroque palaces and we had nothing but our poor town . . . ?"

" . . . why do you not draw on us Croats for officials?" asked Valetta. " . . . But how can we let you Croats be officials?" spluttered Constantine. "You are not loyal!" "And how," asked Valetta, white to the lips, "can we be expected to be loyal if you always treat us like this?" "But I am telling you," grieved Constantine, "how can we treat you differently 'til you are loyal?"

It is an absolute deadlock; and the statement of it filled the heart with desolation. Constantine . . . said, "Valetta, I will tell you what is the matter with you. . . . Here in Croatia you are lawyers as well as soldiers. You have been good lawyers, and you have been lawyers all the time. For eight hundred years you have had your *procès* against Hungary. You have quibbled over phrases in the *diploma inaugurale* of your kings, you have wrangled about the power of your Ban, you have sawed arguments about *regna socia* and *partes adnexae*, you have chattered like jackdaws over your rights under the Dual Monarchy, you have covered acres of paper discussing the Hungaro-Croatian compromise. And so it is that you are now more lawyers than soldiers, for it is not since the eighteenth century that you have fought the Turks. . . . But now we are making Yugoslavia we must feel not like lawyers but like soldiers. . . . You must cast away all your little rights, and say that we have a big right, the right of the Slavs to be together, and we must sacrifice all our rights to protect the great right."

Valetta shrugged his shoulders once more. "What have you against that?" roared Constantine. "I will tell you what is the matter with you. You are an intellectual, you are all intellectuals here in the bad sense. You boast because Zagreb is an old town, but that is a great pity for you. Everywhere else in Serbia is a new town, and though we have novelists and poets and all, they have now been in no town no more than . . . one generation. . . . So what the peasant knows they also know. They know that one must not work against, one must work with. . . . But in the town you do not know that, you can go through life and you can work against all. . . . So you are intellectuals. The false sort that are always in opposition. My God, my God, how easy it is to be an intellectual in opposition to the man of action! He can always be so much cleverer, he can always pick out the little faults. But to make, that is more difficult. . . . *Ach*, in all your little ways you are very terrible!"

For a time Valetta did not answer. . . . "You would say we are well governed here?" he asked presently. "You would say that nobody is arrested without cause and thrown into prison and treated barbarously? You would say that nobody has been tortured in Croatia since it became Yugoslavia?" He was trembling, and such sick horror passed across his face that I am sure he was recollecting atrocities which he had seen with his own eyes, at which his own bowels had revolted. Constantine nearly cried. "Ah, God! it is their fault," he pled, indicating my husband and myself. "These English are hypocrites, they pretend they govern people without using force, because there are many parts of the Empire where they govern only people who want to be governed . . . in India where the people do not want to be governed many people are beaten and imprisoned. And for that I do not blame the English. It must be done if one race has to have power over another; that is why it is wrong for one race to have power over another, and that is why we must have a Yugoslavia, a self-governing kingdom of the South Slavs, and why we should make all possible sacrifices for Yugoslavia." "I see the argument," said Valetta; "we are to let Serbs torture us Croats, because under Yugoslavia we are not to be tortured by the Italians and Hungarians." "Oh, God. Oh, God!" cried Constantine, "I am glad that I am not a Croat, but a Serb, for though I myself am a very clever man, the Serbs are not a very clever people; that has not been their business; their business has been to drive out the Turks and keep their independence from the Austrians and the Germans . . . my God, my God, do you know what I feel like doing when I talk to you Croats? I feel like rolling up my coat and lying down in the middle of the street and putting my head on my coat, and saying to the horses and motor cars, 'Drive on, I am disgusted.' What is so horrible in this conversation is that you are never wrong, but I am always right, and we could go on talking like this for ever, till the clever way you are never wrong brought death upon us." "Some have died already," said Valetta. (West 1940:89–94, quoted from Strauss 1959:169–73)

When we follow Constantine's suggestion that contradictions in the ideology and practice of English rule might provide a clue, what have we learned about the relation between nationalism and cultural production under British colonial rule? Could this knowledge constructively inform our response to a soliloquy delivered by a middle-aged "mixed race" woman in the East Coast Demerara region of what was once British Guiana, but is now the People's Co-operative Republic of Guyana, where the descendants of emancipated African slaves and ex-indentured laborers from India, Portuguese Madeira, and China still struggle with one another and with a handful of surviving indigenous people (that is, Amerindians)?

"There ain't no people like your own villagers to talk bad about you and to sell your character low. I'm just not able with Black people. They play friends but they don't know what it is to be a real friend. As soon as they say [M——] is a nice girl, they mean [she] is a fool that they believe they can use. They come to your house to search and spy, all the time skinning their teeth [smiling] and talking about buddy friend, ahwe sister friends. They see this [picking up an object] [and they say] please for this [give it to me]. I see you have a lemon also. They ready to carry something. And bring back? [Punctuated with tooth-sucking] They don't know about bring back. When you go to ask them for it, you got to quarrel 'pon dem to git back you t'ing. No, I tell you and I tell them straight, I ain't able with Black people.

"They are a people who lacks discipline. They are always minding everybody's business but their own. I am not able with Black people because they are too nasty and boderation. They are always looking for a way to wipe their feet on you or wash their mouth on you. Let them talk but I da [there] with the Yankees and the Canadians because they are a more disciplined people. It takes discipline, not complaining, to get a job done. I [have] worked [a] long [time] with the Yankees and Canadians and I still da between the Yankees and the Canadians. [Throughout these comments the speaker moves between her seat and the window, inquiring of her listener information on those passing by outside. She comments on their appearance, morality, family background, and their "pretenses."]

"I'm not like some, disloyal to my country, always running to somebody else's country. Everyday you see them [returned migrants] with this shoe and that jersey [tee-shirt] and all such nonsense, trying to buy prosperity when they have none. They come back and don't wear shoes, they wear the shoes bores [labels]. They go out and get big. They buying prosperity with their fancy Yankee clothes and stereos and records, and their 'hey baby dis and dat.' A set of fools, you ask me! They lack the discipline to work for what they want, so they hustle and go outside [abroad], selling out their country to buy prosperity. [Punctuated with another tooth-suck].

[Reaching under her straw hat to pull out a braid:] "You see how long my hair is? I got [Amer]indian in my veins. I ain't able with Black people and their stupidness. I surround myself with Bucks [Amerindians] [and] [East] Indians, and I go long my way. These people are disciplined and they work hard. They mind their business and live a simple life. I don't believe in trying to be what I ain't. [Removing her hat.] You see this hair I don't press it. [Sucks her tooth.] People waste too much time trying to be what they ain't. They run to church talking peace and love but they just talking, they can't put it in practice."

[Before leaving, she asks her cousin for a straw mat the cousin had promised to make for her and gives the cousin car fare to pay her a return visit.] (Comments of a woman from Linden, visiting her cousin at the field site, excerpted from fieldnotes, July 27, 1980)

What, might we suggest, do two chunks of Yugoslavian meat have in common with this leaf of a Guyanese onion? For that matter, what have these ingredients of an East European and a South American brew in common with the reported actions of that Polish-American grain of rice, councilwoman Barbara Mikulski, who, after admitting that she had once considered changing the spelling of her name from the Polish "Mikulski" to the Irish "McClosky," charged, as late as 1970, that the North American United States was not a melting pot but a "sizzling cauldron"? (See Stein and Hill 1977:126.)

Whatever we might have told the above characters, what their actions, and the actions and commentaries of multitudes of others in different "pots of physical proximity," have told us is that the grains of rice and the leaves of onion never become mere grains and vegetables; they remain troublesome, often violently resistive, masses of humanity. The chunks of meat and the splinters of bone do not become the scraps of subhuman creatures, but rather—through identification both by others and by self—form parts of the protective outer shell and internal framework of, as Constantine struggled to make clear to Valetta, "true human beings" in their "God-given shape." Furthermore, when we have too quickly attributed such bounded definitions of humanness to prenationalist "primordial sentiments," we have often been forced to recant because we have found in huge, long-simmering pots of vichyssoise not identifiable lumps of potato and leek, but, suddenly, chunks of meat and skins of apples that were not present when the lid of a "common political system" was capped.

In addition, as we listen more closely to the cacophony of voices emanating from these not quite homogeneous brews, the implied neutral, well-seasoned brew of Akzin's extended metaphor is not so characterized by all the voices. Some of the people involved charge that the melting process involves a daily devaluation of their cherished cultural beliefs and practices. Although we may note that major features of the "subcultures" to which they refer are often as likely to be recently *traditionalized* as they are to be historically *traditional*, such peoples nonetheless claim that devaluations of these features of the national brew occur for the sake of a simultaneous overvaluation of the creativity and creations of other peoples sharing the same pot of physical proximity. Hence, whatever we might tell the world about its struggles, one of the things many peoples of that world persist in telling us is that the flavor of these brews tends always toward the essence of a single ingredient: an essence frequently so overpowering of all other ingredients that even decades after its removal the most identifiable taste is a bitter aftertaste.

Yet, as Strauss (1959) points out in his analysis of the Valetta-Constantine dialogue, peoples in these brews who are identified with their less powerful ingredients find their sense of taste (that is to say, identity, self-worth, and modes of evaluating their own status and the status of others) inextricably bound up with interpretations of the essence of that overpowering single ingredient, however bitter the aftertaste. Personal identities and conceptions of self-worth are enmeshed with group identities which are themselves historically constituted dialectical reflections. Valetta and Constantine share a history out of which they define their oneness as Slavs, but the divergences within that history also wreak havoc with their individual senses of where they have come from, where they are now headed, and, more important, how they will get there. In his interpretation of this dialogue, Strauss suggests that

[t]he Croatian looks back across the centuries and sees the oppression of his people, and of the Slavs in general; and now sees a continuation of this oppression by one of the Slav people. If anything, the current oppression is a worst form, hence his confrontation of the Serb with accusations of betrayal. Valetta, the Croat, rises to his strongest pitches of anger and revulsion when he insinuates or hurls these accusations, and especially when Constantine paradoxically accuses the Croati[a]ns of disloyalty to all Slavs. To Valetta, Yugoslavia ought to mean freedom; but freedom cannot signify merely free from the Austrians, the Hungarians, and the Turks; it must mean a true lack of oppression by anyone. We may hazard, also, that since Valetta believes the Croats represent a high point of civilization, he also believes Croatians ought to be the true leaders of the Slavs. Real freedom cannot be gained at the expense of loss of those civilizational values. These latter are not merely "education" and "schooling" but as Constantine himself suggests constitute dear possessions, deeply rooted in the Croatians' conception of themselves.

Constantine's identity is equally linked with the centuries, but if anything appears more complex because the Serbs had changed from an age-old status ("oppressed by non-Slavs") through another ("leaders of the victory over the outsiders") to the current one ("rulers in cooperation with fellow Slavs"). Victory in the battle for freedom justifies the Serb as a man of action, for the highest goal was freedom from oppression. Previous concessions wrung from the oppressors, by legal means, are forgotten or not recognized by Constantine; history is perceived as leading up to the final great right, the right for all Slavs to be free together. Those who are, so to speak, handed their freedom, who never really earned it, should at least cooperate in building a great Slavic country. At this juncture of history, the important thing is to forget specific identities and be a "true Slav." They are all born Slavs, but the essence of the true Slavic identity is that it is earned. The Serbs earned theirs by winning the victory, and by working toward a great and united Yugoslavia. In a certain sense, Constantine regards the Croats as traitors: they have not been instrumental in winning the victory; they are not cooperating now that victory is won; and they are all the more culpable because they are the best educated of all Slavic people. (Constantine himself is a poet and an intellectual.) At the same time, we might guess, the stress placed upon the Serb as a man of action could not be so pronounced if the legalistic Croat did not exist as a vivid and exasperating contrast. Constantine's vulnerability—the dilemma confronting him—is that he is now one of the rulers whereas all his life he has been styled as, and has styled himself as, one of the oppressed. The transition has left him open to charges of treachery, of being no different than the Austrians—except infinitely worse, because he is a Slav. Such accusations strike at the roots of his being, for he and the Serbs are the defenders and liberators of all Slavs. Slavs have not been free for centuries but now they are. Rebecca West has probably caught accurately Constantine's moments of greatest anguish and fury when he is accused of betrayal. His sensitivity to the problems of British rule, and to the images of backwardness held of Yugoslavia by wealthier countries, is part of his transition from oppressed to ruler. This is a transition unquestionably fraught with anxiety. The Serbian history of oppression does not yield many cues for handling this unaccustomed new status. Perhaps the rule of the British does? (Strauss 1959:173–75)

Strauss's analysis of this passionate dialogue brings forth for us both the value of, and the problems involved in, attempts to develop historically informed analyses of linkages between personal and group identities, and the significance of these linkages for an understanding of relations between territorial and cultural nationalism. His analysis underscores the complexities of any notion of shared historical experience in pots of physical proximity as we note how these agents retrospectively place different symbolic stress on aspects of experience, thus creating, within the same stream of time and experience, multiple historical disjunctures. It also makes clear that these disjunctures are at the same time conjunctures. The specificity of

Serbian and Croatian identities is forged in these disjunctive conjunctures of political oppression and struggle. That is to say, they are
located in the generalities of a Slavic identity defined in interpretive
opposition by Serbs and Croats. The existential dilemma implied in
this process is nicely summed up in the words of Rabbi Mendel of
Kotzk: "If I am I, simply because I am I, and thou art thou simply
because thou art thou, then I am I and thou art thou. But if I am I
because thou art thou and thou art thou because I am I, then I am not I
and thou art not thou."[1]

Yet, as poignant as Mendel's dialectical image of identity is,
the I-thou dichotomy it implies is also highly problematic. In the
Constantine-Valetta dialogue, Constantine the Serb struggles to play
Caliban to Valetta's Prospero, while Valetta, the Croat, in turn, struggles to play Caliban to Constantine's Prospero.[2] Valetta, as colonizing
colonized, has been able to carry on a legalistic struggle against
Slavic oppression behind the shield of Constantine, the colonized
man of action. Equally, Constantine, the colonizing colonized, has
been able to conduct the battles of the man of action, at least in part,
in the civilized spaces provided by the legal maneuvers of the colonized Valetta. Both men, as emblems of disjunctive Slavic identities,
have been and continue to be both Prospero (the good colonized)
and Caliban (the bad colonized). They now carry within the core of
their separable but (for reasons of territorial nationalism) interdependent identities the consequences of their multidimensional historical
experience. That Constantine is forced in the end to confront what
he earlier recognized but underplayed—that Valetta as Croat has
been both lawyer and soldier, whereas Constantine as Serb has
earned his right to the God-given shape of a "true human being" by a
single criterion—further alerts us to the problem of dichotomy.
Though he does not consider Serbs a clever people, Constantine the
Serb, as educated poet and intellectual, is a clever man. Yet, as a Serb,
he nonetheless stands for the man of action, for centuries fighting
battles against external oppressors, only recently a resident of the
town, for all that that signifies. Under these conditions, he must,
therefore, base his Serbian claim to priority in directing the struggle
to form the Kingdom of South Slavs on the fact that he, like other
Serbs, knows what the peasant knows. What the peasant knows, has,
and does, however, are not the shiny things that impress those one
ought not to have to, but must now, impress.

Thus, it is in the context of ties between territorial nationalism and international political structures that Yugoslavia is an unchic peasant state in search of shiny things to impress outsiders (some of whom were once oppressors) if it is to have any hope of acting as a political equal in the international arena. It is also in this context that the Croats, with their double criteria for Slavness (that is, lawyer and soldier), become both brothers and disloyal, potentially dangerous subjects. Nonetheless, it is with reference to such criteria as the age of Zagreb and the significance of education and schooling, and through Croatian evaluations of these criteria and of themselves in relation to them, that the Serbs may, as Constantine stresses, raise questions about Croats' oneness with Serbs who have earned their Slavness solely by being men of action. These criteria also bring Zagreb and the Croats closer to being among the shiny things respected by those outsiders who otherwise despise all Slavs. We are reminded by Poliakov (1974:19) that "while the Slav is a 'slave' in western languages, the western emperor is the 'king' in the Slav languages." It is, therefore, the Prospero *in* Caliban—not the pure dichotomized confrontation between Prospero *and* Caliban—that poses the greatest problems for these men as they try to locate and appropriately to value or to legitimate the conjunctures in the disjunctive generalities of their historical experiences.

Hence, if history, even history made behind men's backs, be the siren that calls them to particular identities (personal and group) under conditions of territorial nationalism, it does so always while, at the same time, pleading the contradictory cases for dissolution *and* maintenance of the specificity of these identities; a specificity through which individuals may claim to have earned their place in a historically constituted social world of generalities—generalities which, in the case of our Guyanese informant, flow through the culturally constructed blood in her veins, displaying their conjunctures and disjunctures not only in the particulars of her behavioral choices (Azkin's "heat of social and cultural interchange"), but also in the very hair on her head!

The meaning our Guyanese informant finds partially lodged in the hair on her head has a parallel, albeit a complex one, in the meaning of a name that Barbara Mikulski considered changing, and in the efforts of the Bemba to hold on to the symbolism of a long-gone tradition of military glory as a symbol of their place in the class-stratified ethnic hierarchy of contemporary Zambia (see Epstein

1978:113–38). These meanings are constructed along paths well trod by Europeans centuries earlier as they fashioned themselves into different races, nationalities, and nations.

It is, therefore, in listening to voices of this type that we have gained a sense of the kind of material out of which we must construct our representations of how peoples actually struggle. We have learned that, if we are to provide informative accounts of these struggles and their relation to the consciousness the world must attain, we must take into consideration the complexities of historically constituted interpretations of the nature of social and cultural interchanges. This is especially so if such accounts are to assist us in understanding the interpenetration of such solidarities and identities by a class consciousness necessitated by, and formulated in, pots of territorial nationalism.

In the Pot of Physical Proximity

Efforts, however, to account for the relation between political, economic, and cultural integration have been conducted under certain largely unexamined assumptions. As Akzin's extended metaphor and a voluminous literature on nationalism[3] suggest, one key assumption has been that political identity, conceived of in terms of territorial nationalism, should and must take precedence over other means of defining identity and unity. Under the lid of a common political system, heterogeneity, if recognized at all, was to give way to some form of homogeneity forged and stabilized through processes of assimilation and acculturation.[4] Commenting on the dichotomy between "primordial" and "civil" ties to which this assumption led, Barnett states:

Having postulated a conflict between "primordial" and "civil" sentiments it is an easy step for politicians and social scientists to argue for the substitution of one (civil ties) for the other (primordial ties). Even when theorists are careful not to postulate a dichotomy, primordial ties are believed (their modern recrudescence notwithstanding) to be "traditional" and "civil" ties to be modern. However, if all nationalisms (ideologies of national unity) are infused with notions of blood and soil and specifically evoke these emotional "primordial sentiments" at the first sign of the "nation in danger," the dichotomy (or near dichotomy) of the civil and primordial falls apart and with it accepted notions of political identity and political integration.

If the loci of political identity (cultural unit versus nation-state) are not necessarily concommitant [*sic*] with the nature of the "tie" or loyalty (i.e., routine versus affective or rational versus non-rational) [then] the primordial-civil distinction may be a clumsy way to distinguish the competing elements which precipitate a political identity crisis. As Nehru so perceptively saw, what is at issue are two forms of nationalism, one a cultural nationalism which defines the relevant political community as coterminous with a cultural community and the other territorial nationalism which defines the relevant political community according to territorial boundaries as defined by the nation-state and the international community. But is one form of nationalism traditional and the other modern? What are the distinguishing characteristics of the two nationalisms? Why does one nationalism, with its attendant locus of political identity develop and not the other? What is the relevant level of analysis of these two nationalisms? In the process of modernization will territorial nationalism inevitably replace cultural nationalism? (M. Barnett 1974:240)

Whether our goal is to understand class solidarities in the older nation-states of Europe or to explain the relation between ethnic identity and class or national identity in newly independent states such as Guyana, on which this book will focus, we must analyze the historical development of nationalist ideologies to clarify the meanings they give to race, class, and culture in relation to territorial nationalism and homogeneity. In a prelude to her case study of the "invention" and the unification of a "non-Brahman" political identity in South India, Barnett, building on the work of Kohn (1955) on nationalism and of Dumont (1970) on the interaction of opposing ideological orientations in Indian history, makes an interesting contribution to such a clarification. First, she notes with Kohn that, beginning around the eighteenth century, ideologies of nationalism that developed in conjunction with Western European definitions of nation-states demanded that the supreme loyalty of the individual was due the nation-state. And,

as the nation-state idea was evolving, European philosophical development was moving in the direction of individualism and therefore a "social contract" as the link between antecedently autonomous selves and the state. The concepts of natural law, the social contract, and individualism provide the ideological basis for granting sovereignty to the nation-state. At the heart of this is the concept of the individual as the basic unit of society. (M. Barnett 1974:241)

She concludes that nationalism in the modern West was predominantly a political movement to limit government power and to secure civic rights. This was a movement and an ideology that, Kohn suggests, in "English nationalism became identified, to a degree unknown anywhere, with the concept of individual liberty" (Kohn 1955:9, quoted in M. Barnett 1974:241).

Second, noting that these ideas spread, via the dominance of Western nations in shaping world political culture, into non-Western nations of markedly different political, economic, and cultural structures, she agrees with Dumont (1970) that their introduction set the stage for a confrontation between holistic (collectivist) ideological orientations and individualist ideological orientations. On empirical grounds, however, she rejects Dumont's contention that as ideal types these opposing orientations (that is, collectivism/hierarchy versus individualism/egalitarianism) adequately differentiate traditional from modern society. Nonetheless, she concludes that Dumont's focus on the interaction between these two ideological stances does provide the basis for a theory of cultural nationalism that would allow for an emphasis on the structure of cultural systems rather than on the nature of personal ties to political communities. She cautions, however, that in the construction and application of such a theory, we must keep in mind that the particularities of social, economic, and political factors are crucial determinants of whether a group stresses a collective identity. Moreover, the emergence of a cultural nationalist perspective articulating a communal political identity, in a context where the potential exists, depends on the additional factors of leadership, ideology, and a sense of relative deprivation, which she defines as "an invidious comparison of one's group status to that of a reference group" (M. Barnett 1974:242). Although she concludes that "territorial nationalism and cultural nationalism may each derive from their own historical and socio-cultural contexts, in fact they may be dialectically rather than dichotomously related," personal and group identities are constructed in the intersection of these nationalisms (M. Barnett 1974:243).

Ideologies of nationalism, which linked territorial unity to cultural homogeneity and individual rights within, and loyalty to, such entities, therefore posed both pragmatic and conceptual difficulties before their introduction into non-European societies. As Schermerhorn's (1978) work suggests, ideological contradictions, and the stage for the oppositional and dialectical interaction of these contradictions, were set *within* the initial ideological precepts[5] as these ideas and concepts spread into Central and Eastern Europe. He concludes that

[n]ormative monism was the order of the day for dominant powers speaking in the name of nationalism. However, their subjects also appealed to the same ideology in the name of freedom: if uniformity was good and pluralism was bad, then they asserted their autonomy as nations and demanded separation, independence and the right to set up new sovereign states with their *own* uniformity and homogeneity. Such annexed peoples having their own language and set of institutions, their awareness of a common historical past, and an awakening to the possibility of a new independent status under the potent influence of the nationalist ideal, came to be known as nationalists rather than nations. The more loosely organized Austro-Hungarian Empire never attempted to organize an overarching national state but the wave of nationalist ideology from the west transformed their annexed peoples into nationalities—Czechs, Hungarians, Croati[a]ns, Serbs, etc. The treaties of Versailles and Trianon after the first World War recognized the rights of self-determination for nationalities, many of which became full-blown nations as a consequence. (Schermerhorn 1978:134–35)

The boundaries of these new nations did not enclose homogeneous populations defined in the aforementioned preexisting terms. Consequently, against what Schermerhorn refers to as the "norm of homogeneity," the concept and the struggles of the "minority group" developed as "nationalities" further fragmented into smaller groupings looking back with different eyes across centuries of experience in physical proximity and using the ideological precepts of nationalism to express their differing visions of identity, self-worth, and rights, which they saw in the particularities of historical conjunctures and disjunctures. Within Central and Eastern European nations there were nonhomogenized nationalities, and within these nonhomogenized nationalities there existed also smaller groupings of nonhomogenized minorities based on language, locality, and other culturally constructed factors. Schermerhorn (1978:135) thus maintains that "in the post-Versailles crop of new Central European nations . . . the notion of minority rights became a belated supplement to the idealistic demand for national self-determination which proved to be an illusory attempt at creating uniform states."

Just as this belated supplement was grounded in the particular ideological precepts European powers used to link territorial and cultural nationalism through the norm of homogeneity, so, too, this norm developed in relation to earlier conceptions of race and blood purity which had long served as criteria for distinctions among peoples within and across the politically bounded cultural terrains of Europe (see Poliakov 1974 and Ross 1982).[6]

The ideological contradictions, the cultural struggles engendered through their mediation, and some of the political processes through which these were institutionalized in Central and Eastern Europe reverberated through twentieth-century Western European nations and their dominions. The coming home of colonial chickens to roost amid a growing and diverse influx of Eastern and Southern European, other Mediterranean, and Middle Eastern guest laborers resulted in a proliferation of nationalities, minorities, races, and religious groups in the putatively homogeneous nation-states of Western Europe. These collectivities, many of whose members at least initially considered themselves temporary immigrants, were like chocolate drops in Toll House cookies—they softened but did not melt. The host societies, as they came to be called, did not expect these immigrants to melt because they viewed them as temporary guests.[7]

As the guests became permanent residents and naturalized citizens, they utilized contradictions in the nationalist ideology and took advantage of the ways these contradictions had been mediated elsewhere. In the arguments coined for self-determination and for sovereign independence, they found parallels adequate for the development of economic strategies. In this sociopolitical environment, these economically motivated strategies soon took on an ideological edge directed at maintaining cultural autonomy while the guests demanded the right to live, to work, and otherwise to participate in the sociopolitical life of states that still conceived of themselves as culturally homogeneous *nations-as-states*. These were not, ideologically speaking, "immigrant societies." Instead, they were "nations" (that is, peoples of the same blood) sharing states (that is, politically defined territorial units). Their major policies generally assumed an identity of territorial nationalism and cultural nationalism. Hence, while legally the "others"—the aliens—could become "naturalized" citizens of the politically defined state, ideologically they remained alien to the nation as a biologically defined body politic.

In these states, despite conclusions of biological and social-scientific writings on race and culture, during and after the Age of Enlightenment, ideologies continued to locate the source and the meaning of cultural differences in the "blood" of different human populations. The cultural homogeneity of politically defined territorial units directly contradicted preexisting European ideas about nations as different races of inbreeding blood groups, each producing cultures, that is, levels of civilization, consistent with its innate character. Concurrent with the development of territorial nationalism was an interwoven development of ideas that maintained a conflation of racial differentiation with hierarchically related assessments of cultural differentiation. Moreover, although attention must always be paid to the historical particulars of different European national origin myths, these myths had, as part of the developing ideological intersection of territorial and cultural nationalism, an additional conflation of race and class, making the superior races both the superior classes and the producers of the superior standards of civilization. Biogenetic superiority, like cream, rose to the top. Speaking of the assessed superiority of the Germanic roots in an early French national myth of origin, Poliakov (1974:17) notes, "[t]his was a superiority both of race and of class, because the two notions of upper and lower classes and of superior and inferior races, which are quite distinct today, were not so easy to disentangle when it was a question of contrasting conquering peoples with those they had conquered."

Cultures had not been removed from the "bloods" of mankind, nor had blood been removed from the "cultures" of mankind. Thus, behind both forced cultural uniformity and pluralistic resistance lay ideas about how cultural differences reflected innate propensities. Economically motivated struggles—the strategies for resource competition and for civil rights—were, in part, necessitated and shaped by the continuing structural linkages between occupational role allocations and the conflation of race, culture, and class contained in modern ideologies of nationalism. From the "love it or leave it" slogan of the United States to the "one people, one nation, one destiny" motto of Guyana, we often find a velvet-gloved fist of hegemonic dominance controlling the broader process of cultural homogenization in contemporary nation-states. Central to this process is an effort to delimit politically the criteria out of which standards of civilized conduct will be fashioned and against which any remaining cultural heterogeneity will be judged. Increasingly central, to both dominant groups' hegemonic constructions of homogeneity and subordinate groups' resistance to homogenization, is a selective traditionalism out of which a diversified set of identities is maintained, recreated, or invented in conjunction with the particulars of political and economic struggles.

In the European dominions, changing economic conditions, combined with responses to the cultural and ideological struggles and to the achievements of the new immigrants, awakened linguistic and regional minorities previously presumed homogenized or "dead" (see Allardt 1979). Within Europe, the terms "ethnoregionalism," "neonationalism," and "internal colonies" were spawned in discussions of emerging politicocultural struggles among the Basques, the Bretons, the Flemish, the Irish, and the Scots, to name but a few.[8] Thus supplementing, and sometimes distinct from, narrow economic motivations, these "minority/nationality" groups also maintained competing conceptualizations of race, blood purity, and cultural homogeneity. Although these conceptualizations had developed out of, or were greatly transformed through, interregional European contact and overseas colonial encounters, they also retained elements that preexisted the homogenized content of those contacts.

How these groups selectively pick among historical conjunctures and disjunctures to recall a world presumed to have existed before they were drawn into larger internationally defined territorial, political, and cultural units is nicely captured in Grasmuck's (1980:482) analysis of Scottish Nationalist Party (SNP) ideology: "[T]hrough some paradoxical symbolic inversion, the SNP activists cast politics of class, class identification, and class mobilization in a reactionary light, as an atavistic, alien influence—associated not with an outmoded political program but with a *psychological predisposition.*"

SNP ideology relates this psychological predisposition to its own nationalist resistance of class consciousness, labeling it a cooptation as it moves back through history picking up the fragments believed to be parts of selves formed outside the conflation of British territorial and cultural nationalism after the Union of 1707. First,

[w]hat may be distilled from . . . [the] comments of SNP activists is an association, in the nationalists' minds, of class consciousness with one of two attitudes: among the rather well off, with upper-class snobbery, imputed to the "anglicized" Scottish rich who imitate the English and ridicule Scottish folkways; or more commonly, among the less affluent, with an attitude of

inferiority, with believing oneself unequal to fellow Scots, inferior in an almost philosophical sense. (Grasmuck 1980:482)

And then,

[T]he ever-accommodating myth of Scottish democracy rationalizes this shift [from class consciousness to Scottish nationalism]. The old "equality" of the Kirk, the clan system, and the Scottish comprehensive educational system are all brought forth as evidence that equality and democracy are somehow at the heart of the genuine Scottish tradition. Further, it is claimed, the whole notion of "class," with its inherent connotations of conflict, combative communities, and industrial strife, goes against the Scottish grain. More important, this whole business of class solidarity as opposed to national brotherhood is posited as a foreign, imported notion, in particular, as a decidedly "English-way-of-thinking." We have here a clear illustration of the Scottish ambiguous relationship to metropolitan culture: "a desire to dominate it in the only way open to a provincial—by understanding and mastering its ideology—and an enduring suspicion that this path might, after all, be blocked by a socially-selective clique." (Grasmuck 1980:481).

Grasmuck points out that this contemporary resurgence of Scottish nationalist ideology, if allowed to run its course, would result in a false consciousness, thereby undermining socialist strategies for the political and economic transformation of a class-stratified society. Yet, if we focus on understanding why people actually struggle rather than on how we assume they ought to struggle, we may also note that this ideological deemphasis on class differentiation as an English import provides these Scottish activists, looking backward for positive conjunctures, with symbolic material more conducive to their immediate anti-imperialist task than class-based images of themselves as colonized middleman colonizers in a decaying British empire.

If we extend the line of analysis back past contemporary scholarly disentanglements of the conflation of race, class, and culture, we confront the continuities between this resurgence of Scottish nationalism and what Daiches refers to as the paradoxical cultural consequences of the Union of 1707. In *The Paradox of Scottish Culture: The Eighteenth-Century Experience* (1964), he argues that the Union of 1707 made possible a special kind of Scottish national feeling, but the dominance of the English and their contentions of cultural superiority restricted the effective working of this feeling within Scottish culture. As a result, he maintains, during the late eighteenth and nineteenth centuries, Scotland developed a cultural schizophrenia in the context of which patriotic Scotsmen sublimated their Scottish-ness into a comprehensive Britishness. It is his further contention that the Edinburgh philosophers in particular "were patriotic Scotsmen, making their contribution to the cultural life of Scotland's capital city, yet they thought of their country as 'North Britain' and saw Scotland's vindication as the vying with or even surpassing of England in the production of a common British culture" (Daiches 1964:73).

The economic problems of Scottish Prosperos and Calibans are real but need have no analytic privilege over how they define their struggle against this reality and how they fashion personal and group identities out of the historical conjunctures and disjunctures pro-duced out of these struggles. Grasmuck recognizes, but gives only mythical credence to, this possibility when she states that "[t]he economic and political decline of the U.K. has been instrumental in bringing about an increased confidence on the part of many of these Scots. It is a paradoxical 'relative' rise of confidence, which demands and thrives on a backdrop of decay" (1980:485).

Hence, her conclusion that this nationalist ideology is a contem-porary mythical manipulation encouraged by a self-interested politi-cal group does not explain why this kind of manipulation has been either possible or effective sometimes but not always. To limit the analysis of this struggle to class-differentiated economic determinism is to ignore the very long and complex ideological history out of which Englishness, Britishness, and Scottishness have been con-junctively and disjunctively constructed. What were the characteris-tics of the Britishness to which some eighteenth-century Scotsmen had sublimated their Scottishness while vying to surpass England in the production of a common British culture? Why did they vie with the English in this regard, and why should political and economic decay two centuries later produce a "paradoxical 'relative' rise" in Scottish confidence? In short, which continuities and disjunctions in the ideological underpinnings made meaningful these responses?

Tracing changes in the ideological bases of English self-identifica-tion as a race, Poliakov notes that, although the last invasion of the British Isles took place in 1066, for two millennia preceding the Norman invasions the Isles had been colonized by waves of Iberians, Celts, Romans, Germans, and Scandinavians. This sequence had resulted in a complex cultural situation that, he maintains, "became more so with partial francization which followed." Consequently, co-existence between Celts and Germans, Britons and Anglo-Saxons was extremely turbulent. But little by little it brought about a near identity of the terms "British" and "English." From the very beginning the kaleidoscopic population of the islands had to learn the art of compromise, of which the greatest achievement without any doubt was the fusion of tongues which produced the English language. English humour, that interior compromise of the self with oneself, no less than the notion of *fairness*, may well derive from this primal source. During the Middle Ages, King Arthur, that legendary conqueror of the English, became their national hero, and Richard Coeur de Lion, whose favorite oath was "Do you take me for an Englishman?" was only slightly less popular. In a period of nationalist fervour, an English author was comforted by the thought that Arthur and Richard were, after all, British heroes (though perhaps that touch of humour was involuntary). (Poliakov 1974:37–38)

Viewing themselves as the amalgamated product of the commingling of all the races of Europe, Poliakov maintains, gave the English four genealogical mythologies—the Greco-Roman, the Celtic, the Germanic, and the Hebrew—out of which to produce their own national origin myth. Although it was the Germanic and the Hebrew genealogical constructions that became the mainstays of their mythical inventions, changes in the international status of other European nations linked to these genealogical myths, and against which the English measured themselves, resulted in historical shifts in the emphasis they placed on these in their origin myths. An initially analogous, then sometimes carnal, descent from the Jews was replaced by an emphasis on the Germanic origin of the English, only later to be subordinated as the rise of the Germans to a position of first among nations made of the English the increasingly poor relation (Poliakov 1974:52). Ultimately, it was to be on the Jewish analogue—God's chosen people—that the English were able to stabilize the ideological construction of their origin and their place among the races of Europe. They were a new people: out of five races had been produced a new, valiant, divinely chosen people. In conjunction with their eighteenth-century rise in political and economic power, they invented, reinvented, and reformed English cultural institutions, judging them naturally superior to all others as they took upon themselves the burden of civilizing the world.[9] Out of impurity had been born an ideologically defined purity of biogenetic type as the embodiment of a new culture.

It was against such a developing and expanding sense of English-ness that Scots had pitted themselves before the Union of 1707, to which they sublimated their Scottishness after the Union, and in conjunction with which twentieth-century SNP ideology may be understood as part of a long-term construction of Scottishness (that is, itself a cultural and political label for those who, before their fifth-century migration, had been Irish) in the intersection of territorial and cultural nationalism (see, for example, Mitchison 1980 and R. Campbell 1980). Speaking of the fourteenth-century Scottish struggle for independence against the English, Trevelyan remarks that "in Scotland, contemporaneously with the very similar doings in Switzerland, a new ideal and tradition of wonderful potency was brought into the world; it had no name then, but now we should call it democratic patriotism. It was not the outcome of theory. The unconscious qualities of a people had given it reality in a sudden fit of rage" (1942:164).

In Trevelyan's estimation, however, the "fit of rage" served only to spur on the Scots to an empty victory, though a victory Constantine would have gladly applauded.

Her democratic instincts had prevented her from being annexed to England, who would have given her wealth and civilization. But her democratic instincts had done nothing else for her politically, had not kept her feudal nobility in order, still less found expression for the national feeling in any representative system. Her alliance with France, useful militarily against England, was unnatural culturally, and could be no true substitute for the broken connection with her nearer neighbour. What then had Scotland gained by resisting England? Nothing at all—except her soul, and what-soever things might come in the end from preserving that. (Trevelyan 1942:164)

For the sake of civilization it is better, it seems, to sacrifice the soul to an unholy alliance with the perpetrator of the Hundred Years' War than to foster an unnatural cultural alliance.

The Heat of Social and Cultural Interchanges

Although contemporary collectivities preexisted the introduction of nationalist ideological precepts, others were born of the struggles engendered by the institutionalization of nationalism in relation to

specific economic and political structures. The existence and bound-
edness of still others were the product of a combination of the
motivated activation (often by a small elite stratum) of preexisting
sentiments and common experiences resulting from their struggles
either to resist or to accommodate to the institutionalization of these
ideological precepts. Thus, it is important to know whether particular
collective identities existed before, were a creation of, or were fundamentally reshaped by responses to the development of nationalist
ideologies and the particular economic and political structures within
which these ideologies were fashioned. Because, as the Constantine-
Valetta dialogue should have suggested, when a "people" work to
construct the intersection of territorial and cultural nationalism,
never is that "people's" common historical past so common that it can
be easily and inevitably prostituted to just any reckoning of homogeneity. Neither, as our Guyanese informant's soliloquy should have
suggested, is heterogeneous blood, once culturally constructed, easily and inevitably subject to alternate conceptualizations of place,
status, and conduct.

In a piece entitled "*El Mestizaje:* An All-Inclusive Ideology of Exclusion," Stutzman (1981) provides a marvelous analysis of the role of
heterogeneous blood in the construction of contemporary Ecuadorian nationalism. Race and class, which Poliakov contends are distinct
today in the European cases he describes, are shown by Stutzman to
be interwoven in an Ecuadorian nationalist ideology. This ideology is
rooted in the condensed symbols of *El Mestizaje*—the intermixture of
blood and cultural traditions resulting from a history of miscegenation believed to have produced a new type of human being. Neither a
transplanted European nor of pure indigenous descent, the true Ecuadorian is the son of the soil who gives up ethnic identity for a
commitment to national goals. The goals, however, are defined in
terms of bringing Ecuador into the modern civilized world of developed nation-states, and it is in regard to these goals that the miscege-
nated bloods and the heterogeneous cultures that course through the
veins of the true Ecuadorian take on different political, social, and
cultural meanings.

Stutzman maintains that becoming Ecuadorian is, therefore, a selective process through which "subordinate peripheral heterogeneity
[is assimilated] to the dominant homogeneous center": "[t]his 'selective process' is referred to as *blanqueamiento*—a putative lightening or

'whitening' of the population in both the biogenetic and cultural-behavioral senses of the term *blanco*. The cultural goals, the society, and even the physical characteristics of the dominant class are taken by members of that class to be the objective of all cultural, social, and biological movement and change" (1981:49).

In Ecuadorian nationalist ideology, everyone has mixed blood and everyone ought to be on the way to *blanco* because it is the blood and the cultural traditions of *la raza blanca*, the most valuable of the three races (that is, *india, blanca,* and *negra*) that make up *El Mestizaje* (that is, the biogenetic/cultural amalgam), which provide the foundation for progress, national development, and, hence, the movement toward higher civilization. In these terms, the history of miscegenation has also been the history of the blood of *la raza blanca* absorbing the best of *la raza india* while subordinating its weaknesses (sometimes cruelly), thereby creating past (though Spanish, not Ecuadorian) injustices with which the new nation must contend. In this regard, Stutzman reports that Ecuadorian politicians, policies, and textbook accounts eliminate the "Indian problem"; for, on the one hand, all are part Indian, and, on the other hand, all that is left of the Indian is the legacy of decay that resulted initially from Spanish exploitation and ultimately from the natural tendency of a lower civilization to give way to a higher one. As for *la raza negra*, from "those who were not even owners of their own bodies," textbook accounts provide no evidence of cultural contribution, and the proof of contribution to the blood of *El Mestizaje* is nothing more than the "proliferation of *castas*, terms used to designate the multiplicity of racial crosses that arise when mixed types mate" (Stutzman 1981:63). The character of these past contributions is embedded in stereotypes of the social significance of different races and cultures believed to have passed on undiluted in the bloods of persons who are identified with them.[10]

As Stutzman's case indicates, to understand the continuing consequences of the conflation of race, class, and culture in many of the contemporary nationalist ideologies created by the diverse inhabitants of the new postcolonial states of Africa, Asia, Latin America, and the Caribbean, we must also recognize that the processes through which cultural homogenization—the "not quite homogeneous" homogeneity—was institutionalized were, and in most places continue to be, the same processes through which racial and cultural superiority were heralded; first, among Europeans themselves, then, between them and their colonized subjects, and subsequently, between the strata of colonized colonizers who have taken charge of the "civilizing process" in new nations. It was, thus, with or against the grain of such processes that the inhabitants of these states developed personal and group identities and continue to assess the relative worth of these identities.

Hegemony and the Homogenizing Process

Whatever we are to learn about the role and the implications of ethnicity in the production of, or resistance to, cultural nationalism as an aspect of the construction of social selves and their political consciousness will be located in these intersecting processes. Given that ethnic identities and loyalties are forged in the "heat of social and cultural interchange," generated out of a particular brand of territorial nationalism, and confronted with ideologically trumpeted cultural homogeneity,

[t]he lesson of ethnicity is that we see as problematical the manner in which different kinds of interests and relationships—symbolic and material—will combine in producing social and political solidarities. . . . The concept of ethnicity emphasises that more is at work in this process than a logic of deduced material interests. The latter are an important energising factor. But this energy is most effectively expressed in consciousness and action through a symbolic and affective discourse which creates in actors shared convictions of their *worth* and *potency.* These convictions often encourage solidarities that confound the assumptions of class analysis. (Norton 1984:432)

That the ethnographic reality of these convictions has so often confounded the assumptions of class analysis is, in large measure, a consequence of our own ideological efforts to (prematurely) disentangle race, class, and culture, and to give analytic and political priority to class analysis and, for Marxist scholars, to class struggle. We have done so without adequate attention to the difference between political projections or programs and analytic descriptions of the lived experiences of those we encounter. Whether we have treated the interrelations of race, class, and ethnicity from the standpoint of pluralist, assimilationist, or socialist political projections, we have had more to say about what ought to happen to this interrelation than we have said about the nature of the interrelation. Albeit for different reasons, from all of these analytic perspectives, ethnicity as a particular label for the more general phenomenon of identity formation is viewed as a kind of reactionary bridge to the past, a wall against the future, or a simple disengagement from both the present and a particular future.

In conjunction with these stances, we now find in the past two decades of literature on ethnicity conclusions that proclaim ethnicity to be an economically determined boundary-constructing process strategically used in political and resource competition; a process stimulated by and employed as a communal bulwark against the alienation of mass society; and a process engendered by state expansionism, which provides a strategic disengagement from the contest for, and subordination to, an illegitimate state apparatus (or vice versa).[11] The problem with these conclusions is neither that they are inadequately supported by ethnographic data nor simply that, when proclaimed in universalist terms, they are contradictory. Instead, the difficulty seems to be that there is a documentable and generalizable ring of truth to each of these conclusions. Moreover, this ring of truth is increasingly sustained by the conscious adoption, in identity constructions and in strategic manipulations, of one or the other of these stances by those whose lived experiences we seek to analyze.

The solution to our analytic muddle is not to be found in a stubborn insistence on the analytic priority of race, class, or ethnicity. Instead, where our goal is to understand how personal and group identities are constructed and transformed in the intersection of territorial and cultural nationalism, we must first produce ethnographic accounts of the manner in which race, class, and culture have been entangled in the historical development of particular ideological fields.[12] Rather than insisting on class analysis, if our interest is in disclosing how inequalities stemming from objective conditions are exacerbated or left unremedied by nationalist ideologies and ethnic reactions, we must provide detailed accounts of how ideological fields operate to sustain the pragmatic subordination and the divisive intents of a diverse population.

Both tasks require us to attend carefully to the microsociological details of the ways these entanglements and inequalities are manifest in the social organization of interaction, as well as in the symbolic representation of status within and across the personal and group identities constructed during objective struggles. In these terms, there is no object, act, or idea too insignificant to provide valuable insights into this process. All such objects, acts, and ideas contain within them diverse representations of political and economic differences entailed, first, by how they relate nations and groupings within those nations to the international politicoeconomic arena (the order of nations). Second, their analysis can disclose the impact that this relation has on the policies and the practices through which nationalist ideologies aim to homogenize heterogeneity. As Gilsenan comments, "[E]nglish furniture? Well, yes. Furniture, ways of sitting, modes of dress, politeness, photography, table manners, and gestures overturn societies, too. Such conventions, techniques, and ways of acting in and on the world are as important as any religion, and changes in them may be as dislocating as changes in belief" (1983:20).

Where the national process aimed at homogenizing heterogeneity is fashioned around assimilating elements of that heterogeneity through appropriations that devalue them or that deny the source of their contribution, it establishes what Gramsci referred to as a transformist hegemony.[13] Under these conditions, those groupings associated with objects, acts, and ideas treated in this manner are placed at both a pragmatic and an ideological disadvantage. If they continue to insist on the root identity of their selves and of the objects, acts, and ideas associated with those selves, they are not "true" members of the ideologically defined nation. They are, as Stutzman comments, marginalized persons and groups more often than not viewed as holding back the nation in its efforts to accomplish the goals that define it and its potential place in the order of nations. If, on the other hand, such groups do not insist on identifying the roots of the appropriated elements but instead aim to reduce their marginalization by adopting elements whose roots are ideologically attributed to other groups in the society, they may (and most often do) stand accused of riding to the pinnacle of civilization on the coattails of its real producers. The ideologically defined "real producers," though class-stratified in objective terms, are ideologically conjoined in such a manner that, when they adopt the products of the marginalized other, they are able to do so without experiencing the same pragmatic and ideological consequences to which the marginalized others are subjected. That is not to say that they confront no ideological consequences as a result of this maneuver. Instead, it is to say that the possibility of ameliorating any negative effects lies in the greater control over legitimated interpretations of the meaning of these appropriations attained by such persons in relation to the control of the political and economic structures of the society maintained by an elite stratum with which they become allied by virtue of their identity. For example, in Stutzman's case, Ecuadorian ideology admits that the Spaniards assimilated Quiteña (that is, *la india*) blood in the development of *blanqueamiento*—the civilizing process—but they also decided what significance was to be attributed to this appropriation in the civilizing process.

Thus, in a transformist hegemony, the limits of public debate on all issues are established around a set of criteria and a mode of interpreting those criteria that aim to render illegitimate attempts on the part of marginalized others to expand the criteria or to insist on a different mode or even range of legitimate interpretations. Within a transformist hegemony, the marginalized citizens of the state may continue to value highly objects, to adhere to practices, and to maintain commitments to ideas that are devalued in the putatively homogeneous brew. As long as they lack the political and economic power necessary to insist on a redefinition of what are ideologically defined as the core or the central ingredients of that brew, or to insist on a revaluation of the status of their group identities and their cultural productions, these remain outside the "mainstream." Their new cultural products are either excluded from or absorbed into the homogeneous brew in ways that do little to reduce their marginalization.

Although they remain marginalized, the heterogeneity they represent is never eliminated from the system. Instead, these sources of diversity are combined with two other sources of heterogeneity— that which stems from structural variations in objective conditions, and that which stems from acts of interpretation. In the face of these tendencies toward heterogeneity, even where the homogenizing process achieves a naturalized (that is, taken as given in the natural condition of things) transformist hegemony, heterogeneity remains an essential aspect of the production of culture as a logico-meaningful system in human societies.

Humans are dependent on these systems, and the construction, the maintenance, and the transmission of these systems require developing the means for making the arbitrariness of the systems' constituent elements appear nonarbitrary. Any procedure developed to decrease the apparent arbitrariness of the constituent elements is also dependent on interpretation. In turn, interpretation is influenced by the perspective from which it is made. And, although thinking human beings obviously can adopt different perspectives at different times, their adoption of any perspective is always partially shaped by their objective conditions. Structural variations in the conditions experienced by different groups of the society thereby assure the continued production of heterogeneity in even the most stable transformist hegemony.

In this regard, Gramsci has suggested that any hegemony stemming from a homogenizing process might ultimately take the alternate form of an expansive hegemony. Within an expansive hegemony, goals of the homogenizing process would be different from those of a transformist one. When the momentary definition of homogeneity contradicts the goals and the objectively defined interests of different strata of a population, an expansive hegemony would expand the set of criteria and the range and mode of interpretation to achieve a positive resolution of the contradiction.

To speak of any homogenizing process without reference to its tendency toward one or the other of these hegemonic outcomes is to ignore the political aspect of cultural production in the intersection of territorial and cultural nationalism. Efforts to fix the nonarbitrariness (that is, the momentary, historically constituted givenness) of otherwise arbitrary symbolic constructions are always struggles among perspectives. These perspectives are generated out of a combination of objective structural variations, ideologically defined distinctions, their differential links to alternate interpretations, and potentially different modes of interpretation. Culture—treated as a logico-meaningful system of signs, symbols, identities, statuses, and structural coordinates—is always a representation of the momentary outcome of power struggles over different perspectives and possible alternative interpretations.

Regardless of the type of economic system, cultural struggles are political struggles because, as Gramsci intended in his use of the expression "war of position," the control of a system of meanings and of changes in the value to be attributed to different elements of that system is always linked to the objective conditions shaping the distribution of wealth and power. However, just as there is no one-to-one correspondence between the production and the distribution of wealth, so, too, there is no one-to-one correspondence between who produces the cultural elements assimilated to this system and who controls the assimilation of elements and what they will mean in the system.[14]

From this theoretical standpoint, to analyze the interrelation of race, class, and ethnicity (that is to say, the unity of Constantine's God-given shape, the criteria of loyalty, and the quest for the respect due shiny things) as they are manifest in the lived experience of persons interacting in ideological fields constructed in the intersection of territorial and cultural nationalism is to cut continually into the homogenizing process from different perspectives. It is to recognize, at the same time, that the homogenizing process we seek to represent through these analytic movements within and across perspectives is, in its political aspect, also a hegemonic process. Consequently, as we move among the kaleidoscopic perspectives constructing representations of how people actually struggle, we are also interested in what the actuality of these struggles, which take place in the intersection between territorial and cultural nationalism, tells us about the potential for movement between transformist and expansive hegemonies. Ultimately, our subject of investigation is neither race, class, nor ethnicity per se, but instead the mutability of the ideological structures of dominations constructed out of these distinctions.

The Politics of Cultural Struggle in the Conception of a Guyanese People

The People's Co-operative Republic of Guyana (formerly British Guiana)[15] is located in the northwest corner of South America. It is bordered on the south and southeast by Brazil, on the east by Suriname (formerly Dutch Guiana), and on the west by Venezuela. It encompasses 83,000 square miles with a northeasterly facing coastline that stretches approximately 270 miles along the Atlantic Ocean and extends about 450 miles south to the Brazil border. The total population is roughly 800,000.

The country's territory can be divided into three major zones—the coastal strip, the forest, and the savannah—each characterized by additional variations in soil, climate, geology, and economic utilization (Mandle 1973, Smith 1962). The coastal strip varies in width from forty miles on the Corentyne River coast (the eastern border with Suriname) to less than a mile at points along the Essequibo coast. This 1,750-square-mile zone is the center of Guyana's agricultural enterprise. Immediately to the south of this strip is a forest zone covering nearly 70,000 square miles. This white-sand zone is the location of the country's primary (bauxite) and secondary (gold and diamond) mineral resources, as well as of other forest extractions such as balata and a variety of timber. In the far southwestern corner is the Rupununi Savannah, about 6,000 square miles primarily used for cattle grazing. The remainder of the country's territory is composed of an intermediate savannah along the Berbice River.

Most important ecologically, the entire coastal strip, with the exception of elevated sandbars, lies some six feet below sea level and is subject to inundation by waters from the country's three major rivers, numerous tributaries, and the Corentyne River. The reclamation and maintenance of this zone made necessary the construction and ensuing maintenance of an intricate and costly drainage and irrigation system that must not only keep out seawater but also control the entry and the expulsion of fresh water for irrigation and drainage. These requirements are met by the construction of a front dam (the seawall) to keep out the seawater and of a back dam and conservancy linked to a maze of cross-cutting trenches through which the level and the flow of fresh water are controlled by opening or closing "kokers" (sluice gates).

Historically, economically, and culturally Guyana shares much with the British Caribbean Islands. Initially, the colonies of Essequibo, Demerara, and Berbice (now the names of its three counties) were established by Dutch traders under the Dutch West Indian Company and were not officially ceded to the British until 1814. Effective British control, however, is usually dated from 1781 (Smith 1962). In 1831 the British united the three colonies to create British Guiana, which developed a plantation economy heavily dependent on sugar cane cultivation by African slaves. After emancipation in 1834 the African labor force was augmented by the importation of indentured laborers from China, Portuguese Madeira, India, and the West Indian islands.

The British maintained control until May 26, 1966, when the colony gained its independence. The period from 1960 to 1964 was marked by civil strife when the People's Progressive Party, founded by

Cheddi Jagan and Forbes Burnham, split into two parties, the People's Progressive Party (PPP) and the People's National Congress (PNC), with Jagan heading the PPP and Burnham the PNC. This split, and the accompanying disagreements between Jagan and Burnham, allegedly divided the population along the lines of its major ethnic segments, with Africans supporting the PNC and East Indians supporting the PPP. In 1962, 1963, and 1964 further disagreements over political and economic issues were accompanied by racially oriented violence.

By 1979 large-scale violent confrontations had given way to suspicion, distrust, political assassination, allegations of massive electoral fraud, and a range of other intimidation tactics, as racially oriented political competition continued. Under the paramount party leadership of the PNC, approximately 80 percent of the economy had been nationalized. Unfortunately, despite the socialist orientation of the major political parties, the nationalization of major industries, and other measures intended to decrease dependency on foreign imports, the country had experienced no real economic growth since 1970, and an estimated 30 percent of the labor force was unemployed.

As economic historians (for example, Adamson 1972, Mandle 1982, Rodney 1981, Thomas 1984) have amply demonstrated, during the colonial era of "emergent capitalism" in Guiana the allied strata managed to control the political and economic apparatus while justifying their dominance in terms of intellectual and cultural superiority and the naturalness of practices stemming from such justification.[16] State legal and judicial coercive forces were frequently brought to bear against workers where their interests conflicted with those of the owners and managers of the major sugar and bauxite industries. Moreover, the policy decisions favoring the owners of these industries were phrased in nationalized terms (nationalized in a Gramscian, not an economic, sense). That is to say, though objectively a small sector of the population benefited most from the decisions, policies concerning the allocation and the use of resources were discussed in terms of the "national good" or "the welfare of the total society." Under both proprietary and multinational corporate ownership of plantations, conflicts of interest between labor and management were resolved in favor of the interests of management (Thomas 1984). By combining control of the means of production with state-mediated control of workers and finance, consciously al-

lied elements of the historical bloc were able to manipulate productivity and, hence, profitability in relation to fluctuations in world
market prices (Thomas 1984). It was in conjunction with this transformist hegemony that cultural productions were evaluated and sub-
verted or appropriated and rearticulated.

In contrast, the elite that assumed power after independence faced
different conditions for the formation of a historical bloc that could
nationalize its interests in transformist terms (Middle 1982). In 1979
an African elite and other ethnically identified individuals pragmatically allied to it had assumed the mantle of European institutional
domination through control of the political apparatus. Through political control they had nationalized 80 percent of the economy and
thereby had gained greater official control over it. Even so, they had
not yet managed to combine effectively these aspects of the society
to produce a hegemony the naturalness of which was given in practice and in the ideological interpretations of that practice. Yet, as
Mandle notes, to the extent that they were able at all to represent
their interests as *the* national interests, they had done so through
appropriation of a previously nationalized discourse—socialism.

To understand why they had not achieved a legitimated transformist hegemony requires an examination of the means they used to
gain control of the political apparatus, and, "in the last instance," why
they had been unable to dress their control over the use of power in a
nationalized clothing that is consistent with their interests. As Mandle states:

the transition to "socialism" reflected the pursuit of self-interest by a group of
lawyers, teachers, professionals, and small businessmen—who came to political office with Independence. Fundamental to this situation was the fact
that this class of political leaders had no direct economic interest in the
dominant industries in Guyana. Both sugar and bauxite were foreign-owned.
Thus, the institutional base for their power was not economic, but rather in
their control of the state apparatus. Under these circumstances the bias of
their rule was toward centralization. For in vesting increased control in the
hands of the state, this class would, through their positions in government,
also accumulate increased influence and power. (1982:112)

Following this line of reasoning Mandle suggests that this group
not only economically nationalized major sectors but also, through
the use of a socialist discourse, managed partially to ideologically
naturalize their interests, because

[w]hen the [economic] nationalizations occurred, they were described as part of a "socialist thrust." In employing such an ideological defense for their actions, government officials were able to capture the positive benefits to be derived from identifying themselves as socialists. At the same time, they were able to avoid having to defend acts of nationalization on the much less attractive ground that such acts were part of the process by which a local governing class was extending and solidifying its base of power. (1982:113)

Hence, they nationalized their interest through the appropriation of what had, in the course of the independence movement, become a legitimated anticolonial framework for defining appropriate modes of competition and cooperation. Within this socialist discourse, however, they transformed the objectives of worker control over resources and over decision-making procedures into the reality of state capitalism by firmly dominating these rather than by institutionalizing full worker participation (Mandle 1982, Thomas 1984). Even, as Mandle notes, cooperativism, this power bloc's designated mechanism for a socialist transformation of social relations of production, became in practice no more than another form of wage labor within which relations between labor and management followed the pattern established under emergent capitalism.[17]

In light of these achievements, and without assuming a complete absence of sincere interest in socialism, we may conclude that the failure of this elite stratum to produce a legitimated transformist hegemony is rooted in its inability, thus far, to transform the major agricultural sector of the economy in a manner that affords it control over national productivity and over the production of a range of goods and services to distribute to the subordinate classes (Mandle 1982). To the extent that hegemonic expansion and legitimation depend on the transformation of the rural agricultural sector in order to increase productivity and, thus, to be able to reward, however unequally, supporting coalitions, the symbolism of ethnicity and its production remains a problematic aspect of the elite stratum's effort to link political and economic control with moral and intellectual leadership, an accomplishment that Gramsci (1971) identified as an essential condition for transformist hegemonic dominance. Again, Mandle points to the underlying disjunction between political and economic power and its link to the elite stratum's desire to manipulate ethnic marking when he states, "[t]he fact, however, that this new state-based ruling class is largely urban and of Afro-Guyanese descent, has meant that it is poorly equipped to promote successfully the country's economic development. A successful development strategy in Guyana depends on the harnessing of the energies of the agricultural work force. To date, the country does not possess a government capable for making that critical linkage" (1982:124–25).

By contrast, the agricultural work force is predominantly rural and East Indian. It would be a mistake, however, not to recognize that this government is poorly equipped, not solely because it is Afro-Guyanese and urban. Though it nationalized its interests through a socialist discourse, it also continued to institutionalize capitalist patterns of labor to management relations to maintain a particular articulation of ethnicity and mode of production. Labor unrest associated with this system of relations partly accounts for the government's inability to engender a level of productivity that would allow it to strengthen the ties among the diverse members of the historical bloc by delivering greater material rewards. It must, therefore, maintain control through the contradictory combination of socialist and ethnic discourses.[18]

An emphasis on ethnicity is a powerful instrument because it extends the composition of the historical bloc to include (consistent with Gramsci's definition of historical bloc) those social groupings consciously allied to one another as well as to other social groupings that, confronted with these conditions, develop everyday practices that complement and, therefore, become part of the mechanism of control available to the most powerful coalitions among the consciously allied strata.

Even so, the hegemonic process produces a very tangled web because, as we shall see, the complementary nature of the symbolism of ethnicity and associated practices (for example, the ethnic marking of cultural productions, the linkages between ethnic identity and the relative fitness for particular economic tasks and leadership roles) are not divorced from their origin in the past ideological interpretations of appropriate patterns of interaction between members of the dominant and the subordinate strata. Hence, it makes as much sense to say that in 1979 the government was Afro-Guyanese because it was poorly equipped as it does to say that it was poorly equipped because if was Afro-Guyanese. That is to say, unable to deliver on its socialist promises, it relied on ethnic divisiveness. Let us turn now to the country—the processes of hegemonic dominance and the efforts to dismantle it—in the community of Cockalorum.

2

Cockalorum:
Spatial Boundaries,
Economic Limits,
and Cultural
Constraints

Cockalorum is located in East Coast Demerara about twenty-five miles east of Georgetown, the capital city, and a little more than three times that distance west of New Amsterdam, Berbice. It is one of a chain of densely populated settlements stretching from Georgetown in the west to Rosignol in the east. A public road bisects Cockalorum; it traverses the coastal region and serves as the artery of communication between coastal localities and the river ports connecting these with northwestern and southern interior mining, lumber, and fishing areas.

Cockalorum and other settlements along the east coast can be easily reached within an hour or two by private car, bus, or the many "hire cars" (licensed vehicles) that regularly ply this route. Although there is a bus stop on the public road at the entrance to Cockalorum, most residents prefer to take one of the faster, locally owned hire cars that regularly leave the central area of the settlement for the east coast car park (that is to say, the equivalent of a taxi stand) in Georgetown, where they can get transportation to go farther west. They also prefer to transfer there to get a car to travel back to eastern localities beyond Cockalorum or to the Rosignol "stelling"[1] (wharf), because, although one can wait by the side of the public road to hail a car, hire cars are usually filled beyond the legal limit by the time they leave Georgetown. Unless special arrangements are made, local hire-car operators do not regularly carry passengers farther east than Cockalorum.

The core of the unit is the two-village strip approximately one-

Figure 2.1. Cockalorum Residential Area

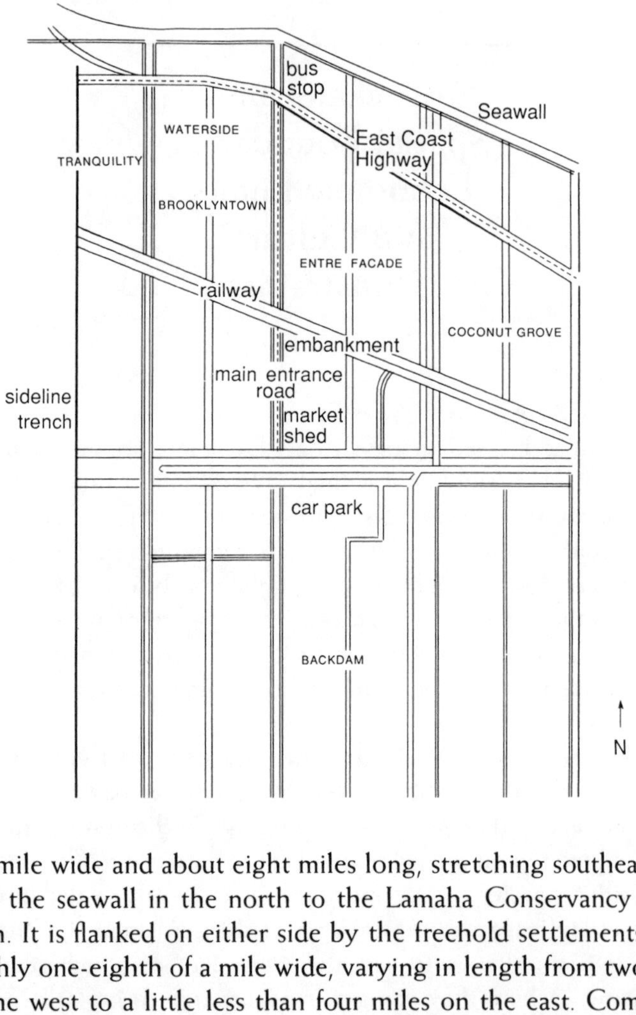

half mile wide and about eight miles long, stretching southeastward
from the seawall in the north to the Lamaha Conservancy in the
south. It is flanked on either side by the freehold settlements, each
roughly one-eighth of a mile wide, varying in length from two miles
on the west to a little less than four miles on the east. Combined,
these sections cover an area of approximately 5,600 acres (see Figures
2.1 and 2.2).

The eastern and the western sections are the physical boundaries
of what residents recognize as a moral community based on locality—people are "born and grown between one another" and therefore "belong to the same place." Although each section is named and
persons identify themselves as belonging to a particular section, they
also recognize a shared identity across these parts, defining Cockalorum as a social and moral unit distinct from adjacent territories.

Figure 2.2. Cockalorum Residential Area
and Farmland

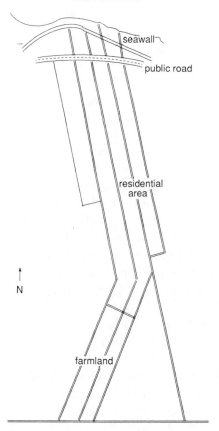

Recognized landmarks and drainage trenches further divide these four sections into five areas north to south: from the seawall to the public road; from the public road to the old railway embankment; from the railway embankment to the Mahaica Canal, which runs through three of the four sections; from the Mahaica Canal to the first polder (reclaimed farmland); and from the first polder to the Conservancy. The first four areas are residential; the last consists of farmland and savannah.

Tranquility, the smallest of the four named sections, about one and one-half miles wide by two miles long, serves as the western boundary of Cockalorum. The backland (a farm area in most coastal settlements) is not owned by Tranquility residents; it is part of the adjacent plantation to which Tranquility belonged. This residential area was initially settled by Africans and by time-expired East Indian indentured laborers who bought, leased, or rented small plots of land on which to build houses and to plant vegetables while they continued working on the plantation.

The plantation (now a privately owned coconut estate) produced coffee until the mid-1820s. When coffee was no longer profitable, the estate merged with two smaller adjacent cotton-producing estates to the west of its boundary. Under several different owners, this amalgamated estate produced sugar until the second decade of the twentieth century, while the freehold area continued to develop as an attached residential community.

The population of Tranquility grew until the 1940s, when it began to decline. Repeated flooding forced residents to seek house lots in other sections of Cockalorum or elsewhere in the east coast region. During the 1962–64 disturbances both Africans and East Indians fled the section to take up residence in one of the less racially integrated sections of Cockalorum or moved out of Cockalorum altogether. Furthermore, in recent years individuals have migrated to Georgetown, the United Kingdom, Canada, and the United States. Today, in all of Cockalorum, there are few families who do not have at least one or two relatives who are temporary or permanent residents in these countries.

There are many vacant lots and several abandoned houses in Tranquility. Of the sixty-seven lots of differing sizes, only forty-two have occupied houses. Some lots have more than one household; thus, the forty-two lots have fifty-two households, making Tranquility the least populated section of Cockalorum. It is also the most poorly drained section. Roadways and paths are unpaved and become almost impassable during the wet seasons, at which time it must be entered by "corial" (boat).

To the immediate east of Tranquility, separated by a trench and a footpath, is Brooklyntown,[2] an area approximately three miles wide by eight miles long. This section was settled in 1849 as two communal African villages. The eastern part was purchased by three Africans with $10,000 contributed by seventy-two persons, who were then given shares in the residential area and in each of the farmland polders. The western portion was purchased by four persons for a sum of $7,000 (*Daily Chronicle*, February 2, 1960). They were amalgamated within the same year of their purchase and thereafter operated as one communal village. After an 1859 survey residents received separate deeds for their shares.[3]

Consistent with this past pattern, Brooklyntown is now divided into a residential and a farm area. With the exception of both the poorly drained, unused area between the seawall and the public road and an open area between the public road and the old railway embankment, the northern portion of Brooklyntown is residential. It has 554 lots, many of which are used for gardens. A few are vacant, and still others, with and without houses, belong to persons residing abroad in the United States, Canada, and the United Kingdom. The balance of Brooklyntown (about three miles wide by six miles long) is reclaimed farmland and savannah. Although I did not systematically collect information on land ownership, informants contend that most inhabitants own or have rights in "children's property" (that is, impartible property inherited by a set of siblings) in both the residential and the farm area. The few residents who are most likely not to own or have rights in farmland are the very indigent and those families who, for several generations, have engaged in nonagricultural occupations.

Entre Facade, the next section to the east, is roughly three miles wide by seven miles long. Like Brooklyntown, it is divided north to south into a residential portion and farmland. Also like Brooklyntown and Tranquility, the area between the seawall and the public road is poorly drained. It is vacant except for a water pump that serves all of Cockalorum. The residential section from the public road to the first polder contains a government housing scheme separated from a once-incorporated proprietary[4] village by the embankment of a defunct railway.

The housing-scheme land has been state owned since the plantation was abandoned around 1918. Twenty units are occupied and several others are near completion, but a proposed school and playground have yet to be started. A wooden building, intended as a recreation center and public meeting hall, is nearly complete and presently serves to store equipment and supplies for persons who are working on their own houses. A health center (also part of the housing-scheme plan) is complete and has been operating for several years. Some roads have also been graded and surveyed, but a third of this area, which floods easily and is usually wet, has yet to be cleared of grass. In principle, residents of all sections of Cockalorum have access to it for grazing livestock.

South of the railway to the first polder is the residential section of Entre Facade, the old proprietary village. Although all informants questioned agreed that Entre Facade was an East Indian settlement by the third decade of the twentieth century, they differed over the racial composition of the settlement that developed immediately after the sugar plantation was abandoned. Most likely, it followed a pattern similar to that described for Tranquility. Some informants, mainly Africans but also a few elderly East Indians, argue that Africans from Brooklyntown and from nearby estates bought land from the plantation owner and settled on it while the plantation was still functioning. When it was abandoned, all the land not owned by the individual proprietors became state land, which the government then sold by the acre to time-expired East Indian indentured laborers who had relocated from other estates in the region. African informants claim that, as East Indians moved into the area, Africans who had purchased land there sold it and left to take up residence in Brooklyn- town. Some East Indian informants agree, but others maintain that, once abandoned by the plantation owner, Entre Facade was always an East Indian settlement. Nevertheless, even by these accounts a few African families always owned land in and resided in what became Entre Facade.

Including the housing scheme, Entre Facade is divided into 290 lots that are used for housing, gardens, various commercial structures, and communal facilities. The large majority (203) of these lots have more than one house and household, making Entre Facade the most densely populated section of Cockalorum, with few vacant lots and still fewer unoccupied houses (see Table 2.1). To the south of the residences is farmland where most villagers, but few housing-scheme inhabitants, own plots. Entre Facade was not originally a communal village; consequently, residents acquired house lots and farm plots separately rather than through distributed shares.

Coconut Grove, the eastern boundary of Cockalorum, is approx- imately three miles wide by four miles long. Part of it, like Tran- quility, was once a freehold residential community attached to a sugar plantation, with each plantation owner selling or leasing additional house lots and provision plots to East Indians and to Africans. When the plantation was finally abandoned in the first decade of the twen-

Table 2.1. Population of Cockalorum by Section

Section	Number	Percentage
Tranquility	200	4
Brooklyntown	2,000	40
Entre Facade	2,500	50
Coconut Grove	300	6
Total	5,000	100

Note: Data included in tables 2.1–2.4 are the result of a household survey conducted by the author.

tieth century, the government assumed control over it and eventually sold most of the remaining land to a single proprietor from whom the current owners, an East Indian family, purchased the estate. This family maintains a house in the area and employs an overseer to look after the coconut grove.

The land between the seawall and the railway embankment remains state owned. Unlike the other three sections of Cockalorum, the northern area between the seawall and the public road is sufficiently drained for habitation. In the past few years it has become rather densely populated, because individuals from all other sections of Cockalorum moved there, buying lots and building houses. Because of floods and the salinity of the soil, this part of Coconut Grove is primarily residential, with few gardens and no communal or commercial facilities. Some East Indians occasionally plant rice on the land situated between the public road and the railway embankment; between rice crops, they, and others, also use it for pasture.

From the railway embankment to the first polder is the main residential area. The Mahaica Canal, which divides it north to south, marks a further division between the old freehold settlement and a new residential area, most of which has been inhabited only since the current proprietors took control. Because much of this northern land still belongs to the proprietors, residents either rent house lots and farm plots or compensate the owners by maintaining the drainage trenches. Many of them moved here during the disturbances after fleeing Brooklyntown, the racially integrated part of Tranquility, and the southern freehold section of Coconut Grove.

Overall, the combined sections—Brooklyntown, Coconut Grove,

Table 2.2. Racial and Religious Composition of Cockalorum
by Percentage of Households (N = 794)

Race	Percentage	Religion	Percentage
African	45.0	Christian	54
East Indian	48.0	Hindu	36
Portuguese	0.6	Muslim	10
Mixed	6.4		

Entre Facade, and Tranquility—have a population of about 5,000 inhabitants distributed among 794 households. The racial and religious composition of the community is typical of Guyana's rural coastal regions. Table 2.2 presents the racial and religious composition of Cockalorum. Table 2.3 and Table 2.4 present the racial and religious affiliations of households according to their distribution across the four sectional divisions.[5]

The population composition of each of the sections continues to reflect the racial identity of its initial settlers. Informants, however, claim that before the political disturbances of 1962–64, the racial composition of each of the four sections was slightly more integrated than it is today. During this period many individuals relocated to a section where their race predominated. In each section one or two racially outnumbered families remained. These say they did not move because they had "lived well" with their neighbors, who protected them by threatening or by actually attacking persons who sought to drive them out because of their racial identity. Others who left have since returned, and still others have bought or are renting houses in sections where they are racially outnumbered. Thus, although no major part of Cockalorum is composed entirely of one racial segment, one group tends to predominate and others form segregated clusters within each section.

A paved entrance road divides Brooklyntown and Tranquility on the west from Entre Facade and Coconut Grove on the east. The point where this road crosses the Mahaica Canal and its "dam" (filled-in roadway) is the nucleus and commercial center of the settlement. It is the busiest, most public area of the settlement and includes the shed where morning market is held, a paved turn-around where hire cars pick up and discharge passengers, several shops and bars, the

Table 2.3. Racial Distribution of Households
by Section (N = 794)

Section	African	East Indian	Portuguese	Mixed	Total
Tranquility	29	23	0	0	52
Brooklyntown	233	11	3	26	273
Entre Facade	5	255	2	13	275
Coconut Grove	83	100	1	10	194

village office, and the trade school. Several churches and the community high school are also located in the immediate vicinity.

Other commercial and communal facilities are distributed
throughout Entre Facade and Brooklyntown. With the exception of a
cemetery in Tranquility and of a coconut oil factory and one general
shop in Coconut Grove, these two settlements have no commercial
or communal facilities. Their residents worship in churches and
attend schools in either Entre Facade or Brooklyntown.

Although all inhabitants of Cockalorum use most of the facilities
located in Brooklyntown and in Entre Facade, such as the post office,
the health center, and the police station, they prefer to worship,
attend school, drink, and shop in establishments situated in their own
settlements. However, of the four Christian churches located in Entre
Facade, only the Canadian Mission church has a predominantly East
Indian congregation. Though the Entre Facade elementary school
(built by East Indians following the disturbances) now has a mini-
mally integrated staff and student body, residents of all the sections

Table 2.4. Religious Affiliation of Households
by Section (N = 794)

Section	Christian	Hindu	Muslim	Total
Tranquility	32	5	15	52
Brooklyntown	266	1	6	273
Entre Facade	44	196	35	275
Coconut Grove	103	89	2	194
Total	445	291	58	794

still refer to it as the East Indian school. The field with an adjacent bandstand (considered to be part of the school) ideally serves as a playing field for all Cockalorums, but it is used mainly by East Indians.

Whereas all large and scarce items must be bought in Georgetown or in Melanie Damashana, a shopping center about ten miles west of the community, its inhabitants try to make all other purchases at local shops owned by members of their racial group. This practice can date back only a short time, because until the 1940s all shops in the community were owned by either Portuguese or Chinese shopkeepers, and shopping patterns tended to be influenced by the quality of social relationships between particular shoppers and particular proprietors.[6]

Today, even with this ethnic diversity in shop ownership, it is seldom possible for residents to adhere strictly to their preference for shopping in their own section from shopowners of their own race/ethnic[7] group. Shops differ in the range of goods they regularly stock, and shopkeepers differ in the connections they manage to develop, which allow them regularly to obtain goods in chronic short supply. Further, shopkeepers frequently refuse to sell short-supply items to any but their regular customers. Others are either told that because they are not regular customers, they are not entitled to purchase or that the stock is already sold out. Even regular customers are often required to buy one or more goods for which there is less demand before they are permitted to acquire items in short supply. Stock differences and these selling practices encourage residents to try to establish trading relations with several shops. They also account for why all residents trade at the largest, best-stocked shop, although it is owned by a Muslim East Indian family and is located in Entre Facade.

Unlike the old pattern, according to which each settlement was an autonomous unit of the centralized local government administration, all four sections are now part of one local government unit. As a consequence of this change, informants thought that, in the first decade of the twentieth century, the freehold settlement of Entre Facade became a country district controlled by the local government department. Its councilors, charged with tax collection and the maintenance of public works, were appointed by the local government board. By 1920 Entre Facade was incorporated and became a village district (also known as a local authority), and its council was composed of one appointed and at least two elected councilors.

In 1856 the incorporated village of Brooklyntown also came under the control of the local government board. Before that time it had operated as a communal village, selecting its own headman and councilors. After its integration into the local government administration, it had one appointed and several elected councilors responsible for collecting taxes and for maintaining public works. Entre Facade and Brooklyntown continued to function as adjacent villages with their own village councils until 1930, when the local government administration unified them in the name of creating a larger, more effectively governed district. This amalgamation was short-lived. It was dissolved in 1933 by the colonial secretary in response to petitions and to a protest march organized by some residents of Brooklyntown, who argued that the arrangement placed Africans at a political disadvantage.

The villages operated as separate local authorities until 1969, when they were again amalgamated as one unit of the Grove-Haslington Local Government District. Elected councilors currently represent the two villages and the freehold areas of Tranquility and Coconut Grove on the local government board. Unlike these village sections, until 1968 the freehold settlements were unincorporated and, therefore, did not have a local government structure, nor did their residents pay taxes. Now they, and all residents, pay their taxes at an office located in Brooklyntown. One overseer is still in charge of tax collection and public works throughout the four sections.

Making a Living: Economic Options as
First-Order Limitations

As in many Caribbean communities, individuals in Cockalorum simultaneously pursue several income-producing activities (see Mason 1970). Residents divide their efforts into two broad categories: "working for self" and "working for others." Generally, working for self is preferred to working for others, and nonagricultural enterprise is preferred to agricultural labor.

Since the late nineteenth century small-scale provision farming has been increasingly devalued relative to petty entrepreneurship, wage labor, and salaried labor. Even so, peasant agriculture continues to play an important role in the community's economic base and serves at least as a partial source of income for a majority of Cockalorums. Its links to slavery, indenture, and the colonial era have contributed to its devaluation; however, one must recognize that it is also extremely difficult to make a living at farming. Yet, because working for oneself is more highly valued than working for others, agriculture, with its tie to land ownership (a symbol of independence and of personal worth in colonial Guiana) is also an activity associated with an ambiguous evaluation of prestige. Farming, in a symbolic sense, is "real" (essential) work in ways that other occupations and income-producing activities are not. In practical terms, therefore, Cockalorums typically express the view that, as an occupation, it is a losing proposition—" 'e caan pay"[8] (translation: it does not [re]pay the effort one expends).

In the late nineteenth century and in the first decade of the twentieth, before surrounding estates stopped producing and grinding cane, many farmers in Cockalorum and in the region grew cane, which they sold to the estates. According to informants, over the past sixty years they have not produced commercial cane because, as most of the nearby estates folded, the transport distance and time involved increased, making the venture unprofitable.

At the same time rice cultivation developed and expanded as a cash crop, and many Cockalorum families began to grow rice for income and for personal consumption. This venture, too, proved unprofitable. Nowadays, the land in the front section of Coconut Grove, designated rice land, more often than not lies fallow. Informants say that there have been only two rice crops since 1975. Instead, those who now farm regularly or intermittently raise root crops and vegetables and tend a variety of tree crops. Farmers seldom have more than three or four beds of one-quarter to one-half acre each in use at the same time, because the amount of land cultivated depends on a sufficiency of family labor. Paid labor is too expensive for most, and, for all practical purposes there is no exchange of unpaid farm labor ("day-for-day" labor).

As either an alternative or a supplement, many informants reported raising poultry for cash at one time or another, though few succeeded for any length of time. Some of them went out of business because they were unable to obtain drugs to treat diseased stock; others had to sell out because feed was unavailable or too expensive. Most felt that poultry farming is not a business for "small men" (ordinary men) because the few large producers can afford to sell below the government-controlled price for a period of time long enough to drive the smallest of the small competitors out of business and limit those who remain to selling retail to customers in their own communities.

To supplement other sources of income, many households in Cockalorum also sell farm produce and other consumer goods. This includes wholesale marketing of goods produced by the marketer, retail selling of goods produced by the marketer or bought from other producers, and retailing of domestic and imported manufactured goods. Differences in age, gender, and ethnic affiliation influence the type and the extent of involvement in these activities. For example, men, women, and children of all ethnic segments engage in the wholesale and retail sale of farm produce, but middle-aged women generally predominate, while among women East Indians are most likely to market produce wholesale. Because of differences in household composition and in domestic organization (see Smith and Jayawardena 1959, Smith 1956), which affect the amount of family labor available for cultivating, East Indian women have larger supplies to sell. These women, in contrast to their African and other counterparts, are more likely to be directly involved in farm labor and, hence, are unlikely to want to spend the amount of time necessary to retail their goods. Across ethnic lines, marketers who have smaller supplies are most likely to engage in retailing. Typically, they sell part of their supplies in the local morning markets (held every day except Sunday) and transport the rest to Georgetown to sell in the large marketplaces there or at specific sites along the city sidewalks.

Men, alone, with their mates, or with some family members, may also be involved in marketing. Younger men (approximately aged twenty to thirty) often center their attention on purchasing and reselling "water" (green) coconuts. They sell these wholesale to a vendor or retail to customers as a typical form of refreshment. Other males in the same age category, along with a few females, may buy manufactured goods to sell on the sidewalks of Georgetown. These pavement sellers concentrate on imported goods, mainly items banned by the government. The most enterprising among them try to gain enough capital to finance buying trips to nearby countries (primarily Suriname, Trinidad, and Barbados) to purchase such items as cigarettes, candy, and canned and dry goods. Although this form of marketing has been tried by many and is the goal of many more, few actually succeed. The cost of buying the required foreign currency on the black market, the risk of having goods confiscated by officials, or having to pay bribes to avoid confiscation can each make this a difficult venture to sustain.

Young children and teenagers may also engage in marketing either to earn a small "pocket piece" (spending money) for themselves or to contribute to the family income. They frequently assist their parents, but they may also work alone, selling fruits, vegetables, and cooked food to villagers—especially on their midday break from school and in the early evening hours when many residents go out for a stroll. Industrious children plant small gardens that they tend, harvest, and market. Others, particularly very young boys, build small carts and purchase ice and flavored syrup in order to sell "shaved ice" (snow-cones).

Comparing the range of possible options, many Cockalorums declare shopkeeping a vocation of the highest status. Opening and stocking a shop, however small, is an expensive venture, and most aspirants never manage to do more than sell from their homes a variety of small items such as ice, cigarettes, candy, homemade sweets, and so forth. The largest of the seventeen operating shops began in this manner, expanding when their proprietors could afford to enclose the "bottom-house" (the area underneath an elevated house) and to develop enough connections to stock supplies regularly.

With the exception of two small shops that sell only candies, sweet drinks, and beer, all are family-run units. Either male or female family members may control the daily operations and the purchasing of stock. None of the shops carry major consumer goods such as furniture or large appliances. All the shops offer roughly the same stock of food, dry goods, patent medicines, and small tools or household implements. The proprietors who have better connections for procuring goods, especially those in chronic short supply, do the best business because, as mentioned before, they sell these only to regular customers and usually only if customers purchase one or two items that are difficult to sell.

Most shops are licensed to sell beer and liquor, but "rum shops" specialize in selling liquor. In general, these bars are family businesses, though one of the largest is operated by some unrelated young men who regularly sponsor disco dances and who sometimes also serve cooked food. They supplement their income by sponsoring weekend outings and "socas" (socials), and by working as disc jockeys for house parties in Cockalorum and in other communities.

Even the owners of the largest shops, however, must supplement this income with wage labor or with other forms of self-employment. Some join other self-employers as hire-care operators, carpenters, electricians, midwives, religious specialists, private teachers, independent "porkknockers" (diamond and gold prospectors), seamstresses, and tailors. Hire-care operators probably make the most money, but they also need sufficient capital to purchase and to maintain a vehicle, making this a difficult form of self-employment to start. Occasionally, an individual may find work driving someone else's car for a share of the daily earnings. Although rare, when this occurs it is often an arrangement between close kin who believe one another to be honest.

Porkknocking is the form of self-employment most glorified and the most subject to windfall gains. However, unless one joins a crew in which the crew leader puts up the cost of transportation and supplies, becoming an independent porkknocker requires a substantial initial outlay of cash. In most instances, the high cost of food, brothels, and bars in the bush, as well as in-camp theft, cause porkknockers to return home nearly penniless if not in debt. Nonetheless, work histories collected suggest that porkknocking is most popular with young, unmarried African males. They usually become involved by running away to join a crew against their parents' advice or without their knowledge. The dangers and the risks are such that most men give up porkknocking after a couple of "quarters" (a quarter equals three to four months), especially if they become husbands and fathers. Currently, there are two African families who have regularly engaged in porkknocking since the 1920s. The males in these families spend most of their time in the interior, returning home during some holidays or for the wet season. In the past, East Indians from East Coast Demerara communities did not engage in porkknocking, but today in Cockalorum a few young East Indian men have joined one of the African crews.

Sugar and rice production are mainstays of the Guyanese economy. Two government-operated estates produce sugar in the East Coast Demerara region; rice is cultivated in the nearby Mahaicony-Abary Creek area. Although both sources of employment are within easy commuting distance of the community, residents rarely work there. Except for a few Africans who were employed on these estates during the 1963 strike, most residents under forty have little direct experience with sugar work. Occasionally, males who need a little quick money work for short periods in the rice or sugar industries, but most informants describe even this level of involvement as more a past than a current pattern. Sometimes, East Indian and African women earn wages breaking coconuts for copra production on nearby estates. As with sugar and rice work, this wage labor is most often sought to pay for special expenses. The only other local source of non-government-related wage labor is available in a small Brooklyntown factory that produces candles and shoes when it has materials. It employs five to ten persons.

Non-self-employment is also usually nonagricultural wage and salaried labor in the public or private sectors of the national economy. Salaried positions as teachers, civil servants, nurses, and as military and paramilitary personnel prevail. Thus, other than the teachers and the school administrators who work in the community schools, most of Cockalorum's wage laborers commute daily to Georgetown and to other East Coast Demerara communities. A few younger males lucky enough to have connections in Linden (previously named McKenzie) work in the bauxite industry. They usually find housing there, periodically returning to Cockalorum to visit friends and relatives.

Despite the range of income options and the variety of ways they can be combined, most Cockalorums, if not unemployed, are underemployed. Young adults (approximately eighteen to thirty-five), especially those from families not regularly engaged in farming, work at occasional odd jobs. Some of them actively pursue leads and social connections that they hope will result in stable employment; others are persons-in-waiting. Some of these are waiting for the opportunity that will allow them to be self-employed without first having to work for someone else; others for the opportunity that will place them on the road to migration and a chance to "make life" "outside" (abroad). Still others—males and females—are waiting to find someone who might be persuaded to support them. Individuals labeled "limers" (idlers or "anti-social" types) are simply waiting and hoping for a new day. In the meantime, they steal or live off their relatives in the community and abroad.

Making Life: Ethnic Stereotypes as
Second-Order Limitations

In any society a person's sense of self-worth and quest for status among peers are constrained by the availability of employment and the prestige accorded to different types of work. The work one actually does, and the amount of income derived from it, are always part of the criteria employed to evaluate residents' status claims. Yet, from the standpoint of their everyday evaluations of one another's status claims, it is necessary to examine such criteria against the background of how a particular people view work (regardless of type and of income potential) as an activity that competes for time with other, non-income-producing activities.

Cultural interpretations of the place of work in social life took a particular form in societies built on slave and indentured labor. In these societies the individuals and the groups who enjoyed the highest status not only worked the least but also acquired their material worth and their social position by forcing others to labor for them. Although differences in the cultural interpretations of work as an activity existed across these societies, in general everyone participated in a social system in which ambition and concern for improving personal worth centered on attempts to avoid work and to benefit from the efforts of those who could not avoid it (Goveia 1965, Patterson 1967, Knight 1978, Braithwaite 1971). Further, the large majority of those who had to work tried to reject or to minimize their involvement in the most denigrated forms of labor (for instance, agricultural tasks). As the same time the most economically successful among them viewed themselves as exceptions to the ideological links, drawn by the European elite, between race and suitability for particular economic tasks (see, for example, Glasgow 1970).

In early postslavery, postindenture Guiana these past conditions and cultural interpretations of them influenced the ideas of both the elite groups and the subordinate groups about the place of work in human activity. Although correlations among attitudes about work, freedom, independence, and status were often overdrawn (for example, when the behavior of ex-slaves was explained as merely a rejection of work in favor of indolence and poverty), it is reasonable to say that linkages among these attitudes served as preconditions for contemporary conceptions of what it means to be "somebody" (a person of high status) and for those that defined the most acceptable way to accomplish upward mobility. Past attitudes continue to inform current views of the relations between different forms of work and such factors as racial or ethnic identity, and the social and moral worth of an individual (Smith 1963, Graham and Gordon 1977, Bartels 1977).

Moreover, the subsequent economic and political constraints faced by estate and village residents encouraged subordinates to develop a system of values centering on egalitarian principles (see Hickerson 1954, Jayawardena 1963 and 1968). As members of a community of equals, persons striving to improve their material well-being and status were often accused of greed, jealousy, and insensitivity to others' well-being. In addition, the past allocation of economic roles along racial or ethnic lines (Bartels 1977) further affected the ability of an ethnically identified individual to engage in certain forms of work without damage to his[9] status (Rodney 1981).

Cockalorums' ideas about these factors are part of their responses to available income-producing options, and they also account in part for variations in residents' attitudes toward work as an activity and the place they give it in their views of the social and moral life of individuals as members of ethnic groups. Ideas about work, types of labor, and the potentially negative or positive impact that involvement in these has on identity and on status claims enter into evaluations of personal and ethnic group status.

Residents gloss the problems involved with a distinction they make between "making a living" and "making life." Most often, when they refer to someone's ability to make a living, they are speaking of the person's industry, skill, and ambition, all of which result in material rewards. When they speak of someone's ability to make life, they are referring to their own assessment of the individuals' interest in the socioeconomic well-being of others and his inclination to balance work against sociability—the enjoyment of life through participation in organized and casual forms of socializing, on the one hand, and conspicuous consumption, on the other. In making a living to make life, everyone should, Cockalorums say, try to make the most of their talents and opportunities to achieve a better standard of living for themselves and for their families of orientation and procreation. To make a living, individuals should try to combine as many opportunities as possible; they should develop their talents and take advantage of opportunities through a pattern of cooperation and of reciprocity. In other words, they should be ambitious, but their ambition should be solidly grounded in a concern for others and achieved through an acceptable pattern of social interaction.

In this regard East Indian informants frequently claim that the Black man does not know how to make life, and, just as frequently,

African informants say the same of East Indians. Both African and East Indian informants tend to agree that Portuguese do know how to make a living. This does not mean, however, that they necessarily approve of the way Portuguese are presumed to make money. As one might expect, Portuguese informants find both Africans and East Indians lacking in the ability to make life. By such statements African and East Indian informants mean that members of the identified ethnic segment typically do not manage to strike what they consider to be a proper balance between an emphasis on work and sociability, defined in terms of their group's differing definitions of freedom and independence. Stereotypes of an ethnic segment's relative emphasis on work sum up these contentions: East Indians live to work, Amerindians work to live, Africans work when all else fails, and Portuguese and Chinese work only long and hard enough to accumulate sufficient capital to let it work for them. (Subsequent references to the creation and use of these stereotypes in Cockalorum will be limited to locally represented ethnic segments: Africans, East Indians, and Portuguese.)

Generally, these stereotyped behaviors are thought to be genetically transmitted. When individuals claim or are recognized to have a particular ethnic identity but behave in a manner that is not stereotypically associated with it, their deviant behavior is explained in two ways. First, the behavior of the person who has been long or intensely associated with persons of another ethnic identity is assumed to result from socialization—"living between" or having been "cared" (for) by people of another ethnic segment. Second, where evidence of this kind of socialization is absent and cannot be reasonably postulated, such behavior becomes the presumed outcome of hidden genetic transmission. Somewhere in the individual's genealogy there were relatives who belonged to the ethnic segment stereotypically associated with the displayed pattern of behavior. Such explanations are applied alone or in combination, and they are self-applied as well as applied by others.[10]

Informants argue that despite ethnic socialization, racial/ethnic heritage "will out" (that is, manifest itself) in the long run: what is in the "blood" will sooner or later show in one's behavior. A shopkeeper, angry with her teenage son for neglecting his chores to spend the day socializing with friends, yelled at him, "You should have been born in a nigger yard! Doogla [mixed race] is wasted on you." From the standpoint of her identity preference for him, she effectively charged him with improper emphasis on sociability while reminding him that he had "grown a Doogla" because he was born into a Doogla, not an African, household. An industrious middle-aged African farmer, remarking on his work habits and on why he annually conducts a "jhandi" (a type of Hindu thanksgiving ritual), concluded, "I am everything a coolie" (translation: For all intents and purposes, I am a coolie). To account for his behavior and because his mixed heritage was not obvious from his appearance, he then proceeded to trace out his genealogy to identify non-African ancestors. He felt that this genealogical source of deviation was further substantiated by his brother's behavior. His brother, a man who had always scorned East Indians and who, as they were growing up, had ridiculed him for close association with them, chose a "mad" East Indian woman as a common-law mate after his African wife deserted him and emigrated to the United States. The farmer summed up his argument by wondering why, other than "heritage coming out," his brother ever would have taken an East Indian mate. Following the same logic, a young woman of mixed heritage explained that she chose shopkeeping as an occupation because she was "part Potogee." Her lack of success, she further explained, was partly due to a "war" among "all de races in [her] veins!"

Thus, while in making life individuals are interested in improving their economic well-being, they are also concerned with maintaining and substantiating their ethnic identity claims. In general, residents attempt to strike an ethnically appropriate balance between work (type, frequency, degree of emphasis) and sociability.[11] Different types and combinations of income-producing activities offer different possibilities for striking a proper balance. Africans, who object to being stereotyped as lazy, do not care to be seen as so hard working that they can be charged with behaving like a coolie or with being a slave to the job. A prestigious, well-paid occupation or combination of income-producing activities is good as long as job performance and concern for performance do not give the impression that one is enslaved by work. From this point of view, accepting economically beneficial but very demanding jobs may be counterproductive to the employee's overall status claims. One ideal, especially prevalent among young African males, is to seek a source of income that allows one to appear nonchalant about work and to have ample time for socializing—an attitude summed up in the slang expression, "When ah wuk, ah wuk." Literally this means "When I work, I work." Figuratively it is best translated as either "When I am working, I work well and when I am not working, I am not concerned with work" or "When I work, I work well and, therefore, when I am not working, do not bother me about work."

Older African informants, like most older people who voice grievances about the young, frequently complain that younger African males and females do not know how to make life—they either do not understand or do not care about a proper balance between work and sociability. In their view the young are lazy and unambitious, concerned only with socializing and conspicuous consumption. Ironically, this is the stereotype that other ethnic segments apply to all Africans. Yet, among Africans, conclusions about whether a particular person is "punishin' 'e se'f" by working for work's sake, is too concerned with saving for the future in general or for some particular investment, or is simply greedy depends on the individual's particular responsibilities and obligations.

Young males and females who pull their weight at home and who occasionally work to earn a "pocket piece" (money strictly for their own use) are not likely to be considered either greedy or unambitious. However, a child, for example, who regularly sells shaved ice or who hustles fruits and vegetables may be seen as overly ambitious, even showing early signs of love of money, especially if he is thought to prefer work to playing with others his own age. Similarly, an older but unmarried male who works as hard and as frequently as men and women with numerous responsibilities may also be judged greedy or overly ambitious. If, however, he plans to marry soon, he is considered to be exhibiting the proper ambition for one about to take on the responsibilities of a wife and a home. On the other hand, if he has such plans but continues to emphasize socializing and conspicuous consumption similar to that of his age mates who lack such plans, he may be deemed not serious enough about making life or his intended marriage. Anyone continuing an inappropriate balance between work and sociability may then be evaluated as lazy or simply ignorant about how to make life. Hence, the African version of the cross-ethnically shared cultural construct, making life, presumes that an ethnically proper balance between work and sociability should involve placing equal emphasis on both or a greater stress on sociability. Nevertheless, actual judgments about whether individuals exhibit the appropriate balance are situationally determined by considerations of age and responsibility.

East Indian and Portuguese stereotypes of the African emphasis on sociability are as extreme as African and Portuguese stereotypes of the East Indian emphasis on work. Other ethnic segments see East Indians as particularly capable of making a living under the worst circumstances. East Indians are considered to be extremely well organized, efficient in gaining financial stability, and capable of progressing by using the available income-producing activities. In the view of other ethnic segments they do not, however, know how to make life. In other words, they do not understand that the purpose of human existence is neither work for work's sake nor work to amass and to retain wealth for wealth's sake.

East Indian informants generally agree that as a people they stress work over sociability, but they disagree with the distinction they say Africans and Portuguese make between work and sociability as these relate to the purpose of human existence. First, East Indian informants draw the line between work and sociability less clearly. Second, they (especially Hindus) view work as a part of the process of character-building and of improving one's humanness, which they take to be a fundamental part of the purpose of human existence. Moreover, although work to complete a task for material rewards is a recognized aspect of the East Indian definition of work and working, work as activity is also considered pleasurable. Whether working to build one's character or, for the Hindu in particular, to improve one's humanness and one's chance of a better rebirth, the work itself should provide pleasure. Just as one may gain pleasure from dancing or playing ball to exhaustion, the same should be true of tiring, difficult work. From this East Indian viewpoint, it is the enjoyment of work in making life that the Africans and the Portuguese do not understand. East Indian informants contend that Africans and Portuguese falsely and absolutely divorce work from pleasure and, hence, can find joy only in sociability. Some go further so say that the Portuguese can find pleasure only in having money to hold.

Attending a movie, going to a party or to an outing, taking a holiday, or, for males, drinking and gambling with friends are as much forms of socializing for East Indians as they are for members of other ethnic segments. Yet other activities are less easily dichotomized. For example, Hindu and Muslim religion-based rituals, such as "jhandis" and "jhags" (types of Hindu thanksgiving rituals), are considered both work and sociability. Although such events are recognized as social occasions, the sponsor of such activities refers to them as "doing a work." Thus, among East Indians achieving the ethnically appropriate balance between work and sociability requires creating parity between work as the completion of a task for material reward (pleasure aspect included) and work as the sponsorship of formal religious occasions for group socializing. It weighs the time involved in both types of work against that spent in less formal, more individualized forms of sociability.

Consequently, East Indians may judge one another as stressing work inappropriately by showing too much concern with work for material gain (the pleasurable aspect notwithstanding) and too little concern for sponsoring "works." A person so judged would be considered greedy—a money lover who does not understand how to make life—a stereotype that African and Portuguese informants tend to apply indiscriminately to all East Indians. Such a person may also be stereotyped as one who places too much emphasis on individualized forms of socializing over one or both conceptions of work. Ultimately, whether someone sponsors works frequently enough and on a proper scale will depend on others' calculations of that person's financial capability because, as with Africans, among East Indians the emphasis appropriate for a particular individual is situationally determined. Unlike Africans, however, the East Indian who places too great an emphasis on sociability, especially individualized forms of socializing, over work and works may not be considered a true East Indian (see Chapter 7).

East Indian and African informants agree, for somewhat different reasons, that Portuguese do appear to know how to make life if their behavior is evaluated across their life span. Informants from both these ethnic segments contend that, in the short run, the alleged Portuguese love of money results in an inappropriate emphasis on work over sociability. From the African standpoint, Portuguese "punish" themselves in order to accumulate money and fail to enjoy even the basic comforts of life. Further, East Indian informants claim that Portuguese reinvest to the point of robbing themselves, for unnecessarily long periods, of essential goods and of opportunities for sociability. In the East Indians' view, not only do the Portuguese rob themselves and their families of basics but, more important, they do not engage in (or even have) culturally dictated forms of group sociability. The Portuguese emphasis on work is unidimensional. According to East Indians, it is also the strength of the Portuguese love of money that prevents them from developing intrafamilial cooperation and intragroup sociability as forms of status acquisition, which is therefore reduced to making money.

Thus, both East Indians and Africans stress an innate Portuguese love of money, willingness to punish themselves, and to exploit others for the sake of accumulating capital. Nonetheless, in this regard members of these two ethnic segments raise different issues about the Portuguese pattern of making life. East Indians ask, what is the point of hard work if one's efforts are not reflected in the well-being of the family or economic unit or in its relative status? Africans ask, what is the point of working oneself to death if one cannot enjoy one's earnings while in good health?

As Africans and East Indians puzzle over their stereotypes of Portuguese behavior, they admit that their stereotypes are based on stories from the indenture period and immediately thereafter. Informants alleged that Portuguese habits and living conditions began to change after 1940 as they gained control of the local rum and grocery shops. Today, they say that most Portuguese do not have to scrimp and save because most of them are well off, and that it is no longer true that most Portuguese spend money only for basic goods. Now, wealthy Portuguese do not sacrifice all sociability for work and capital accumulation or fail to buy luxury goods. Yet, informants still argue that a "true Potogee" is always concerned with making money and will willingly punish himself and exploit others in any situation that promises profit.[12]

In contemporary Cockalorum, however, the Portuguese do not form an ethnic enclave as do Africans and East Indians. Although there are a few individuals who identify themselves, and are identified by others, as "true or pure Potogee," they do not live in Portuguese households, nor do they interact predominantly with others of Portuguese descent. They have intermarried or cohabit with Africans and persons of part-African ancestry, and though some of the heads of household are Portuguese, most are generally considered African in culture. Such individuals' most intense interactions take place within predominantly non-Portuguese social and kin networks. Consequently, their conceptions of what it means to make life are assessed in terms of whether they consider themselves Doogla, "Santantone" (Portuguese-Black), "really African," or, rarely, "really East Indian."

On making life, these individuals stereotype East Indians and Africans in much the same way Africans and East Indians stereotype one another. Depending on their self-identity claims, they view the associated stereotypes as negative or positive. In Cockalorum, how-ever, the more general tendency is for these persons to note both positive and negative features of both African and East Indian stereo-types. For example, they may stress the positive importance of a concern with family progress over individual interests and comforts while also noting the value of enjoying life. Negatively, they feel that neither East Indians nor Africans know how to make life because neither group's conceptions of making life include any appropriate mix of family and individual concerns that would suggest that mem-bers of these groups know when to emphasize one concern over the other. This Portuguese perspective stresses, as do African and East Indian views, the importance of personal circumstances for all evalua-tions.

Among those who consider themselves part "Potogee," reference to their Portuguese heritage is often used as a way to distance them-selves from what they consider to be the negative aspects of their chosen identity. For example, it allows a person who otherwise claims to be African to justify an ethnically inappropriate emphasis on work over sociability without running the risk that this emphasis might be mistaken for an East Indian orientation. Although there is no well-developed model of the Portuguese conception of making life di-rectly applicable to the situation of Cockalorum Portuguese, it is generally assumed that "having Potogee in de veins" leaves one dissat-isfied with the typical East Indian or African pattern for making life. As in the case of the young female shopkeeper, claiming a Portuguese heritage often implies an expectation that the heritage should some-how make a difference in behavioral orientations and in success at ventures consistent with the Portuguese stereotype.

Sometimes it amounts to nothing more than a frustrated sense of having failed one's heritage or having been failed by it. A middle-aged man drinking with two companions—one ostensibly part "buk" (Amerindian) and the other ostensibly African—bemoaned being stuck with a "wuthless Potogee 'title'" (surname). He asked,

Iz me Potogee? Naa me, everyt'ing wan Blakman! So why oi mus' kai dis Potogee title fo' mek mesef wan rass? Naa so 'caus Potogee deh in me veins? But what good 'e dus do me? Me ah still everyt'ing wan Blakman.

(Am I Portuguese? No. I am an African, a Blackman. So, why must I carry this Portuguese surname that makes me an ass? It is not because I have some Portuguese ancestors or blood? But what good does it do me? I am still only, or behave solely like, an African.)

His part-Amerindian companion agreed that it was a shame for him to be stuck with a Potogee title and nothing to show for it. His African companion, however, laughed and poked a bit of fun at him when he replied, pointing to a beer bottle in the man's hand, "Blakman deh[13] too strong fo' lil biddy Potogee!"

Making a Living to Make Life:
Ethnicity, Freedom, and Independence

Why a certain balance between work and sociability is considered to be appropriate is explained by ethnically different informants in terms of their group's conceptions of freedom and of independence, conceptions through which they attempt to interpret the contemporary significance of their divergent histories. African and East Indian practices and verbal statements suggest different definitions of freedom and of independence when these are related to work and to a concern for the quality of job performance. The African conception of freedom centers on controlling both the amount of time one must spend working rather than socializing and, when working, the constraints imposed on one by job-related obligations and regulations. Independence centers on not being subjected to regulations subordinating the worker to the direct authority of bosses, of customers, or of political dictates. In contrast, the East Indians' conception of freedom is focused on their contribution and, thus, their right to enjoy the privileges of membership in a unit (for example, domestic group or, more broadly, kin group). In essence, their conception of independence is one of equalized interdependence—over the course of an individual's life, one can gain independence in this sense by contributing to the family unit or kin group. To make little or no contribution to the unit is to remain a dependent within and on that unit regardless of one's age and of other connections to the unit. To remain a dependent is to have to obey the commands of others in the household, with few opportunities to make demands of one's own.

Therefore, for Cockalorums, the quest for status is influenced always by variation in the possibilities different types of employment offer for striking an ethnically appropriate balance between work and sociability. Individuals are concerned with the degree of fit between their conceptions of freedom and of independence, on the one hand, and the structural requirements (that is, hours, duties, obligations, and hierarchies) of a job, on the other. Obviously, they cannot select employment strictly on the basis of these concerns. Such concerns, however, do inform how they feel about and respond to the constraints imposed by different kinds of work. They frequently weigh the income potential and the prestige of an occupation against its impact on their status, judged according to their ethnic group's conception of what it means to make life.

Africans prefer income-producing activities that allow maximum control over the amount of time the worker spends working or forms of employment that entail minimal dependence on others for assistance or approval. Informants of all ethnic identities often saw the United States, Canada, and the United Kingdom as places offering more lucrative opportunities for making a living but fewer possibilities for making life. Making life is difficult in these places, they say, because one must work five days a week, nine to five, while constantly worrying about pleasing a boss. Many Cockalorums hope to emigrate to one of these countries to make a living and then return to Guyana to make life. They see this hope dimming with the decline of Guyana's economy and the increasing difficulties of gaining the money and the official permits needed to emigrate.

It is in relation to these stereotypes and to these concerns for an appropriate balance in making life that we must understand the relative status attributed to nonagricultural wage and salaried labor relative to agricultural labor, because the latter is associated with degradation, while the former is associated with education, urbanism, and a relatively stable income. Yet, because wage and salaried jobs also entail working for someone else, they offer Africans less freedom to decide when and how long they will work. For this reason, to African informants, such employment is generally less prestigious than all but agricultural self-employment. This, at least apparent, contradiction poses a dilemma.

Africans respond to this dilemma in different ways. Some simply forego the prestige and the income of wage and salaried labor in favor of greater freedom and independence. Middle-aged and younger

African informants who have engaged in wage and salaried labor say that such employment is "too troublesome," either because one needs too many "lines" (personal connections) to get, to keep, and to advance in these types of work, or because one may have to suppress negative opinions about government policies or even become a card-carrying member of the People's National Congress (PNC). Those who voiced this complaint were as leery about becoming a puppet on a string to the PNC as a boss, as they were vexed with any PNC policy.

As a temporary expedient, some may forego freedom and independence, or emphasize work and job performances over sociability, to acquire sufficient capital for self-employment. To distance themselves from the charge "slave to a job," some of these individuals discuss their involvement as temporary and detail their future plans for self-employment. If they show concrete signs of getting involved in some other income-producing activity that might lead to self-employment, others tend to accept their justification. In this sense, the acceptance of nonagricultural wage and salaried labor parallels attitudes toward temporary emigration as an access to more lucrative opportunities for making a living, by providing income that they might later use to make life properly.

Finally, Africans who accept nonagricultural wage and salaried employment as a long-term, permanent source of income, treating it as an integral part of making life, respond differently to the need to compensate for their loss of freedom. They are likely to devalue job performance and openly express a disinterest in being a good employee. For example, retail clerks, bureaucrats, nurses, and others sometimes ignore those seeking their services while they socialize with fellow employees or with friends who have dropped by to visit them on the job. Occupants of such positions often state that, although they have a boss, "the customer is not the boss." They endeavor to give the impression that service is a personal favor, rather than a duty or a job responsibility. Likewise, teachers (especially young, unmarried ones) may show their independence through absenteeism—using all sick days whether ill, taking all allotted personal leave whether it is really needed, or losing pay to go to a movie with friends. They openly justify their actions as resistance to having their lives regulated by a job or argue that such actions are job "benefits," which they often cite as reasons for preferring one form of wage or salaried employment over others.

Although Africans typically engage in such behaviors and factor them into their model of what it means to make life, they do see the problems such patterns pose. In the ever-present discussion of the relative progress of the different ethnic segments, Africans consistently say that these stereotyped patterns of behavior are detrimental not only to individual advancement but also to the relative progress of Africans as an ethnic segment. In fact, some who consider working for others a permanent and integral part of their lives and who stress the importance of quality job performance contend that Africans must redefine their conceptions of freedom and of independence. They feel that the current attitudes are part of a colonial mentality that must be rejected for a maximum contribution to national and to ethnic progress.

East Indian informants also say that some forms of nonagricultural wage and salaried labor are generally more prestigious income-producing activities than agricultural labor. Like Africans, however, they also note that working for someone else offers less freedom than does self-employment. Nonetheless, they suggest that a person's primary concern should be to integrate one's activities into the overall pattern of income production for one's particular family or economic unit. Employment should not be sought solely for its prestige or for its income potential.

Involvement in any income production is a contribution to the unit and so justifies one's rights to membership. Balancing work and sociability are lesser factors in work choice. However, it should be noted that younger East Indian males, especially those who are part of integrated peer groups, appear to place a greater emphasis on sociability over work than do older East Indian males and younger ones involved in nonintegrated peer groups. In the former category, some who work as farmers occasionally assist one another with weeding, planting, or harvesting on a cooperative, nonpaid basis in order to have more time for socializing with peers. Others engaged in wage and salaried labor say they work very hard on the job to convince their employers of their value, hoping to be granted extra personal leave by the employer who wants to reward their efforts, and, in the employer's view, increase their loyalty. Thus, these individuals manipulate the stereotype of how an employer should manage an East Indian employee to make him hard working and loyal. These East Indians claim that they are then able to socialize with their peers, taking time off with, rather than without, permission, therefore not jeopardizing their contributions to their families or economic units. Such manipulations suggest an interest in validating status and social worth in terms of both the African and the East Indian models of what it means to make life.

These tactics are not missed by Africans and Portuguese, who often remark scornfully that, despite appearances, all East Indians ultimately emphasize work over sociability. They say that if an East Indian socializes during work hours, it means he has already completed his work. In contrast, they assume that an African in the same situation is taking time to enjoy life even if he has not completed his work. When presented with contradictory examples, informants argue that the individuals in question were either not what they appeared to be ethnically, or that their behavior was only temporarily unnatural.

African informants also complain that East Indians who use the aforementioned tactics while working as wage and salaried laborers make other employees look bad. In their view such tactics increase the difficulty that non–East Indian workers face in attempting to manage an ethnically appropriate balance between work and sociability. Although they contend that in making life East Indians do emphasize work over sociability, East Indian informants also maintain that, even if this were not the case, in wage and salaried employment they must work twice as hard and be more concerned about job performance than Africans and Portuguese because, when their employment is controlled by these racial groups, East Indians are subject to discrimination. More often than not, Africans in Cockalorum agree that East Indians are correct in their assessments, but they add that such treatment results from the East Indian's emphasis on work over sociability. If unfair tactics were not used, Africans argue, employers would always seek the hard-working East Indian, making it difficult for others to compete without becoming "slaves to the job."

Africans, thus, justify discrimination as a means of "equalizing opportunities" among people who place different emphases on work in an economy offering few lucrative options. Yet, they also recognize that the use of this justification not only substantiates the East Indian stereotypes but also reinforces the general process of ethnic competition that stereotypes relations between ethnic identity and the appropriate means for balancing work and sociability, thereby, in the long run, paradoxically further limiting Africans' access to the full range of economic opportunities. Likewise, young East Indian males, intent on undermining the stereotypical images of their ethnic group as a people who do not know how to make life, cannot afford to relinquish too quickly the stereotype of themselves as a hard-working people. Consequently, though no one can take advantage of an option that is not available, cultural conceptions also place constraints on views of "availability." The accessibility of an option may depend on who one is or on what one is trying to be or become or both.

3

Status Stratification
and Status Signaling

Max Weber defines status as:

a quality of social honor or a lack of it, [which] is in the main conditioned as well as expressed through a specific style of life. Social honor can stick directly to a class-situation, and it is also, indeed most of the time, determined by the average class-situation of the status-group members. This, however, is not necessarily the case. Status membership, in turn, influences the class-situation in that the style of life required by status groups makes them prefer special kinds of property or gainful pursuits and reject others. A status group can be closed ("status by descent") or it can be open. (1958:405)

In a manner logically consistent with Weber's definition, Cockalorums define status as (1) the ease with which individuals are perceived to gain and to enjoy the material and social benefits of Guyanese and international life, and (2) the ability and the willingness of individuals to use their social connections to assist or to thwart others. Unlike Weber, they make statements about different status categories that refer less to the ability to engage in different overall lifestyles than to the relative ability of persons to approximate the same lifestyle as measured by degrees of deference and of respect demanded and received in interaction.[1]

To understand how Cockalorums link their sense of honor to status categories, what criteria they generate and use to make distinctions among such categories, and how they place one another in them requires careful consideration of the relations among identity, locality, and the historical images that adhere to and inform their contemporary conceptions of honor and of status categories. As a consequence of their belief in notions of ethnic distinctiveness, groups have divergent histories that may serve as sources of status criteria. In addition, the spatial grid on which they move has a history shaped by divergences in ethnic histories, so that it, too, serves as a source of status criteria. In combination, Cockalorums integrate and evaluate criteria from these two sources with other criteria associated with a person's material accomplishments and ethical conduct.

Status and Social Geography

Among the factors that Cockalorums use to begin evaluating one another's relative status are links they make between locality classifications and stereotypes of residents' psychological and social character, their ethnic or racial identity, and that of the founding settlers of that locality. The status implications of residence in a particular locality fall between those based on achieved status criteria (for example, material accomplishments or personal reputation) and those that are ascribed (for example, kin ties or racial affiliation). Everyone is born in a specific locality, a fact that Cockalorums believe influences a person's basic character and potential moral worth. Individuals may change their places of residence and assume the behavior pattern of persons born there. However, Cockalorums think such behavioral changes are superficial in much the same way as we think that "You can take a person out of the country, but you can't take the country out of a person." Further, in Guyana the link between status and locality is often conflated with the relationship between geography and the spatial distribution of ethnically identified persons. For example, most coastal dwellers consider the interior regions of Guyana lower status localities, not only because they are removed from coastal social life but also because they are viewed as the natural dwelling places of Amerindians, to whom they accord the lowest status in an ethnic hierarchy. (See Chapters 6 and 7, and Drummond 1974, for additional comments on attitudes toward the "bush" as a locality type.)

In addition to the usual urban-rural spatially related status divisions, Cockalorums further divide rural space into six locality types—"bush" (interior), "estate" (plantation), village, freehold settlement, housing scheme, and squatter settlement. To these types they accord different values in their assessment of residents' status. With the exception of the bush, these locality types rarely coincide with social units in East Coast Demerara because the latter are most often composites created of different settlement patterns and, therefore, are identifiable in terms of several locality designations. In Cockalorum, portions of the spatial area are identified as freehold, village, and housing-scheme locality types. Each of these resulted from different historical patterns of land acquisition, and each has different implications for the assessment of residence as an aspect of interpersonal status evaluation. Thus, persons identified as countrymen on the basis of shared residence in a recognized social unit may be accorded unequal status on the basis of where they reside within it.

In general, freehold settlements, housing schemes, squatter settlements, and estates, in roughly that order, fall between villages as the most prestigious and the bush as the least prestigious in the status ranking of rural locality types. Consistent with the historical relations between individuals, land, and power in Guyana, justifications for the status ranking elevate personal autonomy, land ownership, and the exercise of self- (local) government. For Cockalorums, historically these locality types represented different potentials for independence from the plantation social structure. These differences continue to have salience in status evaluations because Cockalorums contend that persons who resided in these different localities developed different personality characteristics, which they transmitted to their descendants. They base this presumption on a worked-out view of settlement histories and their relation to the development of contemporary character types and socialization patterns.

From this perspective, in postemancipation Guiana, villages contrasted with estates as the symbols of free, intelligent, progressive individuals seeking greater economic independence and control over interpersonal relations versus the less intelligent, less progressive persons and their descendants who remained on the estates. Among estate dwellers, further status distinctions were made between those who lived in plantation-owned housing and those who built homes on plantation-owned land or in attached freehold communities. Freehold settlers, referred to as individuals "living free," were accorded a higher status than plantation dwellers who lived in plantation-owned housing but a lower status than persons who inhabited either communal or proprietary villages.

Two factors that distinguished freehold settlers from village dwellers and served as further justification for their status below villagers were their questionable relation to the land on which their homes were located and their lack of formalized self-government. While some freehold settlers bought plots from the estate owners, others built houses and planted gardens on land belonging to the estate, from which they could be evicted if they failed to cooperate with the dictates of the plantation management. Even in those settlements where most of the residents purchased their plots, they rarely formed local governments by electing a headman and councilors. Ignoring the fact that not all communal villages established a formal self-government structure, Cockalorums say that, compared with villages, freehold areas were more "lawless places." Everyone was "dar pon 'e own" without formal means for resolving interpersonal conflicts and for maintaining public works.

Some African informants conflate the status of postdisturbance squatter settlements with racial stereotypes. Many of them believe that the first inhabitants of those settlements were East Indians. More particularly, they were the weakest, most cowardly East Indians who, rather than fight for their homes in villages and in freehold areas, accepted the inferior housing and the squalor of these residences. Although East Indian informants are familiar with the racial stereotypes associated with these squatter settlements, they disagree with the stereotype, pointing to the racially integrated character of those with which they are familiar. Where such examples prove inadequate, they may agree with the negative stereotype but note that the East Indians in question were Madrassi, thereby hoping to diminish a general negative impact on their ethnic group status. As a category of East Indians, Madrassi are South Indians whom North Indians consider inferior to themselves. Non-Madrassi East Indian informants' ranking of Madrassi within the East Indian segment is based partly on their tendency to have dark complexions and wavy hair, and partly on notions of rank (based on a North-South division) that were already established among the immigrants before their departure from the subcontinent. When there was little ground on which to claim that those of questionable character and status were Madrassi, informants were likely to argue that they were Dooglas, or persons who had lived "bad" with neighbors and relatives. The latter persons, having no other place to turn in their time of crisis, fled to squatter settlements.

Cockalorums' assessment of housing schemes are ambiguous. The schemes are usually accorded a higher status than squatter settlements but a lower status than villages and freehold areas. The informants who ranked housing schemes below villages and freehold settlements referred to independence and to land ownership as important criteria. They argued that housing-scheme residents are like slaves, with the government as their master.[2]

Ownership of property in housing schemes is thought to be "false," both because the land in housing schemes belongs to the government and because, during their lifetimes, residents have limited control over the houses they build and cannot will them to their children or to anyone else. The occupation of many housing-scheme dwellers further contributes to the view of these as low-status localities. They are Guyana Defense Force soldiers, and individuals who become soldiers are considered to have been morally inferior persons who only now appear to be morally upstanding. Informants who voiced a dissenting view of the status of housing schemes pointed to the general good quality of the housing, and to the lines that they believe afford the residents easier access to goods and services. As with the racial stereotypes associated with squatter settlements, the assessment of housing schemes suggests that the status of the locality type is raised or lowered by the stereotypes of its inhabitants, which, in turn, influence the status-related stereotypes of the residents.

Within Cockalorum, the identification of the sections as villages, freehold areas, and housing-scheme settlements is an aspect of interpersonal assessments of status. It cannot be overstated that this criterion, like other criteria, is an aspect, not a determiner, of status rank. Persons who are "born and grow" in one of the village sections consider themselves (and under certain circumstances are considered by others) to be higher status individuals. These distinctions are attended to less today than they were in the past when intermarriage and property ownership across locality types were discouraged. Elderly informants claim that in the past, whenever Brooklyntown residents discovered a courtship between one of their youngsters and any Coconut Grove or Tranquility resident, they refused to give their blessing to and assistance for a marriage. Fights also regularly occurred between young males from the different sections who transgressed sectional boundaries seeking recreation.

East Indian informants from Coconut Grove and from Tranquility contend that East Indians from Entre Facade, whatever their economic position, still consider themselves superior to Coconut Grove and to Tranquility residents simply because they are "villagers." Freeholders maintain that arranging marriages between their children and villagers' children still poses difficulties because of the village-freehold distinction. Nor are well-to-do freeholders happy to arrange marriages between their children and the offspring of materially equal or wealthier villagers for fear that such arrangements would give the impression that they, too, believe villagers to be superior to freehold inhabitants. Yet, they are not inclined to marry their children to those of estate dwellers because they hold that settlement type in low esteem.

Although informants commenting on the village-freehold distinction associated it with conceptions of status differences between locality types, a few felt that although this was so in the old days, today it is merely a surface excuse that masks a belief that most Tranquility and Coconut Grove East Indians are of lower castes,[3] less racially pure, or less culturally traditional than Entre Facade residents because they have long lived "between African people." Furthermore, Coconut Grove and Tranquility informants complain that, although Entre Facade East Indians insist that East Indians are one people and should behave with racial solidarity, they are reluctant to accept invitations to attend social functions in the freehold sections. As proof of their attitude of superiority, a local Hindi teacher claimed that he was thwarted in his effort to provide a Hindi class for local youngsters because parents in Entre Facade refused to send their children to Coconut Grove where he was conducting the lessons in the bottom-house of a well-to-do East Indian family. He said they agreed to send their children to class only when he gained permission to move the class to the Sanatan temple located in Entre Facade. In a similar vein, another East Indian resident of Coconut Grove reported that she experienced serious difficulties arranging a marriage between her daughter and a young man from Entre Facade even though it was the young man who initially expressed interest. As a qualification to these cases and others like them, in any such situation there are always factors other than section of residence that contribute to the problems encountered. Even so, the sectional divisions are recognized as potential barriers among status equals and as factors exacerbating other forms of status inequality. Consequently, some East Indians from the freehold areas also said they do not go out of their way to attend functions in Entre Facade, because, despite what these villagers say about solidarity, they know how Entre Facade people "stay" (typically feel or respond) toward freehold dwellers. Avoiding situations where, however subtly, they will be treated as inferior, they accept invitations only when extended by a kinsperson or by a close friend, in which instance not attending would look very bad.

In addition to the spatially linked aspects of status distinctions, Cockalorums also associate a north-to-south division, which cross-cuts all but one of the major sections (that is, Tranquility, where it has no practical significance because all houses are located in the back-dam area), with status differentiation. The Mahaica Canal divides the community north and south into two areas—"waterside" and "back-dam"—viewed as high and low status residential spaces. This division is related to the historical design of plantations in which the big house and the manager's quarters were located near the front of the settlement, whereas the laborers' quarters and the farmland were located at the rear.

Entre Facade and Coconut Grove residents recognize the division and its status implications, although they believe that in the recent past (as in the present) it was always considered more important by African inhabitants of Brooklyntown than by residents of other sections. Brooklyntown informants, on the other hand, say that, in the past, the waterside-backdam division was dubbed "North and South Korea" because of the negative relations and the fights between their inhabitants. Interracial marriages across the division were discouraged, and social interaction was more frequent and multiplex among households within than between those outside an area. When cricket and boxing matches were regularly arranged across boundaries, they often ended in melees when audiences or participants disagreed with the official outcome.

Today, although residents belong to the backdam or to the waterside, depending on where they were born, relocations and marriages have resulted in most households having kin ties across the divisions. However, visits and cooperation among kin-related households across the division are still less frequent than among similar households located within the same area. Some waterside informants, especially those who consider themselves above average, boast of rarely visiting any backdam resident. In a similar vein, some backdam informants complain that relatives and friends who move to the waterside stop interacting with backdam residents and, in turn, that socializing at waterside homes makes them feel strange. Even though their ill-ease is partly related to the particular status they accord to the household visited, backdam residents of roughly equivalent economic position may feel inferior to similar waterside residents just because they live in that space.

The implications of the waterside-backdam distinction center on stereotyped conceptions of differences in styles of interaction. Informants think that the distinction is a legitimate criterion for establishing expectations, responses, and explanations of one another's behavior. According to backdammers, watersiders are pretentious, sneaky, deceptive, and prefer to hold grudges, talk behind a person's back, and cheat in commercial transactions. In contrast, their counterparts judge them to be unnecessarily quarrelsome and uncouth, and less knowledgeable than themselves about European norms and mores (they lack "manners," as the saying goes). Instead, they are more versed in non-European Guyanese customs (they are said to be "rude" in their general pattern of conduct).

These residential divisions are further divided into "squares." Squares, formed by the intersection of drainage trenches and paths throughout the community, are the smallest extra-household units defined in terms of space and of proximity. Individuals who are born and raised in a particular square are perceived to be more like one another than residents of other squares within and outside the section. They develop characteristic styles of interaction that differ slightly from one square to the next. Hence, inhabitants of a particular square may be stereotyped as being more or less direct, sneaky, or contentious. In other words, they are thought to share certain basic features of reputation and of personality.

These stereotyped differences are seen as aspects of status differentiation, and they condition the deference and the respect that parties owe one another. Although sections and intrasection spaces differ slightly in their physical characteristics and in quality (for example, drainage and upkeep of paths or the size and the quality of houses), in addition to historical relations between locality type and size, the status differences associated with them are based on conceptions about differences in personality characteristics and in inbred patterns of interaction. These assumed differences establish expectations and influence responses and evaluations of both behavior and status across spaces.

Persons born in different locality types and in different spaces within these types do not, then, begin the quest for status from the same vantage point. In addition to these baseline features of status differentiation, Cockalorums use ascribed and achieved criteria to define hierarchically related status categories and to rank families and individuals across these categories.

Status Categories: From Truly Big to Small Small

The major status categories recognized in Guyanese society are those of big and small men: a division between those who can comfortably afford to enjoy life and those who "punish" (suffer and struggle) to make a living and to make life.[4] This division is between those who have power, authority, and wealth and those who do not. The two categories are contrasted in the cynical but astute comment, "Big people have lines; small people stand on lines." In the first instance, the lines are the social connections that facilitate the acquisition of goods and services; in the second, they are the queues that form for short-supply goods and services (or are simply a reference to the necessity of going through regular channels to obtain them).

With few exceptions, the people of Cockalorum are small men. Consequently, after a brief description of the major distinctions among big men as elements of a national system of status stratification, we shall focus on describing the hierarchical ordering of locally recognized distinctions among small men.

In the words of one informant, "None body naa big fo' all body; 'e mus' gaa fo' se sir to somebody." All big men are big in relation to the category of small men, but not all big men are equally big, nor are all big men big in every social context. It is, in part, the ability to retain one's status as a big man as one moves from one social context to the next, even when the change means a move from regional to national to international circles, that distinguishes "truly big men" from "small big men."

"Truly" big men, it is thought, purchase the best of whatever is available in whatever quantity they desire. While they are not immune to the national problems of shortages and of a very limited range of goods, services, and occupations, they manage to short-circuit regular channels of acquisition through social connections and personal authority, obtaining goods and employment when others must do without. They can enjoy whatever they consider the best that Guyanese and international social life have to offer. In their relations with others, truly big men are able to exercise authority within and outside family and kin circles on a regional and a national level. They can gain the unwilling assistance of others in ways deemed possible only when one has great wealth and important social connections.

The social circles of the truly big man center on other members of the national elite, and they have significant ties to members of an international upper-middle class. Thus, the truly big man is one who will be recognized and accepted as wealthy and socially significant wherever he travels. In the language of proverbs, they are the "fowl cocks" (roosters) and small men are the cockroaches: "When fowl cock gie dance, cockroach naa gaa business." Nationally, the number of people who can claim to be truly big men is small—primarily the prime minister, a few other high-ranking government officials, and a few wealthy businessmen. In these terms, no inhabitants of Cock-alorum qualify as, or are perceived to be, truly big men.

Locally and nationally, most persons who self-ascribe big-man status, or who are recognized as such by others, are small big men. Their status, power, and authority are more firmly anchored to the national hierarchy than those of the truly big men. Whereas it is accepted that there are international circles of wealth, power, and authority in which the truly big men of Guyana are reduced to small big men, such a reduction in status occurs most often for those who are not truly big men. The social circles of small big men usually include some ties to truly big men, in part defining their right to big-man status, but they are likely to have little access to highly signifi-cant members of an international upper-middle class. The power and the authority they wield is directly linked both to the important positions they hold in national and in regional bureaucracies and businesses, and to the influence they gain through their ties to the truly big men, who are likely to be their business associates, personal acquaintances, and kin. Apart from their wealth, small big men achieve their status as big men as much from perceptions of what they can do to and for small men as from what they can do for themselves and for other big men.

Yet, if having lines, as opposed to standing on lines, distinguishes truly big men from all small men, it is the end result of standing in lines that distinguishes small big men from ordinary small men. Small big men, or their representatives, may stand in line, but they usually do so only after having obtained an agreement from someone of authority that they will receive what they are seeking, often in quantities greater than allowed persons without such connections.

Two Cockalorum families are generally considered by community members as small big men, but neither family lives permanently in the community. Although they maintain a family home there, they also have residences in Georgetown. Several members of the East Indian family that owns most of the land in the Coconut Grove section are professionals and businessmen trained at some of the best North American and European universities. They have homes in Georgetown but occasionally visit the family place in Cockalorum, which is regularly occupied by less wealthy members of the family. They count among their relatives upper-middle-class permanent residents or citizens of other countries who, along with non-kin members of the Georgetown elite, comprise the center of their social circle. The African family recognized as small big men has a similar relation to the community and to the urban elite. It maintains a family home that is occupied by an elderly cousin who retired to the community after spending many years in Brazil, but its members spend most of their time at their residences in Georgetown or outside Cockalorum. Their visits to the village are usually brief—a day in the country or the occasional attendance at a ceremonial event sponsored by a relative. On these visits they may interact socially with community members who were their close friends or schoolmates before they left the community.

Individuals and families at the top of the small-man category— big small men—lack sufficient material wealth, educational achievements, or social connections to claim an unquestionable position among big men. Their accomplishments, however, are considered adequate to place them above the ordinary small man. They are the resident notables, yet their ability to purchase goods and services, to participate in a range of social activities, and to justify claims of connections to and interactions with big men are constantly questioned and carefully scrutinized by others in about the same position as well as by those less well off.

The ability big small men have to exercise authority outside their family and kin group is linked to their occupation and to the significant social connections that they develop through these positions. Their authority is much more anchored to occupation than that of the small big man. Like the small big man, their status derives from others' perceptions of what services they can render and what disservices they can do to those who are less well off. They are persons who can grease the paths to "getting through" (accomplishing a difficult task) anything that involves contact with bureaucracies and with the small big men who run them. They also are perceived as persons who, if rubbed the wrong way, may block the acquisition of goods and services or, in general, may make getting through more difficult. Ordinary small men believe they are big enough so that bigger people "hear them when they speak"; they "have voice." Big small men also have a stable source of income, often with several household members employed in skilled or semiskilled occupations. This category includes the larger landowners and shopkeepers, some teachers, nurses, soldiers, civil servants, hire-care operators, some religious specialists, and the most prosperous small farmers.

As big small men attempt to develop more and better links to bigger people, their social connections and interactions continue to be with persons who are less well off than themselves. They form local and regional ties, through marriage and forms of cooperation and of reciprocity, with individuals of similar status. The development of these ties and of those to bigger people helps to stabilize their status, because, as noted above, others look to them as persons capable of utilizing these connections on their behalf.

Each section of Cockalorum has several families that are generally labeled big small men. The subjective nature of status placements always causes disagreement among informants over the objective basis of such families' status claims. As one might expect, individuals who have been assisted (or thwarted) by one of these families are more likely to identify them as "big ones," whereas others remain skeptical of their claims. Even so, one recognizes the status of big small men in the demeanor they assume toward their status inferiors and in the deference their status inferiors consider appropriate when interacting with them.

Most Cockalorums consider themselves ordinary small men— members of that segment of the total population that "punishes" (that is, suffers) to survive from day to day. Their housing is usually adequate and, by local standards, comfortable, though they are not likely to have such conveniences as indoor plumbing, refrigerators, or gas stoves. Their homes are more likely than those of big small men to be in need of repairs, of painting, or of expansion to accommodate better the number of persons who share them.

Although ordinary small men identify themselves as people who punish to make life, they also recognize further distinctions in their ability (1) to take care of their basic needs, and (2) to acquire some consumer and status symbol goods, especially imported goods. Ordinary small men must work (or hustle) harder for the same goods, services, and recreation; they have greater difficulty in striking the appropriate balance between work and sociability while improving their financial position. Their income is usually less stable than that of big small men because they are more likely to have only one household member, if any, who is employed regularly in a skilled or semiskilled occupation. Whenever they have funds from occasional employment, an especially good harvest, or remittances from relatives abroad, they are able to improve their housing, to purchase desired consumer and status symbol goods, and to take part in social activities that they usually forego. Frequently, these families can also improve their financial position for short periods by operating small bottom-house shops, by raising pigs and poultry, and by selling cassava, "cassareep" (a sauce made from the bitter cassava), or copra.

Work histories of men in these families follow a pattern of intermittent involvement in a range of income-producing activities that remains cyclical rather than eventuating in increasingly lucrative and stable sources of income. For the most part, their income derives from the less stable sources of intermittent farming and of retailing either what they grow or what they can buy wholesale from other local cultivators.

Although ordinary small men are linked to big small men, and sometimes (often through kinship) to big men, their most intense social interactions are with other ordinary small men. Lacking significant social connections, they are likely, even with much running back and forth, to be only partially successful in "getting through with the business." Thus, differences in the quantity and in the quality of their social connections rather than absolute differences in power and in material accomplishments distinguish them from big small men.

Beneath the ordinary small men is a category of persons referred to as "bottom-class people."[5] These are the residents of Cockalorum who have the greatest difficulty in meeting their basic needs. They are people who are unquestionably outside the mainstream of the community's social and material life and those who get the least respect in interactions. They have little or no cash most of the year, subsisting on produce from kitchen gardens and on occasional handouts from relatives and friends. A few households in each section of Cockalorum fall into this category. The reasons for their predicament are almost as varied as the number of individuals and of families who belong to the category.

First among the category of bottom-class people are the elderly, infirm pensioners (some of whom report receiving as little as U.S. $2.50 to $5.00 per month from the government, supplemented in a variety of ways) who live alone and who have few relatives in the community. In some instances, their relatives have emigrated to other countries or have moved to other areas of Guyana. In other instances, they have relatives in the community but are not on good terms with them and, thus, refuse to accept their assistance. A second group in this category is the female-headed household with children who are too young to be of financial assistance. For a number of reasons, these women may only occasionally receive funds from their children's father(s), and relatives and other affines may provide very limited assistance to them.

A third group in this category is composed of the middle-aged and younger men who, for one reason or another, live alone or "batchee" (in a house with other unmarried men). Some of the older men suffer from debilitating physical and mental illnesses, whereas others have missed one opportunity too many or they simply never have made the transition from "sweetman" (meaning playboy in this context although, in general, sweet may also mean drunk or tipsy) to family man. The younger men are unemployed, and most of them have never had a job of any kind. The majority of these men spend their time drinking up the few dollars they acquire from gambling or from stealing. Some have families who continue to assist them, but others are deemed ne'er-do-wells whose relatives have given up on them. Members of this latter category can demand deference only from very young children and, in turn, do not grant deference to others, taking what Cockalorums call a "doan-kay-dam" (don't give a damn) attitude toward the whole issue of status competition.

Strategic Interpretations
of Status-Signaling Criteria

Although Cockalorums recognize these status categories and their hierarchical ordering, the ranking of local families is based on the evaluator's knowledge of the families' overall situations and on the types of interactions that have occurred between the evaluator and those families. Specifically referring to relations among small men, residents are less concerned with what has been achieved quantitatively than with how these achievements have been accomplished and, therefore, with how such achievements have influenced the achiever's behavior toward other members of the community.

This is not to argue that quantitative differences among small men based on relevant criteria are not important for determinations of their status differences. Obviously, they are key features of status differentiation. Instead, it is to say that apparent quantitative differences discussed above as defining different abstract categories are manipulated and interpreted in interpersonal status determinations. Hence, in local interactions, references to status differences and their implications for deference and demeanor center on evaluations of the differences between appearance and substance. As a basis for the recognition of status claims, appearance cannot be taken at face value. Further, everyone must try to "appear to be somebody," if ever one expects to "become somebody." In other words, substantive accomplishments are believed to require the assistance of others who are thought to be most willing to cooperate with those persons who seem to be somebody—that is to say, someone who, in turn, will be able to render assistance. The stress on the appearance of success is essential to actual achievement but makes it difficult to know "who is what."

In interactions, determining "who is what" requires evaluating quantitative and qualitative differences. In these assessments, material accomplishment can only signal the need for an appraisal or for a reassessment of the status claims presented during the interaction. What interpretation is made of this signal is determined by the strategy used by those involved to evaluate status claims based on material worth. The aim of the interactors is to disclose (or to manipulate prior assessments of) the link between the apparent and the real.

To illustrate some of the basic features of this process, we will now examine how Cockalorums interpret the contribution houses make to the acceptance or to the rejection of overall status claims. How they treat this highly visible objective criterion of difference parallels how they view other quantitative differences, and it is similar to how they determine the value of moral aspects of status acquisition and differentiation. Cockalorums focus on how individuals increase their material worth and on the implications of their methods for status recognition or denial. Houses, like other criteria, are symbols (not signs) that signal potential status differentiation.

In Cockalorum the size, the type, the quality, and the general appearance of houses are important criteria for evaluating relative financial position and provide potential verification, or the grounds for a rejection, of status claims. As in other Guyanese settlements, the Cockalorum house design is uniform. Houses are square or rectangular structures elevated on five- to seven-foot piles. Although the use of cinderblocks has increased recently, most houses are constructed of wood, and those constructed of cinderblocks and clay bricks retain the general design of the traditional wooden houses.

The interior of the house is divided into a living room and one or more bedrooms. Some houses include a kitchen in the main body of the house, but most have a detached kitchen shed or a kitchen area under the house. The latter (bottom-house) may be enclosed or left open when it is used as a kitchen.

The typical roof is an inverted V. A few of the older houses that have not been modernized have an old-fashioned "flat-B" roof. On these houses, at the front, above and behind a separate veranda or landing roof, is a rectangular facade with one or more small windows that give the appearance of a second story; hence the name "flat-B." A few of the more recently built houses, especially the large cinderblock constructions, have flat overhanging roofs made of "zinc" (corrugated tin) with pipes along the sides to drain off the rainwater. Most roofs are painted red, though a few are painted aquamarine or have portions that are made of aquamarine fiberglass.

Houses generally have two entrances—one at the front and another at the rear or side—with several steps leading up to them. It is not unusual to find houses with steps to only one of the entrances because the owner is waiting for funds or materials to build steps to the other. At the top of the front steps of most houses is a veranda or a landing. Where there is a veranda, it may stretch the length of the house or may simply be a small square bordered by a railing or enclosed by some decoratively carved boards about four feet high. For the largest ones, windows are added that can be opened to admit cooling breezes or closed against blowing rain. Because of the in-

creasing costs and a chronic shortage of glass, tarpaulins and plas-
ticized sheets that can be rolled up have become popular substitutes.
The steps may also be covered with a roof of zinc sheets or of
corrugated fiberglass.

Doors are of three basic types: a single panel that opens vertically,
two vertical panels that open in the center,and the Dutch door. They
may be painted or otherwise finished to harmonize with the rest of
the house. Still atypical are sliding glass doors and plate glass windows found in some of the larger cinderblock and theater-front
houses. A returning migrant is said to have introduced the sliding
glass door to Cockalorum, after it was already noticeable in Georgetown. The theater-front house has a high, imposing square or rectangular front that is purely decorative and is patterned after the
building design of movie houses.

Any house feature may be used to evaluate relative financial positions and status claims, but Cockalorums do not do so primarily by
computing its monetary value. Instead, they are interested in the
extent to which the house is a true indicator of the occupants'
statuses. If the house is not rented, they consider the kind of ownership, the overall style of the house, and its size and height. Whether
both entrance steps are complete, whether the steps are covered, and
whether the veranda and the bottom-house are enclosed are other
indicators. They consider how long it took the occupants to bring
the house to its current stage of development. In addition, because
sources of income differ in stability, Cockalorums also analyze the
source of the funds used to complete construction.

Houses may actually be children's property, in which instance the
co-owners have only a share in it and use-rights. In one such case,
during a dispute with her brother, a woman threatened to remove the
veranda and the front entrance steps. Although the woman occupied
the house, it had been willed to the disputants as children's property.
The sister had added on the veranda and the front steps, which she,
therefore, had a right to remove. Even though she lived in the house
and was its co-owner, those who knew the details of the situation
agreed that the contribution the house made to her status was only
equivalent to an undefined share of the original house plus the add-
ons. The matter was further complicated by the fact that she had
financed these with "one-time" (windfall or temporary) funds rather
than with monies derived from a stable source of income. To an

uninformed passer-by this house appeared to signal greater than average status; however, to knowledgeable Cockalorums it contributed negatively to their appraisals of her status.

Two other cases that occurred during the field period involved houses built on rented land that was part of children's property. In one of these cases, the landowner needed the land for a relative (a co-owner) who, returning from abroad, wanted to construct a house on it. Because the land was children's property, the landowner had no choice but to set aside the informal rental agreement. The family that had rented the land and that had erected a house on it was obliged to dismantle the house and to store it in a relative's yard until such time as they could obtain another location for reconstruction. This event sparked much gossip and led to reassessments of the renting family's status and its previous "pretenses." In the second case, a dispute arose between two brothers. One brother, who had been willed the land but not the house located on it, insisted that the other, who had inherited the house, remove it. The house was dismantled, and while the houseowner sought another location for reconstruction, he was forced to move into a rented house—an occurrence that again resulted in others reassessing his previous status claim.

When a house is clearly owned by its occupants, analyses may begin with the overall style and quality of the house. A modern, well-built and maintained house is a potential indicator of the occupants' statuses. Occasionally, houses are renovated solely to modernize some feature considered old-fashioned. In two cases observed during the field period, completion of a house was delayed because the owners decided to renovate a part of the house in order to add a feature that had become popular or that had been included in the home of a person with whom the owners wished to be directly competitive.

For these reasons and as a result of such acts, it is not unusual to see adjacent houses that are identical to the last painted board. Informants explained that things that are different are more difficult to evaluate than those that are the same. A man who wishes to signal to his neighbors and to his status competitors that he is of equal status may most effectively do so by acquiring an item that is a duplicate of theirs. In the case of houses, this goal is best accomplished by quickly building a house that is larger than, but otherwise identical to, houses of one's status competitors.

Nonetheless, a person who considers himself a member of a particular status category on the basis of house type or quality may attempt to signal an improvement in his status by introducing an innovative feature. Such an individual is more likely to succeed if the innovation has already been introduced elsewhere in Guyana and is accepted as modern (for example, cinderblock houses, theater facades, and sliding doors), or if it can be clearly associated with the outside (abroad), especially the United States, the United Kingdom, or Canada. Despite government efforts to encourage pride in local manufacture, foreign goods and styles still are held in higher esteem than are local products.

Successful manipulations of evaluations based on specific objective criteria must be maintained by giving the appearance of being able to keep pace in other respects with persons in the same status category. That is, Cockalorums must show some change in their situation indicative of improvements in their overall worth. They must continually manipulate their relationships to criteria that define potential membership in a status category, and they must adjust to changes in the set of criteria. For example, as house size, quality, and style become more uniform across all status categories, they become less useful as criteria for distinguishing between status categories because, as informants put it, "when everyone has a thing, that thing tells you nothing about anyone." It is partly due to the increasing uniformity in house size and quality that Cockalorums now pay greater attention to the time it takes to bring a house to different stages of completion. Although anyone may eventually be able to build a large, modern house, individuals do so with greater or less difficulty.

During the field period there were five houses that had been under construction for long periods: three of them for more than two years and the other two for about one year. These two houses were being built by persons living abroad, who periodically sent funds to relatives for the purchase of additional materials and who planned to return to Guyana when the houses were completed.[6] The other three houses (though already occupied by their owners) needed doors or windows and, in one case, the front walls and a portion of the roof. Informants believed that one family had sufficient funds to finish its house but had been unable to do so because materials were in short supply. The overall status rank of this family was, therefore, higher than that of the other two, which were thought to be waiting to save enough money to conclude their projects. Yet, even though the first family could not control its shortage problem, the failure to obtain the required materials was also an indication of its "size" (status): had its members been bigger, they would have had the right lines to obtain even short-supply items.

Even when a house is complete, this does not rule out the possibility that others will consider the time factor in their evaluations of the occupants' statuses. A house builder who expands a house or who builds a big house in stages as he can afford to do so is likely to be considered wealthier and of a higher status than one who builds a house of equal size and quality over a shorter period. Informants reason that, unless the second builder is a firmly established big small man—a designation difficult to achieve unquestionably—the first builder is probably more financially sound despite his outlay to finish the house. They also reason that the person who took longer to build the house probably did so with surplus funds, whereas they believe that the other overspent, leaving himself impoverished with a "lavish-lavish" (luxurious) house and little to live on.

Consequently, a big house is a meaningful criterion only if the occupants can show other signs of living that are congruous with the style suggested by the house. The situation and the comments of one informant serve to underscore this aspect of status assessments. When first encountered in 1977, he and his family of five were living in a two-room house with a lean-to shed for cooking. By 1979 he had built a five-bedroom wooden house with sliding glass doors, a large veranda, and an enclosed bottom-house that was used for a kitchen. He complained that he had not been able to save much money since moving into the new house, and he included inflation, black market prices, and the expense of paying for weddings for both a son and a daughter among the reasons for his predicament. Yet, he concluded that he could live more cheaply except for the fact that "in dis lavish-lavish house, we mus gaa of' live lavish-lavish, nuh?"

This man had worked hard as a fisherman, a boat builder, and a rice farmer. He "lived poor" (openly scrimping to save) for a long time. As a result, it was generally accepted by those who knew him that he could afford both the house and the style of life it suggested. For him to fail to live up to their expectations would have detracted from the status he gained by building the house. One part of his status substan-

tiation resulted from his ability consistently to give the appearance—
the accurate appearance—that his stable source of income was congruous with the house as a symbol of his success. His ability, however,
to substantiate this appearance was made easier by his ethnic identity.
The stereotype of East Indians as stingy and frugal weighed in his
favor with those African evaluators who took it for granted that even
East Indians who seem to be very poor probably have some money
hidden away. African informants, thus, argued that, as an East Indian,
he would not have built the house if he could not afford to do so and
remain financially stable. Of course, his East Indian neighbors, relatives, friends, and competitors, less convinced of the stereotype, took
into consideration a wider range of the criteria available to all Cockalorums as they scrutinized the relation between appearance and
substance.

In other instances, questionable sources of funds for building a
house are a potential cause for rejecting a status claim. An individual
who has slowly expanded a small house or who has built a large one
with his own capital (or with contributions from closely related
household members) is likely to be accorded a more secure status
rank than one believed to have built his house over the same period of
time using remittances from relatives abroad or one-time gains. In the
latter case, the money is spent with little assurance that the opportunity that provided it will ever reoccur. The use of remittances is
risky, informants reason, because, if the relatives who provided them
return to the community, they might eventually quarrel with the
homeowner and claim part of the house or demand reimbursement.
Even if this does not occur, they say such a homeowner is like the
man who spends all his savings on a lavish house, leaving himself
without the means to take care of his basic needs or to live in the style
suggested by the house.

No one criterion determines the status ranking of individuals or of
families. The point here is that, whatever the criteria, status evaluations involve assessing a range of information about the personal
circumstances of those being evaluated. Cockalorums grant or with-
hold deference and respect in interactions on the basis of these
essentially indeterminate situational interpretations of spatial boundaries, status signals, and ethnic stereotypes. For them, identifying
practical links between status as a quality of social honor and of class
situation, and generating criteria to evaluate the "average" class situation of the status-group members, are no mean feats.

Although Cockalorums basically perceive themselves as all belonging to the general category of small men, they by no means perceive all small men as status equals. Instead, they attempt to determine strategically what relevant signals symbolize and how they should interpret them in interactions. Types of interactions and the amount of information available to any particular party to an interaction about other parties to that interaction are limited; therefore, they must also depend on reputations—funds of secondary information based on previous evaluations of these parties. In reputations and in assessments of them, histories of space and of group identities are wed to histories of personal and family patterns of interaction. Who's who is inextricably bound up with where, in the broadest sense, one "came from," to where, in the broadest sense, one is trying to go, and how, in the strictest sense, one tries to get there.

4

The Art
of Becoming
"Somebody"

Despite differences in wealth and in the stress placed on appearing better off than one may actually be, in relation to big men, Cockalorums consider themselves to be in the same politicoeconomic situation. The general welfare of the community and every individual's hope for substantiating the appearance of success depends, they say, on group solidarity and on interpresonal cooperation and reciprocity. The condition of the total community is believed to be linked to cooperation and solidarity between its most and least well-to-do members. Without the assistance of those capable of giving a helping hand, no real progress is possible.

Although individuals and families should try to improve their material conditions in both absolute and relative terms, they are also expected to do so without breaching local norms of equality, solidarity, and reciprocity. Their efforts at self-improvement and at status competition are judged against moral criteria that again primarily pertain to how they go about reaching goals and presenting status claims based on their achievements. Individuals cannot avoid judgment by being noncompetitive, because persons who exhibit a lack of interest in status competition and in the acquisition of material goods or who claim to act for the general public interest are, at best, considered "strange" and, at worst, hypocrites who believe themselves superior to others. In this regard Cockalorum is not peculiar. As Bailey (1971) notes, in an egalitarian society such figures ideally stand for the community, for altruism against egotism; yet, as he also notes, they are likely to be mocked. They are not only thought to be too good, they are considered stupid. "It may also be that no man can be a prophet in his own country and that in small communities people know too much about one another, about one another's antecedents, for it to be possible to find someone pure enough to remain, respected, outside the competitive arena" (Bailey 1971:21).

Jayawardena's comments on the preference for mass action as opposed to leader-organized procedures among persons committed to egalitarian ideological precepts extend Bailey's conclusions and ground them more fully in the structural and ideological relation between the local community and the broader social system. He argues specifically that the distrust of leaders—those who would claim to act for the public good—and the preference for mass action are rooted in community members' recognition of the very real limits of their power to force powerful members of the broader society to act in accordance with norms of equality and solidarity generated out of their egalitarian precepts. It is not simply that no man can be a prophet in his own country because others know too much about his antecedents. It is also the well-founded belief that the conditions under which altruistic attempts are made favor an eventual betrayal of that intention.

For their part, Cockalorums analyze the morality of status competition in general and evaluate particular persons' status claims through two related cultural constructs: "face" and "name." Face is primarily concerned with a moral evaluation of an individual's self-presentation in social interactions. Assessments of face focus on individuals' behavior, paying particular attention to whether there are inconsistencies in their patterns of interaction with other community members. A person's face is the reputation he or she develops among peers as one who respects and who adheres to local values and norms. However, though it is possible and useful to speak of the overall reputation of an individual or a family, it is also necessary to recognize that most individuals interact with one another on the basis of partial reputations developed out of their own experience with a person. Thus, no person can be said to have only one reputation or even a composite reputation accepted by all. Therefore, when Cockalorums speak of a person's reputation (or " 'ow 'e stay"), they refer to conclusions based on their personal experience with that individual as well as on gossip to which they have been privy. In contrast, and with the same cautionary stipulations, name refers to the composite reputations of persons who share a surname through genealogical connections to a common ancestor, that is, broadly speaking, to families.

An individual's face contributes to the overall reputation of a family (name), whereas a family's reputation influences the evaluation of a person's face apart from his own actions. Both face and name develop from the adjudged moral quality of his strategic interactions with others as he makes a living, makes life, and competes to improve his status. Evaluations, then, of individuals' and of families' socioeconomic positions are implicitly linked to a moral continuum, the explicitly stated end points of which are "lives well" and "lives bad" with others. Thus, in Cockalorum, placement on the moral continuum becomes a salient aspect of how claims to status superiority based on criteria of wealth and social connections are evaluated.

Living Well: Egalitarianism, Hierarchy, and Competition

Competition for status takes place in a social context where community members value norms of egalitarianism, solidarity, and reciprocity as well as norms of hierarchy, competition, and individualism. Scholars, and to some extent rural Guyanese residents, have viewed these contradictory values as principles that organized interpersonal relations among common plantation laborers, as opposed to those that organized interpersonal relations across social strata of the total society. In his study of status competition and conflict on a Guianese plantation, Jayawardena (1963) noted that, within the socioeconomic structure of plantation communities, individuals were clearly identified with a particular social status. Membership in a particular social stratum depended on occupation, dress, and lifestyle, as well as on wealth and power. The social status hierarchy was clearly linked to the occupational and power structure of the plantation, and within this structure common laborers were a more homogeneous category than management (junior and senior staff).

Jayawardena further argues that in plantation communities, on the basis of their shared poverty, powerlessness, occupations, and lifestyle, the community of common laborers developed an ideology of egalitarianism. This ideology expressed, through the concept of "mati," organized laborers' interpersonal relations and competition around principles of solidarity and of cooperation. Mati essentially defined those presumed to share equal social status and poverty. Ties between such persons, rooted in their association at work and in their shared equality of opportunity, resulted in expectations of amity, cooperation, and solidarity with mati as members of a close-knit social group within which minor material differences were subordinated to a shared political predicament. Material differences were considered to result from luck rather than from any ascribed or achieved superiority. Mati relations were further affirmed through conviviality and conspicuous consumption, which served as redistribution mechanisms for those whose luck allowed them to achieve noticeable material advantage.[1]

It is not, however, egalitarianism alone that shapes this attitude. In the status evaluation process, it is the specter of hierarchical ideological precepts that makes necessary and possible this playing off of material and moral attributes. As members of the broader society, the community of common plantation laborers were also simultaneously exposed to, and developed commitments to, contradictory values consistent with hierarchical ideological precepts that encouraged individualism, status competition, and the recognition of hierarchy among themselves. As Jayawardena (1963) concluded, interest in success and concern with prestige heightened competition within the group, which threatened group solidarity, contradicted egalitarian ideological precepts, and made it difficult to establish patterns of action and interaction consistent with those precepts. Yet, he notes, it was not inequality in the form of individual success or achievement per se that posed the threat. Persons whose success moved them beyond the category of mati could be applauded with pride as local success stories. Their success was an example for others to follow, a support for the hope that others could succeed. The threat to egalitarianism and the source of disputes and friction devolved from prestige demands made by members of the mati category lacking the wherewithal to substantiate their claim to membership in a higher status category. These status claims were contested and led to "eye-pass" disputes: arguments in which one disputant accused the other of an attempt to belittle and to humiliate him, to lower his dignity and his prestige through a rejection of the equality implied in the humanity and in the general socioeconomic and political predicament shared by mati compared with members of other social strata. The humiliation resulted from behavior that the offended party took to be an unjust and unwarranted demand for deference or from demeanor that granted the offended party less than equal deference (see Jayawardena 1963:70–72). The problem was not success, but instead how to know when one had moved beyond the mati category, how to accomplish that move without breaching the local moral code, and how to claim the status implied in such accomplishments without alienating and angering one's neighbors and relatives.

Although eye-pass disputes were commonplace on the Guianese plantation, it was easier within the social structure of the plantation than it was in the villages and in other settlements established apart from that structure to determine who occupied which status category and who belonged in all respects to the mati group. In the villages and in the freehold settlements, the status hierarchy was less clear-cut, and the criteria for placement were less determined by an overarching authority structure. Because individuals had opportunities for greater occupational diversity, they could act more readily on their commitment to norms of hierarchy, competition, and individualism. The conflict between norms associated with egalitarianism, and those associated with hierarchy and status competition, intensified among persons who in most ways remained mati relative to the elite and powerful members of the broader society. Moreover, although the difficulties posed for patterns of interaction that were based on egalitarian ideological precepts increased in the villages, they were by no means uniform. Variations in the characteristics of villages, the range and lucrativeness of income-producing options, the distribution of individuals across this range, the type of established governmental structure, and the opportunities it provided for persons to assume prestigious roles apart from those defined by occupation and wealth, all served to influence the character of competition within villages and to shape the differing emphasis villagers placed on egalitarian and hierarchical ideological precepts (see Jayawardena 1963:129).

Whereas greater socioeconomic diversity weighed against the exclusive use of an egalitarian ideology in the organization of interpersonal relations among villagers, other factors favored the persistence of some form of egalitarian ideology. Within the broader social system, the majority of villagers remained part of the least powerful social stratum. With reference to the status categories discussed in Chapter 3, they were the ordinary small men of the Guianese social system. Their quests for greater personal and economic autonomy from the plantation structure, which they waged through mass negotiations, required solidarity. Reciprocity and cooperation linked to small-scale farming, to marketing, and to the maintenance of public works further favored the persistence of an ideology based on norms of equality (Smith 1955, Jayawardena 1968, Adamson 1972, Rodney 1981).

Nonetheless, this increasing economic diversity and the lack of clear-cut structural relations had serious consequences for villagers' conceptions of equality and the emphasis placed on differing criteria of equality. Increased differentiation, combined with the continued political need for mass action, resulted in an intense emphasis on human equality as an organizing principle, as opposed to the attention given to *social* equality defined in terms of an equality of opportunities and sociopolitical rights (Jayawardena 1968). The egalitarian ideological precepts, which emphasized rights to a minimal degree of respect and deference based on shared humanness, provided a source of values and norms for the organization of interpersonal relations and of social interaction among small men sharing a similar history and current circumstances. Ultimately, it also served to mediate relations across hierarchically related status categories defined in terms of economic and political differentiation.

In short, conceptions of the two forms of equality and degrees of inequality were not mutually exclusive in colonial Guiana. They were interwoven to produce what S. Barnett (1977) calls an ideological field (see Chapter 1, n. 12) in which Cockalorums now operate. To understand the implications of this field for their patterns of interaction and their evaluations of one another's conduct, it is necessary to recognize that both aforementioned definitions of equality, and the competing hierarchical and egalitarian sets of ideological precepts from which they are generated, are simultaneously relevant to all persons in all social contexts. It is this simultaneous relevance that shapes Cockalorums' efforts to integrate both the competing definitions of equality and the ideological precepts from which they stem.

Recognizing the simultaneous relevance of the sets of ideological precepts and of the differing definitions of equality they entail does not, however, imply that they may not be fruitfully analyzed by distinguishing them because, as Jayawardena also notes, "intrinsic or human equality seems to prevail in inverse relation to the prevalence of social equality. Typically, notions of human equality are dominant in a sub-group to the extent that it is denied social equality by the wider society or its dominant class" (1968:414).

Hence, there persist in the impoverished community of Cock-alorum (as in other rural Guyanese communities) egalitarian ideolog-ical precepts that define and emphasize equality in terms of shared historical experience, locality, kinship, and humanness. As a commu-nity of small men, Cockalorums remain the least powerful stratum of Guyanese coastal society. In this stratum, differences are ideally subordinated to members' shared history and current experience of being "those who punish to make life." Although the earliest meaning of the concept of mati, which defined a category of equals according to the precepts of egalitarianism embedded in an otherwise hier-archically ordered society, receives expression and emphasis in con-temporary use, the concept has been further elaborated to include the idea that "true" mati are those persons who, in the past ("slavery times" and "colonial times"), worked in the fields and who today still gain part of their livelihood working the land. On the basis of these criteria, Africans and East Indians define one another as "the same kind of people" (true mati), whereas they exclude Portuguese, Chi-nese, and Amerindians, who, they say, did not experience the praedial labor regime and who, as a consequence, do not now experience the same work and life conditions.

Cockalorums also consider themselves to be equal because they belong to the same locality. Sectional divisions notwithstanding, they contend that everyone born in the locality here identified as Cock-alorum is equal and should interact accordingly. That is, each person should express and demonstrate a concern for others' welfare and should be willing to respect and cooperate with them. More specifi-cally, when threatened by an external agent or when a choice must be made between "countryman" and "stranger," they should act in a solidary fashion.

The idiom of kinship, as expressed in the frequently heard com-ment "We 'z awl wan famali," expresses an additional criterion of equality as "sameness"—a single unit morally obligated to act soli-dary. Cockalorums believe that, beginning with any individual, one can ultimately link that person to every other person in the commu-nity. They apply this idea most often to intraethnic relations, but they also say such links, though more difficult to trace, can also be dis-covered across ethnic boundaries. The latter belief is part of a more general one that states that, despite individual claims of racial purity, all Guyanese have "mixed blood." "In truth," they say, "we are the same people."

The sense of equality expressed in the notion of "wan famali" is not, however, limited to real or fictive genealogical ties. Although within a family unit members differ in their roles, in the authority they can exercise at different stages of their lives, and with regard to their achievements, they are still part of one unit bound by expectations of concern for one another's welfare and, therefore, as in most societies, they are expected to respect and cooperate with one another simply because they are kin. It is this view of "family" relations that is part of what is meant by "wan famili" and that serves as one model for defining the nature of moral equality among all socially unequal persons.

As human beings, all persons are ideally deserving of some unspecifiable degree of respect, cooperation, and concern from others simply because they are human. Consistent with Jayawardena's earlier findings, in Cockalorum social inequality is further mediated and redefined as an equality of shared humanness. Human equality transcends historical experience, locality, kinship, and status based on subjectively interpreted economic differences. As with the other criteria of equality, the degree of respect a person deserves simply because he is human is left unspecified because it can never be fully delimited. Yet, humanness represents a bottom-line criterion of equality because, in all places and at all times, human beings are, as human beings, deserving of one another's concern, respect, and some minimum of cooperation. Moreover, despite the impact of ethnic affiliation on status (to be discussed in Chapters 5 and 6), the notion of human equality transcends ethnic boundaries. For example, when an African lawyer who had accepted an East Indian man's case failed to show up for the court hearing, those standing around, assuming that he would not have acted the same with an African client, agreed that he went "too far wid de race t'ing." They argued that it would have been fair (though racial) for him to refuse the man's case because he did not want to work for an East Indian, but, they contended, having taken on the case, it was not right to treat the man as he did. As one onlooker commented, "Iz true 'e coolie, and dem coolie people ah racial fo' true. But consider dis, naa so 'e ah human, and when you consider de t'ing you mus' gaa fo' treat 'e so, nuh?" (Translation: He [the client] is a coolie and all coolies are racist. However, consider this: are they not also human and, when you recognize that they are human, are you not bound to treat them as such?)

Yet, ideologically and in practice, even this criterion of equality is problematic. As noted above, all criteria are part of an ideological field, aspects of which, when subjected to situational interpretations, indicate inequality as readily as they do equality. Although each serves as a justification for solidarity, cooperation, reciprocity, and respect, certain aspects of each are also potentially divisive because they suggest differentiation and inequality.

Whereas the concept mati assumes that all small men are equal relative to big men, it can also be employed to justify inequality: Africans and East Indians as true mati are the "backbone" of the economic order. As true mati, they possess the attributes that, they argue, ought to give them the right to national positions of power and authority over Portuguese, Chinese, and Amerindians who, though mati in other respects, cannot, they contend, claim these particular "true mati" attributes. Second, though "countryman" unifies persons sharing a locality, the interpretation of spatially related status differences frequently results in redefinitions of the "in-group" and allows for differences in behavioral responses. Third, whereas the idiom of kinship implies equality in a broad moral sense, it is an equality tied to a recognized authority structure of inequality. Fourth, although biologically one is either human or not human, sociologically the matter is more complex. Persons who consistently disrespect their own and others' humanity come to be considered less than human and undeserving of being treated as human.

Earlier, we concluded that potential signals of economic differentiation and of status inequality are indeterminate. We may now add that ideological conceptions of equality are equivocal. Social interactions take place in an ideological field where both hierarchy and egalitarianism are recognized and valued. Cockalorums competing for status and for the hierarchical rank it implies are also concerned with maintaining social solidarity by adhering to norms of egalitarianism. As members of a moral community—a community of persons who accept one another's right to make judgments about proper and improper conduct—they are interested in balancing these countervailing concerns.

Individuals and families are expected to attempt to improve their economic situation and their relative status. Those who show little or no interest in economic improvement are called "doan-kay-dam" people, as are those who show little or no concern for improving the moral quality of their relations and interactions with others. Families and individuals ought to rise above the "average" to "mek demse'f somebody," but they must do so while "living-well wid de people dem." Thus, in day-to-day interactions, the morally worthwhile individual is concerned with being seen as one who willingly shares any good fortune with friends, with neighbors, and with kin. Friendship and actively recognized kinship are most often defined in terms of reciprocal respect, generosity, and cooperation. Persons who achieve the assessment of "agreein' well" with their neighbors and with their kin are also likely to have a general reputation for living well wid de people dem.

Individuals who live well with others are careful to avoid charges of "acting big," of "flaunting" good fortune, of unfair use of power or social connections, and of being jealous, greedy, covetous, or unduly quarrelsome. With regard to interpersonal conflicts, those who are morally worthwhile try to behave in such a manner that others will feel that they want to avoid conflicts whenever possible but, when this is not possible, that they will seek open and rapid resolution of disagreements. Such persons are as concerned with demanding as with giving "satisfaction" (arriving at a just solution as required by the situation), both of which they try to gain without recourse to the formal legal system.

In sum, the morally worthwhile person is one perceived (through the precepts of egalitarianism) by others to want to balance the obligation to give against the right to receive—either goods and services or intangible deference and respect. Thus, one of the most damaging charges that can be brought against the reputation of a person who desires to live well with others is that of eye-pass—a blatant disregard for the worth (human equality) and the personal accomplishments (social inequality) of another. The damage wrought by such a charge is matched perhaps only by the contrasting charge of "duppy"—a person who, so concerned with generosity or the obligation to give, allows others consistently to disregard his human worth by taking unfair advantage of the benefits of his personal accomplishments. In brief, the morally worthwhile individual seeks to give others their due and to gain from others what is due.

Eh-eh, 'e T'ink 'e Wan Big Wan, Nuh?

Living good makes it hard to live well. Coming from those with above-average material goods, the smallest impertinence becomes a sign of acting big. Cockalorums frequently comment that, in practice, it is next to impossible to improve one's economic situation, to claim higher status, and to remain for long a person considered to live well with others. They complain that people are too greedy, jealous, and covetous; they make life "hard" because they are too quick to "mind one another's business." They describe intraethnic social relations and interaction with a variety of negative metaphors. Some Africans and East Indians refer to East Indians as "crabs"—deeply entwined in one another's lives, and jealously clawing and pulling one another down. Some East Indians and Africans describe Africans as "dogs"—individualistic, greedy, and quick to fight over a bone. Members of both groups refer to "Dooglas" (a term applicable to all Guyanese of mixed race, but most often used to identify those of combined African and East Indian descent) as "crab-dogs," presumably having acquired the worst traits of both ethnic worlds. Detached from ethnic affiliation, these same metaphors are also used to describe the general quality of social relations among all Cockalorums—"dog eat dog" or "crabs in a barrel."

This tenebrous view of Cockalorum social life is further darkened by the fact that seldom a day passes that is not liberally punctuated by public " 'busings,"[2] charges of " 'vantage" (advantage), of "eye-pass," and of denied satisfaction in the many ongoing disputes and formal court cases. Public quarrels draw crowds of varying size to observe intense displays of emotion and, occasionally, shocking incidents of violence. The public displays, along with more covert disagreements, become focal points of concentric circles of gossip about "who is what," as people try to assess the credibility of individuals' faces. Actions and counteractions are judged against knowledge of histories of interaction between the parties and who has whom "up his sleeve" (who is holding a grudge). Neither persons nor apparent sources of conflict or congeniality are taken at "face" value, so that, to use a mixed metaphor, one quickly gains a sense of social life in Cockalorum as a mine-filled, eggshell existence in which the margins for error are minute and the consequences for face are immense and interminable.

Yet, Cockalorums just as readily offer another image of the character of social life among mati, "countryman dem," and nationals. They are, they say, the "most hospitable people in South America"—generous, hospitable, convivial, and willing to come to one another's aid in times of personal distress and public conflict. Hosts take pride in offering their guests the best of what they have and try to laden them with choice goods as "prags" (gifts) to carry away. When comparing themselves with their characterization and their experience of North American and European social life, they consider themselves to be more interdependent, communal, and concerned with one another's physical and social well-being. This more positive assessment of the character of social life also finds ample support in the daily interaction and exchanges that take place among Cockalorums.

As one would expect, the hard surfaces of social life for individuals and for the community lie somewhere between these contrasting views. In their development and presentation of face, residents aim, as consciously as an interviewee trying to make a good impression on a potential employer, to give the impression that they closely approximate the hospitable image, while protecting themselves from charges of contributing to behavior associated with the contentious one. With reference, however, to others' evaluations of a person's moral quality and to the linkages between morality and status ranking, all actions are ambiguous and are subject to equivocal interpretations. For example, actions that an individual intends as displays of generosity and cooperation may be, and are often, interpreted by others as pretentious flaunting of good fortune and as attempts to interfere in another's business. Further, to the extent that the person making the evaluation holds a grudge against the party being evaluated, any action is likely to be treated by others as just another instance of that party's contribution to the negative character of social life and of his low worth as a member of the moral community.

The presentation and maintenance of a face, consistent with ideals of living well with others, are made all the more difficult and tenuous by the astute attentiveness that community members give to one another's public behavior and to gossip about one another's private dealings.[3] Cockalorum attentiveness to, and scrutiny of, others' public conduct centers on gathering and evaluating information indicative of the person's self-respect and the respect that person shows others. Self-respect, as the maintenance of one's right to the basic deference and respect that should be accorded to all known morally worthwhile human beings, is evaluated in terms of the individual's display, in his daily interactions, of "shame"—a desire to protect his face and name (surname) from "stains" (charges of public or private misconduct). In other words, the scrutiny given to others' behavior in public is an effort to determine whether they consistently display a concern for developing and maintaining a face that says they live well with others. The goal is to play off material and moral attributes against one another in order to maintain a complexly defined equality: not because no man can be a prophet in his own community, but because every man's action is prophetic of the rise or the decline of the total, internally stratified and externally dominated, community.

Thus, individuals, whatever their assessed economic worth, may behave in a manner that raises questions about, or affirms, their basic humanness and moral worth. All behavior has both negative and positive consequences for others' willingness not only to accept a status claim based on economic achievements but also to cooperate with others in their efforts to improve further their economic situations. A sense of the continual scrutiny and evaluation during public interactions lends a guarded, highly conscious, and indirect air to public conduct and exchanges. Without implying there is rampant paranoia, I would suggest that Cockalorums are consistently concerned with what others may be saying behind their backs. Through gossip networks and microscopic attention to the interactional responses of others, they also expend a great deal of energy trying to find out and to keep track of what others think of them. They are equally cautious about what they say to others to their faces and behind their backs.

Caution is more than justified because remarks are often easily misinterpreted, and both advertently and inadvertently passed along. Frequently, this leads to distortion because proper contextualization is lacking. Consequently, misunderstandings are often lengthy and difficult to resolve, resulting in open confrontations, in one party's having another up his sleeve, or in both parties' "not talking" (refusing to engage in any form of cooperation). Also, lest others overhear what was not meant for their ears, public discussions, unless intended to "broadcast" a message or to "throw hints," are conducted in quiet voices or at a safe distance from others.[4] Likewise, at night on dark paths, approaching footsteps are signals for a break or a change in conversation until the person approaching is again out of earshot. Moreover, the language of such discussions is made as vague as possible—sometimes so vague that it takes participants several attempts before both understand what is being discussed.

In descriptions of their own actions in interactions, individuals also take care to describe their actions as defensive, especially in assessments of public quarrels and other confrontations. Though this often leads to wide discrepancies between accounts of the same event, it is an expected maneuver that community members discount as "making a case for one's self"—only a fool or a doan-kay-dam person does not attempt to make a case for himself. Making a case, however, must be done within reasonable limits. To paint one's self too much the innocent victim may result in face-damaging charges of " 'e too liar" or " 'e dus go too far." Hence, as with most aspects of interaction and of making life, the local focus is on balance. To breach that reasonable balance is to invite face-damaging charges.

Interactors must take care not to appear too eager to damage others' faces even to protect their own. Thus, though gossip is essential to discovering and consolidating information about one's own and others' faces, it is also very risky. One protection consistently taken by Cockalorums is to "talk story" (the details of an event) without "talking name" (calling the personal names or surnames of parties involved). The names of those involved may be obvious to all parties to the conversation, but, by not calling the name, one decreases the risk of subsequent involvement in a "dem-say-she-say story," or of having to instigate a "provin' story" (get a third party to clarify and to substantiate what one did or did not say about another party). As an added precaution against charges of unfairly giving another a "false face" (a face one is unwilling to accept and that the accuser cannot prove accurate), at various points in a conversation the speaker may typically clarify the frame (Goffman 1974) and his involvement by stating, "Me ah talk story, me naa talk none body name."

Where the names of other parties are necessary to an account (usually when an individual hopes the listener will act as a go-between to help resolve an ongoing dispute), the speaker may still attempt to define the frame as nonmalicious or unintentional talking name by stating, "Iz me own story me ah talk. Me naa gaa time fo' other people story." He thereby excludes himself from the category of persons who "talk name fo' name sake," that is to say, "ladda mo'f" or "wallah mo'f" people. Of course, where the person being discussed is labeled doan-kay-dam or as one whose behavior is thought to be so outrageously offensive that little risk to one's own face is likely to be incurred from talking name, names may be called. Even in this situation, however, the speaker will usually take care to affirm that talking name is not his typical behavior: "You know me long, nuh? Me naa talk name, but. . . ."

Face: Since Beg Pa'don Come ah Fashun Small Boy Mash (step on) Big Maan Foot

Manners, "sense" (competence in applying appropriate behavior across social contexts and under differing circumstances), and "shame" (sensitivity and susceptibility to feelings of guilt and degradation when behaving inappropriately) are the boundary conditions for successful interactions among morally worthwhile persons seeking to live well with others. An active interest in what constitutes good manners and making a consistent effort to improve one's skill in displaying appropriate manners across contexts and circumstances are the hallmarks of the mature, morally worthwhile adult. Evaluations focused on individuals' most consistent responses to manners and to shame are also the dividing lines between moral categories referred to as "shame-faced" and "bold-faced."

Not only are shame-faced persons susceptible to feelings of guilt and degradation when behaving inappropriately, they also vigilantly attend to whether their own behavior and that of others toward them results in embarrassing negative evaluations of their personal and, by association, their family name. When such individuals behave inappropriately, as in frustrating situations or in the heat of an argument, they try to rectify the situation and to convince others that it was only a momentary lapse of good manners, sense, and shame. In such situations, actors often later excuse their lapse with such expressions as "Me git wild," or " 'e mek me wild." During exchanges they may also signal a potential breach by saying, "Naa git (or mek) me wild." In contrast, bold-faced characters consistently behave in ways that show an almost total disregard for manners and a lack of interest in whether their behavior and that of others toward them is shameful. The bold-faced rarely make any effort to improve negative assessments of their public and private conduct. Those individuals and families who are economically better off are expected to be shame faced, but this is not always the case: bold-faced persons may be found in àny of the economically defined categories. Yet, apart from temporary lapses in which the shame-faced behave like the bold-faced or, more rarely, the bold-faced behave like the shame-faced, there are others whose consistent pattern of behavior is too complex to fit either of these labels. Such persons, most often males, are frequently referred to as "viragoes."[5]

In many respects, the term virago coincides with the U.S. Afro-American designation "bad-ass nigger."[6] In this sense, a virago is a person who is quick to anger and equally quick to settle disagreements violently. Unlike bullies, viragoes do not usually instigate fights, but like them, when confronted or "crossed" by others, they are unlikely to seek a compromise resolution to the disagreement. Viragoes expect loyalty from family and from friends and in return are loyal to them, coming to their aid without regard for what others think of their social conduct and their status in the community.

Although somewhat like the doan-kay-dam and the bold-faced, the virago is not simply a doan-kay-dam, bold-faced person. For instance, unlike many doan-kay-dam persons, viragoes are less likely to be thieves, liars, and "wallah mouths" (here, meaning general gossips). Instead, they are often hard workers, acutely concerned with being viewed as honest individuals whose word can be taken as truthful and binding. Perhaps even more than those labeled shame faced, viragoes mind their own business and insist that others do likewise. What further distinguishes them from shame-faced and bold-faced persons alike—and what makes of them a type of folk hero—is their uncompromising adherence to their own code of just responses, regardless of what good manners and legal statuses dictate.

Ultimately, it is "having manners"—displaying competence and skill in behaving appropriately for context and situation—that categorizes individuals morally and relates them to the ideal of living well with others. Good manners, as the saying goes, hide many faults and afford all the opportunity to present a face that is less than accurate: a face that others, unless willing to risk damage to their own reputations, must respond to until time and circumstances allow them safely to reveal its falseness. Manners allow all to present themselves as morally worthwhile and afford each individual the ability to challenge the moral worth of others. The small boy who, whether inadvertently or advertently, steps on the big man's foot and "begs pardon" excuses his inappropriate behavior and places the big man in a position where he must accept limits on the retaliatory use of his status, power, and strength or risk others' negative evaluation of his moral worth. In other words, the big man who ignores the remedial work implied by the child's action responds unjustly and may suffer the consequences of being unjust. (See, for example, Goffman 1971:95–187 on virtual offenses and remedial work.)

From the standpoint of moral evaluations, the recognition that manners are both a presentation of one's own moral worth and a challenge to the moral worth of others makes them especially useful in status competition. Hence, like any behavioral response, they are subject to two-way interpretations informed by the contrasting views of the character of Cockalorum social life discussed in the preceding section. For example, although greetings are minimal features of the recognition of others' human equality and are part of what can indicate a desire to live well with others, exchanged between members of a solidary, cooperative community, they may also be taken as prime indicators of a striving toward status superiority and a challenge to the moral worth of the parties involved in the exchange. This is the case because greetings, no less than other aspects of public conduct, may be interpreted as flaunting good fortune and as unjustly or justly claiming higher-than-average status.

While conducting a house and lot survey in one of the predominantly East Indian sections of Cockalorum, I was assisted by an elderly East Indian man. Approaching each yard, he called out the greeting "pandit" (pundit) even if no one in the household functioned in that religious capacity. He explained that he did so as a way of showing respect because he feared that people would be jealous of his association with me and would later accuse him of acting big. His use of pandit as a greeting allowed him, at least momentarily, to elevate their status relative to his own in the hope of allaying their suspicions about his motives and, hence, avoiding future conflicts.

This greeting, and others so employed, are important aspects of face-to-face manipulations of interpersonal status claims and evaluations of moral worth within and across ethnic boundaries. Although pandit is often used as an initial greeting among East Indian males, it is (for fairly obvious reasons) less often used by females and by Africans among themselves. Sometimes, African males, interacting with East Indian males, greet them in this manner as a sign of respect and as a means of easing concerns over status differences typically associated with ethnic affiliation. Likewise, "swami" (teacher), professor, doctor, and other occupational designations are employed as greetings because they have the potential of elevating the status of the hearer relative to the speaker. By contrast, cousin, aunt, uncle, sister, neighbor, schoolmate, mati, and countryman may be used to suggest shared identity and equality.

Whether such greetings gain for the interactor the identity "morally worthwhile person who respects others" depends in large measure on the quality of preexisting relationships. Between parties who are not "agreein' well," both status-elevating and status-equalizing greetings may be taken as sarcastic, belittling comments intended to put the person in a position where he must acknowledge what he considers to be the "false face" of the other party. Even greetings that are not specifically concerned with status elevation or equalization are potentially dangerous to the face of those involved in the exchange, because the quality of previous interactions makes it more or less easy for parties to guard against behaving in a manner that suggests flaunting good fortune and engaging in blatant status rivalry. Thus, responses to an initial question "How are you?" usually fall into two defensive categories: those that aim to minimize the respondent's good fortune relative to the greeter and to others not present, and those that try to reduce the respondent's accountability for undeniable good fortune. Typically, replies of the first type are, "Not so fine as you," "Me just here trying," or "Just ordinary," whereas those of the second type give credit to fate or to the supernatural, "All right for the time" (the present), or "Fine, by the grace of God."

Between interactors who recognize one another as status equals and who are "agreein' well," these greeting forms are merely polite, formalized modes of exchanging pleasantries. Between those who question one another's status claims or who are not agreein' well but have not reached the point of not talkin', attention to tone of voice and to body glosses often results in a conclusion that the other party is being sarcastic and belittling—a message that is often consciously intended. In the latter situation, one "dig" often leads to another, not infrequently serving as the opening salvo for a more direct confrontation during which long-standing grievances are brought to the fore as both parties try to maintain a defensive posture for the sake of face-evaluating observers.

In addition to greetings, most formalized features of proper public conduct allow Cockalorums the opportunity to present a morally worthwhile face and, indirectly, to challenge the moral quality of others. Transporting goods in public, requesting favors or gifts, showing gratitude, and giving compliments offer all residents similar formalized means for presenting themselves as morally worthwhile persons—that is to say, as those working to improve their socioeconomic standing within the moral constraints of local norms of equality, solidarity, and generalized reciprocity. (In generalized reciprocity, the emphasis in exchange is on the long-term, rather than on the short-term, balance between giver and receiver. See Sahlins 1965). For example, material goods transported in public should always be obscured from public view. Cockalorums explain that not making an effort to cover goods in public is flaunting one's possessions in front of those less fortunate. Perhaps the most extreme example of this polite behavior occurs when someone moves from one house to another. The polite mover waits until dark to move and, whenever possible, all residents make arrangements to take delivery of large purchases such as furniture after dark, thereby avoiding possible charges of flaunting their possessions. And, we might add, at the same time such persons avoid providing others with accurate information about their economic worth.

Although morally worthwhile individuals are expected to be generous and to engage willingly in generalized reciprocity in response to shared features of identity and equality, those making demands on them also are expected to do so in a manner that does not take unfair advantage of others' obligations to give. Requesting any favor or gift is referred to as "begging." Apart from humbling body glosses, tones of voice, and attention to how often one makes demands of others as opposed to offering assistance to others, whenever possible requests should be stated in terms general enough to allow the other person to fulfill the request according to his means. For example, requests for gifts of produce are generally stated as "Please for two," where "two" is not to be taken as an exact quantity. The giver may then give what he thinks is a fair amount based on his circumstances.

Children play a very important role in decreasing tensions and in facilitating the exchange of gifts and favors among adults without loss of face. Whenever possible, adults prefer to send a child to initiate requests for favors and loans, or to request their repayment. Children are always expected to be humble before adults, and as intermediaries they should not react to refusals or to the quantity and quality of what is given. As the proverb "When picni sen' fo' errand, foot cold, but heart hot" suggests, children are often sent to make requests where adults are particularly leery about the expected response. M., having twice unsuccessfully requested that a neighbor for whom she had done some sewing pay her for the work, decided to send one of her children to make the third request in the hope that she might receive her pay without a confrontation. When the child returned empty-handed, she resolved to confront the neighbor publicly at the earliest possible opportunity with a charge of "'vantage" (unjust treatment). During the pubic confrontation, which occurred several days later, the neighbor still refused to pay, claiming she had not been satisfied with the work. This left M. to charge eye-pass and to seek satisfaction for this disregard of herself as a person who deserved either to be paid for the work as done or to be given the opportunity to complete the work satisfactorily.

Favors granted and gifts given may result in conflict if the giver's generosity is not properly acknowledged. As Mauss (1967) notes, giving creates a situation in which the receiver is potentially at a momentary status disadvantage relative to the giver—making the acknowledgment of generosity, from the standpoint of status competition, a risky business. Thus, as Cockalorums state, although it is necessary to acknowledge others' assistance and generosity, it is also to one's advantage to do so in a manner that suggests the long-term equality of the transaction as part of an ongoing relationship in which the receiver has often been the giver and will again be the giver in future transactions. Hence, though it is good and necessary to be humble, to be too humble is to imply that one might be undeserving of others' generosity. Parties to exchanges are, therefore, concerned to underscore their right to receive as an aspect of their obligation and their willingness to give. They may immediately offer a specific item or service in return, but they are more likely to make statements to the effect that they deserve others' assistance because they are persons who readily give assistance to others.[7]

For instance, "housepeople" (persons who are members of households linked through economic cooperation on the basis of kin or affective ties) often offer the telling tongue-in-cheek acknowledgment "Me would sey t'anks, bu' if me do me naa git again." Likewise, givers play down the value of what they give in order to gain the moral benefits of their generosity. Those who do otherwise are not seen as generous; instead, they are viewed as self-serving, giving only so that they may later brag about what they have given. Of course, givers and receivers desiring to comment indirectly and negatively on another's generosity may behave in the opposite way. That is, receivers may elaborately offer thanks, whereas givers may accept thanks without any effort to minimize the temporary inequality suggested by the transaction.

Giving or receiving compliments is as complicated as acknowledging others' generosity in the exchange of gifts and favors. Compliments on physical appearance, dress, and other material possessions are most readily exchanged among long-term friends who are on very good terms. Cockalorums argue that giving and receiving compliments is risky because one cannot know what is in the heart of another, and that all but one's closest friends are likely to misinterpret one's intentions. It is an accepted fact that those who give compliments may well mean the opposite of what they say. In other words, the exchange of compliments, like the exchange of greetings, is seen as a prime opportunity for throwing hints. A compliment on one's appearance or possessions, for example, may be an indirect statement made to those who overhear it that the giver believes that the receiver considers himself above average in appearance or to possess goods of above-average quality, an assessment the complimenter does not share.

However, a greater risk to the face of interactors stems from the association made between compliments and the scrutiny of others. Although all Cockalorums are acutely aware of others' attentiveness to their appearance and their conduct in public, each tries to appear disinterested in others' conduct and possessions. In complaints, it is always the other community members who are too concerned with, and who are too quick to "interfere" (to be negatively involved) in, others' private affairs. Yet, in order to compliment a person, one must at least indirectly acknowledge that one is paying careful attention to that person. Complimenters, however sincere their intentions, thus run the risk of suggesting that they harbor jealous and covetous thoughts.

Individuals may attempt to guard their faces against such implied offenses by limiting the exchange of compliments to close friends whom they believe less likely to misinterpret their intentions and their attentiveness. In various other ways, they also try to protect themselves and their possessions from the presumed negative effects of others' jealous scrutiny. Parents of healthy, beautiful babies, for example, shield them from bad or "evil-eye" by prominently placing "tikas" (black dots) on their foreheads to attract attention away from their beauty. Owners of especially healthy, beautiful animals keep them from harm in a similar manner by tying red or blue strings around their necks. Gardens are protected by an appealing construction placed in the midst of the plants to attract the attention of passers-by away from the plants. In this way, the gardener hopes to avoid injurious effects to the plants that might be wrought by the jealousy and covetousness of those whose gardens are less productive. In addition, gardens may be protected from the covetousness of others (and faces from charges of greed and stinginess) by giving one's neighbors the best of one's first fruits.

These protective moves, as one might expect, are not without their difficulties. When P. gave his neighbor a beautiful squash as first fruit, the neighbor was insulted and accused P. of unfairly charging him with being covetous. Despite the fact that P. insisted he was only being a good neighbor (trying to live well with people), others on the square took the neighbor's side, contending that P. had a long-standing disagreement with this neighbor and chose this way to show his true face. Otherwise, they said, "Naa so 'e ah wait one time fo' gie bhagi [vegetables] to all two ah 'e neighba dem, nuh." (Translation: Is it not true that if he had not intended to insult him, he would have waited until he had enough vegetables to give some to both of his neighbors at the same time?)

Most who commented on the disagreement argued that P., as a big man (an adult), should have anticipated the reaction his action would receive because he and his neighbor were not agreein' well. Thus, because they felt P. should have known better ("been sensible to his actions"), they decided that he must have deliberately intended to insult his neighbor. Those who were more charitable did not question P.'s sincerity but instead concluded that he did the right thing at the wrong time with the wrong person—that is, that P. made a strategic error. P., aware of the damage done to his face, later made a more successful overture to the same neighbor by inviting him to a ritual event. The neighbor, still contending that P. had deliberately sought to insult him and that he probably still had him up his sleeve, attended the event because he felt, if he refused, others would believe he was being unnecessarily "hard" (difficult, stubborn, egotistical). This judgment, in turn, would damage his face while improving P.'s as a man willing to put aside disagreements in an effort to reestablish cordial relations.

Individuals differ in the competence, the skill, and the sincerity with which they employ formalized procedures for the presentation and maintenance of a morally worthwhile face. The task of all but doan-kay-dam people is made even more difficult by evaluators who rarely assess an action to have been merely a strategic error. As in P.'s case, the majority is far more likely to determine that the negative consequences of an action were deliberate. Although the tendency to interpret errors in judgment as intentional is often part of a person's attempt to improve his face at the expense of another, the matter is also more complex. As previously stated, Cockalorums consistently express two views of the nature of social life, one positive, the other negative, linked respectively to precepts of egalitarianism and to precepts of hierarchy.

Therefore, with reference to these competing sets of precepts, an individual's actions are always subject to at least two contrasting interpretations. Any action raises the question whether the person is trying to adhere to egalitarian norms of equality, solidarity, and generalized reciprocity, or to hierarchical norms of inequality, individualism, and competition. For example, from the perspective of egalitarian precepts, covering goods transported in public is considered a polite expression of one's desire not to be seen as flaunting one's good fortune and inciting the jealousy of others. However, from the standpoint of hierarchical norms, the same action is frequently interpreted as a rude attempt to hide one's possessions from others in order to avoid sharing them, or to decrease the accuracy of information available to others about one's true economic worth in order to make it more difficult for them to reject one's claim to above-average status.

This potential for double-edged interpretations results in considerable testing of others' concern for one or the other set of values. These testings are focused on assessments of others' willingness to seek a behavioral balance between acts of competition and acts of cooperation. The information adults gain from children is often of critical importance in the testing of others' generosity. Generally, children (the most frequent visitors to neighboring households) report to their parents detailed information about their neighbor's possessions. In turn, parents often send these children to beg for items that they know their neighbors have and that the neighbors know the children know they possess. It is much easier to question another's generosity successfully if one is sure the other possesses what one has requested.

On several occasions my weekly purchase of kerosene was delivered to my house when one of my neighbors' children was visiting. Each time, this neighbor later sent back one of the same children to "beg lil' kerosene." Interested in the implications of her actions, I discussed the matter (without calling name) with one of my primary informants. He advised me that, although it was good to be generous, always to comply with another's requests would result in unreasonable demands and in ultimately being labeled a "duppy" (one impracticably and overly concerned with generosity and cooperation, a fair mark). Consequently, when my next supply arrived, in full view of my young visitors, I put the kerosene into my stove. When they returned to request kerosene, I regretfully informed them that I had put it all in the stove and could only retrieve it by dismantling the stove— leaving unstated that I had no intention of doing so. Although it was a flimsy excuse, this indirect message was accepted. I continued to loan her kerosene and other items; the primary difference was that subsequently, when requesting something from me, she often sent something in exchange, thereby acknowledging the relation between generosity and reciprocity in testing another person's generosity.

It is extremely difficult to climb the socioeconomic ladder while maintaining a morally worthwhile face, but many individuals and families succeed for long periods without serious disjunction between their overall status claims and what others find acceptable. Those who are most successful take care to maintain a balance between adherence to the norms of egalitarianism and to those of hierarchy. Morally worthwhile persons cultivating links to others of higher status are careful to maintain their previous ties with ordinary small men and to engage in reciprocal transactions with neighbors and friends. Most important, they try to make clear to all their willingness to use their newly formed social connections to help others improve themselves. To behave otherwise is to open oneself to intense scrutiny, criticism, and a reluctance on the part of others to cooperate and to accept one's status claims as valid. Such persons are most likely to experience what Wilson (1973), Bailey (1971), and Cockalorums refer to as the "crab antics" (attempts to level all who rise above average) of "back-to-back" societies.

Moreover, neither clear indications of greater-than-average economic worth nor physical removal from the community places countrymen beyond the pale of Cockalorums' evaluative links between economic worth and moral quality. Residents stress that, however fortunate a person may be at a given time, fate, ill health, or other adverse circumstances may result in one's return to the average. Further, they believe that no one survives and certainly no one rises above the average without the aid of many helpers, whose help they should acknowledge in concrete fashion. "Wan hand cain wash." Those who depart often leave behind poorer kin whose ability to gain assistance from others is adversely affected by moral evaluations of the absent relatives. If, in their zeal to rise above the average or to emigrate, they fail to balance cooperation and competition, they leave behind an indelible stain (damage to an overall positive evaluation of the moral worth of a surname) on their family name. Also, if they return to the community, it is their kin links to "family" that serve as the first point of evaluation for those with whom they will have to interact. Thus, whatever an individual's face and economic worth, his surname and its links to other surnames within and outside Cockalorum are key elements in shaping others' responses and evaluations.

Name: The Dirt That Falls on the Heads of the Parents Rests on the Shoulders of the Children

For better or for worse, Cockalorums feel that an individual's behavior will ultimately approximate the overall reputation of the family to which he belongs. The morally damaging actions of a person from a morally worthwhile family are likely to be seen as temporary. If the individual is young or unmarried, it is generally expected that, when older or married, he will settle into a pattern more consistent with the moral worth of his surname. Likewise, persons from less morally worthwhile families who behave in a morally worthwhile manner are less likely to be given credit for their behavior, as others are likely to expect that they, too, will ultimately return to a pattern of behavior more consistent with the overall reputation of their surname.

When the daughter of an ordinary small-man family observed the daughter of a big small-man family in a compromising situation with a young man, she spread a rumor about what she had observed. Upon confronting the gossip who admitted that she had spread the rumor, the wayward girl's mother filed charges against the gossip, suing her for slander. The gossip's mother then went to her counterpart, asking to settle the matter out of court, to which, after much discussion, the other mother acceded. A "paper" (written agreement) was drawn up in which the gossip admitted that she had spread the rumor, and her family agreed to pay fifty dollars for damages. The gossip's family was able to settle the matter out of court because the other family respected its good name and decided that the family should not suffer the greater expense of a court case because of its daughter's loose mouth.

As the gossip had no witness to what she claimed to have observed, it was assumed that she would not prevail in court; the truth of the rumor, thus, was not central to the outcome. And, although the matter was settled out of court, thereby saving her family the greater expense of hiring a lawyer, the family name was stained because the agreement implied an admission of guilt. The truth of the rumor was not disproved; consequently, the other girl did not escape without at least minor damage to her personal reputation. Note, however, that the resolution of the conflict stressed name and differences in the families' resources rather than the truth of the gossip's accusation.

In cases where resources are more equal, the quality of name remains an important factor. Two young boys from different families were caught stealing coconuts from a man's backdam trees. The owner of the trees decided not to take the matter to the police because he believed that the boys' families, like himself, were "poor, but honest people" who did not condone thievery. He also reasoned, however, that something should be done to encourage the families to control their children's behavior better. As the boys were too young to have any personal income and the families would have to pay the court costs, he thought that it would be unfair to impose on them this expense simply to get across his message. He decided, instead, to inform the families that he would not take the matter to court if they would each pay twenty dollars, which, he felt, was sufficient penalty to encourage them to restrain their children. The owner was an elderly man who had turned over the care of his trees to his own son.

It was his son who caught the thieves, and it was his son through whom he transmitted his settlement offer. Even though no papers were drawn up, both families accepted the offer and sent the owner the payment.

Several days later, the owner returned the payment to one of the families while retaining the other's. In the interim, he had learned that one of the thieves was the grandson (daughter's child) of a man for whom he had great respect. It also had been brought to his attention that this boy was living with his grandfather and that the grandfather had paid the penalty. Because the child carried his mother's married name and because the owner had not personally delivered his settlement offer, he had not connected the child with the grandfather or his reputation. Once he knew of this connection, he reasoned that the payment was an unnecessary stimulus. On the basis of his knowledge of the grandfather and his family name, he believed that every effort would be made, without reference to the penalty payment, to correct the child's wayward behavior. He had no such respect for the other family and, therefore, retained their payment in order to impress upon them the need to regulate their child's behavior.

Thus, in practical terms, surnames and their links to assessments of moral quality influence individuals' patterns of cooperation with one another. Although there are always risks involved in assisting another—mainly that, when needed, the other will fail to reciprocate—Cockalorums say one's greatest security in such transactions comes from the knowledge one has of the reputation of the other party's surname. Put another way, knowledge is one's assessment of the family's long-term concern with balancing acts of cooperation against acts of competition. In each generation, family members must be concerned that their actions and the faces they maintain do not permanently stain their surnames. Stains result from moral and legal transgressions and from the failure either to confront or to gain satisfaction, or both, from those who physically or verbally transgress against one of those whom one represents.[8]

Apart from maintaining a morally acceptable face (one relatively free of sustainable charges of moral or legal transgressions), the individual must protect his name by confronting and satisfactorily resolving conflicts where others unfairly attack those whom he represents. To represent another means to relate to the other as one responsible for intervening in and mediating conflicts between that person and another party capable of taking advantage ("'vantage 'pon") of the person. Criteria for the role of "representer" are age, role, status, and, of course, kin ties. With the exception of infants, everyone is representer to someone else.

Under circumstances in which neither party is considered to have an advantage over the other, individuals should represent themselves. That is, they are initially responsible for resolving their own conflicts, either one-to-one or through the informal and formal mechanisms available to them. Yet, even between adults, the intervention of a representer is often justified on the grounds of 'vantage where one party is of a higher status, has greater economic resources, or has more powerful social connections. Older adults in conflict with younger adults have the assumed advantage of more experience and, hence, greater skill at strategic manipulations, as well as the very real advantage of etiquette, which requires the younger person to respect the elder and, thus, to forego certain "moves" that might otherwise be acceptable. Where conflicts go beyond words, the greater physical strength of one party may also constitute 'vantage and justify the intervention of a representer. Likewise, a person known to be of subnormal intelligence or "not at himself" is at a disadvantage in conflicts with others of normal intelligence and, therefore, may require representation.

In the protection of names from stains, males as husbands and as fathers are responsible for intervening in and mediating conflicts between others and members of their nuclear and extended households. When conflicts result from disagreements between young children, however, women more often play the initial representer role in attempts to resolve them. Yet, who acts as representer varies, because defining the beginning of a dispute is always difficult, as it is usually connected both to previous ones and to current relations between the interactors and their respective families. If one parent feels that the dispute is connected more with his relationship to the parties involved, then that parent is most likely to intervene initially. From records kept of sixty cases entailing an initial conflict between young children that subsequently involved adult intervention, a female always played the role of representer. In twenty-one (33 percent) of these cases, where the efforts of the female failed to bring the matter to a satisfactory close, males then represented both the child and the female. In twelve of these twenty-one cases, it was the husband or the father who played this role. When the husband or father was absent (the other nine cases), an older brother or some other older male relative took the role.

In keeping with a preference for the most indirect and subtle means to resolve conflicts, Cockalorums say that males, as the most powerful representatives of their households and their names, should be the initial actors only in extreme cases of 'vantage. Otherwise (to avoid charges of being "hard" or "going too far"), it is best to allow the next most powerful family member to intervene. That is, initially the power of this party should match the seriousness of the conflict. If the first effort fails to resolve it, others may attempt its resolution before formal authorities such as the local police or the regional court are called upon. Further, where no one comes forth, it is incumbent upon the injured party to seek a mediator for the case before going beyond informal procedures. Not to do so would inevitably result in a charge of eye-pass because one would have failed to give an appropriate party the opportunity to try to settle the conflict before the family name was "carried to the station or court."

In children's disagreements siblings should first act on behalf of one another. Most specifically, older siblings are representatives for their younger siblings and should move to resolve difficulties where they believe the other party has an advantage. Among siblings, brothers, especially older brothers, should come to the aid of their younger sisters. Although these big brothers should limit their assistance to situations in which their sisters are in conflict with males of the girls' own ages or older, they may also reasonably intervene when both parties are female, if the circumstances indicate a clear condition of 'vantage. Most situations, though, are ambiguous, resulting in claims and counterclaims of 'vantage from both sides.

In the broader context of kin relations and the protection of names from stains, kinspersons are all representatives for one another and intervene whenever one of them is deemed to be at a disadvantage. When direct intervention is considered inappropriate, they should still try to influence those whom they represent to seek a fair and speedy resolution to the problem without recourse to the police or the court. Those who feel that their kin have been wronged, however, may encourage court action and may raise funds to help cover the cost should the matter go to court.[9] Individuals and families, on the other hand, who develop a reputation for openly intervening unjustifiably in conflicts damage rather than protect their name. They are judged ignorant of knowing how to live well with others or how to accomplish a fair resolution to conflicts. They are said to "play big," placing themselves above the local norms of just interaction among members of a moral community.

In contrast, those who fail to act as representatives, consistently allowing others to take advantage of and to eye-pass them and their kinspersons without a concerted effort to gain satisfaction, in the short run, damage their face and, in the long run, their name. They, like "play big people," are among those whom others refer to as having "dropped out of society"—persons thought no longer to have shame or to care about the adjudged quality of their names within the local community. Members of this category should not be confused with those who are said "not to have sense." Individuals who do not have sense remain concerned about their face and name but are consistently unable to resolve conflicts through appropriate means and in a manner advantageous to themselves. They simply lack the skill and the competence to engage successfully in strategic manipulations to benefit themselves and their surname.

The expression dropping out of society has a literal and a figurative meaning that applies to both individuals and families. In its literal sense, it means a resident withdraws from normal social interaction or physically leaves the community. Each Christmas for more than ten years, Mrs. G., an African, has cried for her son, who was arrested and jailed in Georgetown. The charges (unknown or vaguely remembered by most who told the story) later proved false and he was released. While in jail, he met another person from Cockalorum. Fearing the disgrace he would confront when this bold-faced person informed others that he had been seen in jail, he refused to go home when released. Some informants say that for several years he stayed in Georgetown, avoiding Cockalorums. Whenever he wanted to give gifts to his family, he sent them or brought them as far as the public road at the entrance to the community and left them to be picked up according to a prearranged message. When members of his family finally discovered his whereabouts in Georgetown and tried to persuade him to return home, he refused and disappeared from Georgetown. Later, rumors circulated by returning porkknockers claimed that he had been seen in Bartica, a town on the Essequibo River, where he was said to be living with an Amerindian woman and her children. That the woman was said to be Amerindian was taken, by those who told the story, to be just another indication of his drop from society. "Why else," they asked, "would a well-respected, socially mobile African male take up with an Amerindian woman—one with children as well?" Although not all Amerindian-African unions are considered to be drops from society, these informants felt that under the circumstances their interpretation was logical.

When these rumors reached his sister, she went to Bartica to look for him, but she was unable to find him. He apparently saw her because, a few days after she returned to Cockalorum, his mother received a telegram informing her that he was doing well and that she should cease sending others to search for him. In the years that followed he periodically sent money to his mother but successfully avoided attempts to discover his whereabouts. When rumors circulated that he was dead, his mother was in great distress. He somehow heard them and sent her a telegram informing her that they were false. Now, each Christmas when the family gathers, Mrs. G. cries for her missing son who has dropped out of society. Some informants argue that the son would have been kinder to let his family believe he was dead.

Dropping out of society in the literal sense need not engender a physical departure from the community, nor need it be as abrupt as in the case of Mrs. G.'s son. A young woman from a moderately well-to-do family was caught stealing a chicken from a neighbor (see B. Williams 1983: chap. 8, for additional details). She had never been involved in any such incident before, and her family was well respected. No one knew why she stole the chicken; there seemed to be no extenuating circumstances. Though her family compensated the neighbor for the chicken, the young girl never overcame her own shame. She gradually ceased interacting with her peers and with most of her kin, remaining a dependent, never marrying, and rarely venturing outside her home. When many years later she died as an old woman and her kin announced her wake and funeral, informants claimed they were surprised to learn that she still lived in Cockalorum. She, too, was said to have dropped out of society. An elderly man living alone, who, informants claimed, had not been seen outside his house for years (though they did not recall why he withdrew) was also referred to as one who had dropped out of society.

Although both Mrs. G.'s son and the young woman are thought to have dropped out of society, in each case the actions resulting in the drop-out had different consequences for the family name. The case of Mrs. G.'s son is viewed as an unfortunate misunderstanding. Informants contend today that his reaction (sense of shame) would be considered extreme even for the well-to-do, because young males who happen to be at the wrong place at the wrong time are likely to be arrested as chronic "limers" (loiterers) even if in actuality they are only enjoying leisure time with friends. They say damage to face and name today would depend both on the type of charge and on public opinion about its fairness and the likelihood of its being true. Moreover, because Mrs. G.'s son was a respected member of the community before his arrest, the fact that the charges proved false meant that no permanent stain was left on the family name. Though there would always be a few who believed the worst, others said the son should have realized that the incident, if not soon forgotten, would at least not be damaging to his face and name. In contrast, the young woman's behavior stained her family name. Although this case was first brought to my attention during discussions of the meaning of dropping out of society, it also came up later as an example of the low moral quality of members of that family when told by persons in conflict with one of them. Even though the family had compensated the neighbor for the loss of the chicken, there was no credible excuse for the young woman's action. Consequently, the family could not possibly protect its name from the stain brought about by her deed. This incident is, therefore, passed down as an indicator of the "true" moral quality of those who now carry the surname.

These cases represent the most dramatic and literal meaning of dropping out of society. More typically, dropping out of society is gradual and figurative. It results from a general failure of family members to maintain morally worthwhile faces, causing a slow erosion of others' confidence in the family's concern with living well with others. When families that are physically present and engaged in social interaction are said to have dropped out or to be in the process of dropping out of society, people mean that others attempt to limit severely their transactions with them. A proverb often used to sum up the situation—"'af yam naa kay shovel dig um" (translation: a yam, already cut by the shovel, does not care if it is cut again)—suggests that the carriers of a name stained to the point of dropping out of society have little to lose by failing to live up to their agreements or by failing to seek a just settlement in their conflicts with others.

In essence, among the small men of Cockalorum, it can be reasonably argued that differences in wealth and in accomplishments are boundary conditions for the definition of status categories based on hierarchical precepts, but it is the assessment of moral quality that ultimately substantiates and stabilizes (lends certainty and determinancy to) status claims in interactions. Furthermore, when we keep in mind that Cockalorums believe (with ample historical justification) that the potential for social mobility among small men is linked to solidarity, to cooperation, and to the willingness of those most able to assist others to grant such assistance, we need not limit our understanding of the resulting patterns and conflicts to metaphors of thoughtless crabs indiscriminately pulling down anyone who rises above average. Instead, the goal of those who simultaneously reject the materially based status claims of certain individuals and negatively evaluate those who reject competition may be apprehended more accurately when viewed as an effort to reinforce a local code of conduct that demands of mati a balanced concern for hierarchical and egalitarian precepts.

II

Ideology,
Ethnicity, and
Anglo-European
Hegemony

5

Ideology and
the Formation of
Anglo-European
Hegemony

Thus far, our primary focus has been on individuals and families (surname groupings) and on the criteria, evaluation processes, and patterns of interpersonal interactions through which Cockalorums attempt to place one another. We will now direct our attention to the meanings they attach to differences in ethnic affiliation and to the significance of these meanings for other aspects of social interaction.

Drummond, in his analysis of Pomeroon Amerindian ethnicity, argues that "the concept of ethnicity is the ideological focus of Guyanese life and the mainspring of Guyanese thought" (1974:49). He states that in addition to its sociological dimensions, ethnicity is a set of associations that "are not determined by features of social organization alone" (p. 49). Further he contends that

the ethnic stereotypes involved here are broken loose from social organiza-tion—they no longer identify particular groups—and become ideas that men use to create a social world around them. Ideas about ethnicity—the set of stereotypes that make up the ethnic myth—are not tied to actual social groups and individuals in the way that say, a traffic sign derives its meaning from features of the highway. These ideas are rather partially independent of the social setting that produced and sustains them; they are symbols rather than signs. As symbols they are what people think with, and also what is available to think (I will not say that they think themselves). (1974:51)

Yet, to understand how and why Guyanese think with symbolic conceptions of ethnicity, how and why they do tie stereotypes to particular groups and individuals, and how and why they tie these groups back to the historical particulars of social organization, one must examine several interrelated features of Guyanese social and economic history. First, what were the historical conditions under which ethnically identified groupings of individuals came to share common geographical space and to participate in a single economic and sociocultural order? Second, how were the European elite's rationalizations[1] of their own economic and political dominance linked to particular interpretations of the meaning of ethnic identity and ethnic cultures? Third, at different times and under different circumstances, how did subordinated ethnic groups incorporate, reinterpret, and add features to this ideological framework competitively to justify their own rights relative to the dominant European elite and to other subordinated ethnic groups? Only through an exploration of these interrelated factors can we begin to understand the current meanings that Cockalorums attach to ethnic identities and culture, and how these meanings influence local evaluations of individual and group status.

Heterogeneity, Economic Structure, and Stereotypes

The Europeans who began entering Guiana at the end of the sixteenth century brought with them ethnic diversity.[2] They were Dutch, British, French, and Spanish nationals who represented the religious and cultural diversity of Western Europe. They also encountered ethnic diversity in the Aboriginal inhabitants. Though European settlers noted few differences among the indigenous peoples in their physical appearance, they concluded that the groupings had only a few words in common and fought among themselves. According to Menezes (1979:4), European settlers saw Caribs and Arawaks as sworn enemies, both despising the "timid Warraus, distinguished among all tribes for their 'filthy habits'." Although it was a commonplace European contention that all tribes considered themselves free people, it was also, according to these early stereotypes, the Caribs' "past warlike reputation" that had purchased them the "crème de la crème" rank of this indigenous hierarchy (Menezes 1979:4). These intertribal stereotypes, differences in skills, and patterns of environmental exploitation were important identifying features for early Europeans interested in trading with the indigenous population. Such stereotypes, the patterns of interaction they engendered, and the policies that would eventually attempt to capitalize on them were the beginning of the ideological process that ultimately produced the collective categorization of Aboriginal peoples now known as the Amerindians.

These two heterogeneous groupings (European and Aboriginal) were also the first racial segments of Guianese society. Defined in opposition to one another, their heterogeneity faded into a homogenized "purity" of types. These types were ultimately blended to produce new types. For while there was intertribal breeding (especially among Caribs and captive Arawak women), from the standpoint of the developing colonial society the "Bovianders"[3] produced by the union of European and Aboriginal peoples may be considered the first elements of a social category currently called "No Nations"[4] or "Doogla."

As the heterogeneous seventeenth-century European population turned from a primary emphasis on exploration and trade to the development of a plantation economy, they added African slaves to the racial diversity. The first African slaves entered Guiana soon after the founding in 1621 of the Dutch West India Company. By 1803 there were about 60,000 African slaves in Guiana. They, and those who followed them, were mainly West African but were linguistically and culturally diverse. Despite enslavement and the seasoning process, their presence and diversity contributed to the developing Guianese cultural complex. Interbreeding among these segments continually added to the physical diversity. Unions between Aboriginal peoples and Africans (most often, escaped slaves) added those whom, Pierronet (1798) claims, were dubbed "Carib-ogres,"[5] whereas African and European unions produced Mulattoes. Among Mulattoes, finer distinctions, based on physical attributes and on parentage, were recognized and accorded different social status.

After emancipation planters began importing contract laborers from the continent and the West Indian islands. A small number of Europeans of English, German, and Irish stock were also imported in the experimental phase of the indentured labor scheme. These sources proved unsuccessful and inadequate for the plantation needs as defined by planters. The continuing search for a viable source of labor resulted in the importation of indentured laborers from China, Portuguese Madeira, Malta, the Azores, and India. Immigration figures for the period 1835 to 1880 are shown in Table 5.1.

By 1891 Africa-born Africans, Guiana-born Africans, and other West Indies–born Africans totaled just under 42 percent of the total

Table 5.1. Postemancipation Immigration, 1835 to 1880

Period	Indian	Portuguese	West Indian	African	Chinese	Others	Total
1835–40	396	429	8,092	91	—	278	9,286
1841–50	11,841	16,908	4,806	10,528	—	—	44,083
1851–60	22,381	10,406	—	1,965	6,665	21	[41,438]
1861–70	38,717	1,533	10,180	1,476	5,975	—	57,881
1871–80	53,327	2,170	12,887	—	903	—	69,287
1835–80	[126,662]	[31,446]	[35,965]	14,060	13,543	299	[221,975]

Source: Rodney 1981: 241. Addition corrected for the sums of columns 1, 2, 3, and for line 3, for a total of 221,975.

population of 278,328. Indian immigrants accounted for nearly 38 percent of the population. Europeans continued to equal less than 2 percent. In fact, Amerindians, Chinese, Portuguese, and all other Europeans combined numbered just over 10 percent of the total and were slightly outnumbered by the "mixed race" category, which accounted for just under 11 percent of the total population (Rodney 1981).

The introduction of African slaves had shifted the ethnic composition from an Aboriginal and European numerical predominance to an African and Aboriginal numerical predominance. The introduction of laborers from Indian again altered this composition, soon changing it to an East Indian and African numerical predominance. In addition, the European population, composed of English, Irish, Scots, French, and Dutch, was soon outnumbered by Portuguese. Although they were officially distinguished from other Europeans, by 1891 more than two-thirds of all European members of the population were Portuguese.

By 1964, less than two years before British Guiana gained independence, the end of significant immigrant repatriation and group differences in birth and death rates had resulted in the ethnic/racial population composition shown in Table 5.2. The current population of Guyana continues to reflect this ethnic/racial distribution. East Indians are now more than 50 percent of the total population, followed by Africans and persons of mixed ancestry. Since independence in May of 1966 the non-Portuguese European component of the

Table 5.2. Population Composition of British Guiana, December 1964

Racial Group	Number	Percentage
East Indian	320,070	50.2
African	199,830	31.3
Mixed	75,990	12.0
Amerindian	29,430	4.6
Portuguese	6,380	1.0
Chinese	3,910	0.6
European	2,420	0.3
Total	638,030	100.0

Source: Rauf 1974: 35.

population has continued to decline, until only a few expatriates associated with church organizations or with development projects and diplomatic services remain. A largely uninvestigated but important shift has also occurred in the composition of the mixed population. Exact figures were not available, but it is highly unlikely that the majority of the mixed population now is of European and African mix, as reported by Rauf (1974) for the early 1960s. As one would expect, these mixtures now are some combination of African, East Indian, Amerindian, Chinese, or Portuguese. As early as 1912 even the Boviander category was no longer primarily composed of European and Aboriginal mixes (Rodway 1912:179). Terms distinguishing types of Mulattoes have given way to those distinguishing types of Dooglas, such as "Cabbaculas" (African-Portuguese or African-Amerindian), "Santantones" (Portuguese-African), "Coolidooglas" (East Indian–African or other), and "Chinnidooglas" (Chinese-and any other). Or any of these mixtures may simply be called "No Nations" or "Cosmopolitans."

Economic Structure and Ethnic Diversity: Anglo-European Rationalizations of Linkages between Ethnic Identity, Contribution, and Place

In *British Guiana: The Land of Six Peoples* Swan maintains: "It would take, I imagine, half the lifetime of a social anthropologist to define the structure of Georgetown society accurately; to plot the relationship

between the various peoples, the Chinese, Indians, Negroes, coloured people, high coloured people, British and Portuguese, not to
mention the results of miscegenation between all, would require the
subtlety of a Guianese Proust" (1957:49). Although his reference is
specifically to Georgetown society, the matter and its investigation
are no less complex in the rural areas, nor have time and shifts in
proportions of persons in the different social categories diminished
the need for subtlety in analysis and for caution in generalizations.
Yet one factor, the relationship between economic structure and the
meanings of diversity, remains the most cogent point of departure for
such efforts. For, as the Reverend L. Crookall wrote, any equality in
British Guiana was

> not equality amongst the people; for in that respect we have the most glaring
> inequalities. Here the planter has long been the lord of the soil, if not the
> lord of creation. He has made our laws, and to a large extent administered
> them. And he has always had an eye to his own interest. In fact, he considers
> he has made the colony, *ergo* the colony ought to exist for him. He is the
> universal sweetener. But for him we should have "no cakes and ale." He is the
> one-eyed man in the kingdom of the blind. (1898:47–48)

In Crookall's comments are the nodes of an ideological framework—referred to herein as an ideological field—which was both a
scaffold for and a product of European rationalizations, and, subsequently, other ethnic segments' rationalizations of linkages between
contribution, place in the social hierarchy, and senses of a just distribution of goods, services, and power. It is in the ideological rationalizations of contribution to economic and cultural development ("he
considers he has made the colony") and their links to assumptions
about just allocations of economic rewards, burdens, and power ("*ergo*
the colony ought to exist for him") that the roots and an understanding of current local conceptions of ethnicity, place, and the rights of
ethnic groups must be sought. It is not so much a matter of "the one-
eyed man in the kingdom of the blind" as it was, in the first historical
disjuncture, the single-minded planters' making a world consistent
with what they considered to be the functional prerequisites of a
particular form of agricultural production, with a supporting cast of
administrators who had particular ideas about the necessity of trans-
ferring European civilization to non-European laborers and "benighted" indigenous charges. And in the second historical disjunc-

ture, it was more a matter of well-sighted subordinates' having ideologically reinterpreted and incorporated the planters' myopic perceptions of the texture of the emperor's new clothes.

In other words, the beginnings of the ethnic/racial diversity in British Guiana also marked the beginning of the unequal allocation of economic rewards and its administrative and cultural rationalization. In their quest for items of trade value, the Dutch quickly recognized differences in Aboriginal skills and in how they exploited their environment. When the Dutch turned to agricultural pursuits, they initially attempted to enslave the Aboriginal population to make the land (which they had appropriated from them) productive. Despite the claim that the Aboriginal population was not particularly suited for agricultural production, as defined by the Dutch, other factors were of greater importance in the cessation of Dutch attempts to enslave them. The Aboriginals, unwilling to submit passively to enslavement and having a better knowledge of the territory, could easily escape Dutch control. But, equally important, the Dutch had an alternate source of labor (African slaves) and a more urgent need for Aboriginal friendship and military cooperation.

First, they needed the military aid of the Natives to defend themselves against external attacks from the Spaniards, the French, and the British. Second, as settlers, they required peaceful relations with the Aboriginal population if they were to survive and to develop their agricultural interests. And third, as they expanded agricultural production using imported slave labor, they could call upon the Natives to help put down slave rebellions, to fight as guerrillas against escaped slaves, and to act as guides on missions to recapture escaped slaves. Menezes (1973:65), calling up one of the more positive stereotypes of the Dutch settlers, concludes that "summing up the situation, the shrewd businesslike Dutch mapped out a definite policy" toward Amerindians designed to enhance internal and external security. They formed treaties of alliance and friendship with the chiefs and developed a system of annual presents to be granted for services rendered by the Native population. To administer this policy, they created a series of posts in the interior: administrators, known as postholders, were to foster good relations with their local Native population, "attach" them to the post, and, when necessary, lead them on expeditions against escaped or rebelling slaves.

"Attaching" Natives to the post included encouraging them to request Dutch assistance in settling their intertribal disputes and their conflicts with the Spaniards, plying them with rum, and giving them plots of land near the Dutch settlements. This policy and other unofficial exploitative practices engaged in by postholders ultimately resulted in a Native population "physically and morally degraded by being made to depend on presents and organized killing" (Henfrey 1965:263). The Dutch policy became the basis of European perceptions of the Native population as a military reserve and an interior police force whose loyalty and invaluable aid could be bought with an annual distribution of trinkets, symbols of office, payments for killings, and promises of exclusion from slavery.[6]

When the British took control, their needs were much the same as those of the Dutch. External security remained a problem, and internal security was even more urgent. These requirements and the British view of themselves, however, were in conflict. Although they immediately saw the wisdom of the Dutch solution and continued the policy in practice, philosophically they objected to being "held in fee by a small native population." As Menezes notes, whereas the Dutch had been in a position of minor strength, the British, full of their own military glories, found it "unthinkable that such a nation should kow-tow to the natives of a small colony in South America" (1973:73). Anxious to rid themselves of the stigma and the financial burden of paying tribute, they sought to gain the needed assistance of the Natives without suggesting that they had a right to be rewarded. Their first rationalization was to call what they gave a boon, not a right—a reward for past good conduct, not a purchase of future loyalty. Their second rationalization was an argument that the Natives would always be more than willing to offer military assistance against Africans, a people toward whom it was believed they had a natural animosity.

Although this approach may have been somewhat successful as regards the granting of titles and symbols of office to Natives designated chiefs and captains, it was unsuccessful with respect to the annual distribution of presents and of direct payments for military service associated with slave control. The Natives' pride in their freedom and their willingness to go to any length to avoid their own enslavement may, as British colonial administrators argued, have left them with a negative image of the alien enslaved African. Nonetheless, there is little evidence that this view alone guaranteed their

military assistance against escaped African slaves. For example, re-
negade African settlements sometimes existed for as long as fifteen
years before they were destroyed by a combined European and
Native force. The Native population's knowledge of the forest and
their skill in "discovering" these settlements when adequately rewarded by Europeans casts some doubt on natural animosity as a sole
or primary motivating force. Further, Natives more than once threatened to refuse further assistance against slave rebels when promised
payments were withheld or too slowly delivered. In fact, an attempt
in 1831 to discontinue annual presents was met with strong resent-
ment and, more important,

> some of the most intelligent among them were heard to declare that, in case
> the negroes revolted, they would assist them instead of fighting against
> them. Moreover, the Indians affirmed that "the whites["] have done them no
> service; the country is theirs—they have their own laws and wish not the
> whites to govern them. (letter from Rev. John Hynes to Governor Car-
> michael Smyth, July 10, 1834, quoted in Menezes 1973:82)

Nonetheless, in the British perspective, where no previous treaties
existed and when internal and external security allowed, such boons
were to be withheld in the name of fiscal responsibility and to
discourage the further creation of an indolent, dependent Native
population. In fact, however, such alterations in policy remained
merely philosophical throughout the slave era. Fear of insurrections
and actual slave rebellions continually resulted in the British promis-
ing and reluctantly paying the Native population for services rendered. As late as 1823 Natives helped put down a slave rebellion in
Demerara. Yet, between these periods of fear and slave rebellions, the
British continually attempted to define the Natives as an idle, indolent population who contributed nothing to the colony. They ignored their own appropriation of land and its interference with
Native patterns of subsistence—the payments and trinkets given
were hardly useful nor adequate compensation for the Natives' loss of
life and the crops they abandoned to render military service (Menezes 1973).

It was not until after emancipation (1834) that the British developed an adequate substitute for the Natives' role as an interior police
force. During the apprenticeship period (1832–34) they needed their
help to control the rebellious apprentices anxious for complete free-

dom. With emancipation, planters and administrators considered both Native assistance and the postholder system inadequate to stem what they believed would be the mass withdrawal of Africans from the coast to creek and river areas. They sought to solve this potential problem by creating superintendents of rivers and creeks. Persons appointed to these positions had two key functions. First, they were to replace the Native population as an interior police to check the flow of Africans away from the coast. Second, they were to control the relation between the coastal society and the Native population. As Menezes also notes, this solution was deemed best both because it was fiscally responsible and because "to the Court it was indeed a more prudent policy to pay salaries to one's own officials than to hold oneself in fee to native tribes" (Menezes 1973:83). Further, Menezes reports that "in late 1839, a Police Force was established in place of the scrapped militia" (1973:83).

Some administrators, such as Hillhouse, ostensibly interested in the welfare of the Native population, objected to the establishment of the superintendent position. Others objected to the vagueness of the bill that created the position because of the leeway it left for the abuse of power by appointees. But administrators were less concerned with Native rights and their protection than with an effective means of controlling Africans' "lapse into barbarism," that is, withdrawal from estate wage labor or any other attempt on their part to establish more autonomous forms of subsistence.

From this point forward, efforts to define the Native population as idle, indolent, noncontributing peoples in need of paternal guidance and undeserving of financial reward for their indolence were more successful. In less than three decades financial awards to Natives were fully redefined as donations considered a "waste of Public Money" (Menezes 1973:84). It turned out that the superintendents were not needed to stem a mass exodus of Africans from the coast, but the creation of the position did help to control and to redefine the Native population (Menezes 1977). The governor sent out instructions to the Pomeroon superintendent of rivers and creeks, W. C. F. McClintock (an avid, if paternalistic, supporter of his "benighted children"), to prevent their coming to town to receive donations. With external security less volatile and the Africans free and remaining on the coast, Native assistance was no longer essential. Though for many indigenous peoples the river and creek areas had been home for more than two centuries, they were passively and actively encouraged to *return* to the wilderness. "Thus the Indians were put in their places, and *back* to those places they went in the wilderness" (emphasis added; Menezes 1973:84).

However, it is a myth that their only primary contribution to and involvement in colonial society had been that of a security force or that, when no longer useful, they willingly withdrew to the wilderness and returned to a preferred, so-called carefree, indolent existence. In the initial era of European settlements, the Native population formed a more integrated part of the social and economic organization of the colony:

The Amerindians acted not only as allies and soldiers of the Dutch but also as their servants. They were employed as boatmen, pilots, guides, and field labourers. Large numbers of Amerindians were also employed by the Dutch in well-established fisheries along the whole coast from the Essequibo to the Orinoco, including the mouths of the Waini, Barima, and Amacuro rivers. They were in the habit of encamping in the mouths of these rivers and catching turtles and large quantities of morocot. (Daly 1975:19)

Further, "formerly the Dutchmen took wives from the Indians, with the result that many of the half-breeds owned plantations and were important personages on the rivers. Some had been sent to Europe for their education and were gentlemen of the old school and yet [are now] degenerates in almost every respect" (Rodway 1912:182).

As late as 1912, Rodway reports that in these areas the descendants of Bovianders continued to have traceable rights to land which, though no longer worked as plantations and long depleted of valuable timber, supplied them with some cash income from the sale of low-grade firewood. In addition, Amerindians continued to seek wage employment. They worked for licensed and unlicensed woodcutters, balata bleeders, and later for diamond seekers and gold diggers, all of whom, unfortunately, exploited them either by failing to pay promised wages or by paying them in rum. Moreover, in 1842, a few Natives (some apparently because of the encouragement of W. C. F. McClintock) were also employed as canecutters on sugar estates in the Mahaica-Mahaicony area (Menezes 1977).

Despite these forms of early and continued involvement, European planters and administrators ideologically defined the Aboriginal groups as "children of the forest," denying or ignoring their previous involvement in and contributions to the colonial economy, and they awarded them economic benefits accordingly. When they no longer needed them as an interior security force, they redefined their contributions and their rights and withdrew their rewards. But their ideological and actual relegation to a position physically and socially outside the colonial economic order exceeded passive neglect. Notwithstanding Daly's charges to the contrary, it was also more than a paternalistic relegation to museum pieces left to the "benevolence" of missionaries interested in Christianizing noble savages (Daly 1975).

In 1844, recognizing the baneful effects of past patterns, a few notable individuals among the Europeans argued that the Native population should be brought into the "pale of civilization" and, in the language which had come to link contribution and place, that they should be "made to contribute to the economy of the country." They proposed the allocation of funds to establish an experimental Native agricultural settlement. Instead of trinkets and rum, the Natives would be supplied with land, agricultural tools, and training. Just as in the earlier period, however, the emphasis on large-scale plantations and their need for a large, cheap, tractable labor force (better filled by transported African slaves) resulted in Natives' being excluded from the plantation. It was also at this point that members of the Combined Court, who opposed and disallowed the experiment, saw a more desirable use for the funds in the importation of indentured labor. This time, indentured laborers, rather than a Native interior police force or Native agriculturalists, were better suited to the influential planters' aim of controlling Africans' economic opportunities, one aspect of their broader goal of maintaining a cheap, tractable plantation labor force.

The result was that no effort was made to integrate or to gain any economic contribution from the Native population. Their segregation was rationalized as the protection of a "fallen race" who preferred a carefree existence in its natural environment—the wilderness. After emancipation, then, the Native population was not so much dropped from a rank in the social hierarchy next to Europeans to one beneath Africans and East Indians (Daly 1975:185) as it was excluded from coastal society and its economic structure. Both the language Rodway uses and the logic that leads to his conclusion are ideologically consistent with a framework of contribution and place when he states:

The native Indian can hardly *be reckoned as a member of the community*, he is, however, useful to the traveller, the gold-digger, and balata-bleeder. As a boatman, wood-cutter, or huntsman, *he is in his place*, but his sturdy independence prevents him from becoming a reliable servant. Make him your friend and he will do anything in his power for you, but he takes orders from no one. (emphasis added; 1912:194)

Thus, the interior became the Natives' physical place and the symbolic source of their rights and privileges within the total sociocultural order. It was a paradoxical position he was in. Ideologically, standing apart from the plantation labor regime and living beyond the coastal pale of civilization, the Native could not be reckoned a member of the community, yet he had found an occupation that placed him in the total economic structure. Hence, a curious blending of stereotypes proclaiming his independence of character, on the one hand, and his easily purchased loyalty, if not servility, on the other, left him defined as a helpless child and as a museum piece somewhere outside of real society.

Consequently, efforts, often more restrictive than beneficial, were made to protect him from exploitation and to allow for his return to his so-called carefree existence as a "child of the forest." He had been reserved for subsequent conservation. This policy was only moderately modified by Ordinance 22 of 1910, which established ten reservations. Though rationalized as protection for the Native population, these reservations and the regulations pertaining to them not only restricted the Natives' ability to continue "traditional" patterns of subsistence but also provided no policy of transition or integration (Henfrey 1965). When, thirty years later, reports of exploitation and ill-treatment prompted an investigation, the report and the suggestions made by P. S. Peberdy, the welfare officer appointed to conduct the survey, were largely ignored or treated in a manner that had the same result. That is, where policy suggestions that would have been economically beneficial to the Native and that might have served ultimately to integrate the Native population into the colonial economy conflicted with the interests of private ranchers and the Booker Brothers' legal monopoly of the balata business, they were ignored.

Subsequent reports and ordinances in 1948, 1951, and 1961 emphasized social transition and economic integration but actually left matters largely unchanged (Henfrey 1965). This policy and its ideological framework and rationalizations were inherited by independent Guyana along with the past patterns of exploitation and racial division (Ridgewell 1972). The new state also acquired a problem inherent in the ideological rationalizations that conserved a people by reserving a physical space for them that, by its creation, reckoned them not to have a "place" in the developing social order.

The interior and the reservations it later contained, as the physical place and the symbolic source of Amerindians' rights, take on added significance when related to another peculiar feature of the country's economic history and ecology. The emphasis on large-scale plantations for cane cultivation, coupled with the rapidly diminishing fertility of interior soils, resulted in a movement of agricultural settlements to the coast. On the coast planters were not mere "lords of the soil," as Crookall had dubbed them: technologically, they were its creators. The poldering of the coast ideologically created two Guianas—a natural Guiana of the interior, originally appropriated from its Aboriginal inhabitants, and a man-made Guiana reclaimed from the sea.

The whole of the territory now brought into cultivation upon the coast is *made*-land. It has been placed—I had almost said created—by the hand of man, and is only preserved to his use, by constant toil. Numerous ditches and canals are cut to drain the water from the common surface, and the land that is planted, is only the mud and clay thrown out of these channels. (Pinckard 1806:389, vol. 3)

Never shy in the appropriation of interior land, with respect to the coast the European envisioned himself as owing the Native population neither apology nor privilege.[7] Moreover, this coastal belt, on which 90 percent of the Guyanese population still resides, was the center of the social and economic order. Europeans judged the worth of different groups from the standpoint of what their activities contributed to the development of plantation agriculture. They attempted to allocate rights, privileges, and assistance on the basis of these judgments. Just as the Amerindians were relegated to the interior and then defined as noncontributors to whom (apart from humanitarian sentiments) nothing was owed, Africans who sought to move away from the estates to establish other forms of subsistence were viewed, from the same standpoint, as idle or indolent by the European elite. Work and industry, at least for subordinated non-Europeans, were defined as direct involvement in the plantation labor force. Refusal to accept European definitions and allocations of appropriate roles was defined as a preference for indolence and a lapse into "barbarism." Thus, activities on the part of Africans or Amerindians that were disapproved of or not directly related to the development of plantation agriculture were deemed a burden on the colony and its financial resources.

Despite the centrality of plantation labor and the resulting policy of nondevelopment of other sectors of the economy (Adamson 1972, Rodney 1981, Potter 1982), other economic and administrative activities were necessary to the overall functioning of the society. Where it was impossible to avoid such developments, planters, aided by public officials, in both philosophy and practice sought to allocate these roles in a way that enabled them to control the majority of the population, which they desired to keep dependent on plantation wage labor.

For example, during the slave era, free Mulattoes served as a buffer between the large slave population and the small ruling European population. In addition to participating in the military control of slave rebellions, Mulattoes filled needed functions and were granted opportunities, roles, and rights that increased their identification with and loyalty to the European population. After emancipation, putting Mulattoes into these roles was more problematic; unlike the Native population, they were physically and socially a part of coastal society. Their agitation for increased economic, political, and social integration for themselves and, at times, for the emancipated population decreased their usefulness as a buffer and a source of labor control. Moreover, aid granted them to develop other economic sectors could not be fully separated ideologically from emancipated Africans' view of available opportunities.

Although the emphasis on the racial component in the European ideological rationalizations distinguished Mulattoes from pure Africans and pure Europeans, based as it was on the presumption of shared biogenetic substance, it tied Mulattoes to Europeans but was incapable of entirely severing ideological and practical linkages between them and the non-Mulatto emancipated Africans who were their other counterparts. Consequently, members of the European elite feared that, although the Mulattoes' identity placed them in a category apart from the newly emancipated non-Mulatto slaves, how they were treated and the successes that stemmed from such treatment might serve as a model for members of the emancipated non-Mulatto population who were trying to decrease their own dependence on plantation wage labor.

It is also in this light that the Europeans' treatment of the Portuguese immigrants must be understood. The planters became interested in the Portuguese, as in other immigrants, for their potential as plantation laborers. And, despite an initially high death rate, Portuguese did adapt to the plantation regimen and were productive plantation laborers for short periods (Daly 1975). In fact, their susceptibility to disease and their high death rate was, in part, considered to be the result of their willingness to overexert themselves and to emphasize saving over the purchase of food, medical supplies, and adequate clothing.[8] Yet from the beginning, these immigrants, like the emancipated slaves they were intended to replace or to supplement in the plantation labor force, exhibited a lack of interest in long-term plantation labor. They also showed little inclination toward establishing themselves as small-scale farmers. At best, plantation labor and other agricultural pursuits were viewed as short-term sources of capital necessary to establish themselves in the retail trade. Why then did planters, in spite of these clearly demonstrated tendencies (which planters recognized and about which they frequently complained) and the subsequent direct refusal of Portuguese immigrants to be bound to any labor contract, continue to support the payment of bounty for the introduction of Portuguese?

Moore (1975) argues that racial affinity and solidarity were the overriding determinants of the European elite's treatment of the Portuguese and account for the high status the Portuguese had in colonial society. He maintains that the European elite acknowledged a racial affinity with the Portuguese and, in the interest of European solidarity, acted to assure Portuguese prosperity. Whereas Moore's argument appears reasonable on the surface, Wagner (1975, 1977) notes that the high social status of the Portuguese was evident only during the last third of the nineteenth century. Initially, they were chided for their greed and filthy habits and, as Catholics, despised for their religious preference. Even at the height of their prosperity, they were distinguished from the rest of the heterogeneous European population as the "other Europeans" (Smith 1962). Resistance, subtle and direct, to their full social integration also continued. Hence, as Wagner (1977) argues, the extent to which the Portuguese were recognized as a high-status group came after their commercial success. Therefore, though racial affinity and a hope for European solidarity in conflict situations played a role in the continuation of Portuguese importation and in elite conceptions of Portuguese abilities, cultural propensities, and the rights to be accorded to them, these factors cannot fully account for Portuguese success or for the Anglo-European elite's responses to them.

Instead, the European elite's efforts to help the Portuguese, and the subsequent Portuguese commercial success, must be understood in relation to (1) the elite's shifting but continual need for a buffer population, (2) its ideological rationalizations of the allocation of that role, and (3) Portuguese efforts on their own behalf, which were not entirely congruent with what the Anglo-European elite (composed of planters, merchants, and administrators) may have considered to be consistent with its own diverse, structurally defined interests. Their need for a buffer population and the same process that structured the European elite's relations with the Native and Mulatto populations served to structure their interaction with the Portuguese immigrants.

At the time the Portuguese were introduced, they were an ideal buffer population. First, any interest in and talent they had for commercial ventures directly complemented the European elite's need for a means to close off these opportunities to other segments of the population. Second, as Europeans, their success could be more easily rationalized and dismissed as an inappropriate model for African aspirations. Third, as Europeans, they also augmented the European population and made reasonable the hope that in conflicts they would naturally align with the European elite. Their race was, therefore, an important aspect of their suitability as a buffer population, yet, as Wagner (1977) notes, the need for a buffer population would have resulted in some segment of the population fulfilling this role, however less than ideal it may have been.

It was this concern that resulted in the continuance of bounty payments for Portuguese immigrants, some of whom were not bound to contracts. Once the Portuguese arrived in British Guiana, the grand English merchants provided them with inexpensive credit, and laws were written or altered allowing the Portuguese to gain a competitive advantage over the Africans and the Mulattoes (Daly 1975, Wagner 1977). At the same time, credit previously granted to Africans and to Mulattoes was withdrawn. The allocation of these roles to the Portuguese was openly discussed as an essential source of labor control (Laurence 1965). The worth of the Portuguese as a group was defined primarily in terms of this indirect contribution to the maintenance of the plantation system.

By 1853 the essential elements of the Portuguese monopoly of the retail trade were in place. More important, also in place was the rationalization that they had achieved their commercial success on the basis of their cultural values for thrift and industry, their previous commercial experience, and their superior innate abilities. That Africans and Mulattoes had failed to compete was likewise attributed to culture and values: they were said to lack appropriate values, previous experience, and innate ability. In both language and logic, Adamson's (1972) conclusions about Africans' failure to compete with the Portuguese reflect what had become an accepted link between cultural values and economic success. Although he notes the difficult conditions under which Africans attempted to develop a marketing system, he concludes that under any conditions their success was unlikely because they lacked the necessary background and experience in commerce. As he proceeds to account for the Portuguese success, however, the ideological roots of his analysis surface.

[The Portuguese] had the advantage of a cultural background in which buying and selling and saving were familiar categories. When their indentures were served they avoided the trap of the small peasant holding, and most of those who had any savings moved into trade. Raymond Smith suggests that at least part of their mercantile success stemmed from their "marginal position in society and the absence of any relationship with their customers other than a straight market relationship." (Adamson 1972:68)

Although neither the sacrifices made by the Portuguese nor their previous experience and cultural background should be discounted as factors in their success, Wagner is correct to point out that these factors could contribute to Portuguese success because their success was consistent with the elite-defined needs of the plantation system at that time. One has to account for how they "avoided the trap of the small peasant," for the relation between their cultural background and experience, and for the other material and ideological factors that made their experience and background relevant in colonial Guiana.

Likewise, Portuguese marginality must be explained as an integral feature of the process of role and geographical space allocation within the plantation economy. To view their marginality as a determining factor in their success is, as Wagner characterizes Moore's racial affinity argument, to put the cart before the horse. What must be kept in mind is that the actual complex of conditions resulting in the commercial success of the Portuguese was obscured by ideological emphases on differences in cultural background and stereotypes of behavior. Such emphasis deflected attention from the interplay between these factors and the constraints and conditions directly rendered into law and into notes of credit, and those indirectly engendered by rationalizations the European elite ultimately used to explain Portuguese success.

This is not to say, however, that the Portuguese success remained within limits and forms wholly acceptable to the European elite stratum and the diversity of interests it included. Instead, the Portuguese sought to consolidate their position and to gain increased social and political rights on the basis of their role and success. By their expansion into urban areas and into wholesale trade, by their exploitative business practices, and by their behavior in conflict situations, they, like the indigenous and Mulatto populations who had earlier served as buffer populations, showed that their primary loyalty was to themselves and to their own business interests.

Although the Portuguese consistently withheld credit from striking workers (an act beneficial to themselves and to the European elite), there is little evidence that they made any other direct effort to assist the European elite. During the Africans' anti-Portuguese riots, the European elite often complained bitterly that Portuguese merchants did little to protect their own property. Knowing that, in the aftermath, they could claim compensation for property damage, these merchants sensibly sought safety. The colonial government paid the compensation from funds collected through a regressive sales tax on items consumed primarily by Africans and by East Indians (Wagner 1977), a registration tax, and fines collected, sometimes through forced labor, from Africans found guilty of riot-related acts (Daly 1975:189). After the most widespread and destructive of these riots (1856), rumors circulated that some Portuguese merchants had even encouraged the destruction of their shops to claim exorbitant compensation. If the rumors were true, the behavior would have been consistent with a recognition of their position as scapegoats for hostilities that might otherwise have been directed at the European elite.

Within the system, to effectively serve as a buffer population, a Portuguese monopoly was most critically needed in the rural areas and in the retail trade. When the Portuguese developed interests in urban and wholesale ventures, Europeans again feared that Africans and East Indians, desired as plantation laborers, would take advantage of openings left by Portuguese urban migration. Although a small number of Africans and Mulattoes were able to take advantage of these openings, the timely arrival of Chinese immigrants again allowed the European elite to maintain control over these opportunities.

In large measure because of their numerical insignificance, little systematic attention has been given to the rise of the Chinese elite in Guiana. They initially received treatment similar to that given other indentured immigrants. As estate workers, they were considered industrious but dishonest and difficult to control (Clementi 1915, Daly 1975). Some of these immigrants, having been falsely led to believe that they would be allowed to ply artisan trades, rebelled against the plantation labor regimen. A few who felt that they had been misled in this manner took to gambling, thievery, and petty trade, which resulted in a temporary stereotyping of all Chinese as troublemakers and thieves. The bulk of the Chinese immigrants who survived, however, completed their indentures and turned to farming and shopkeeping. Their willingness to remain in the rural areas and to combine farming, wage labor, and shopkeeping ultimately resulted in their being considered the perfect settlers (Clementi 1915, Rodway 1912).

In 1865 the British Guiana government granted land and financial assistance to O Tye Kim, a British subject of Chinese origin sent to Guiana by the Church Missionary Society for the establishment of Hopetown, an agricultural settlement for time-expired Christian Chinese. This settlement soon became a refuge for time-expired Chinese immigrants. The postindenture success of Chinese immigrants appears to have been largely due to the time of their arrival and their ability to take advantage of the opportunity structure resulting from the previous interactions between the European elite and the Portuguese. Again, the complex of factors that may have contributed to their success was generally reduced to differences in culture, in past experiences, and in innate ability. In this vein, the Chinese, like the Portuguese and unlike the African creoles and the East Indians, were considered cunning and highly intelligent with a cultural background conducive to making the best of any available opportunity.

Hegemonic Process in Stereotyping

Because this process (role allocations and their subsequent ideological rationalization in terms that increased pragmatic consent, thereby decreasing the need for direct coercion) was primarily aimed at controlling the African creole labor force, this group was initially most constrained by it. The failures of African creoles at other ventures were rationalized in negative stereotypes centering on a lack of appropriate values—ignoring the fact that they had, for the most part, learned these values from the most successful segment of the population, the European elite. As they continued to struggle for greater autonomy and demanded greater compensation for their labor, however, planters increased their emphasis on East Indian immigrant labor. Although African creoles were still considered best suited for the most arduous tasks and for the skilled, best-paid factory positions, planters relied on East Indians as the core of the estate labor force. Under contract, these laborers were cheaper, easier to control, and hence more reliable.

The African creoles' exodus from the estate and the level of their involvement in estate wage labor was, thus, as much the result of exclusion as of their own preferences (Adamson 1972, Despres 1969, Rodney 1981). Nonetheless, when not involved in estate wage labor, they were considered idle and lazy by the European elite. The decline of African village settlements and the Africans' lack of upward economic mobility were attributed to presumed cultural habits and values. Apart from being considered dim-witted and too easily mislead, they were said to be too concerned with social pretensions, luxury items, and aping the upper circles. During the same period that Farley (1955) accused elite planters of establishing an inappropriate model for Africans to follow, it was the African villagers who were stereotyped as prone to a preference for "shadow over substance." It was they, not their socializers and role models, who were seen as Cockalorums in search of Cockaigne (that is, self-important little people intent on enjoying a land of luxury and ease without putting forth the honest exertion required to produce the bounty).

As their contracts expired, East Indians, too, aspired to other enterprises and sought greater autonomy from estate wage labor. Planters were again faced with the need for a buffer population, this time to control East Indian access to other opportunities. Strategies such as the bounty for reindenturing, the access to small plots of land for provisions and, later, for rice crops, the right to keep livestock, and, eventually, the establishment of land-grant villages were all utilized to keep East Indians in the rural areas and dependent on plantation wage labor as their primary source of subsistence (Potter 1982). Encouraging the maintenance of cultural differences, physical segregation, and the employment of African creoles in security positions served to divide further the rural laboring population. In conflict situations, depending on the circumstances, one or the other group was encouraged to align with the European elite. This encouragement was not always direct or consciously conspiratorial but often stemmed from a group's perceptions of its own interests under structural and ideological constraints resulting from the differential allocation of economic roles and burdens (Rodney 1981).

Ideological rationalizations have little force if they do not become lodged in sites significant to the everyday struggles of those who might ultimately come to see their world through them. Hence, formal policies and informal practices of both the dominating Anglo-European elite and the subordinated diverse elements of the non-elite population combined to form a framework of objective and ideological constraints within which the racial/ethnic groups developed different adaptive strategies for subsistence and social mobility.

With reference to Africans in the latter part of the nineteenth century, differences between the marketable skills of Africans and of East Indians gave Africans a competitive advantage in urban environments and in new industries developing at that time. The African, longer a part of the social system, was more Europeanized, had a better command of Guianese English, and longer had been educated in the Christian-run schools. For these reasons, and in conjunction with the planters' interest in controlling East Indian access to these opportunities, "large numbers of Africans were recruited to fill positions in the public service bureaucracy, in business houses, in the communications media, and in industry" (Despres 1969:40). Others turned to the developing gold, diamond, and bauxite industries in the interior. They exploited these advantages to accomplish, as did the Portuguese with retail trade, a short-term virtual monopoly of these opportunities (Smith 1962). East Indians, temporarily lacking these skills, exploited to their benefit advantages stemming from the planters' efforts to keep them locked into the rural environment.

In the process, those aspects of both groups' social practices conducive to consolidating and improving their economic well-being were also strengthened and "traditionalized" as they became symbolic of their identity and place in the socioeconomic order. These practices, especially those that could be linked to cultural divergences based on place of origin, became "core elements" of ethnic cultures. Once these differential adaptive strategies had developed, the European elite rationalized them as the natural outcome of cultural differences and of differences in ethnic/racial groups' innate intellectual and physical capabilities. The proof was in the pudding. Puddings might differ in taste and in quality, but their character was always traceable to the competence of the cooks, rather than to the types, the quality, and the quantity of ingredients available to the different cooks.

East Indians' greater success in the rural areas (relative to that of African villagers) was attributed to their greater intellectual ability, their cultural values that encouraged thrift and industry, and their cultural institutions, presumed to have positively organized their patterns of interpersonal interaction. It was generally accepted among the European elite that East Indians naturally preferred a rural existence. They were as much a "people of the land," with a natural love of agricultural pursuits, as the Amerindian was a "child of the forest," with a preference for a hand-to-mouth, carefree existence. In contrast, the elite argued, the African, "corruptly" socialized to European values and wants, not only lacked values for saving, sacrificing, and planning for the future but also naturally sought the excitement of the urban environment and the adventure of the interior. Even those, like the Reverend Cropper and Judge Hewick, who noted the constraints that influenced African and East Indian patterns of adaptation and relative success in the rural area, tended to consider differences in cultural background and associated value orientations to be determining, rather than contributing, factors in the way different groups confronted these constraints (Cropper 1912, Hewick 1911). Neither, of course, considered the dialectical interplay between "East Indian-ness," "Africanness," and the Anglo-European policies and ideological rationalizations within which these, as well as "Europeanness" and status stratification within and across all these categories, were being constructed.

Hence, though geographical space and economic roles were never fully ethnically segregated, from an ideological standpoint they came to be viewed as the natural provinces of different ethnic groups. The contributions of these groups to the social and economic order and their social worth both were largely defined in terms of their histor-ical relation to the maintenance of the plantation system and their subsequent economic contributions within a structure of ethnically related geographic and economic provinces. Just as Amerindians had been excluded from integration into coastal society and Africans and Mulattoes had been effectively barred from trade, when East Indians began to develop other skills and sought opportunities outside the estates and rural occupations, colonial officials, planters, and mission-aries warned of the potential for ethnic clashes because Africans were expected to guard jealously their provinces.[9] These conceptions of group provinces and competitive jealousy were further buttressed by an administrative policy that recognized group interests over the public good and, if only passively, encouraged communalism and ethnic boundary maintenance (Tinker 1982). Ethnic identification became both the conjunctive (that is, common oppression) and disjunctive (that is, differential experiences, strategies, and symbolic encoding of their significance) historical linkages between personal and group identities, and the sense of social worth and status attached to these identities.

As post facto rationalizations, stereotypes (including stereotypes of the European elite) served to obscure the actual conditions that resulted in different patterns of adaptation, in relative degrees of success in particular endeavors, and in a group's overall economic progress. Across time, subtle shifts and/or reinterpretations of ethnic stereotypes coincided with changes in the group's activities and in the European elite's perceptions of the value of these activities for the maintenance of the plantation system.

Viewed from the top down, ethnically identified groups operated in an ideological field in which elite Europeans saw themselves as culturally and intellectually superior to all other groups. On the basis of their political and economic dominance, they claimed to have made Guiana; they reserved for themselves the right to allocate economic roles and social privileges and to manipulate patterns of interaction among subordinated ethnic groups. Robinson (1970:54) argues that the European elite's economic and political dominance was the proof of cultural and racial superiority. Beginning with slavery, she notes that the logical sequence of rationalizations began with "economic domination, this led to cultural domination which was interpreted as meaning cultural, and then racial superiority; which is then turned into a justification for the original domination." Moreover, this view of racial/cultural superiority included a conviction that Englishmen represented "justice and impartiality and protect[ed] the less fortunate from the consequences of their own shortcomings" (Smith 1962:101).

Following the same logic, the elite, after it had manipulated the allocation of economic roles, justified the successes (or failures) of different ethnic groups by their alleged relative racial (physical and intellectual) and cultural (value orientations and institutional forms) inferiority. Hence, in postemancipation Guiana the initial black/white, African/European racial and cultural poles were altered to create a hierarchical framework within which subordinated ethnic groups were not simply inferior to the European elite; relative to one another, the elite viewed them as culturally and intellectually suited to certain economic roles and as more or less deserving of economic and social advancement (Smith 1970).

Anglo-Europeans were the purveyors of civilization. Ideologically, if not in their actual behavior, they set the standards for civilized conduct against which all were to be judged. They established a hegemonic order—an ideological and practical framework in which Anglo-European control of the economic and political apparatus of the society meant that subordinates could neither fully institutionalize practices (that is, those associated with egalitarianism in village communities) resulting from their alternate interpretations nor legitimate those they managed, in part, to institutionalize. The established hegemony was a transformist one because it included neither ideological precepts nor practical mechanisms through which criteria for civilized conduct emanating from other sources could be accommodated. It was an Anglo-European transformist hegemony, because where other European patterns of conduct (that is, those of the

Dutch and the Portuguese) differed from the Anglo-European standard, they, too, were excluded from the realm of legitimated civility.

Instead, cognitively, the hegemonic conditions under which both dominant and subordinate strata operated were reproduced through ideological rationalizations whereby persons' prototypical understandings of their experiences became stereotypical ones. Rationalizations of this sort account for Drummond's conclusions that stereotypes are broken loose from ties to specific types of situations and material processes. That is to say, in accordance with these rationalizations it appears that identity can be explained apart from its formation in the social organization of power and economy. However, this break was possible only because at the same time it developed, the stereotypes paradoxically also became tightly tied to the production of groups, of group identities, and of patterns of conduct among members of these groups. In addition, to maintain this break across generations, it was necessary to link the prototype-to-stereotype transformation to some factor presumed to be independent of everyday experience. Otherwise, in a generation it would again appear that persons allocated different roles and operating under different conditions were developing patterns and behaving in accordance with the material conditions and ideological constraints they experienced.

Race and culture, as "biologically" reproduced determinants of the economic role allocations and performance in them, supplied the "grains of truth" about individuals' predecessors and the manner in which "place" was transmitted to their successors. "Blood types" had been created out of socioeconomic diversity. Thus, the conditions under which interactions between dominants and subordinates, and between different types of subordinates, took place were hidden in plain sight, in that each individual embodied the break between experience and its ideological rationalization in the developing Anglo-European hegemony.

It is worthwhile to contrast the position taken here with Schermerhorn's classification of racist ideologies and their implications for the order of ethnic relations.

Racism is an ideology that sees an invariable connection between cultural behavior and physical type. Hence it defines specific outgroups as having characteristic traits (usually detestable or in some way inferior) that are inherent outgrowths of their biological constitutions. While not all ethnic relations have a racist component, a great many do. . . .

It is quite likely that the most common form of racism is a doctrine of group supremacy or superiority couched in physical terms—as Ruth Benedict puts it, "the dogma that one ethnic group is condemned by Nature to hereditary inferiority and another group is destined to hereditary superiority" (Benedict, 1943, 98). This is the sort of racist belief that accompanies and rationalizes a dominant power position of substantial magnitude, where the contrast between upper and lower statuses is clear and unmistakable. Metaphorically speaking, this is vertical racism with the upper incumbents looking down at the lower and characterizing them as inferior, relatively or absolutely. Where the distinction is relative, vertical racism is minimal, i.e., appearing without rigid segregation; where the distinction is absolute or extreme, it is possible to speak of maximal racism and its manifestation is the compulsory separation of segregation or apartheid. (1978:102–103)

He goes on to apply this view to multiethnic situations with the following qualifications:

where several ethnic groups of distinctly different physical appearance coexist in the same territory without any one of them monopolizing a power position, a kind of mutual or reciprocal ethnocentrism results, with each group stereotyping the other in its own way. While it is the cultural practices of the "others" that have salience, these are eventually attributed to their unique inheritance, i.e., are racially imputed. Since there are several groups making an attribution, no one of them can unilaterally impose its views on the rest, as happens in vertical racism; now the notion of racial superiority, plurally asserted, becomes relativistic and loses its capacity to polarize the society into clearly defined uppers and lowers. . . . this is horizontal racism, differing substantially from the vertical form described above. (Schermerhorn 1978:103)

Schermerhorn's general theoretical insights on the nature of the racial component of the ideological precepts that rationalize domination capture many of the features of the particular processes manifested in colonial Guiana. In addition, his qualifications concerning processual variations and their implications for domination in multiethnic situations point the way into the next chapter, where we examine subordinate interpretations of the meanings of racial and cultural differences and of the stereotypes that encoded these meanings, first in colonial Guiana and later in postindependence Guyana, following the exodus of the Anglo-European component of the population.

Where our ethnographic reality will diverge from Schermerhorn's general theoretical insights is at the point where we must insist that what he distinguishes as different types of situations or time sequences were in colonial Guiana simply different perspectives—dominant versus subordinate—on the same situation and time sequence. That is to say, the range and the type of attributions encoded in the stereotypes of horizontal racism were, viewed from a subordinate perspective, initially fashioned and expanded under the constraints of vertical racism entailed in Anglo-European hegemony. Moreover, the ideological precepts underlying vertical and horizontal racism are not significantly different. What is different, as Schermerhorn notes, is the power to enforce these attributions. It is not simply a matter of how control of economic and political power is ideological linked to conceptions of racial and cultural superiority. Consequently, it is on differences in group power and on the ideological justifications that explain these differences that we must concentrate as we turn to examine the implications of stereotyping for relations among the diverse subordinated non-European population during and after the development of Anglo-European hegemonic dominance. These are the relations that set the terms of the politics of cultural struggle in contemporary Guyana.

6

Anglo-European Hegemony and the Culture of Domination

The process of . . . civilization can now be recognized in its general lines.
The inequality of races has been established.
—Ernest Renan, *L'avenir de la Science* (quoted in Poliakov 1982:62)

In Chapter 2 we noted Cockalorums' belief that ethnic identity ought to predict men's and women's general potentials for social mobility and their abilities to engage successfully in particular occupations. We met a man of mixed racial descent who, after a few drinks in a rum shop, commented on the worthlessness of his Portuguese surname. We also heard his companions attribute this worthlessness to his mixed blood. They maintained that he did not benefit from his Portuguese surname because the African component of his mixed blood was stronger—somehow more determinative of his conduct and his potential—than the Portuguese component. We heard these same contentions echoed in the metaphorical explanation another young woman of mixed descent gave for the setbacks she had experienced as she tried to establish herself as a shopkeeper. She argued that her efforts were undermined by a "war" among the various races in her veins (blood).

We also noted that these particular comments were subsumed by informants' general contention that "race will out." That is to say, they maintained that, in the long run, racial differences, because they denote differences in innate intellectual abilities, in cultural propensities, and in the quality of cultural heritage stemming from them, determine in a complex manner how and to what degree persons as carriers of these heritages may expect to succeed in life. These factors, informants suggest, most influence individuals' potentials for success at the diverse ventures out of which they must make a living to make life.

Against the background of our discussion of the ideological rationalizations and stereotyping process entailed in the formation of an Anglo-European hegemony, we are now prepared further to explore and to explicate the significance of such particular comments and the general convictions of which they are part. We may now ask, how did the non-European, non-Anglo, subordinated population respond to the development and the solidification of Anglo-European hegemony? How did they respond to stereotypes and the stereotyping process that encoded the particularities of their inequality and inferiority, and through which Anglo-European racial and cultural superiority were heralded as justification for this elite stratum's objective domination of the political and economic structure of the society? Under the constraints posed by Anglo-European hegemonic dominance, how did the components of a diversified subordinated stratum respond to one another? What questions, social spaces, and aspects of interaction were left unaddressed by the ideologically naturalized social world of Anglo-European hegemony? How did a diverse, subordinated population actively participate in drawing the general lines of the "civilizing process" to create a culture of domination? Did these lines remain within the ideological boundaries of racial and cultural inferiority, or did they extend beyond these boundaries? In other words, was the social world indeed naturalized? In short, we are now in a position to ask, How did the subordinates carry the "Whiteman's" burden, and how was the burden altered by the postindependence departure of the Anglo-European stratum, the physical representatives of symbolic predominance?

Subordinate Appropriation of Stereotyping: "Givers" and "Takers"

Hegemonic interpretations of the meanings of racial and cultural differences established a sociocultural, economic, and political hierarchy in which Anglo-Europeans occupied the top rank. Existing cultural and nationality differences within the total European elite stratum were either homogenized or ignored as the amalgamated territories became British Guiana. Unfortunately, historians of economy and of culture have also ignored heterogeneity in this stratum, leaving us without an understanding of the particularities of ideological and practical processes through which this homogenization was accomplished.

Based on the scanty evidence available, it would appear that, among Europeans, both the emphasis on "things English" and on the superiority of Englishmen (the self-appointed protectors of inter-ethnic justice and common morality) not only subordinated Europeans of different nationalities (Portuguese, French, and Dutch) but also may well have allowed for the exportation from Western Europe of previously established colonial domination. The emphasis on English tradition over Irish and Scottish contributions to the British content of Guianese culture and development ignored the fact that, in addition to the presence of "wealthy and respectable proprietors from Ireland, by far the largest proportion of the wealth and influence of the Colony [was] vested in Scotchmen [sic] . . . Scotch economy, and Scotch industry, were never more successfully exerted than in Demerara" (Halliday 1837:117–18). Halliday leaves us to wonder about the ideological and cultural implications of his statement, "being in manner and feelings already half-Dutch, they [the Scots] easily amalgamated with the original settlers, and appear very quietly to have stept into their place" (Halliday 1837:118).

We do know, however, that in accordance with these hegemonic interpretations, the Portuguese and all components of the non-European colonial population were deemed racially and culturally inferior to the Anglo-European elite stratum. Their rank order relative to the diverse constituents of this homogenized European elite stratum and to one another was not a worked-out feature of the hegemonic interpretations emanating from the Anglo-European elite stratum. Instead, within this stratum, stereotyped conceptions of the capabilities and the cultural propensities of the diverse subordinated population shifted in conjunction with temporal changes in their economic roles, resulting in complex, contradictory assessments of their worth and their status in the society. It was out of these complex stereotypes that subordinates attempted to generate criteria to formalize and to legitimate a particular rank order of subordinates beneath the Anglo-European stratum, on the one hand, and to reconceptualize the meaning of racial and cultural differences, on the other.

As regards the first task, the formalization and the legitimation of a subordinate rank order, depending on the criteria employed (physical attributes, economic progress, alleged differences in intelligence or in culture) these groups could vie for second place in the social hierarchy. In competing for this position and for the economic benefits associated with it, subordinated ethnic groups, Bartels (1977) concludes, took over racial stereotypes used by the "ruling class." In his view, these positive features were used in self-ascription, whereas the negative features of stereotypes of other groups were used to identify those groups. Thus, "East Indians often came to see themselves as thrifty, industrious, and physically attractive in contrast to Afro-Guyanese, whom they saw as irresponsible, physically unattractive, and lacking in initiative. Afro-Guyanese, on the other hand, often saw themselves as physically strong, Christian, generous, and trusting in contrast to East Indian 'coolies' whom they regarded as greedy, clannish heathens" (Bartels 1977:401).

He argues that these stereotypes took root among subordinated groups after the failure of the 1847–48 strike. Following the strike, subordinated ethnic groups used racial stereotypes of self and other to "'explain' their social and economic successes and failures and to justify their role in struggles against other subordinated ethnic groups for economic resources and political power" (Bartels 1977:401). Although one can reasonably question whether the 1847–48 strike did more than intensify a process that was already operative, Bartels's conclusion seems to represent an accurate summary of certain aspects of relations among subordinate groupings. Conclusions about subordinate acceptance (if only in practice) of the superiority of Europeans and of "things English" also seem to summarize accurately another feature of the ideological framework and its organization of relations between dominant and subordinate strata.[1]

It would be an overgeneralization to assume that subordinated groups merely internalized and utilized elite Anglo-European racial and cultural stereotypes (cf. Bartels 1977:29). From an elite standpoint, we have seen how the shared cultural meanings of "contribution" and "place" and their relation to the concepts of "race" and "culture" have been produced in this prototype-to-stereotype transformation. What remains to be seen is how the diverse subordinated non-Europeans who embodied these stereotypes interpreted and reshaped them in relation to the egalitarian and hierarchical precepts of an ideological field. How did their production and experience of horizontal racism encapsulated by vertical racism influence their production and use of stereotypes?

There is ample evidence to suggest that in Guiana subordinated ethnic segments accepted European cultural domination in practice and, consistent with Bartels's conclusion, utilized racial stereotypes derived from this elite stratum to compete for and to justify their rights to certain economic and political benefits. At the same time, in more general terms, whether intended by the European elite, subordinates also viewed the sociocultural order as a hierarchy of ethnically differentiated groups. This image was reinforced by formal and informal administrative policies that encouraged group competition and a notion that political representation along ethnic lines was essential to protect the interests of the different groups (Tinker 1982).

In relation to the European elite's emphasis on the relative contribution of the subordinate groups to the plantation economy and on the ideological links which that stratum established between cultural difference and economic success, a variety of criteria were employed by the subordinated groups in their own efforts to establish a hierarchical ranking of their groups beneath the dominant European stratum. Criteria advantageous to one group's rank claims were not necessarily similarly advantageous to other groups. Hence, though there was apparent consensus on certain features of the ideological framework (that is, hierarchy and linkages between contribution, success, and the justification for cultural domination that create the vectors of the ideological field), there was little agreement on acceptable interpretations of these shared criteria. Nor was there consensus on the acceptability of other criteria generated within a particular group for determining its rank in an ethnic hierarchy. This perspective stressed historical disjunctures.

Yet, hierarchical interpretations of criteria competed with egalitarian interpretations. For example, in the struggle for independence, some members of the subordinated ethnic groups argued for solidarity and for sharing power previously unfairly usurped by the European elite. They viewed Guiana, its culture and its development, as a conglomeration of the contributions made by all Guianese ethnic groups. They pointed to different ethnic contributions to language, dress, ritual, and cuisine as proof that all Guianese (including the creole European elite) had contributed to the making of Guiana, maintaining, therefore, that the only true goals were those of developing a more just distribution of Guiana's wealth and a more balanced participation of all Guianese in a determination of the nation's future. This perspective stressed historical conjunctures. Even so, it remained within the ideological limits created under Anglo-European hegemony. Arguments were fashioned in terms of linkages between differences in ethnic cultures, variations in ethnic group contributions, and their meaning for sociocultural and political integration.[2]

Nonetheless, nationally, the hierarchical view, with its links to disjunctive experiences and evaluations, continued to influence interpretations of relations among subordinate groups. Guyanese historian Daly's treatment of ethnic differentiation in his *Short History of the Guyanese People* (1975) is typical of this stance. In this work, Daly examines the "sufferings" of each subordinated ethnic group. Often explicit in his discussion is a comparative evaluation of whether different experiences and patterns of treatment by the European elite constituted equal suffering (Daly 1975:185–89). V. A. February (1981:169), summarizing a position he attributes to Guyanese novelist Wilson Harris, notes "the total effect of ritual bounty can be gauged from the manner in which the conqueror has managed to pulverize the conquered into 'a uniform conviction that the reality or play of contrasts is eclipsed within an order of self-deception.'"[3]

Based in subordinate groups' differing assessments of the importance of different types of contributions, a notion of groups as essentially "givers" or "takers" was added to the ideological framework. From this standpoint, certain groups gave little to the overall development of Guiana while allegedly benefiting unfairly by assuming the majority of the high status positions and by receiving the largest portion of the colony's wealth. Central to the identification of groups as givers or takers were comparisons of their participation in the estate labor force and their experiences of the physical suffering and discrimination associated with it. Overall, out of this ideological interpretation subordinates produced an inverted and more complete hierarchy of ethnic groups.

According to this inversion, during the colonial era at the bottom of the hierarchy as takers were the foreign personnel (that is, Anglo-Europeans joined by Anglo-Americans and Canadians) who were deemed to give back little to the colony, although they benefited financially from the exploitation of its resources. Second was the local (creole) European elite, which, as Smith notes, was increasingly viewed as "a privileged group occupying all the most favoured positions and exploiting the resources and labour of the country without putting anything back" (1962:101). Next were the Portuguese, who were (from an African and an East Indian perspective) seen as having contributed little to plantation development and as having experienced less physical suffering and social discrimination than the other subordinated groups. They were thus takers, benefiting unjustly from their trade monopoly.

The idea of givers and takers placed limits on the range of criteria relevant to the rank ordering of subordinated groups. Interpretations of the criteria, however, remained inconsistent and competitive across ethnic boundaries, as each group vied for the top rank, defining their group as the quintessential giver. Hence, the upper ranks of this hierarchy remained unsettled, regardless of the particular ethnic viewpoint.

In African and in East Indian opinions, the Chinese shared to some extent a position with the Portuguese. They assimilated very rapidly, maintaining only the most tenuous ties to China and to Chinese culture (Fried 1956). Yet, although they assumed occupations among the elite within a fairly short time, they were dispersed throughout middle-range higher status positions without monopolizing any one opportunity. They intermarried with all ethnic groups and enjoyed good relations with all groups (Smith 1962). Their success, though patterned on that of the Portuguese, was less directly traceable to the European elite's favoritism. Although their physical characteristics, compared with Africans, placed them closer to Europeans, and although their time on the estates was shorter than that of either Africans or East Indians, the latter groups attributed Chinese success to their diligence and adaptability. Hence, although Chinese numerical insignificance and lack of real political power may partly account for the lack of hostility directed at them by other subordinated ethnic groups, it might also be suggested that the Chinese were model (that is, hegemonically appropriate) Guianese—fundamentally "English" and superficially ethnic. Also, in the eyes of other subordinated groups, their path to success may well have been seen as the most just.

In essence, Cockalorum informants' descriptions of the Chinese social mobility strategies suggest a balance between giving and taking—a balance consistent with the precepts of egalitarian morality discussed in Chapter 4. Africans and East Indians, contrasting the Chinese with the Portuguese, argue that the Chinese worked and suffered on the estates, contributed to plantation development and to cultural content, and through their diligence gained economic benefits from the system without European favoritism or economic monopoly. Perhaps more important, these informants maintain that, once successful, Chinese immigrants did not attribute their success to racial and cultural superiority, nor did they claim any right to dominate others.

When we turn to Cockalorums' views of the Amerindians, we discover that, with respect to the criteria that ordered this hierarchy of givers and takers, Amerindians remained more excluded than ranked. Although they were not takers in the same sense as the European elite or the Portuguese, because of African and of East Indian emphases on criteria most directly related to the development of the coastal strip, the significance of the Amerindians' contribution was minimized (see Daly 1975:18–21). They were credited with having unwillingly given "natural" Guiana and with having contributed elements of their traditional cultures to the content of Guianese culture. In conjunction with stereotypes of them as children of the forest, however, members of other subordinate groups alleged that Amerindians had neither participated in the "making" of the coastal land nor been involved in plantation labor. Moreover, as the least Anglicized segment of the subordinated population, they were thought to be the least politically fit and culturally deserving of any position of dominance. Hence, though they "belonged" to Guiana because the territory on which Guiana was created once belonged to them, benefits they derived from the society were considered by the other subordinated groups to be largely unearned. Any position offered them in society was a boon, a humanitarian gesture.

Thus, whereas Africans and East Indians disagreed on which of their groups should assume justly the top rank of the hierarchy, they agreed that their groups were givers par excellence. In their view, they were the most deserving of economic benefits and of positions of dominance in the society. As the backbone of the labor force, competing interests notwithstanding, Africans and East Indians often saw themselves as mati. Locked into a competitive framework, however, each group also interpreted all criteria to its own rank advantage.

Africans placed themselves above East Indians. They considered themselves the group most justly deserving to inherit Guiana and the reins of power when the European elite relinquished control. Although they recognized certain common interests with other immigrant groups, from a competitive standpoint they concluded that these immigrants were taking over opportunities belonging to Africans. Their sense of justice, as Laurence (1965) notes with reference to their involvement in anti-Portuguese rioting, was offended by any action on the part of the European elite that they interpreted as favoritism toward other immigrant groups.

Above all, Africans maintained that they had made the most fundamental contribution to the development of Guiana. It was their labor as slaves that moved "100 million tons of water-logged clay" (Rodney 1981) to reclaim the coastal strip and to establish the plantation economy. Initially, they were also the most Anglicized and, therefore, by the rules of the hegemonic game, they deemed themselves the most fit of all non-Anglo Europeans to assume positions of dominance and political control. Despite similarities which they acknowledged between slavery and indentureship, they remained convinced that they had suffered most. They had been exposed to the economic system's degradation longer and had borne the financial burden of labor importation and its negative effects on their bargaining power, wages, and opportunities for advancement. Of no less importance to them was their belief that they had been most instrumental in the initial survival and creolization of the immigrant groups—especially the East Indians.

Accepting some of the Africans' contentions, East Indians nonetheless placed themselves at the top of the hierarchy. From their perspective, it was the emancipated Africans' refusal to work regularly, their "pretensions," and their "unreasonable" wage demands that brought the colony to near ruin. It was the labor of East Indian immigrants that not only brought it back from the brink of ruin but also made possible the expansion of the plantation system and economy. If Africans had labored to reclaim the land from the sea, that was, in the East Indian view, no more important than the fact that East Indian labor had generated the capital necessary to refurbish and to expand the irrigation and drainage system that kept it afloat. As the country's "saviors," they maintained that they most justly deserved its economic benefits and positions of dominance.

  In efforts to situate the different ethnic groups and their contributions, even the chronology of immigration is subject to competing historical reckonings. During an interview with a Muslim East Indian man, aimed at dating jumbie stories about Dutchman Massa (that is to say, the spirits of long-deceased Dutch masters), linguist John Rickford recorded the following chronology of immigration with its implications for interaction between Africans and East Indians. Throughout the discussion, Indian refers to East Indian, not Amerindian, and the emphases are those of the particular speakers.[4]

JRR:	[Black linguist] So wuh year i'dis? Dis a when Englishman a come in?
Mr. A:	[Muslim East Indian] Yes.
JRR:	Yuh na a know de nail—de year.
Mr. A:	Na—well . . . me na know de year, and de mont'?
JRR:	But—
Dispenser:	[Black] Yuh can show us de place?
JRR:	Is before . . . ?
Mr. A:	[To Disp.] *Eh?*
Disp.:	Yuh can show us de place?
Mr. A:	Yes! Definitely. Man, me can show you de spot.
JRR:	/Before-Hear, nuh man/ [Overlaps previous line]
Disp.:	De pla—de place is important.
JRR:	Allright. Is before Indian people start fuh come hey? Or after dat?
Mr. A:	No, well—Indian people bin deh before.
JRR:	Bin deh before dis. Eh heh. Good.
Disp.:	Black people still bin slave an'suh?
Mr. A:	No—da time Black people na bin.
JRR:	[To Disp.] All dat done. All dat done.
Mr. A:	No! *Black* people na bin da time. Black people na come in dis country da time. Indian bin come. Chinee bin come. Potogee bin come. A'Right? But Black na bin come. Black a de *las'* people (w)a come.
Visitor:	[Educ. Indian] (Softly) Na-ma(n), Indian is de las' people (wa come).
JRR:	De Black come after Indian?
Mr. A:	Mm-hm.
JRR:	So wait—Black people come, an' dey make them slave?

Mr. A: Well—well—de White people an' de Indian make Black people come as slave.

JRR: [Softly to Dispenser] Ayuh ge' cus, boy! [Laughs] hear duh one sah—Wuh yeh seh dis moring a true . . .

Mr. A: [Continuing] Yuh see, Indian bina rule Black people. At dat time. Make dem [Blacks] come 'denture. Right?

Disp.:   . . . when Indians come indenture, dey were ruling Black people?

JRR: Chubby—(calling visitor, who sucks teeth, says "Don' worry wi dis man, man . . .")

Mr. A: Hear—me—yuh want me till yuh de trut' o' de story?

Disp.:   No—no—

Mr. A: (Over interruptions from Disp.) Watch—dis man bin say—dis man—dis man—

Disp.:   . . . hear dis man good!

Mr. A: Dis man [JRR? Chubby? Disp.?] Him say me insult am, right? But me na wan insult nobody. But Black people when dem come in dis country, de na know dey own strength.

JRR: Mm-hm. [Sounds as though he's addressing me, talking about Dispenser]

Mr. A: Right? When dem bring dem.

JRR: Mm-hm.

Mr. A: An dey start to haul punt. An Indian bina drive dem, fuh haul punt. Now today Black people de pon top awee, aw'awee got fuh rule under Black. No, talk de truth! Awee a Guyanese, man. But dem de(a) 'denture people. Yuh un(d)erstan' wa me tell yuh?

Thus, if the hierarchy were to be stabilized justly in terms of the East Indian perspective, it would appear as shown in Figure 6.1. Looking backward to the colonial era, East Indians place themselves above the Africans, their major contemporary rivals. Looking to the future, they use their alleged superior rank in the colonial era (specified in terms of criteria advantageous to their group) to suggest the naturalness and the justice of their ascending to the top rank. Viewed from an African perspective, the only change in rank order would be a shift in their placement to a position above East Indians.

Even so, Cockalorums from both groups present the image illustrated by section three of Figure 6.1[5] as a future nightmare, and they see in the image illustrated by section two, the wishful thinking of those who have not transcended "colonial mentality." In both egalitarian and hierarchical terms, they conclude that ethnic groups, like

Figure 6.1. A Hierarchy of "Givers" and "Takers"

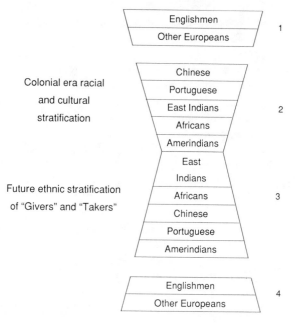

the individuals of which they are composed, must for the moment recognize that "wan hand cain wash or clap." For, unlike the Anglo-Europeans, who had combined control over the political, economic, and cultural life of the colony, today Guyanese of all racial and cultural backgrounds are locked in an ideological contest, the resolution of which, for better or worse, is vitiated by the clear reality of economic interdependence and by the absence of legitimated criteria to transform this interdependency into ranked relations of dominance and subordination. Valetta and Constantine's agony (see Chapter 1) are Guyanese agonies played out in relation to different criteria of conjuncture and disjuncture.

Any reconceptualization of the meaning of racial and cultural differences influences how ethnically identified persons can justify their claims to positions of status and prestige unconstrained by their ethnic identity. The identity between English cultural patterns and standards for civilized conduct in the presentation of middle- and upper-class status claims, hence, placed economically progressive East Indians at a status disadvantage during the colonial era. Their wealth, initially based on rural agricultural ventures, demanded less acculturation to English cultural standards. In the wider social context, their economic successes in agriculture did not, therefore, gain for them the status and the prestige enjoyed by others less wealthy but more acculturated. Speaking specifically of East Indian Hindus, Smith notes:

> Their reaction was to form self-assertive "Indian" organizations like the Arya Samaj in which they defensively insisted upon the glories of Indian culture, but at the same time condemned the "barbarism" and "superstition" of traditional Brahmanical Hinduism. Furthermore these religious organizations . . . became the focus of the practice of all those patterns of behaviour in which the Indian felt himself to be at a disadvantage vis-à-vis the Negro and Coloured groups. (1962:110)

The glorification of Indian culture offered East Indians another avenue to and standard for evaluating status and prestige, thereby lending a new dimension to their efforts to produce a hierarchy of ethnic groups. The East Indian no longer sought simply to raise himself through Anglicization; he also aimed to raise the value and worth of Indian culture as a "mode of expression of his desire to be treated on terms of equality within a Guianese universe" (Smith 1962:111).

The resurgence of an emphasis on a positive evaluation of "things Indian," and on Indian contributions to the Guianese sociocultural order, preceded but also combined with a more general political emphasis on the fitness of all Guianese for independence and self-determination. It also all coincided with and further encouraged efforts on the part of other ethnic groups, especially Africans, to do likewise and to deemphasize the superiority of "things English" by placing them on par with other ethnic cultures and with their contributions to the development of Guiana and its culture. International events such as India's independence, the Chinese Revolution, the Black Power movement in the United States, and Ghana's independence have all been significant in this regard for different segments of the Guyanese population. These events reinforced claims for a positive evaluation of the non-English content of Guyanese culture and behavior patterns. In their struggle for independence, it was out of a variety of internationally defined historical disjunctures that they constructed their independence discourse at the same time that they sought to produce a conjunctive egalitarian Guianese identity.

Thus, whether one views the ideological framework from the vantage point of the Anglo-European elites' or the subordinated ethnic groups' interpretations, two facts seem clear. First, from either vantage point, interpretations made possible by the ideological framework served to obscure the actual conditions that resulted in ethnically differentiated patterns of adaptation, progress, and interaction. Second, the ideological linkages between criteria, such as race, culture, and contribution, served to rationalize differences in economic roles and power, which then influenced subsequent patterns of adaptation and interaction that were themselves partially the result of such rationalized differences. Neither the linkages and rationalizations nor the patterns resulting from them were aimed at providing the ground on which to establish separate ethnic states. Instead, the criteria, the interpretations, and the rationalizations they made possible, all aimed to *place* groups within a single sociocultural and political order and to legitimate their right to participate in all aspects of society and economy. These criteria proposed particular and competing intersections of territorial nationalism and cultural identities. Yet, equality within a single universe was always a significant feature of the ideological field in which hierarchy dominated in the construction of the extra-village, colonial order.

Egalitarian and Hierarchical Images
of the Sociocultural and Political Order

Cockalorums treat ethnic cultures as the repositories of the collective *contributions* made to Guyana's total sociocultural diversity and economic development by the ancestors of contemporary Guyanese or by groups, such as Englishmen and other Europeans, who were once segments of the colonial population. They consider these respositories of ethnic group contributions to be *owned* by groups of contemporary Guyanese who can claim genealogical or other types of links to a particular category of ancestors. They interchangeably label these categories of ancestors and their contemporary descendants as ethnic groups, races, nations, peoples, or castes.

Their interests in which ethnic group contributed what, and in which ethnic group owns which features of Guyanese culture, are the surface manifestations of their deeper interest in the nature of sociocultural and political integration. They are concerned with differences in links drawn between ethnic identity, individual achievement, and access to the middle- and upper-class ranks implied in different images of sociocultural and political integration. Their intense interest in determining the ethnic source of particular contributions, in the implications of differences in the historical experiences of ethnic groups, and in the relative *quality* and *distinctiveness* of ethnic cultures is part of their struggle to formulate and to legitimate criteria that can serve as the bases for a just system of political participation and a just allocation of economic rights and obligations. In the struggle to resolve these issues, they simultaneously generate solutions out of two competing contradictory sets of ideological precepts—egalitarianism and hierarchy—that have different implications for how they can envision the sociocultural and political order.

First, rooted in their past and present experience as the most economically interdependent and politically powerless social stratum, egalitarianism provides Cockalorums of all ethnic and racial backgrounds with a code allowing them to interpret ethnic group differences in nonhierarchical terms. From this ideological perspective, they argue that the presence in Guyana of ethnically identifiable cultural and economic contributions is simply proof that Guyanese of every race and every ethnic background have made and continue to make significant contributions to the nation. On the basis of this proof, all Guyanese are to be represented and involved in the political order, and in the formulation of policies to guide the future economic and social development of the nation. Out of a combination of disjunctive and conjunctive intersections between territorial nationalism and cultural identities, a "homogeneity" of rights and obligations is to be formulated, whereby access to all economic opportunities is based solely on individual merit. Personal inclinations rather than ethnic group identity are to determine Guyanese involvement in different types of ethnically marked practices. Furthermore, in Guyana the very idea of ethnic purity is to be considered ridiculous on the grounds that everyone is Doogla, a contention believed to be easily proven by a few moments of "tracin'" (genealogical reckoning). Thus, according to this egalitarian view, group differences, ethnically marked cultural elements, and persons are simply the historical residue out of which one can reconstruct the story of how these elements were introduced to Guiana, and how the peoples associated with them became Guyanese. They are neither grounds for a rank ordering of ethnically identifiable groups nor a legitimate source of criteria for determining privileged access to different economic opportunities or positions of political authority.

Second, egalitarianism also provides Cockalorums with a code against which to assess the moral and social worth of particular individuals. From this perspective, they conclude that the only just way to judge a person's worth is to evaluate his or her material attainments against an assessment of his or her face (personal reputation) and name (family reputation). However, as noted in Chapter 4, labeling this perspective egalitarian does not mean that Cockalorums demand economic equality for all individuals. Egalitarianism, as a set of ideological precepts, is a code for conduct stipulating how one should accomplish social mobility, and how one should interact with those who are less accomplished than oneself as one moves up the socioeconomic ladder in a class-stratified society.

Egalitarianism is not, therefore, a set of precepts aimed at specifying the conditions or mode of conduct for absolute equality. Instead, as noted in Chapter 4, it is (in proverbial language) a code requiring individuals to recognize that "wan hand cain wash or clap." That is to say, everyone should understand that all accomplishments and their enjoyment are made possible by assistance attained from others; therefore, everyone should be willing to assist others. As they struggle to become somebody, they should struggle equally hard to demonstrate, through their everyday actions, (1) their respect for the human dignity of others without reference to class position, (2) their willingness to engage in generalized reciprocity, (3) their desire to avoid actions that damage their own reputations and those of others, and (4) their willingness to submit to and participate in processes of mediation that treat formal litigation as a last resort. The characteristics of social action are necessary because all humans, as humans, deserve one another's respect. In short, ignoring for the moment ethnic identity, we may note that egalitarianism, when applied to evaluations of individual differences and of interpersonal conduct, provides criteria for a moral stratification of the social order that Cockalorums attempt, with limited success, to align with the economic criteria on which class stratification is otherwise based (see Chapter 3).

Returning to the issue of ethnic identity, these perspectives on egalitarianism allow Cockalorums, on the one hand, to envision a national sociocultural and political order in which the ethnic identities of cultural elements and of peoples are simply historical residua—components of a story about how these elements and these peoples became Guyanese and of the case to be made for all Guyanese to have an equal right to participate in the cultural, political, and economic life of the nation. On the other hand, those perspectives permit them to envision a communal order encapsulated by a class-stratified hierarchy. According to two-dimensional interpretations derived from egalitarianism, relations between images of the national order and images of the communal order are mediated by a stress on moral stratification assessed in terms of a resident's adherence to cooperative restrictions on competitive actions.

In the present as in the past, however, hierarchy and class stratification are also analyzed in terms of the unequal significance of ethnic group contributions, the unequal quality of ethnically marked cultural elements, and the presumed unequal innate intellectual and physical capabilities of racially identified peoples. From a hierarchical perspective, Cockalorums generate an alternate contradictory conception of the nature of national sociocultural and political integration that also influences their images of community relations.

From the standpoint of hierarchical ideological precepts, Cockalorums maintain that, although all ethnic and racial groups have contributed to Guyana's cultural and economic development, some groups have contributed more. Moreover, some of these contributions have been of greater importance for national development than others. Therefore, at times, Cockalorums argue that ethnic cultures (repositories of ancestral contributions) should not now be treated as equal because the contributions of which they are composed were not historically of equal economic significance and moral worth for national development. In addition, Cockalorums consider differences in the significance and in the moral worth of contributions to be the result of differences in the innate intellectual and physical capabilities of the racial groups that contributed the ethnic cultures. In these terms, an intellectually superior racial group produces a superior culture that provides the best source of social, cultural, and political practices and that ought, therefore, to serve as the national standard—the homogeneous norm of civilized conduct—against which the conduct and the status of all Guyanese are judged.

Interpretations based on these hierarchical presumptions treat putative differences in the quality of ethnic cultures and the innate intellectual capabilities of the peoples associated with them as criteria for a rank ordering of ethnic groups and as grounds for unequal access to economic opportunities and to positions of political authority. At the same time, they serve as the basis for evaluating interpersonal status claims. Some individuals are considered *unfit* by ethnic identity to engage in certain tasks or to assume political authority over those of other identities. Images of a national order are generated hierarchically. Accordingly, access to a distribution of economic roles and political power is to be made available along ethnic lines, with the most lucrative and powerful positions going to members of the presumably highest ranking ethnic group. Any consideration of individual skills and qualifications for these social functions is to be restricted to an effort to select the most qualified member of the aforementioned group. Interethnically, particular skills are deemed less important than general *moral fitness*, which is defined in terms of presumed genetic and cultural inheritance.

On the point of contribution in the hierarchically defined national order, members of the ethnic group that has contributed most to national development should benefit most from what the nation now has to offer its citizens. Moreover, because members of this ethnic group have the most at stake, they should be more highly represented in the political order and more actively involved in the formulation of policies to guide the future social, cultural, and economic development of the nation. Members of lower ranking, intellectually and culturally inferior groups should willingly accept whatever range of economic opportunities and political positions the ruling members of the highest ethnic group deem suitable for them. They should also restrict their involvement in cultural practices to those of their own ethnic culture or, when adopting cultural practices of other ethnic groups, should admit that they prefer others' practices because they are superior to their own.

This last stipulation is the most pertinent to an understanding of the way hierarchical precepts influence evaluations of interpersonal status claims. In addition to being repositories of ancestral contributions, ethnic cultures are also viewed as sets of values and norms. Inferior cultures have bad values and ineffective, immoral norms. Superior cultures have good values and effective moral norms. This conception of ethnic cultures is encoded in stereotypes and is projected onto their members as the surface manifestation of these individuals' character. Hence, members of inferior cultures are innately lazy, incompetent, and promiscuous. They create cultural norms that encourage and reproduce malfactors (that is to say, members of bad-bodied groups, the innate character of which is displayed through their inefficient work habits, poorly organized family forms, irrational and uncivilized patterns of social interaction, "spendthriftness," and their tendency to substitute the appearance of achievement for actual efforts to succeed). Rationalizations based in these stereotypes become both a long litany against this reproduction and a psalm for the subordination of such malfactors. Members of superior cultures are innately hard-working, competent, and chaste. They create cultural norms that encourage efficient work habits, well-organized family forms, rational and calm patterns of social interaction, thriftiness, a sincere effort to achieve, and so forth. Moreover, through the same type of rationalization, the values and the norms of the superior ethnic culture make possible the genuine achievement of middle- or upper-class status.

Stereotypes of these cultures as inferior or superior influence Cockalorums' evaluations of one another's class status claims. Two persons, one identified with a superior ethnic culture and the other with an inferior one, who appear to be equally prosperous will encounter different difficulties in validating a claim to middle- or upper-class status. The apparently prosperous members of a superior culture are likely to have their claims readily accepted, whereas those identified with the inferior one are thought to be "buying prosperity"—that is, pretentiously living beyond their means. It is in this regard that African informants contend that an apparently impoverished Portuguese or East Indian has money tucked away somewhere for the future while he and his family suffer unnecessarily in the present. They apply the same logic when they, along with members of other ethnic groups, maintain that an apparently poor African is genuinely poor, whereas an apparently prosperous one is presently living beyond his means, and that he and his family will eventually suffer from his imprudence.

Where a person's apparent poverty or prosperity contradicts his ethnic identity and the presumed potential of his ethnic culture to produce middle- and upper-class persons, the search begins for evidence that the individual in question is living according to the

dictates of another culture. In Chapter 2, we note how these stereotypes influence Cockalorums' ideas about work, freedom, and autonomy—the acquisition of material goods. We now turn to how Cockalorums interpret ethnic differentiation in their explanations of how
class stratification is produced.

7

The "Ethnic Production" of Class Stratification

Now, Children, you don't think white people are any better than you
because they have straight hair and white faces?
No, sir.
No, they are no better, but they are different, they possess great power,
they formed this great government, they control this vast country. . . . Now
what makes them different from you?
MONEY! (Unanimous shout)
Yes, but what enables them to obtain it?
Got it off us, stole it off we all.
—Lawrence W. Levine, *Black Culture and Black Consciousness* (p. 124)

Ideological links between ethnic identity and the quality of ethnic
cultures do not mean that only members of the superior culture
achieve the economic prerequisites for middle- or upper-class positions or that all members of the superior culture achieve these class
positions. They do mean that a person's achievements are judged in
terms of presumed innate tendencies that may be either suppressed
or nurtured through the respective adoption of another culture or
through adherence to one's own culture.

The person born to a superior culture who does not achieve a
high-class position is deemed to have failed either because he is
sacrificing so that, in the future, his children will be able to make the
best of their intellectual and cultural potential or because he has
adopted the inferior culture of another ethnic group. From this
hierarchical perspective, an individual born to an inferior culture who
does achieve a middle- or upper-class position poses even less of a
problem for interpretative consistency. His success, if it is taken to be

real rather than apparent, simply means he has suppressed his innate characteristics by adopting the superior cultural practices of another group. Consistent with interpretations established under Anglo-European hegemony, it takes intellectually superior racial groups to create these practices, but a few of the more intelligent members of inferior racial/ethnic groups may successfully adopt and benefit from these creations. Such persons are, however, always at risk of sliding back down the socioeconomic and moral ladder should they fail to hold in check their innate tendencies or should they return to their own cultural practices.

In Cockalorum, apart from any direct competitive economic benefits derived from ethnic mobilization, ethnicity is part of diverse symbolic conceptions of the nature of the sociocultural order and ethnic groups' "place" within it. Ethnicity is the vehicle that persons of different racial stock and cultural background use to conceptualize their contribution to the development of a sociocultural order that is more than the sum of its ethnic parts. On the one hand, meanings attributed to ethnic differentiation allow groups to justify gaining from the society by pointing out what they have given to the society. On the other hand, these meanings encourage a sense of "ownership" through which the cultural content of Guyanese society and different aspects of its economic structure are claimed by particular groups. Cultural products such as religions, cuisine, rituals, and economic roles are conceived of as "belonging" to one ethnic segment or another—either by reference to a historical link to a national origin outside Guyana or to a predominance of one group's involvement in a role or in the use of an item in Guyana.

Ownership never fully coincides with actual patterns of behavior. Cockalorums all adhere to patterns that are still considered "English"; also, in their quest for economic mobility and status recognition, they frequently breach the ideological divide between "things Indian" and "things African." This disjunction between ideological conceptions of the way things are and actual patterns of behavior creates a dilemma—a dilemma that stems from ideological links drawn between contribution and group affiliation, and between ethnic group competition and cultural domination. Consequently, when persons belonging to one ethnic group openly adopt patterns of behavior and engage in economic roles that supposedly belong to another group, Cockalorums express concern about what it means for the evaluation of ethnic cultures, group contributions, and ethnic group rank. Do such actions, they ask, indicate the superiority of the other group's ethnic culture and, by implication, validate that group's right to dominate the other ethnic groups?

Ethnic identity continues to provide the criteria that shape their expectations about individual potential to achieve middle- and upper-class positions. Africans continue to believe that East Indians are always worth more materially than appearance would suggest. Africans, East Indians, and others also continue to believe that Africans are always worth less than appearance would suggest. Persons of Portuguese or Chinese descent, whatever their outward appearance of material worth, are likely to be viewed as upwardly mobile, whereas Amerindians are considered to be among the most impoverished members of the society.

"Getting a Shock": Ethnicity and Status Disjunctions

Disjunctions between expectations that synchronize the potential for individual status achievements and ethnic identity result in what Cockalorums refer to as "getting a shock." This shock is experienced when persons confront a situation in which another person's achievements and apparent status greatly outstrip or fail to live up to expectations based on his ethnic identity. For example, East Indian informants reported getting a shock when confronted with Africans whose material worth they judged not only equal to but greater than appearance would suggest. The shock was most jarring where they could find no proof that the African had adopted some other ethnic culture. Africans were equally shocked when confronted with either very indigent Portuguese who seemed to lack any real potential for upward mobility or with "pretentious" East Indian spendthrifts. However, most recorded examples of shock involved disjunctions between an Amerindian's achievements and status and an African's or an East Indian's expectations that all Amerindians are at the bottom of the socioeconomic hierarchy. Porkknockers (that is, prospectors) in particular reported instances in which, during a sojourn to the interior, they met Amerindians whose material worth, dress, business acumen, or facility with standard Guyanese English they judged not only beyond what was expected but also as having surpassed the achievements of many coastal dwellers.

An African porkknocker described shock as a feeling of dismay, fear, and anger. Once, while working in the interior, he and his partner spotted another man from a distance. The man was too far away for them to ascertain his ethnic identity. Although he could not say exactly why, the porkknocker and his partner assumed the man was Portuguese, Chinese, or at least African or East Indian. They called out to the man to ask the time. The man did not respond but continued to approach them. Several more calls failed to receive a response. When the man finally reached them, he asked, "I say, old chap, did you call to me?" The man was Amerindian. The pork-knocker reported that he and his partner stood dumbfounded, unable to repeat their request. The Amerindian man stood looking at them for a few moments, then bade them good-day and went on his way.

The man who recounted the incident claimed that it took him and his partner a few moments to regain their composure and to decide that they had in fact seen and heard what they thought they had seen and heard. At that point, they both became angry and yelled pro-fanities at the man, who simply continued on his way. This pork-knocker went on to say that he was not sure what made him angry. On reflection, he felt it was probably the man's lack of humility and fear, and his refusal even to respond to their angry profanity. At that time (about 1969), he and his partner expressed to each other their fear that Amerindians would soon get out of "place," and, if the other ethnic groups were not careful, they would find themselves outdis-tanced by such "audacious bucks." Although they swore to each other that, if ever again confronted with such an "uppity buck," they would "knock him good," the porkknocker stated that he had since had several similar encounters, which he now simply found "curious and a little amusing." After all, he concluded, "Iz everybody gaa fo' try fo' dem se'f."

This and other recorded examples of getting a shock may have been exaggerated in the recounting. However, the influence of ster-eotypes on the ease or the difficulty with which indices of class position are recognized as *true* or *apparent* is an aspect of a hierarchical image of a national sociocultural and political order in which it is expected that ethnic identity predicts personal potential for so-cioeconomic mobility.

For example, Cockalorum African informants believe that East Indians as a cultural group are more progressive than Africans. That is, Africans associate East Indian progressiveness with their adherence to East Indian culture. They also maintain that Africans could progress faster and compete more effectively with East Indians if they adopted East Indian culture. As proof of this conviction, they usually point to successful persons who are physically African but whom they see as having adopted an East Indian lifestyle. The following case will serve to illustrate how disjunctions between ethnic identity, conduct, and achievements are ideologically rationalized by those who create the disjunctions and by others who evaluate them.

Mr. L. was born to parents considered to be of African descent. He grew up in the Coconut Grove backdam section, which had always had a fairly even mix of African and East Indian households (see Chapter 2). Members of his extended family had intermarried or cohabited with East Indians, Chinese, Portuguese, and Amerindians. Although he never married across ethnic boundaries, he had East Indian girlfriends and, in general, was viewed as having closer than average associations with East Indians. He says that he always had a "softness" toward East Indian ways—which, he thought, probably indicated some "Indian blood in me veins." When he selected a woman of African descent to marry, he claimed he chose her, in part, because she "appreciated East Indian ways." Overall, he praised himself for his ability to get along with all kinds of people and to understand and make use of their ways of doing things. Even so, others did not question his ethnic identity. Until roughly twenty years ago (when he was about thirty), he considered himself and was considered by others to have "grown and moved as a Blackman."

The event that represented a turning point in his pattern of behavior occurred during the violent upheavals of the 1960s. He was accused of murdering two East Indian children. The charge was made on circumstantial evidence that proved too weak for a formal indictment. Nonetheless, in the community, especially among his East Indian neighbors, he was still considered a murderer. The matter was made worse because the murdered children's parents were his neighbors and had been his friends.

Mr. L. had always been a hard worker, mainly a farmer, but had occasionally joined his father and brothers for a quarter (that is, approximately four months) of porkknocking. After this incident, he says that whatever he tried seemed to go wrong. He simply could not prosper. He took this as a sign from God that he should do something for children, that he should let people know that he was not a man to commit such an act against children, whatever their race.

He began by inviting a few children to accompany him and his family on outings. He was always careful to include East Indian as well as African children. Also, his neighbors' children were always welcome at his home. People soon noticed this pattern and, as their confidence in him grew, more parents allowed their children to attend his outings. East Indian and African neighbors also brought their children to his wife to look after while they worked on their farms or went to sell in the market. His cross-ethnic associations increased and diversified. He was soon invited to jhandis (that is, the most typical ritual form for thanksgiving pujas conducted by Sanatan Dharma Hindus), to East Indian weddings (both Hindu and Muslim), as well as to other social occasions. He shared farming knowledge, equipment, seeds, and labor with his East Indian neighbors. Both he and his East Indian neighbors relate that they grew to respect him as a hard-working, fair-minded person whom East Indian informants half-jokingly call a "coolie fo' true."

Each year the number of child visitors grew until he had to rent several hire cars to carry them to the outings. It became a very expensive venture, but one to which he felt his increasing prosperity and more congenial lifestyle were linked. His wife, fearful of the carelessness of some of the hire-care drivers and of their own inability to give careful supervision to such large numbers of children on an outing, convinced him that instead of the outings they should prepare a dinner for the children at home. He accepted the idea, and the annual outing became an annual dinner. He argued that East Indians "appreciated" what he was doing "more so than me own African people dem," and they began to help out with offers of food and serving utensils. Hindu East Indian women also came to assist him and his wife with the preparation and serving of the meal.

About four years ago, two other changes took place. Mr. L. claims some of his East Indian friends were teasing him. They told him they all worked together and they could really appreciate what he was doing, but they thought it curious that he found it in his heart to invite only children to his thanksgivings. He took the hint and let it be known that the following year the dinner would be for children and adults. When one of his East Indian male companions heard about this change, he told Mr. L. that he should not "do the t'ing piece-piece" (only partially). He should have a full puja (service)—not only to serve people but to let the gods know that he appreciated their assistance. Again he agreed, and the annual dinner became an annual jhandi. Now the cooking was done the night before, and the morning of the dinner he was assisted by East Indian friends in conducting the puja, which followed closely the religious features of the jhandi. He was encouraged to and did join the local Hindu Association, which allowed him to rent (at a nominal fee) the large number of cooking and serving utensils needed for these events.

Hence, as his prosperity grew, Mr. L. took on more and more of what is stereotypically considered an East Indian value for work (see Chapter 2). He also became even more involved in East Indian ritual events. By attending these events, he became part of the system of reciprocity associated with ritual and work. When his son married, the ceremonial activities included a Hindu "Mati Kore" (worship of Mother Earth; see Chapter 9) and a ritual dyeing with turmeric of the groom for purification and protection, as well as a "queh-queh" (African wedding eve ritual) and a disco dance on the same Friday night. The events faded into one another. The food served included items considered to be East Indian, such as vegetable and meat curries and "roti" (breads), as well as cook-up rice, pepperpot, and other dishes credited as African contributions to Guyanese cuisine.

Mr. L.'s actions did not so much raise questions about his "true" ethnic identity as they raised questions about which ethnic group could justifiably take credit for his prosperity and his good character. What is most informative here is that Mr. L.'s success was not simply attributed to his industry, his cleverness, and his living well with others, as it would have been if achieved within the bounds of African ethnicity. Instead, he, African, and East Indian informants viewed his case and numerous others as proof of the greater instrumental benefits of East Indian culture. From "grains of truth" contained in stereotypes of persons and ethnic cultures, members of the competing ethnic groups build ideological castles that house and protect their group's quest for a place in the society. Mr. L. used the "war" in his veins, generally associated with contradictions between individual behavior and ethnic group stereotypes, to remove a stain from his name.

It should not be assumed, however, that Mr. L.'s behavior indicates an attitude significantly different from Africans who do not adopt

"Indian t'ing." Mr. L. expressed most of the negative stereotypes about East Indians. He also voiced the conviction that East Indians' ultimate aim is to "take over Guyana" and dominate the other ethnic groups. He praised himself for his ability to beat them at their own game. Identifying himself as an African, he saw his actions and his success as proof of African intellectual superiority, exhibited, he maintained, in the Africans' ability to adopt and to utilize successfully any other "people's t'ing" if and when they chose to do so. He rejected the possibility that such adoptions implied African cultural inferiority, insisting instead that economic problems fostered by East Indian and Anglo-European collusion during the colonial era made "coolie greed and selfishness," for the moment, the most feasible path to economic success. African culture he believed to be morally superior because the Blackman is naturally generous and intent on cooperating with his fellow man and enjoying his life. If, however, he followed his natural tendencies in Guyana, the jealous and greedy East Indian would soon be well ahead of him, leaving "'e and 'e picni fo' dead out." So he must, at times, suppress his superior moral nature and use his wit to outsmart the East Indians on their own terms.

In this ideological field, pulled between the quest to identity as mati and the desire to protect ethnic patrimony, ethnically different individuals at times seem to interact with one another as merely personified stereotypes. When Mr. K., an East Indian, offered to rent land belonging to Mr. G., an African, Mr. G. refused. Although he needed the money and was not using the land, he reasoned that, if he rented the land to Mr. K., eventually he would be forced to sell the land to him. Mr. G. said that East Indians are a covetous people who want to own all the land in Guyana, that African people like to try to get quick, easy money, and that East Indians take advantage of this African weakness. He, therefore, believed that, if he rented the land to Mr. K., one day Mr. K. would offer to buy the land, saying he could no longer afford to rent it. Mr. G. said he, having become accustomed to the income, would then be faced with losing the income or selling his land for the preferred cash. He did not want to take the risk of putting himself in that position. In his reasoning, he stereotypes the East Indian man and himself, assuming that they would both eventually operate according to stereotyped patterns.

Examples of these types, along with counterexamples of unsuccessful East Indians who are said to have adopted African behavioral patterns, lead East Indians to maintain that their culture makes them more progressive and their ways of doing things more effective for Guyana's economic development. They view their ethnic culture and their group's success as the backbone of Guyanese society and economy. They consider African culture (or Africans' lack of culture) to be responsible for what they see as the Africans' slow economic progress and their alleged insignificant contribution to the overall economic development of Guyana.

Although Africans do not always disagree with East Indian stereotypes of African culture, they do contend that, if adherence to East Indian culture is the price to be paid for economic progress, then the price is too high. On the one hand, they say, to live like a "coolie" is not to live at all. On the other hand, they say, a wholesale adoption of East Indian culture by Africans and by others would amount to a tacit legitimation of what they see as East Indians' quest for hegemonic dominance—combined cultural, political, and economic control over the social order and over the production of status evaluation criteria. To avoid this, African informants maintain that Africans must make their own way. If necessary, the group must revitalize and revise its cultural traditions. They claim all will be lost if Africans give in to "doing other people dem t'ing" without first proving to them that their personal successes and their group progress are not dependent on the adoption of others' cultural traditions. In their effort to revise and to revitalize African traditions, Cockalorums of African descent confront the difficult task of trying to sidestep any solution that could quickly be claimed by other ethnic groups as part of their ethnic cultural heritages.

Hence, it is the manner in which conceptions of both class and ethnicity were synthesized (first, in elite ideological interpretations and, subsequently, in subordinate expansion of the stereotypes and the criteria associated with elite ideological interpretations) that we may begin to understand why consciousness of class position need not necessarily weaken an emphasis on ethnic identity. One of the ironies of ethnicity shaped by such ideological interpretations is that ethnic differentiation within the middle and upper classes tends to lend validity to ethnicity rather than undermine it.[1]

Despite the fact that classes have different interests and that the lifestyle of many economically and socially mobile individuals differs markedly from what is considered their traditional ethnic cultural pattern, the significance of ethnicity or of their ethnic identity is not necessarily undermined, either for the most or for the least successful members of the ethnic group. Instead, Cockalorums believe that any class position above the lower class that a person achieves is the result of his earlier identification with and, more important, utilization of modes of interaction that are presumed to be part of his ethnic culture. They maintain that it is the utilization of ethnic cultures that does or does not afford ethnically different individuals a way to move into these higher class positions, the accomplishment of which they can then display through the conscious adoption of creole English culture.

Thus, even where successful persons are several generations re- moved from adherence to their presumed traditional ethnic cultural patterns, Cockalorums argue that, because these individuals' ances- tors may reasonably be assumed to have gotten their start by follow- ing these patterns, their accomplishments remain a credit to the ethnic culture. After all, they say, success is not a "one day story." In brief, socioeconomic mobility of ethnically identified persons be- comes another criterion by which members of the same ethnic group may aim to rank their group above other groups or, alternatively, to justify a claim to equality of treatment and opportunity in the society. It is one way they can maintain that class stratification is a product of ethnic differentiation. Were it not for racial/ethnic discrimination and political corruption, they contend, the ethnic composition of the middle and upper classes would directly reflect differences in the innate intellectual capabilities of the racial/ethnic groups and in the quality of the cultures each produces.

Social Mobility and the Manipulation of Cultural Content and "Ownership"

Ethnicity, as a criterion for differentiating and legitimating ethnic group status rank, is problematic not merely from the standpoint of a group's ability unquestionably to attribute persons' achievements to their ethnic identity. Formal similarities among features of the "tradi- tional" cultures on which Guyanese ethnic cultures are based often make it difficult for any group definitively to trace and to claim features of the Guyanese cultural complex. For example, rituals, seen as core elements distinguishing ethnic cultures, have features that are so similar that it is difficult to trace them indisputably to an African, an Indian, or a Western European source. Likewise, items of Guyanese cuisine now claimed by a particular group may not be irrefutably traced only to their culture of origin. In addition, because African culture in Guyana tends for the most part to be viewed as a lower-class rural interpretation of English culture, African Cockalorums often contend that others in Guyana who adopt contemporary English culture are now adopting "Blackman t'ing." Others counter that "things English" belong to everyone, and, even where Africans can demonstrate reinterpretation, that does not give them a special claim to these features of Guyanese culture.

This lack of cultural distinctiveness, on the one hand, leads Cockalorums to comment that, culturally, "Awl ahwee a Doogla." On the other hand, it results in intense and intriguing manipulations directed at claiming group ownership or at denying other groups' claims to ownership. Cockalorums say that, unlike the assumed purity of the culture on which Anglo-Europeans partly justified their claim to dominance, the content of subordinated ethnic cultures is obviously "begged, borrowed, and stolen." They frequently draw parallels and try to equate cultural objects and actions. For example, religion is a favorite focus of debate among Cockalorums. They equate religious beliefs, figures, and ritual forms, arguing that these things are really the same; they only appear to be different. They frequently contend that, overall, cultural differences can be compared to lexical differences between languages. That is, different languages vary in the words they include to identify the same objects and actions. The same language often has different "twangs" (dialects), but the objects and actions, and what the different twangs communicate, are presumed to be the same. In this view, Guyanese culture is a composite of different twangs that should not be judged inferior or superior to one another. They are merely alternative forms for communicating the same substance.

Consequently, in an ideal world, Cockalorums conclude, Guyanese should simply be proud of their cultural diversity. Individuals, regardless of their ascriptive identity, should be able to choose among "things Guyanese." That such tolerance and sharing are considered difficult to achieve they attribute to fear and hostility resulting from centuries of racism and discrimination, to current manipulations by such external forces as the U.S. Central Intelligence Agency, and to the actions of the national elite which, they claim, does everything it can to keep "mati at mati throat" in order to maintain their privileges. In a social atmosphere of fear and racism, they maintain that intolerance and competition aimed at linking cultural, economic, and political domination to reestablish hegemonic dominance are inevitable.

In the face of such an inevitability we understand why, when persons are confronted (as frequently they are) with charges that either they or their group have adopted aspects of another group's ethnic culture, they try to discredit such claims in terms of what we will refer to here as denial, recognition, and appropriation.

Denial is an attempt to disprove the accuracy of the charge of adoption. Members of the accused group may attempt to deny the charge by pointing out that whatever is at issue could just as easily be traced to their ancestral culture. In this sense, they claim to be returning to their own cultural tradition. In other instances, the accused person may claim that what is at issue is really part of Guyana's English cultural heritage and, therefore, belongs equally to all Guyanese. Debates centering on the use of denial more often reach a stalemate than a resolution, with each party standings his ground but unable to convince the other party.

Drummond reports an interesting example of denial in a story told to him by an Amerindian man. An African man charged Amerindians with racism toward Africans and simultaneously tried to claim African superiority by contending that Amerindians could not get along without African assistance. Africans, this informant maintained, taught Amerindians everything of worth they know today. The Amerindian man countered that White people were the teachers, and further,

"If you [Africans] say you come here to teach us, it is only that white people send you to show us how to make *dugler* [Doogla] [mixed] children with our women!" And with that he pointed to a boat at the landing, filled with the "outside children" [that is, illegitimate children of another local black Creole and an Arawak woman]. (1977:863)

Drummond goes on to say that, according to the Amerindian, the African conceded the point and they were again friends. This example is especially interesting because, like many debates that begin with denial, this one ends with qualified recognition. Without entirely denying that Africans were teachers, the Amerindian man recognized the role, the Africans' subordinate relation to it, and what he viewed as a negative feature of the Africans' behavior in the role.

In Cockalorum debaters often recognize claims of ownership and the accuracy of charges of adoption but argue that what has been adopted has either had negative consequences or is insignificant for a demonstration of cultural superiority and a legitimate claim to dominance. They try to compel the accuser to prove that the adoption has resulted in positive benefits for the upward mobility of the individual or the group charged with adopting it. The cross-ethnic adoption of ethnically identified items of cuisine, culinary techniques, and features of rituals are often treated in this manner. The accused will claim that the most to be said about the significance of adopted items is that they have been chosen because they are tasty, fun, or lend "brightness" to a particular occasion.

Although, as we see in the next chapter, simultaneous with its negative consequences, this degree of recognition and of credit allows those accused of adoptions to counter that the adoptions are neither significant to their group's economic progress nor proof of the greater fitness of the accusers' groups for positions of dominance. Accusers, faced with this contention, often point to adoption as proof, nonetheless, of the general worth of their culture indicated by the other groups' "appreciation" through adoption.

The issues entailed in some debates are taken more seriously than others, and some debates are more easily resolved than others. The least easily resolved debates center on attempts by one group to appropriate (claim full or joint ownership) what its members admit was introduced to Guiana by another subordinated ethnic group. Although appropriation of any feature of another ethnic group's cultural content may result in heated debates, the appropriation of features of ethnic cultures that have been historically linked to differences in ethnic groups' economic progress are most hotly contested. Because they are very provocative, these debates usually take place among members of the same ethnic group or in mixed gatherings of very good friends who are careful to end the discussion if one party appears genuinely angry.

The focus of such debates is most often the competing claims Africans and East Indians make to the introduction and, hence, to the ownership of values for communalism, and of the techniques and the development of the rice industry in Guiana. In both informant and official political rhetoric, communalism as cooperation and self-help is the foundation of Guyanese "democratic socialism." Most frequently, official political rhetoric credits Africans with the introduc-

tion of these values and patterns of behavior through their involvement in the postemancipation village movement. According to views
expressed in political pamphlets, speeches, newspapers, and radio
broadcasts, at a time when other groups were either passively or
actively aligned with the European elite, Africans were combining
their funds to purchase land and to establish communities in which
they also instituted their own governing bodies.

In local informant debates, the African acceptance of this claim is
countered by East Indians who insist that communalism and cooperation were always part of their Indian cultural tradition. Furthermore,
they contend, in Guiana it was really their pattern of domestic
organization and economic cooperation that was (and, they say, still
is) the "genuine" model of communalism, and representative of a
sincere orientation toward self-help and group progress. Most East
Indian informants insist that the behavior of early African villagers
did represent an interest in communalism, but the Africans' "natural
tendency" toward individualism overshadowed and eventually destroyed these early efforts.

African Cockalorums, viewing such contentions as an effort at
appropriation, counter that, if it appears that East Indians can now
claim ownership of values for cooperation and communalism, it is
only because they learned these from Africans under conditions in
which the East Indians were favored by the European elite and,
hence, were better able to institutionalize and to benefit from the
values. Moreover, they maintain that East Indian claims to these
values as part of their traditional culture are just another example of
East Indian greed, seen as the real feature of East Indian culture
signaled by these efforts. As one might expect, East Indians dismiss
the charge as just another example of African jealousy, which they
consider a major index of the African value for competition.

Similar debates center on who introduced and who can now take
credit for the importance of rice production to the national economy.
Africans rightly claim to have been the first rice growers in Guiana.
East Indians readily admit the accuracy of the claim but counter that
it is irrelevant now. They maintain that Africans missed their chance,
and, whatever the reasons for their failure, East Indians' farming
techniques and diligence established and continue to sustain rice
production in Guyana. Similar and equally acrimonious discussions
revolve around any alleged feature of an ethnic culture that Cock-

alorums consider significantly and demonstrably linked to individual success stories, the comparative economic progress of ethnic groups, or anything deemed a significant contribution to national development.

Neither denial, qualified recognition, nor appropriation guarantee success in any debate. Take, for example, efforts to claim items of Guyanese cuisine. Ethnic claims to the ownership of items of cuisine often begin with the ethnic labeling of procedures. Cockalorums divide culinary arts into two broad categories—wet and dry cookery. Wet cookery includes any process that retains liquor; dry cookery includes those forms of preparation that aim to render the dish liquor-free. Informants associate dry cookery with African cultural tradition and wet cookery with East Indian cultural tradition. The cross-ethnic utilization of these techniques is viewed as borrowing and, hence, provides proof of cross-ethnic teaching and interdependence. When asked about preparation sequences that involve both forms, informants either defined the dish by the final result, historical evidence of national origin, or laughingly said "Iz doogla." With reference to food, however, doogla is more commonly used to identify a mixture of ingredients of roughly the same type (such as when several kinds of greens are combined in one dish).

Claims to ownership of most dishes usually result in a search for its national origin. In this sense, every group can lay claim to some item of Guyanese cuisine. Even the Portuguese, generally considered to have "no culture left in Guyana," can claim "vinga dol" and garlic pork, although today these dishes are rarely prepared by anyone in Cockalorum because they are expensive. There is, however, one claim to ownership that is dependent on neither technique nor national origin but instead is linked to different frequencies among ethnic groups or individuals, who, for vaguely spiritual reasons, prefer "skin" over "scale" fish. Allegedly, East Indians favor skin fish whereas Africans select scale fish. Africans who reject skin fish claim that the consumption of this fish results in illness, nightmares, or spiritual dreams that indicate impending disaster for self or loved ones. In comparison, they say, eating scale fish results in good health, increased fertility, and prosperity. East Indians, who would rather not eat scale fish, give less detailed reasons, simply saying that, like all "rank" (polluting) substances, this type of fish decreases the spiritual purity of the body. In practical terms, some informants argued that, when fish is scarce, this preference-based ownership should be respected, allowing ethnically identified individuals to purchase the appropriate fish.

Moreover, the stereotypes linking ethnic groups to historical conjunctures and disjunctures in the distribution of economic roles and of political rights and obligations not only infuse local debates over the ownership of cultural items but sometimes also provide the analytic scaffold for academic assessments of the roles of different ethnic groups in Guianese history, and for evaluations of current economic policies. For example, Nath, in his *A History of the East Indian in Guyana* (1950), consistently makes explanatory use of elite-derived stereotypes of both Africans and East Indians. He notes certain objective constraints, but he explains African failures and East Indian successes in terms of, for the former, the negative aspects of stereotypes and, for the latter, the positive ones. Hence, he credits East Indians with the industry and thrift said to have made possible the expansion of the rice industry, but he blames Africans for bringing the colony to the brink of ruin by their lack of industry and proper gratitude for emancipation and, above all, by their "unreasonable" wage demands.

However, the interplay between ownership of cultural products and their contributions was never so clear-cut. Hickerson (1954), who offers a fairly detailed description of ethnically related differences in rice cultivation among Danieltown, Essequibo residents, notes that conceptions of the ethnic ownership of these means influenced individuals' ideas about their relative value. He found, however, that who actually uses which procedure was associated with the size of a rice farmer's holdings. He concludes that African techniques based on the use of the hoe and the beating bench were most appropriate and were most likely to be employed in cases where the farmer's holdings were small. East Indian methods centering on the use of the plow and steer for threshing were more appropriate and were more likely to be adopted by farmers with larger plots. Only in cases of medium-sized acreage was there likely to be congruence between ethnic identity and the technique employed.

Nonetheless, rice farming in general and certain procedures in particular continue to be viewed as owned by East Indians. Therefore, when the Jagan government, for lack of other viable options (see Bartels 1974), concentrated on developing the rice sector, it was dubbed the "rice government" and was said, as a result, to discriminate in favor of East Indians. On this issue Bartels (1974) justifiably criticizes Despres (1967) for unwittingly integrating into his own comments on the failure of a rice development project what Bartels refers to as the "PNC-Afro-Guyanese folk model" of the rationale for the Jagan government's emphasis on rice development.

Both East Indian and African Cockalorums refer to the era of the Jagan administration as a period during which East Indians, with Jagan's assistance, attempted to develop the rice industry at the expense of other economic sectors as a step toward economic and political domination. African informants say it was an unfair move, whereas East Indians maintain that, because they were the "most industrious" segment of the population and the major rice farmers, it was only fair and logical that the Jagan government (or any government for that matter) should have invested most heavily in areas that benefited the rural East Indian. To assist the rural East Indians, in their view, is to assure the economic progress of the nation.

These claims, counterclaims, and the unresolved debates that focus on them do little to establish and to stabilize an ethnic hierarchy that would allow individuals to claim status superiority solely on the basis of ethnic identity. At best, they allow individuals flexibility in their choice of instrumental behaviors and in their development of social networks conducive to economic and status mobility. The degree of flexibility available to individuals, however, is constrained by their own beliefs in ethnic cultures, in the group ownership of features of the Guyanese cultural complex, and in the links that they draw between these and their rights to participate in the social system.

In independent Guyana, with the exodus of the ruling European stratum and the "Guyanization" of economic, social, and political institutions, competitive conceptualizations were no longer limited to the strategic ethnic protection of particular economic domains or to a quest for the rung beneath Englishmen on the social ladder. Competitive conceptualizations became means to claim, in all respects, the rung vacated by this ruling elite.

Cockalorums, looking back at the pain and the destruction of the 1960s riots, in voices that range from the shouts of angry resistance to whispers of frustrated submission, speak of the inevitability of racial, cultural, and political domination by one ethnic group through the reestablishment of a transformist hegemony. Ultimately, they say, one group will seize the reins of power to dominate all the others, and one can only hope that it will be one's own group that finds the successful path to domination. The egalitarian precepts that deny the inevitability of a racial and cultural hierarchy are, they contend, parts of a wonderful pipe dream that died in the horrors and the destruction of the 1960s disturbances. Out of this experience, they claim to have learned that it is impossible to know what is truly in the heart of another, even another who has been a good neighbor, "skinnin' 'e tef in you face" (smiling at you) day after day. Moreover, they conclude that the only hope for resuscitating the egalitarian dream lies in biological assimilation. Only when all Guyanese are "No Nations" will they be able to act and interact as a "nation"—persons of one blood, belonging to one state—"racial" and "cultural" differences notwithstanding.[2] Yet, mixed informants, not unlike the Portuguese informants, most often see themselves as waiting on the sidelines until either Africans or East Indians win out, expecting that they will then be able to align themselves with the most powerful group.

In the meantime the struggle to rank order ethnic groups and their cultures continues, producing an increasingly complex discourse of competing criteria and possible modes of causal-functional and logico-meaningful integration. From the perspective of the now numerically predominant African and East Indian groups, it is a quest to establish a set of criteria with which to specify the relation between ethnic groups as a hierarchy of givers and takers. East Indian and African voices are loudest in this discourse, but they are by no means uncontested, as members of the lower-ranked ethnic groups make counterclaims, suggest alternate criteria, and reject the accuracy of African and East Indian criteria and rank claims. Likewise, between Africans and East Indians there are counterclaims, alternate criteria, and disagreements about the ownership of both economic and cultural contributions.

Race, Class, and the Standards of Civilized Conduct

If egalitarianism and hierarchy were mutually exclusive ideologies, they would provide Cockalorums with fundamentally different views of sociocultural and political integration on which to base everyday practices. This, however, is far from the case. Egalitarianism and hierarchy are neither ideologies that become relevant only for evaluations of status and conduct in certain domains of social life nor ideologies to which only some of the community's social categories adhere. The roots of egalitarianism may be traced to the pragmatic actions, first of non-Anglo-European plantation workers and later of their descendants, in response to their experience of economic, political, and cultural subordination by a ruling European elite. Even so, the proprietary and communal village communities they created were always embedded in a broader society. As the least powerful members of this broader society, the rural villagers, trying to adhere to egalitarian precepts, were also exposed to and developed practices consistent with hierarchical precepts. The latter precepts differentially evaluated a person's rights of access to middle- and upper-class positions and assessed a person's potential for socioeconomic mobility in terms of racial and ethnic identity. Hierarchical interpretations were encoded in particular stereotypes, and in a stereotyping process centered on creating linkages among group contribution, the rank ordering of groups, and specifications of their rights in the society.

Within and outside rural communities, these hierarchical precepts influenced both access to economic opportunity and the acceptance by others of status claims based on economic achievements. All non-Europeans and some Europeans (that is, Portuguese) who managed to acquire the economic prerequisites for entry into the middle- and upper-class ranks and who hoped to have their accomplishments recognized had to adopt Anglo-European cultural practices as the standard against which their class-position claims would be judged. Although there was a greater degree of cultural freedom in the private domain, to the extent that private domain practices were based on religious elements of culture, these were also subject to negative evaluations relative to Christian practices, linked, as they were, to Anglo-European culture.

Consequently, individuals who aimed to become respectable members of the middle and upper classes took on, as they moved up the ladder, the practices and symbolic representations of English culture as the homogeneous standard of civilized conduct. Yet, the colonial society in which they lived had a "Starkist" attitude: it had use for people to eat (people who "taste good"), not for people who wanted to eat (people with good taste). So, like Charlie Tuna, these persons' efforts to demonstrate their respectability and their superior status were interpreted by elite Anglo-Europeans, and by members of the subordinated groups, as putting on the airs of their betters. Note, however, that Charlie Tuna's predicament was little better when viewed strictly from the egalitarian perspectives developed in the impoverished rural communities. Here, Charlie Tuna—the socially mobile individual—was likely to be accused of "eye-pass" (disregard for another's human dignity) and "playin' big" as he tried to express a class-position claim consistent with his sense of above-average achievement but inconsistent with the egalitarian code applicable to interactions among mati. Thus, whether Charlie Tuna was a big fish in a small pond or a small fish in a big pond, in the total ideological field he was still a fish—a lower order species.

Contemporary local and national efforts to revalue previously devalued non-Anglo-European cultural contributions notwithstanding, Cockalorums still operate in a social world delimited by the complex interplay of competing, incongruent hierarchical and egalitarian precepts concerning the meaning of racial and cultural differences. What is most problematic is not that these competing ideological precepts exist in the same field, but that neither legitimately predominates in setting the bounds of interpretation. First, despite egalitarian emphasis on the human equality of all Guyanese and the economic interdependence of members of the lowest economic stratum (that is to say, mati), egalitarianism is neither a rejection of hierarchy nor of the class stratification and ethnic ranking it implies. Instead, as noted above, it proposes a set of moral criteria against which to rank individuals hierarchically with respect to *how* they achieve different class positions and *how* they should interact with those who are less successful. At best, egalitarian precepts provide grounds for a moral mediation of problems stemming from economic differentiation and from racial and cultural antagonisms. Second, in contrast, the hierarchical precepts provide two sets of conflated criteria—culture and race—to mediate access to economic opportunities and political power, and against which to evaluate the social and moral worth of individuals and groups in a class-stratified society. According to the precepts of the hierarchical ideological position, moral criteria require no separate treatment; they are embedded in conceptions of race and culture.

Because egalitarianism and hierarchy competitively explicate the relation between class stratification and other types of differentiation,

Figure 7.1. The Ideological Field.

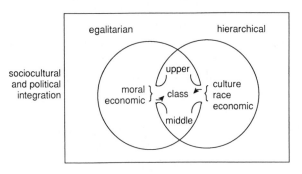

they are not mutually exclusive ideologies; they do not propose wholly different naturalized worlds. They are major components of a single ideological field. This field provides competing, interdependent, ideological solutions to the problem of sociocultural integration (where the term sociocultural should be understood as a reversal of the term causal-functional, with social viewed as functional and culture as causal) and of politicoeconomic integration (where politicoeconomic must be understood as a substitute for logicomeaningful, for it is politicized interpretations of the meaning of economic differentiation and its links to legitimated rights and obligations that are proposed in this form of integration). Thus, to the extent that egalitarianism ignores race and reduces the significance of cultural differentiation to nothing more than proof that all Guyanese have made contributions, and to the extent that hierarchy conflates culture and race, linking the conflation to "fitness" for particular economic opportunities and positions of power, the ideological field can be illustrated by Figure 7.1.[3]

The outer frame represents the total ideological field in terms of the problems it is intended to solve. The inner circles denote, respectively, the competing egalitarian and hierarchical ideological solutions to these problems. Egalitarianism recognizes a particular relation between moral and economic criteria as components that ought to determine an individual's entry into different class positions— indicated by the openings in both circles. It treats the *relation* between moral and economic criteria as the standard for evaluating the validity of a person's class-position claims. The hierarchical perspective recognizes a particular relation between culture (a reified entity embodied in race) and economic criteria as the factor that ought to determine a person's entry into different classes. The hierarchical perspective treats the congruence (that is, conjunctures and disjunctures) of these different criteria as the standard for evaluating the validity of a person's class-position claims.

This static diagram does not, however, accurately depict the dynamics of interpretation and evaluation implied by either of these ideological perspectives. Although egalitarianism provides a stable set of moral criteria against which to judge a person's economic worth and, hence, his status claims, the actual interpretive process linking morality to material attainments, influenced as it is by interactional histories and by the uneven distribution of knowledge, is indeterminate (see Chapters 2 and 3). In Cockalorum, there is little interevaluator agreement on which persons can legitimately claim to live well with people as they move up the socioeconomic ladder. Mr. X., who has been regularly assisted and treated fairly by Mr. Y., is likely to accept Mr. Y.'s claim to be one who lives well with people, whereas Mr. Q., who has been snubbed, cheated, or otherwise mistreated by Mr. Y., is unlikely to accept Mr. X.'s assessment of Mr. Y.'s moral status. Their reactions to Mr. Y.'s class-position claims will be consistent with the differences in their assessment of his moral status. Even if Mr. Y. possesses the economic prerequisites for a middle-class status claim, that does not mean he will have an easy time providing proof of these economic prerequisites. Mr. X. is more likely to accept as legitimate Mr. Y.'s claim to middle-class status than is Mr. Q., who will instead consider pretentious any above-average status claim made by Mr. Y.; in his view, Mr. Y. is just "playin' big."

Thus, whereas the moral criteria for interpersonal status evaluation are stable, their use does not result in a stable class stratification based on a successful interrelation (mediation) of moral and economic criteria. Individuals have many faces and names. Cockalorums have devised ways, including a formal ritual (see Williams 1983: chaps. 7–8), to try to synthesize these multiple reputations to determine a person's "true reputation." However, even the exposures and the distributions of information resulting from such efforts do little to stabilize rank order because the effort to expose (that is, talk name) and to distribute information (that is, talk story) are themselves suspect and subject to moral evaluations (see Chapter 4).

Moreover, although the precepts of the hierarchical perspective provide criteria for systematically interrelating race, culture, and class stratification in a stable hierarchy of ethnic groups and cultures, even during the colonial era these precepts were fraught with lacunas and contradictions. Europeans were racially and culturally superior to all non-Europeans, but Europeans of different nationality were not equal to one another, nor were they all equally able to claim superior class status solely on the bases of race and culture. Recall also that even Europeans of the same nationality were not equally able to claim social superiority on the bases of racial and cultural identity. Race and what counted as Anglo-European culture were ideologically constituted rather than simply the result of physiognomic traits and traceable historical links between Western Europe and its cultural practices. And, most important for an understanding of Cockalorums' contemporary interpretations of these ideological precepts, the Anglo-European elite interpretations did not specify the rank order of subordinated non-European ethnic groups and the criteria on which such a rank order was to be based. Hence, judged by elite Europeans standards, all these groups were racially and culturally inferior to all Europeans, especially Englishmen, but their rank order relative to one another shifted over time with the allocation of different economic roles.

Above all, the culture of domination that developed under Anglo-European hegemony centered on a particular process of stereotyping. Through this process and in conjunction with subordinate uses of different ideological precepts, subordinates could (1) act and interpret the world in accordance with the particulars of Anglo-European hegemonic interpretations, and, at the same time, (2) expand the meaning of ethnic stereotypes by fashioning new stereotypes and competing interpretations. What they were unable to do, however, was to enforce any one of their interpretations or, and this is more important, to legitimate one mode of interpretation (egalitarian or hierarchical) over the other. Although all systems may be said to contain this opposition, problems associated with contradictory interpretation become endemic only where neither perspective has greater social legitimacy and where the relevance of competing perspectives is not limited to identifiable social domains.

In the Guyanese ideological field, neither the selective use of parts of stereotypes nor subordinates' efforts to produce rank-order criteria through the stereotyping process have allowed Cockalorums to draw the lines of the civilizing process beyond the ideological boundaries set by Anglo-European hegemonic dominance. Despite "spaces" left by the lacunas and the contradictions of this hegemony, whether images of the social order and interpretations of the meaning of racial and cultural differences in that order are constructed from an egalitarian or a hierarchical perspective, thus far they remain within the bounds set by links between contribution and place. Proof of group contribution remains a key element in conceptualizations of individual and group rank and rights in the society.

III

*Ethnicity,
Class, and
Cultural
Production*

8

Religion, Class, Culture, and the Ghost of Hegemony

In cultural terms, the impact of Anglo-European hegemony was felt nowhere more strongly than in the area of religious diversity. Variations in religious beliefs and practices, more than any other elements of culture except, perhaps, comparisons of technological inventions and "advances," served as criteria among the elite Europeans for defining non-European racial and cultural groups as morally, socially, and intellectually backward and inferior. Though sectarian and denominational divisions existed among the Europeans, they were soon subordinated to general contentions regarding the superiority of Christianity over non-Christian "pagan" and "heathen" forms of religious expression.

Speaking of the role and the organization of religious differences among East Indian plantation laborers and upwardly mobile junior staff members, Jayawardena argues that "informal pressures," rather than direct coercion, served to define the relative status of Christianity as a feature of "English custom" in opposition to non-English, non-Christian customs.

First, "English" customs had, in the eyes of all Guianese, a great deal of prestige. The upwardly mobile coolie, like his Negro and Chinese counterparts, acquired these customs. Second, there was a growing realization that conformity to "English" customs, values, and beliefs brought certain advantages. For example, jobs as school teachers were open mainly to Christians since most schools were controlled by Christian missions. Moreover, high-status groups regarded the deviant customs of the coolies as "indecent" and "backward." The low status accorded to traditional Indian culture provided another incentive to creolization. (1963:25)

By the early twentieth century, despite less-than-enthusiastic support by planters, managers, and other administrators for the missionaries' interest in converting East Indians to Christianity, East Indian conversion to Christianity had become a "rough but reliable index of creolization" (Jayawardena 1960:98). Creolization by conversion was, however, only one of the ways religion indexed what Jayawardena refers to as informal pressures and what I prefer to call Anglo-European hegemonic dominance. Among upwardly mobile East Indians a low rate of conversion, as already noted, was also accompanied by resistive efforts to reevaluate and to revitalize Indian tradition. Much of this revitalization focused on reestablishing Hindu and Muslim traditions and on re-forming those aspects of these traditions that placed Indian culture in a negative light compared with Christian English culture.

Consequently, Jayawardena notes, it was in the first three decades of the twentieth century that much of this revitalization was initiated. Once it was under way, planters sought to control its structure and its content in order to direct the integration of these cultural elements into the sociocultural order in a politically acceptable manner. They provided favors, amenities, materials for buildings, labor for constructing and repairing religious structures, and stipends and free housing for religious specialists (Jayawardena 1963:22). These supports were buttressed by additional involvement in the organization of activities carried out under the banner of "traditional Indian culture."

[T]hey recognized festival days as holidays. It was probably [management] that persuaded the coolies to conduct their religious activities through associations, with subscriptions, elected committees, and parliamentary procedure for the conduct of meetings. Management helped in keeping accounts, approved appointments to offices and sanctioned the decisions of committees. Elections, minutes, and other association activities were open to scrutiny by management, which also ensured that the associations confined themselves to religious matters. (Jayawardena 1963:22)

Yet, even under the heavy hand of management, religious matters became political matters as religious revitalization and reform became symbolic of non-Christian (especially East Indian Hindu and Muslim) ethnic identity. Religion served as a key element in the East Indians' struggle to demonstrate the equality of Indian culture with

Anglo-European culture as an index of racial equality and, therefore, of their right to equal participation in the sociopolitical and economic order. Although religious and sectarian differences within the East Indian population produced tensions that led to hostile conflict during festivals, in local communities the greatest emphasis was placed on Indianness in opposition to other ethnic identities and to Christianity.

The call for Indian solidarity in the face of religious diversity resulted in (as Jayawardena found for the plantation communities in which he conducted research from the late 1950s to the early 1960s) a tacit agreement to cooperate as Indians. They did not seek to convert one another; religious associations cooperated across sectarian and religious boundaries, and, in religious discussion, assumed commonalities among religious doctrines were stressed. In short, to the extent possible, intragroup controversy was avoided in favor of the creation and maintenance of an Indian identity. Hence:

The basis of this rapprochement is the assertion that both Hindus and Muslims are Indians, in contradistinction to Negroes and Whites, and their religions are Indian, in contradistinction to Christianity. Hinduism and Islam are regarded as alternative ways of being Indian. A close study of their respective customs reveals that a considerable degree of convergence and syncretism has developed. (Jayawardena 1963:23)

In addition to accepting convergence and syncretism, religious adherents and participants in religious rituals concentrated on and tended to find the meaning of their membership in their group identity and in the status it symbolized, rather than in the particular symbols and the symbolic structures of separate religious tradition and distinct ritual events. Rauf (1974), on the basis of fieldwork conducted in 1965, concludes that religious differences did not impede interfaith marriages, generalized reciprocity, or participation in religion-based community events among East Indians in the same community. He reports that the younger generation placed higher value on creolized practices than did the older generations, but that all generations tended to use religion as a racial and cultural marker to distinguish themselves from non-Indians, especially from persons of African descent.

Though intermarriage with Africans and non-Indian Christians, as well as Christianity in general, were seen as threats to the culture, the

morality, and the progress of East Indians, Christianized and otherwise Anglicized East Indians were not ostracized. Nonetheless, as
both Rauf and Jayawardena found, they were sometimes considered
to be less than "real" Indians. They often continued to play important
roles in the religious associations and rituals symbolizing the Indianness of the communities to which they were linked. In fact, Rauf
reports that at one Hindu religious ceremony (a Yagya/Jhag) he
attended,

[t]he religious gathering was presided over by a known Brahman priest who
preached the orthodox ritualistic beliefs of the Hindu religion, quoting ex-
tensively from sacred Hindu scriptures such as the Vedas and the Bhagavad
Gita. His sermon was punctuated with frequent warnings to the audience
that they should remain on guard against Christian catechists who, according to him, were employing surreptitious methods to dissuade them from
their sacred Dharma. While the Brahman priest was sermonizing against the
"undesirable" influence of Christian missionaries, an interesting fact remained unnoticed by the audience—the person who was conducting the
proceedings of Yagya, the headmaster of a local school, was himself a
Christian. (1974:75–76)

It is possible that the religious affiliation of the headmaster went
unnoticed. It is equally possible, however, that given the tendency for
provocative issues to be treated in the indirect language of hints, the
Brahman's sermonizing was motivated by the very presence of this
Christian East Indian. It is also possible that the headmaster's involvement in the ceremony was part of his effort to demonstrate ethnic and
religious solidarity in spite of his, perhaps economically motivated,
conversion to Christianity. In other words, although an emphasis on
ethnic solidarity permitted strategic cooperation and the construction of a sense of identity and of social and moral worth that transcended religious divisions, it did not entirely efface historical tensions between those divisions or fully resolve the status disjunctions
associated with religious diversity in colonial Guiana. And, in postindependence Guyana, religion as a criterion for status ranking, like the
various other criteria we have already discussed, became more rather
than less problematic. Problems associated with ideological links
between religious diversity and social status were especially pressing
for East Indians (the major non-Christian group) as they struggled to
construct a solidary ethnic front and to elevate the culture of their
group in the total social order.

Religious Diversity, Christianity, and the Symbols of Class Status

During the colonial era Christianity was considered the superior form of religious expression. As part of English culture, the institutions, the practices, and the modes of conduct associated with Christianity were the vehicles for the presentation of middle- and upper-class status claims by all members of the religiously diverse population. For the decade before independence, Smith described the situation as follows:

Social stratification in the village is largely in terms of cultural differences combined with occupational status; the school-teacher group, with one or two government employees, forming the village "upper class." The school-teachers even if they are born in the village and work their way through the stage of being a pupil teacher, soon begin to feel themselves different from other people and usually break away from their families and set up a separate household. . . . The hall-mark of the school-teacher is that he wears a jacket and a tie almost all the time, except when he is relaxing at home, and he speaks a more "grammatical" form of English than the local dialect. Above all these are the symbols of his status, but of course they are not the only ones, and a person who merely speaks "grammatical" English and wears a coat and tie does not thereby automatically qualify for higher status group membership. The school-teacher approximates more closely than anyone else in the village to the "white" standards of behaviour, and he is also a specialist in passing on the values of the total social system. Both the church and the school have this function, and the school-teachers are active in both organizations. (1956:206)

The church to which he refers is the Christian church, and the schools are institutions owned and operated by different Christian denominations. For Muslims, Hindus, and followers of less formalized non-Christian religious expressions, this access to the high-status role of schoolteacher required conversion to Christianity.

Nonetheless, the rate of East Indian conversion to Christianity was never very high. For the few who did convert, their conversion was often nominal rather than substantive, because they continued to engage in non-Christian practices. Similar patterns obtained among Amerindians and the earliest Chinese converts. Even among Africans, the most Christianized non-European segment of the population, forms of religious expression contained both elements of West African religious traditions and unorthodox (syncretic) interpretations of Christian practices. Those who openly engaged in such activities, however, risked being labeled ignorant, superstitious, and back-ward—evaluations that made it very difficult for them, whatever their economic accomplishments, to present themselves as persons of middle- or upper-class status.

Interethnically, for those who did not convert to Christianity (a majority of the East Indian population), this linkage between religion and the symbolic representation of class status posed serious concrete and abstract obstacles to social mobility. In concrete terms, it meant that access to the more lucrative economic roles and prestigious occupations required the adoption of the most Anglicized cultural practices in all domains, including religion. In abstract terms, the Anglicization (or creolization) of the most successful non-Europeans was taken as further proof that English culture was indeed superior and, therefore, the better general social foundation (that is, Smith's "values of the total social system"). Just as useful non-English cultural elements could be appropriated and assimilated to English culture (see Chapter 5), so, too, could successful non-European individuals be appropriated and assimilated to the substantiation of an ideologi-cal conception of European/English racial and cultural superiority.

Under these conditions successful persons were of dubious "credit to their race." Anglo-Europeans could argue that it was not these individuals' racial or cultural background, but instead their struggle to become "good Christians," to adopt the ways of their betters, that explained their success. Moreover, it was equally likely that less successful members of their ethnic group would raise doubts about these persons' claim to group membership. Again, Jayawardena pro-vides a telling example from his research among a community of lower-class sugar estate workers:

But while the Indian group is primarily one of descent, cultural consider-ations make important modifications. . . . Patterns of cultural behaviour can make radical changes in status by descent. This is borne out by the status, intermediate between Indian and Negro, enjoyed by Negro Muslims. It is again reflected in the ambiguous status of the highly Westernized Indian of the upper class who is usually a Christian and does not maintain "Indian custom." He too occupies a marginal position in the Indian group; people repeatedly said of certain upper-class Indians, "Dey nah Indian." (1963:12)

Yet, as Jayawardena's comment about the intermediate status of the Negro Muslim suggests, where an individual's class-status claim was incongruent with his or her religious identity, the difficulties entailed in efforts to represent class status symbolically were not limited to interethnic or dominant/subordinate evaluations of this relation. Hierarchical ideological precepts linked race and culture to evaluations of groups' relative "fitness" to enter the upper ranks of the class hierarchy. Religion was an element of culture; therefore, religious differences among non-Christian East Indians also posed problems for their definition of their ethnic group and for their assessment of the quality of the different Indian religions. Given the nature of interethnic competition, they could not simply view Hinduism and Islam as different contributions made by segments of the total East Indian population to its ethnic culture.

These problems were especially difficult to resolve because, from a subordinate/subordinate standpoint, the rank ordering of ethnic groups and their cultures remained indeterminate. With this general indeterminacy, no religion could indisputably claim second rank beneath Christianity. Nor, for the East Indian, would the stabilization of an ethnic group hierarchy, even one in which his group occupied the top rank, have necessarily settled the question of how to evaluate and to integrate religious differences within the ethnic group. If East Indian culture were to be considered equal or superior to other ethnic cultures, would it be best represented by Hindu or Muslim beliefs and practices? If Hinduism were to be favored, would definitions and evaluations be made in terms of Sanatan Dharma or Arya Samaji beliefs and practices? And, the knottiest problem of all, if East Indian culture were to be defined by any one of these non-Christian religions, what would that imply for the internal status rank of East Indians not affiliated with the selected religion?

The problem of selecting, legitimating, and using criteria for rank ordering diverse intergroup and intragroup religious practices was subject to the same procedural vagaries and incongruities characterizing the general effort of subordinates to rank order non-European peoples and their cultures. Among East Indians, intraethnic efforts to resolve this issue were made in an ideological field composed of competing egalitarian and hierarchical precepts. Like the hierarchy of "givers" and "takers," the hierarchy of diverse religious groups among East Indians remained indeterminate, as members of each religious segment proposed criteria advantageous to their segment which they were unable to impose on others.

208 Ethnicity, Class, and Cultural Production

To counter these problems, East Indians of all religious segments did argue that "East Indian religions" were equal to Christianity and to one another. Religions were, in this egalitarian view, simply different paths to salvation; gaining salvation depended on the faith and good conduct of the individual, rather than on the religion to which he belonged. In Cockalorum, the most extreme version of the egalitarian view is most frequently presented by Hindus. They argue that the "Supreme" devised and gave to each "race" or "nation" a particular religious dogma and set of ritual practices ideally suited to the circumstances in which It found them at the time of Its first coming. The ritual practices associated with this religion are the practices through which that race can best communicate with the Supreme. Although there is only one Supreme, known by the variety of names It used when It first appeared to the different races, efforts to communicate with the Supreme through ritual practices other than those divinely given create confusion and make it difficult for the Supreme to understand human messages and requests. Consequently, the conversion of one race, religiously defined, to the religion of another race is not only unnecessary but counterproductive.[1]

Nonetheless, under special circumstances, some individuals might find it necessary to adopt the rituals of another religious "race." In such cases the Supreme will eventually hear and understand the message or request, if the ritual is performed correctly, ideally by a person of the proper religious race (that is to say, one linked to the religion by extranational ancestry rather than by intranational conversion or informal adoption), and if the individual has faith in the efficacy of the ritual. These persons should expect communication difficulties, because the Supreme must first recover from gettin' a shock before it can properly attend to the message. Some East Indian informants, again mainly Hindus, argue that because of extenuating circumstances Africans are in a special position with respect to conversion and the adoption of non-African religious rituals. These informants say that, because Africans were forcibly stripped of their divinely given religious beliefs and ritual practices, the Supreme is attuned to hearing their supplications and propitiations through any religious form in which they have faith.

Hence, interpretations of intraethnic and interethnic religious diversity based on egalitarian precepts neither rank order religions and "religious races" nor attribute greater cultural significance to some forms of religious expression. Yet, as in other areas of social life, individuals who act on these precepts are not unaware of hierarchical precepts, nor do they necessarily deny their validity. Recall, for example, Mr. L.'s continued belief in the inferiority of East Indians, despite his adoption of a major Hindu ritual form, and the generosity and assistance he received from his Hindu neighbors during the enactment of these rituals (see Chapter 7). One finds the same negative hierarchical attitude expressed by Africans and by non-Hindu East Indians, who take spiritually ill babies to an East Indian Hindu "pujari" (a religious leader, especially one associated with Kali Mai) for treatment—in the case of Africans, treatment that often results in the African child's being ritually "given" to East Indian parents for its long-term protection. Although informants contend that such religious practices are more efficacious for propitiating and warding off the evil spirits that cause spiritual illness, they also consider them backward superstitions judged against "orthodox" Hinduism or Christianity.

Mr. F., a middle-aged Muslim, one of my neighbors during my first visit to Cockalorum, was a practicing pujari. He claimed that his curing techniques were based on the religious practices of Kali Mai worship brought to Guyana by South Indian Hindus (that is, Madrassi). These practices, he argued, were backward relative to the true faith of Islam but were, nonetheless, effective for the backward people who still believed in them. Africans who took their children to Mr. F. alleged that the Madrassi-related practices he used were inferior to the West African practices that their ancestors had known but that were now reduced to ineffective fragments, essential knowledge having been repressed by Christian missionaries after emancipation or lost during slavery. In resentful tones they speak of how their current religious predicament resulted from British actions that consistently "favored coolie ways"—a reference to plantation management involvement in the organization and financing of Hindu and Muslim religious associations, temples, and mosques. In this regard, some African informants, though disenchanted with the prime minister's political and economic policies, praised him for what they understood to be his efforts to "treat Obeah [practices based on West African religious traditions] fairly." Some had heard that he even had his own private obeahman.

Interethnic ideas about religion and religious differences are proposed and evaluated in an ideological field that emphasizes "contribution" and "ethnic group ownership," and that assimilates these to egalitarian and hierarchical ideological precepts. An excerpt from one of a 1980 series of articles on religious diversity in Guyana that appeared in the national newspaper, *Guyana Chronicle*, exemplifies the complexity of this discourse:

> If Christianity was seen to be associated with the colonial history of the country, and Hinduism was severe in its restrictions on membership, then Islam, the youngest of the world's great faiths, was a religion of much attractiveness for Guyana.
>
> However, although the number of its followers has been steadily increasing, the rise has been nowhere near to the growth capacity.
>
> One reason no doubt was the past racial polarisation of the country, which led to the erroneous believe that Islam was not only brought to the country by Indian immigrants (who had been converted) but also that it was the preserve of those immigrants.
>
> In fact, long before the first batch of Indian immigrants arrived, Islam had already come with some of the Africans who had been uprooted from their homeland and sent abroad as slaves.
>
> As happened with other religions coming with the Africans, there was a ruthless suppression by the colonial masters.
>
> This impression that Islam belonged to only one of the two major race groups, however, had the consequential effect of alienating other people from the Islamic community, and when orthodox Christianity began to be challenged, it was not to Islam but to the Pentecostal and even newer churches to which the disenchanted turned. (Wilkinson and Monar 1980b:7)

These comments, jointly written by an African and an East Indian, begin with the implicit motivation behind the search for a Guyanese religion, suggesting that Christianity is ideologically tainted because of its past association with colonial inequalities. Second, although free of the ideological taint, Hinduism, as a nonproselytizing faith with no theological provision for conversion, cannot serve as the religion to which Guyanese seeking freedom from religious colonialism might turn. Third, the article treats Islam as ideally suited to this purpose for a number of reasons. It is one of the "world's great faiths," hence, by implication, not a hodgepodge of religious fragments, nor a mere creole (low-status) invention. It permits conversion without reference to the religious affiliation of the convert's parents and it was the contribution of non-European, subordinated peoples. Thus, by logical deduction the growth capacity of Islam is limited only by the percentage of the national population (approximately 8 percent) already estimated to be affiliated with the faith.[2]

Taking the government line that real racial animosity and divisiveness are things of the past, the writers explain why Islam has not lived up to its growth potential. Note that this explanation is phrased in terms of contribution and ownership—terms that ultimately contradict the authors' most general underlying assumption about Islam's appropriateness as the new religion for all right-thinking Guyanese. In setting straight the history of Islam's introduction to Guiana, they describe the religion as a contribution and, therefore, the jointly owned property of the "two major races"—Africans and East Indians. In ideological terms, this contention has the consequential alienating effect of reinforcing the social disadvantage of Guyanese converts of Amerindian, Chinese, and Portuguese descent. And, intentionally or not, it also lends credence to the frequently voiced claim of Africans and of East Indians that, ultimately, what should be accepted as just criteria for legitimacy must emerge from a struggle between Africans and East Indians because they constitute the majority of the population.

Moreover, differences in their racial identity notwithstanding, Cockalorum informants, whom I asked to comment on the article, suggested that the authors' final reference to Pentecostalism and the "newer churches" as the religions to which the "disenchanted" were turning was simply a "racialist hint" about the "superiority" of African forms of religious expression, because these religious forms belong to Africans. They are African property because the majority of the members are Guyanese of African descent, who can also claim a longer association with such churches, and because the religious practices on which Pentecostalism and the newer churches are based result from their reinterpretations of orthodox Christianity. East Indian informants, thus, concluded that for East Indians to convert to these forms of religious expression would entail submission both to Christianity and to African domination. African informants argued that Pentecostalism in particular is a "Blackman thing," and for that reason East Indians and other ethnics would always shun it.

As for the newer churches, Cockalorums considered only Kali Mai (Mother Kali) worship (to which the authors devoted part of an article in the same series) to have the potential to serve as a "true

Guyanese" religion. This, they insisted, was so because, unlike the other new churches, the Kali Mai sect allowed pujaris to be of any race, class, or gender. They also considered it the only religious form based on a syncretic blend of elements drawn from all the religions represented in Guyana, a blend in which no set of religious contributions dominates either quantitatively or in its significance for the effaciousness of the puja (service). And, of equal importance, Kali Mai services are believed to be open to all who care to participate without any requirement that they reject previous religious affiliations.

Whether Kali Mai worship actually fits these ideals is less important than what these ideals tell us about the features Cockalorums consider essential to a Guyanese religion. Taken together, these characteristics suggest a means of recognizing, and of attempting to transcend, the contradictions and the divisiveness contained in both egalitarian and hierarchical interpretations of the meaning of religious diversity. Even so, Cockalorums show little interest in becoming active participants in the Kali Mai church. Why? Because, they say, Kali Mai, with its focus on the propitiation of spirits through individual possession and animal sacrifice, is "backward and superstitious." Guyanese who openly engage in Kali worship, therefore, risk damaging their status because others then question their educational achievements and intellectual capabilities.

There is more to this status evaluation, however, than the link between spirit worship and backwardness. That the religion is considered to be essentially Guyanese (that is, creole) means that, to be positively valued, it must overcome generally negative (at best ambivalent) valuations of things "creole," "inside," or in the word most often used, doogla. Historically, Europeans and non-Europeans alike valued such things less than those they believed to have been transported or subsequently imported from the "outside" world. Despite the historical coexistence of contradictory and ambivalent valuations, and government-proclaimed efforts to overcome this vestige of "colonial mentality" notwithstanding, the ambivalence toward "things Guyanese" persists. Once something is labeled genuinely Guyanese, its status rank must still be reckoned against that of non-Guyanese counterparts—a process from which religion is not exempt. Consequently, although assessments of Kali Mai worship seem to transcend hierarchical precepts by emphasizing its syncretism (that is, its un-

ranked blend of ethnic group contributions and the equal participation of all ethnically identified persons), such a solution does not
resolve more general problems entailed by the wide acceptance of an
internal hierarchy of "nations" and an external hierarchical order of
national cultures.

In addition, participation in Kali Mai does not fully resolve the
problems caused by the linking of religious affiliation and the presentations of class status. It gets tripped up on the egalitarian precepts
that mediate economic and moral attributes of class position. Hence,
even the "inside" view of Kali Mai as a syncretic blend of Guyanese
religious diversity poses as many problems as it solves for individuals
and their efforts to present class status claims unmarred by their
religious identification. For example, Cockalorums treat mati, whom
they believe to be involved in Kali Mai or in other forms of spirit
worship, as potentially greedy, covetous persons who do not intend
to live well with the people. They say such persons are primarily
concerned with "tying spirits" to themselves or to their households so
that the spirits will "work" for them, thereby allowing them to surpass
mati in material wealth and in psychophysical well-being. Moreover,
some informants claim that the effort to gain the cooperation and
assistance of spirits is an effort to reduce one's need for the human
cooperation and assistance implied by the egalitarian precepts underlying communal morality. Others go further. They suggest that spirit
worshipers are not merely concerned with self-help and with their
own social mobility but also use spirits to bring evil, illness, and
material misfortune on their fellow mati.

Cockalorums' inconclusive valuation of Kali Mai reflects the same
lack of true ideological dominance echoed throughout the general
hegemonic process. That is, their debates about the status implications of religious diversity and affiliation reveal a struggle to establish
legitimate criteria and to limit the range of acceptable interpretations
and practices legitimation of these criteria might engender. Their
ultimate interest is in the implications such criteria and their interpretations have for sociocultural and political integration. Nonetheless, if evaluations of religious diversity result in neither a stable rank
order of religions nor an unranked continuum, this does not suggest
that individuals can ignore the consequences of these evaluations as
they aim to represent their ethnic group's rank and their own class
status. Christianity, as one element of or general gloss for Anglo-

European hegemony, remains the ghostly[3] standard around which the production of evaluative criteria and the assessment of their meaning for both individual class-status claims and ethnic-group rank claims are oriented.

Thus, it is not insignificant that the aforementioned series of articles on forms of religion in Guyana begins with Christianity and that four of the eight articles are devoted to different Christian denominations. The series concludes with an article combining brief comments on Kali Mai, the Unity School of Christian Mission, the Guyana Apostolic Mystical Council (Jordanites), and the House of Israel, founded by Black American fugitive David Hill. These alternatives or "other faiths," as the authors refer to them, have not, unlike Christianity, provided the foundation for normal society. According to the authors:

Stories are still told today of persons of other faiths being require[d] to convert to Christianity so as to qualify for certain jobs.

Such legacies of the colonial past have tended to reduce the attractiveness of Christianity in independent, republican Guyana, and have played a key role in the growth of several Pentecostal groups in the country, but it is a fact that Christianity played an important role in laying the foundation for a normal society. Like all great faiths, Christianity may have its bad points, but it certainly also has its good points. (Wilkinson and Monar 1980c: 7)

A central implication of the inconclusive evaluation of other faiths or of local unorthodox forms of Christianity relative to orthodox colonial forms of Christianity is that all Guyanese are caught in a double bind. On the one hand, should someone affiliated with a non-Christian religion choose to exclude from his or her public rituals (for instance, a wedding) actions and objects associated with Christianity, he runs the risk of being labeled one who lacks either taste and manners or the economic means to provide a middle- or upper-class performance. On the other hand, should such a person choose to integrate certain actions and objects associated with Christianity, but also assimilated to English culture, in representations of his middle- or upper-class status, he may be accused of conceding the inferiority of his own religion/ethnic group and, hence, be charged with "aping betters" or with "putting on airs." In either case an individual's racial, cultural, and religious identity are intricately, though inconclusively, implicated in evaluations of his class-status claims.

To flesh out further the ideological and practical consequences of attitudes toward religious diversity, we shall now consider in greater detail intraethnic attitudes toward the religious diversity characterizing the East Indian ethnic group.

Intraethnic Status and Religious Diversity

The major religious division among East Indian non-Christians in Guyana is that between Hinduism and Islam. This division, and its symbolic implications for the legitimation of status differentiation, predates both faiths' experience of British religious colonialism in Guiana and on the subcontinent. Already centuries old when the British began to consolidate and institutionalize their politicoeconomic domination of the subcontinent, the Muslim-Hindu encounter was then, in complex ways, subordinated to that broader political process. And, by the time of the mutiny of 1847 in India, treated by some scholars (see Ahmad 1964) as a turning point in Muslim efforts to expel rather than to submit to the encroaching British domination of the subcontinent, indentured Hindus and Muslims in Guiana already had experienced nearly two decades of accommodating to one another and to British politicoreligious dominance.

As noted at the beginning of this chapter, in Guiana religious practices, interreligious hostilities, and modes of interaction that the two groups had developed in India underwent considerable alteration as a result of the particular structure of the plantation labor process. Although a comparison of the Muslim-Hindu confrontation with British domination in India to that in Guiana would be instructive, such an undertaking is clearly beyond the scope of this work. Here, our exploration is limited to showing how the Hindu-Muslim encounter in Cockalorum is affected by East Indians' general efforts to come to terms with the partly contradictory, partly complementary precepts of the ideological field in which Muslims and Hindus confronted one another in colonial Guiana and in which they continue to operate in contemporary Guyana.

Guyanese Muslims and Hindus interpret religious differences in both egalitarian and hierarchical terms. At times Muslims in Cockalorum and the broader East Indian Muslim community order religions hierarchically, considering Islam superior to all others. On these occasions they argue that Islam teaches them that other religious forms, especially Hinduism and Christianity, are backward misapprehensions of true religiousness. Christianity is a false faith because it misapprehends and overrates the importance of Jesus Christ, one of many early prophets to receive religious messages that would find their final form in Islam. Hinduism, especially Sanatan Dharma, is not only a false faith but also a contemptible one, because it legitimates the worship of idols, physical representations or manifestations (dewas/deotas) of the Supreme Deity. These Muslim informants consider idolatry the lowest, most backward form of religious expression and, therefore, because Sanatan Dharma Hinduism is more closely associated with idolatry than are Arya Samaj Hinduism (a reformist sect) and Christianity, they place Sanatan Dharma Hinduism on the lowest rung of the religious hierarchy. Moreover, as with ethnic culture in general, the religion's place in the hierarchy is assumed to provide evidence of the innate intellectual inferiority of its adherents.

At other times these same Muslims join other Muslims, Hindus, and East Indian Christians in arguing for the equality of all "East Indian religions" relative to one another and to Christianity. From this egalitarian standpoint, religious differences within the East Indian ethnic group constitute the group's contributions to Guiana's initial religious composition. As such, the various forms of East Indian religion are equally valid paths to salvation—the alternative ways of being Indian that Rauf's informants stressed. This egalitarian position is encouraged both by economic interdependence and by a fear of African domination, which East Indians expect will carry in its wake a resubordination to Christianity.

Yet, although the East Indians' concern with intraethnic economic and political cooperation and with the threat of African/Christian domination encourages egalitarian interpretations of their own religious differences, the threat of African/Christian domination also encourages hierarchical interpretations of these same differences. To claim top rank in a hierarchy of ethnic groups ideologically, East Indians must present their rank claims in terms that are difficult for Africans/Christians to refute. All forms of religious expression associated with East Indianness are not equally useful toward this end. If East Indians were to be identified most closely with Sanatan Dharma Hinduism, given its links to idolatry, caste distinctions, and other forms of putative backwardness, as an ethnic group they would find it difficult to claim cultural and intellectual superiority. If the group were identified with Islam, the predictable African counterclaim to Islam would undermine any claim to exclusive ownership and, hence, to cultural and intellectual superiority.

The egalitarian emphasis on all forms of Hinduism and Islam as "Indian religions" and as alternative paths to salvation is, therefore, also combined with a hierarchical emphasis on determining which is the *most Indian* or the best qualified to represent the general status of *Indianness* in postindependence Guyana. These are the grounds on which reformist Arya Samaji claim superiority for their sect. They argue that in addition to having eradicated the corrupting Brahmanical influences on Sanatan Dharma, as an indigenous Indian religion (unlike Islam, which was a foreign introduction to India), Arya Samaj Hinduism places East Indianness in the best light vis-à-vis the issue of African/Christian domination.

The Sanatan Dharma charge of simple self-interest notwithstanding, the Arya Samaj movement in Guiana, like its founding in India, was intricately linked to efforts to raise the status of Hindus and Hinduism relative to other religious groups. In postindependence Guyana adherents of this reformist sect remain concerned to remove from Hinduism practices that they regard as religiously illegitimate and that they consider to be fostering backward superstitions, unnecessary intrareligious inequalities among social groups (for example, vaguely recognized caste distinctions), the degradation of male-female relations, and, above all, the status deprecation of the East Indians. They maintain that neither caste divisions nor the dominance of "born" Brahmans in religious matters has Vedic legitimacy (see note 3, Chapter 3). Brahmanism is, in their view, a matter of individual piety in this life, so that individuals, male or female, who conduct themselves piously can become Brahman and can perform those rituals requiring a religious specialist.

Despite Arya Samaji arguments that their beliefs establish a more ethnically competitive position, in Cockalorum neither the need for intraethnic solidarity and economic cooperation nor the difficulties in sustaining East Indian claims to cultural and intellectual superiority have overcome Muslim and Sanatan Dharma concerns that they will manage to stave off African/Christian domination only to succumb to the Arya Samaj. Both Muslims and Sanatan Dharma East Indians charge followers of Arya Samaj with being Christians in East Indian garb, interested less in East Indian welfare than in their own social aggrandizement and economic advantage.

The Arya Samaji counter by charging Sanatan Dharma, especially Brahmans, with "holding the race back" with their false teachings and their superstitions, and by accusing Muslims of doing the same through their bigoted refusal to intermarry with non-Muslim East Indians unless the latter agree to convert to Islam. Sanatan Dharma Hindus agree with Arya Samaji about Muslims but counter the Arya Samaj charge leveled against Sanatan Dharma by suggesting that Arya Samaji are not "real" East Indians. They are Christians at heart who want the positive benefits of East Indian culture and economic cooperation without "suffering for the race" by exposure to African/Christian discrimination.

In the struggle between Muslims and Hindus, the tacit agreement not to convert each other, noted by Jayawardena, has become a Muslim demand for conversion, voiced as concern for the image of the "race" (that is to say, Indians) in the eyes of the other races and justified by Islamic doctrine. For these reasons, Muslim solidarity occasionally gives way to competing Shi'a, Sunni, and Ahmadi claims that, on the basis of one type of criterion or another, their sect best represents the ethnic group's quest for equality with or superiority to the African/Christian/English conflation.

In the end, interethnic religious differences prove to be neither unranked contributions nor legitimate criteria for a stable rank ordering of ethnic groups and their cultures. And, among East Indians, struggling against the dominance of Christianity still largely taken for granted by African, Portuguese, and Chinese Guyanese, no one non-Christian religious form is accepted as the one that identifies the ethnic group and that represents its status claim in the interethnic social order. Religions, like the ethnic cultures of which they are part, are sources of status criteria that simultaneously emerge from and further serve the ideological struggle from which Cockalorums construct concomitant egalitarian and hierarchical images of sociocultural and political integration.

This brings us to the question to be addressed in the final section of this chapter: Among Cockalorum East Indians, what are the general implications and consequences of all this ideological struggle for the presentation of interpersonal and group status claims through the construction and performance of rituals—viewed as the ideologically central material Cockalorums use to distinguish cultures?

Religion, Status, and the Ghost of Hegemonic Dominance

All public performances in Guyana are occasions for the display of the racial, religious, and class dimensions of an individual's identity, his moral worth (that is, face and name), and associated status claims. During such performances potential conflicts between symbolic representations of different dimensions of identity abound, because (1) cultural elements are linked stereotypically to particular ethnic, religious, and class groupings, and (2) participants and members of the audience alike evaluate the prestige of available cultural elements in terms of their overall assessment of different groups' rank in a national sociocultural hierarchy, and (3) the variety of cultural materials from which such performances can be fashioned is, therefore, intricately bound up with intergroup and intragroup status competition. In turn, individuals' judgments about what counts as a status symbol and how symbols will be evaluated are shaped by their understanding of and interest in that competition.

In a newspaper article entitled "Indo-Guyanese Death Rites," followed by the boldface caption "Ceremonies Too Extravagant," Rooplall Monar examined some of the effects of status competition on the form and content of Guyanese Muslim and Hindu burial rites. A Muslim religious leader interviewed by Monar described religiously appropriate Muslim death rites as simple affairs. The corpse should be clad in unsewn pieces of white cloth, covered with another sheet of white cloth, and placed on a "charpai" (a simple wooden platform). Without further adornment, the body should be carried (by close male relatives) to the burial ground, where it is interred, with a minimum of ritual activity and no crying or wailing. Instead, however, the religious leader reported that Guyanese Muslims favor the "taboo" practice of "shrouding the body in expensive clothes, placed in an expensive coffin." Monar's informant explains these practices in the following manner: "But most [Guyanese] Muslims tend to conduct their burial and after-rites services in extravagance to gain prestige by the community, without knowing that these make it harder for the deceased in its after-life . . . and charity and almsgiving to the needy convey blessings to the deceased, but inviting people on fixed days as [Guyanese] Muslims do on the 3rd, 40th, or the death anniversary for feast-giving is non-Islamic and earns no blessing for anyone" (Monar 1980:10).

Muslims interviewed in Cockalorum recognized the contradiction between their practices and "propa" ritual, but they considered such breaches of religious dogma essential to the maintenance of their face and name, as well as to the competitive status of "Muslim culture" among East Indians. The problem, they say, results from Christian and Hindu convictions that "true" Muslim practices lack "sweetness" (that is, color and entertainment value). To contravene this negative assessment of Muslim culture, Muslims must spend money and put on a good show to prove, in other words, that Muslims are capable of "makin' good services."

Feastings and anniversary celebrations allow Muslims to participate in the exchange of generosity essential to egalitarian concepts of living well with people. As with other Cockalorums, the substance and the extent of extravagant displays by individual Muslims are in part determined by what counts as high-status goods and activities for the social category they wish to impress. Yet, even if a Muslim's only goal is to impress other Muslims with his piety, he cannot afford to limit his ritual presentation to what is religiously appropriate if what is religiously appropriate is read, symbolically and economically, only as a presentation of poverty. Moreover, such a limited aim is rare, because a Muslim also must attend to the status of his ethnic identity and to his own moral and class positions in the community. As we shall see, these status claims cannot be symbolically represented within religious boundaries.

In the case of death rites, if a Muslim's or a Hindu's primary status concern is to underscore the status equality or superiority of the East Indian ethnic group, he is likely to adorn the corpse in the most expensive and religiously appropriate "Indian style" garment he can acquire, preferably an imported one. If, however, the bereaved opts for the representation of class position over either ethnic (that is, Indianness) or religious (that is, Islam or Hinduism) ideological resistance, he is more likely to dress the corpse in an "English-style suit," or in a "creole shirt-jack." Keep in mind, though, that although such a symbolic cut is possible, it is never clean; it always has its ragged edges, which, like a hangnail, are indiscriminate in what they snare. Such a symbolic cut provides others with an indeterminate range of possible and reasonable interpretations.

In short, although at any given moment a person may be more interested in one particular dimension of status presentation, his choice will, nonetheless, have simultaneous implications for the unstressed dimensions. Recall our discussion of interpretations of greed and generosity in assessments of who lives well with people. Just as covering goods transported in public was interpreted both as an egalitarian desire not to flaunt good fortune and as a hierarchical desire to get ahead by greedily hiding one's goods from others who might ask one to share, so, too, an East Indian's emphasis on class status presentation through English/Christian status symbols may be seen both as an individual East Indian's effort to represent his own class status and as his general admission of East Indian cultural inferiority or the inferiority of the particular non-Christian religion he professes. Such presentations are not subject to compartmentalized interpretations; their consequences always ramify across all dimensions of interpersonal and group status.

One must also bear in mind that different religions hold different potentials for status elaboration within the bounds of religious appropriateness. As noted earlier, in this regard the simplicity of Muslim rituals places Muslims at a disadvantage. Hindu rituals, by contrast (sectarian differences notwithstanding) provide ample opportunity for an elaborate display of wealth and generosity. Were the status concerns of a Hindu Guyanese limited to rank within the East Indian ethnic group, he might exclude a good many elements identified with other religious and ethnic groups. As with Muslims, however, this is seldom the case, because individual Hindus also must attend to their class status, which is an interethnic matter. Consequently, from Monar's Hindu informant (a pandit or ritual specialist), we hear an echo of the Muslim religious leaders' complaints: "all the fancy clothes, coffin, tomb and public feasting we see today are contrary to Hindu *dharma*, and were never emphasized by the immigrants" (Monar 1980:10).

In addition to features noted by this pandit, Cockalorum Hindus, in competition with African Christians who, they say, really know how to bury their dead, now hold wakes. African friends are invited to these, and at two wakes I even observed the host asking his African guests to lead the mourners in singing Christian songs to "enliven" the affair. Some Arya Samaj Hindus have organized a band and singing group that, for a small fee, performs at any East Indian wake. When I interviewed the founder of this group, he explained that it served to "liven up" East Indians' wakes and, thereby, to decrease their "jealousy" of African wakes. We must consider that these appropria-

222 Ethnicity, Class, and Cultural Production

tions, transformations, and inventions also coincide with their opposite: efforts to "traditionalize" Hindu rites by introducing practices that are consistent with religious dogma but that were not engaged in by the early immigrants. For example, cremation, considered the most appropriate way to dispose of a Hindu corpse, was not carried out in Guiana until the late 1950s during the general resurgence of Indian traditionalism discussed in Chapter 6.

Given the problems and the prospects thus far noted, one might assume that constructing an elaborate, lively performance within the bounds of one's own religious identity ensures acceptance of that identity claim and garners status points for the religious group. That assumption does not always hold. Let us consider in this regard problems confronted by Madrassi (South Indian) Hindus in Guyana.

East Indian Hindus who identify themselves as descendants of North Indian immigrants take Madrassi Hindus to be their inferiors. This North-South status division had its roots in India; among Cockalorum Hindus, however, it has been assimilated to a race/color, African/East Indian pattern of differentiation and status reckoning (see Chapter 2). Contending that all Madrassi descendants are darker than all North Indian descendants, Cockalorum Hindus who claim North Indian ancestry attribute the color difference to contemporary "race mixing," alleging that most Madrassi have more African than Indian blood, which explains why they are dark and why they are culturally and intellectually inferior. This rationale has a fringe benefit: excluding the darkest members of the East Indian group enables these "north Indians" to reduce the physiognomic distance between themselves and the high-status Europeans, and, thus, to open another potential route to the status position the latter once occupied.

It also has a cost—the loss of ritual features that are high in their potential for elaboration and sanctioned by Hindu dogma but close in style to spiritualist practices attributed to West African sources. Consequently, even though the pandit interviewed by Monar claimed that the dancing and rejoicing in which Guyanese Madrassi Hindus now engage are features of death rites sanctioned by Hindu scripture, Monar's conclusion echoes the opinion of Cockalorum "North Indians": "A survey shows that the Madrassi still practices aspects of these death rites in Guyana, but it is termed 'jumbieish' by others" (Monar 1980:10). Jumbie is a word of West African origin meaning "spirit of the recently deceased." By invoking it here, however, Monar provides a negative assessment of the practice, at the same time symbolically linking the Madrassi Hindus to alleged African racial and cultural inferiority.

To summarize the situation of East Indian adherents of the various non-Christian religions: First, they confront and reproduce a general indeterminacy of intraethnic religious ranking as they struggle to avoid intraethnic religious domination and to represent the East Indian group in the most advantageous cultural light in their competition with other Guyanese ethnic groups. Second, the rituals that are appropriate to the different religions and that provide material to conduct an ideological struggle have different potentials for the elaboration and the presentation of high interpersonal and intergroup status claims. Third, adherents of one religion who adopt ritual features and symbols "belonging" to another, either to borrow their elaboration potential or to construct high-class representations in another manner, simultaneously undermine their own religious identity and the status claims of their ethnic group. And finally, the use by some East Indians of ritual features that are sanctioned by their own religion but that resemble features linked to African (non-Christian) religious tradition may undermine rather than enhance the prestige of their religious identity and its potential for conveying high ethnic group status.

Now let us add to this situation sources of individual status variation. That is to say, the predicament in which individuals find themselves with respect to others' evaluations of the dimensions of their identity—ethnic, religious, class, and moral—within a particular community at a given time. We shall refer to this simply as a status predicament. First, individuals who mount public performances differ with respect to the assessed quality of their personal (face) and family (name) reputations (see Chapter 4). They also vary in the type of locality with which others associate them, and according to which urban areas and city folk are granted higher status than are rural areas and country folk. Within the rural area, if everything else is held constant, different types of settlements imply different relative statuses for their residents. In descending, though not uncontested, rank order, the rural hierarchy moves from village residents at the top to freeholders, estate dwellers, squatters, and finally down to residents of housing schemes. Moreover, within a village or a freehold settlement, watersiders are generally accorded higher status than backdammers (see Chapter 3). And finally, individual Guyanese differ in their material achievements and, of equal importance, in their ability to convince others that their apparent material worth is accurate (see Chapter 3).

Obviously, the content and the elaborateness of any ritual will be affected by how much money a person and his family members can muster to spend, but the above noted aspects of individual status predicaments influence the amount of effort they will put into gathering funds and material, how they spend those funds in constructing the performance, and how, ultimately, others will judge these efforts and expenditures. In the end, it is not a matter that can be judged simply in terms of relative elaborateness and expense or merely as a relative degree of ethnic/religious purity. One must take a microscopic look at the actual character of a sponsor's moral, class, and ethnic identity and the associated status claims and insecurities. What are his strengths and weaknesses, and how does he set about confronting these in relation to the general problem of ethnic group rank and religious competition?

The Ghost Is an Ever-Present Presence

Ritual performances, with their interethnic and intraethnic markings, become part of an ideological struggle through which Cockalorums attempt to establish, to delimit, and to legitimate criteria for the evaluation of different dimensions of their personal and group identity. This struggle contains and is shaped by their understandings of the past Anglo-European hegemony. It also contains and is shaped by conceptions and stereotypes they developed both during and after their initial encounter with one another as subordinates in colonial Guiana. And, though it is difficult to document precolonial factors, we must, nonetheless, keep in mind that certain features of this ideological struggle also predate the Guianese colonial experience. The very formation of the ethnic categories "African" and "East Indian" represents a transformation of previous identities and classificatory distinctions based on factors such as religion, language, place of birth, and other social characteristics that existed among the enslaved and indentured immigrants as they entered Guiana. Further, as the Hindu-Muslim, North-South Indian distinctions suggest, these factors have not lost their ideological force. Yet, for Cockalorums, their current meanings also have been assimilated to the different precepts of the ideological field in which they now operate and they must, therefore, be understood in those terms.

Contemporary interpretations, whether viewed as ideological resistance of as "colonial mentality," continue to be part of a debate fashioned in an ideological field where neither hierarchical nor egalitarian precepts legitimately dominate conceptions of the sociocultural and political order. Consequently, individual Cockalorums acting in any social domain are cognizant of the different ideological interpretations that are simultaneously possible. In public as well as in private domains, their conduct is evaluated in terms of these contradictory, competing egalitarian and hierarchical ideological precepts. Aware of the simultaneous relevance of these precepts, Cockalorums have developed what they refer to as "customary" ways of trying to mediate the contradictory or negative implications of ethnically marked cultural elements while taking advantage of their positive implications.

In this task, as members of particular racial, ethnic, or religious groups, Cockalorums confront different disadvantages with respect to hierarchical precepts and the range of criteria these make available for rank ordering social categories. Their public actions recognize the difficulties posed by their particular vantage points in the politics of cultural struggle. And most important, the symbolic representations of status these actions reveal are displayed through objects and symbols, the prestige and overall meanings of which remain indeterminate and, as such, fundamentally illegitimate.

With these difficulties in mind, we are now in a position to provide a microscopic glimpse of three wedding rituals. Each example is intended to pull us deeper into the culture of domination established under Anglo-European hegemony and the ghostly constraints this form of domination now imposes on Guyanese identity formation and on their efforts to reconceptualize the Guyanese sociocultural and political order.

9

"Bamboo"
Weddings and
the Ghost
of Hegemonic
Dominance

Cockalorum East Indians desire a "real" (that is to say, ethnically pure) cultural performance, but their desire to communicate personal prestige claims and symbols of group status ranking makes it, in effect, impossible for them to exclude all cultural elements "belonging" to other traditions and groups. For an anthropological analysis of any particular performance this means that the analyst must ask what kinds of syncretisms occur and how they relate to participants' efforts to represent symbolically different types of status claims. The analyst must also examine how Guyanese of different ethnic, class, and religious identities who observe these performances react to their constituent parts.

Case I: Christianity, Hinduism, and Communal
Morality in Presentations of Class Status

The first case we will consider is the wedding of a Sanatan Dharma Hindu woman in her early twenties to a fellow teacher around the same age whom she had met while teaching in Georgetown.[1] The decision to marry was not made by the parents, as is still the case for many East Indian marriages, but by the young people themselves. Although the couple shared the same occupation, according to community rumors the groom's family was slightly wealthier than the bride's. The bride's family resided in the backdam area of Entre Facade. Although this locality was more prestigious than other types of rural localities, its status was lower than that of the urban area from which the groom hailed. No specific charges were made against either the bride's or the groom's personal reputation; however, it was rumored that the groom's family was less than pleased with the match. Even some of the bride's close relatives and neighbors insinuated that the groom's parents had acceded to his wishes with less enthusiasm about the marriage than the bride's family.

In addition to the status questions raised by the opposition between urban and rural, and the possible class disjunction based on assumed differences in the wealth of the two households, within the broader community evaluations of the bride's father's personal reputation also influenced the ultimate content of the wedding ritual. The fact that the bride's father, whom we will refer to as J., claimed the moral status of a pious practicing pandit exposed him to questions about the validity of this claim and about its implications for his own and his household's general status. Even among Sanatan Dharma Hindus, Brahmans who are practicing pandits are suspected of exploiting religion for economic gain. The expression "pandits are bandits," frequently voiced by Arya Samaji and the most impoverished Sanatani in Cockalorum, summed up their belief that most pandits are greedy opportunists who falsely claim a Brahman identity and assume the duties of pandit in order to fleece their fellow Hindus. Because of this widely accepted belief, J.'s pandit role did as much to undermine as it did to substantiate any claims to a high status he made for himself and his household. Nonetheless, in the most general terms J. claims for himself and his household a small big man status, that is to say, middle class, defined as higher than the average household in the community.

J. now devotes the lion's share of his time to pandit duties within the community and the rural East Coast Demerara region, while other members of the household run a small grocery shop, take care of farming and petty marketing chores, or work as wage laborers. This variety of income sources gives the family a stable economic base, which has made it possible for the family to build and maintain well a large home and to engage in other forms of behavior associated with middle-class status.

Despite his "good fortune," J. claims for himself and his household the moral status of being among those who live well with the people. In interviews, both he and his wife stressed that as a young couple they had worked very hard, sacrificing for their children and treating mati (kin and neighbors) fairly. Despite rumors to the contrary, they continued to interact with and treat mati fairly. In their own terms, then, they identified their household with what they took to be one of the highest strata of Guyanese society: hard-working, middle-class East Indians who, like them, were maintaining their cultural and religious tradition and were living well with mati and "countryman."

The general rumor mill presented quite a different picture of J.'s personal reputation and Brahman identity as well as of his household's name and class status. According to rumors, J. had not made much of an issue of his Brahman identity until after his marriage to a Brahman, his acquisition of a comfortable material existence, and the birth of sons to assist with agricultural chores. He then began to devote more of his time to religious studies, eventually becoming a practicing pandit. Informants agreed that on the surface he appeared to be a respected member of the regional Hindu elite.

Beneath the surface, however, his status claims were questioned. Informants scrutinized his material accomplishments and his moral conduct and, on the basis of their evaluations, dismissed his claim to middle-class status. They also appraised his religious conduct and knowledge of Hinduism and thereupon rejected his claim to high-caste Brahman status. In short, detractors found interethnic and intra-ethnic grounds on which to question all dimensions of his status and identity claims. Intraethnically, some informants simply said that all caste identity claims in Guyana were invalid, whereas others, focusing on J., argued either that he had acquired his wealth immorally and was therefore unfit to be a Brahman despite his current efforts to live a pious life, or that he lacked adequate knowledge of Hindu religious tradition. The latter detractors were always ready with an example of a gross error they claimed to have observed or to have heard that he committed while performing one religious service or another.

Interethnically, the class status of J. and his household was questioned on still other grounds. From the standpoint of egalitarian precepts of communal morality, some who spoke negatively of J. argued that he had cheated his deceased brother and that he would be worth much less were he ever to compensate fairly his brother's family. As a feature of his overall status, J.'s material worth was, thus, kept in limbo by his failure to confront and to resolve the communal attribution of immorality attached to the way he had acquired it. Still other critics contended that the quality of his extra-community social connections was such that, appearance to the contrary notwithstanding, J. could not interact as an equal among big people of the regional Hindu community (especially its urban members). As the wedding day approached, this last conclusion was frequently voiced by those who knew that the groom was a member of a middle-class urban Sanatan Dharma family.

J. and his family recognized the various contentions surrounding their identity as Brahmans and their status as big people. Like others whose statuses and identities are questioned, publicly they dismissed negative assessments as "sheer jealousy." Nonetheless, behind closed doors the pandit and his wife spoke of their concern not to "shame" themselves before the groom's relatives and the local community. They wanted to provide a ceremony befiting a pious Brahman and a middle-class Guyanese. It was to be a "propa [proper] bamboo wedding,"[2] with proper connoting both correct form and a suitable standard of excellence. Indeed, earlier my informants had insisted that this type of wedding—one in which all primary parties claimed a Brahman Hindu identity—would be a "real" Hindu wedding as opposed to a "mix-up-mix-up" affair, which was the way they characterized non-Brahman weddings.

In the months before the event J.'s preparations were carefully watched by friends and detractors alike. Questions were raised and comments made about the appropriateness of his actions from the perspective of both his Brahman identity and his class position. Was he meeting all the formal prenuptial requirements for the most orthodox Hindu wedding? Could he afford the necessary items, and did he have the social connections essential to acquiring the quantities of food and other materials he would need for a wedding large and elaborate enough to substantiate his class status claims? How long was it taking him to amass a particular item—especially one in short supply—and what did that say about the quality of his "lines" (social connections)? Many goods are in chronic short supply, and obtaining these often depends on the range of ties one has with persons who can cut red tape or can reserve items for particular customers. Hence, attention to the amount of time one takes to acquire such goods is often taken to indicate how well connected an individual is with those of higher status who either control these goods or who have greater access to persons who do control them (see Chapter 3).

The pandit and his family responded to these threats to their status claims by carefully planning for the big event. In addition to the usual preparations around the house and the yard, J. hired the services of a respected older pandit from Berbice, a county whose population Demeraran East Indians credit with being more "traditional" than themselves and other Guyanese East Indians. J. planned for a "Janeo" (investiture of the sacred thread for Brahman males) to be conducted for his unmarried sons, and for a "Satnaran Katha" (sacred scripture reading). These events were held on Sunday, the day of the main ceremonial activities, before the arrival of the groom and his party. The Janeo is allegedly performed only for Brahmans; therefore it underscored the Brahmanness of the occasion. For the wedding and the ritual activities preceding it, all the immediate family members took care to dress in appropriate Hindu Indian-style clothing (dhoti and sari). In short, much effort was expended and care taken to set the stage for and to carry out a proper Brahman Hindu ceremony.

At the same time J. and his family engaged in equally deliberate actions intended to express the class identity of the household as well as J.'s high personal prestige. As a result, compromises between class-related and Sanatan Dharma Hindu–related traditions and status symbols were constant throughout the event and were reflected in many of its syncretic features. Although a complete description of the full range of activities taking place in even the final three days of this type of wedding would be unnecessarily long, several examples drawn from the wedding will illustrate why these compromises led to the inclusion of non-Hindu ritual features and the relation of these choices to the impact hegemonic process has on cultural constructions.

Before the more formal features of the wedding ritual began, community members scrutinized the household from a distance. Once under way, some features of the ritual provided excellent opportunities for residents, even those not invited, to move in for a closer look. The Friday night activities were one instance, because, though the major participants were Sanatan Dharma Hindus, the actions took place on the public pathways, and non-Hindus, especially African women, teenagers, and children, came out to watch. On that Friday night, the first of two nights and three days of activity, a "dig dutty" service (Hindu Mati Kore puja) was conducted to worship Mother Earth and to ward off the evil spirits that are brought forth by the jealousy and the covetousness of community members.

Participation in this service is usually restricted to women. It is conducted alongside one of the many drainage ditches that criss-cross the community. To the Indian-style beat of a female drummer, the women march to this waterside location, where they perform a brief service. The service is followed by a period of dancing during which the women display, competitively, their ability to dance "Indian style."

At the marriage of Pandit J.'s daughter, this routine was disrupted by the presence of a male East Indian Christian hired by J. to drum for the wedding and the dig dutty. The drummer's gender, though atypical, was less the problem than his disdain for what he several times openly referred to as "women's foolishness," thereby ridiculing the ritual's opening public salvo. In addition, he was known for his ability to "beat drum African style," which he insisted on doing even though several of the women asked him to "beat Indian." When I asked some of the women what they thought of his participation and his attitude, among themselves they agreed that he was "boderation" (a nuisance) and lacked "manners." Yet, they also added that they thought it was good to have him perform, because (1) not everyone could afford such a well-known drummer, and (2) it would show Africans that an East Indian could learn a style of drumming that Africans claim as part of their cultural heritage.

With respect to the second reason, it was not simply that he could drum African style; they believed he was so talented that he could teach Africans a thing or two about beating drums. The issue of teaching takes on a special importance because, as noted in Chapter 6, to raise their status rank Africans claim to have taught the East Indian everything of value he knows. In sum, the response of these women suggests that the drummer's presence enhanced J.'s personal prestige and family status, and it bolstered the status of the East Indian group relative to the African group sufficiently to warrant tolerating the resulting breach of Hindu tradition. In essence, to my informants the drummer's presence was less a breach of Hindu tradition than a symbol of family wealth and East Indian talent.

A similar attitude toward an emphasis on the symbolic representation of interpersonal class status and interethnic group rank over religious traditional form was evident in the family's choice of seating for high-status guests. At Guyanese weddings of the type J. aimed to sponsor, it is expected that guests will be seated on the ground, which is covered with flour sacks or sheets.[3] It is considered inauspicious by

Hindus for guests to be seated higher than the bride and groom. The bride and groom are seated on "hasans" (very low stools); thus, only the ground is lower. Despite this religious stricture, J. and his wife provided chairs for some of the urban guests they considered to be persons of high status, "too big" to sit on the ground. These guests, some of them Brahman Sanatan Dharma, were also offered plates and spoons in place of the "traditional" lily leaf, a symbol of Latchmi and of the desire for control over and prudence in financial matters—a theme reiterated for the young couple's benefit throughout the ritual.

When I asked several Sanatan Dharma informants why these guests, especially those claiming Brahman identity, were offered and accepted these "nontraditional" items, they responded, in essence, that it was better to risk the vague consequences of inauspiciousness than to create the more definite opportunity for high-status guests to label the family "backward" or too poor to provide proper (in class terms) seats and eating utensils. In short, although J. had defined the ritual occasion as a "propa bamboo wedding" and had included major features appropriate to that form and to his Brahman identity, and had hired an expert to conduct the ceremony, he and his guests also understood that the occasion, and, as a consequence, his household's class status, would be judged in terms of the presence or absence of cultural elements that historically were features of English culture. As such, they were also the symbols of middle- and upper-class status, for which objects of similar function drawn from East Indian culture could not be used to the same effect. A hasan is a seat, but it is not a chair.

The problem of symbolically representing class status is not limited to the question of which material objects are suitable symbols. Actions are also ethnically marked and, hence, more or less capable of symbolically representing middle- or upper-classness. The same issue arose with regard to the timing of the bride's departure from her parents' home after the conclusion of Sunday's formal wedding activities. In Hindu religious terms, it is considered "shameful" for a Hindu bride to appear eager to leave her parents' home. To avoid this shame, there is usually a lengthy delay before the bride is dressed and the announcement is made that she is ready to depart.

At several weddings I observed, although the bride dressed fairly quickly, the women who attended her waited well over an hour before announcing her departure. Whereas the women dressing J.'s daughter did not want her to appear too eager, they were also concerned that she should not delay so long as to give the groom and other urban middle-class guests the impression that the wedding was being conducted on "coolie time," that is, in a tardy and disorganized fashion. The result was that, although they did not appear rushed in dressing the bride, less than one-half hour elapsed between the time she was dressed and the announcement that she would be leaving. It was better to risk a little "shame" than to stand accused of the backwardness associated with a lack of promptness and the appearance of disorganization, each stereotypically marked as coolie/East Indian/lower class.

Both the selection of ritual features and the participants' interpretation of them show a concern for how best to represent class status under conditions where, even in intraethnic communication, non-Christian ethnic and religious status symbols remain less convincing means of expressing middle- and upper-class status than English/Christian objects, actions, and symbols. Thus, attempts are made to dismantle the hegemonic dominance of Englishness, but the incompleteness of these efforts and the ideological constraints that this type of dominance places on local expressions of class status and on ethnic and religious identity still serve to inspire syncretic ritual performances.

As the wedding ritual draws to a close, the bride's departure, more perhaps than any event in the ritual, provides an excellent opportunity for the family to communicate, interethnically, status messages about its household, religion, and ethnic group. At this time the performance takes place on an interethnic, interfaith stage as uninvited Christians and other non-Hindus come out of their houses, joining Hindus, to stand along the paths near the wedding house to "catch a look" at the bride. At this point and long afterward, these uninvited, though not unexpected, observers discuss among themselves the quality of the bride's attire and her general appearance and comportment. The non-Hindus among these economically, racially, and religiously differentiated uninvited observers consider a style of dress ranked high among Hindus (for instance, an expensive sari) to be not particularly prestigious as a status symbol. They are likely to regard a sari simply as a "coolie thing" of no great prestige. Even in the context of a Hindu wedding, for example, Muslims consider the sari to be the dress of "backward idol worshipers."

234 Ethnicity, Class, and Cultural Production

One can thus easily grasp why it is "customary" for a Hindu bride to exchange the sari she has worn up to the point of her public departure from her parents' house for a Christian/English-style white wedding gown. Even though Cockalorum Hindus symbolically associate white with death and mourning, wearing this garment allows non-Christian East Indians to say, in effect and at the same time, that, although they choose to continue East Indian religious tradition by performing a "bamboo wedding," they can also afford this symbol of affluence and middle-class status.

It is not from a lack of knowledge that they exchange the sari for this type of wedding gown rather than for one associated stereotypically with, say, Amerindians in Guyana. Instead, as noted in Chapter 7 and by Drummond (1980:365) as well, "things Amerindian" are likely to be included only after they have been appropriated—disconnected from their ethnic source—and transformed to accepted (English) elements of a "creole culture." That such a transformation occurs is related to the hegemonic process through which ethnic contributions are evaluated and ranked relative to one another and to the previously dominant "things English." To the extent that the cultural roots of an Amerindian object or action can be severed, those using the object or engaging in the action can avoid a decrease in status; but even then, things Amerindian are not as effective for demonstrating middle-class status as are things English/Christian.

Yet, if exchanging the sari for the white wedding gown allows for the expression of middle-class status but reinforces the hegemony of "things English/Christian," not making the exchange allows for ideological resistance and the assertion of the equality or even superiority of "things Indian" to "things English." It is in this regard that we can most accurately understand J.'s and his wife's conclusions that it was only proper for the daughter of a middle-class Brahman pandit to exchange her ordinary red sari for a more expensive one, but not for a Christian-style wedding gown. In fact, for her departure their daughter donned a gold-threaded red sari imported from India (by way of Toronto, Canada).[4]

Note, however, that the groom, also from a middle-class Brahman family, did not shed his traditional "jarjama" (groom's gown) for an "English-style" business suit. This may well suggest that J., in contrast, was more sensitive about which symbolic representation (class or ethnic/religious identity) to emphasize. For J.'s household, sticking to traditional clothing served to reinforce its Brahman identity and to undermine criticism centered on J.'s alleged lack of religious knowledge. Simultaneously, the choice allowed Hindus who accepted the household's claim to middle-class status to say, as several informants reported to me, that J. could be both middle class and a "real" or "traditional" Hindu. Furthermore, in their judgment the meaning of traditional is limited to a concern with being traditional when it really counts, and when it really counts depends on one's status predicament in the eyes of the community at the time a ritual is performed.

Thus, analyzing the relation of "syncretic" to "traditional" features of a total ritual complex and noting the points during the process when syncretic features are introduced and emphasized gives us a clearer sense of the particulars of the East Indians' ideological struggle to upset the past hegemonic stability of English/Christian cultural dominance. At the same time, we also see how their struggles are fashioned out of the general ideological precepts that delimit how they communicate and represent status ranking in a multiethnic, class-stratified society. Hence, although the particular symbolic manipulations of J.'s household may be understood in relation to his particular status predicament, this should not be taken to mean that his family invented, on the spot, the strategies it used. For such strategies to be effective, other members of the community must already understand certain links between objects and actions and "customary" strategies for presenting personal, ethnic, religious, and class status claims. Only because it has become customary for an East Indian bride to depart in a Christian-style wedding gown as a symbol of her family's affluence can the refusal to do so assume the implications for religious and ethnic group status that Cockalorums now draw from it.

Moreover, as Pandit J.'s concern with the Brahman Sanatan Dharma dimension of his identity and status suggests, in the organization of ritual performances, an individual's class position and his ethnic group's rank claims compete with the representation of intra-ethnic, interfaith, and sectarian claims to status. During major ritual events, broad ethnic stereotypes and solidarities may be dissolved in more particular intraethnic stereotypes linked to religious differences and to adherents' ideas about their relative rank in a religion-based hierarchy.

Let us now look more closely at some of the implications of this intraethnic ideological struggle for the construction of interfaith public events among Cockalorum East Indians. As an ethnographic illustration, we will examine next the marriage of a young lower-class Portuguese–East Indian woman, raised as a nominal Christian, to a Sunni Muslim of approximately the same class. In this case our primary attention is directed to how participants attempted to build into the ritual performance their concerns about ethnic group solidarity in the face of competing claims about the status rank of religious segments.

Case II: Hinduism and Islam in Ethnic Group Rank Presentations

When Mr. G., a Portuguese Catholic, married his daughter to an East Indian Muslim, neither Mr. G. nor the groom's family were considered especially well-to-do. There was little discussion about the moral or material standing of either family—they were "ordinary" people. The groom was from another rural village, and the two were therefore of roughly equal status in terms of locality and economic position. Consequently, most gossip and open discussion centered on Mr. G.'s need to fashion a wedding ritual that would accommodate competing religious identities—Christian, Muslim, and, because of his wife's family, Hindu.

Mr. G.'s daughter, his only child, was the offspring of his marriage to an East Indian Sanatan Dharma. Early in the girl's childhood her mother had died and her mother's sister, an Arya Samaj Hindu, had reared her. This aunt had since migrated abroad and was not available to assist with the wedding. Mr. G. accepted the contemporary Muslim strictures that, for the marriage to occur, the bride had to agree to convert to Islam, receive a new Islamic name, and have the wedding ritual conducted according to "Islamic custom." The groom's family would provide a "maji" (Muslim official) to perform the final features of the service, but Mr. G. was left to handle all other preparations because, as is "traditional" for coastal Guyanese weddings not conducted in church, the ceremony took place at the bride's home.

As a male, Mr. G. knew little about organizing a wedding ritual. Being both Portuguese and a Christian, he knew even less about the particulars of preparing for an Islamic ceremony. For complex reasons related only in part to his ethnic/religious identity, he did not feel free to call on his deceased wife's relatives for assistance. He also had no close Muslim friends in the community to consult about this matter. Instead, he turned to his friend and neighbor, Mrs. R., a Sanatan Dharma Hindu, and asked her if she would preside over preparations for the event. Mrs. R., fond of the girl whose mother had been her friend, reluctantly agreed to take on the task.

She was flustered, however, because she, too, knew little about preparing for an Islamic ceremony. She had never attended one, she claimed, because she believed Muslims "scorned" Hindus and behaved badly toward those who accepted such wedding invitations. Hence, we must recognize that, although she also complained that she did not understand why Muslims always insisted on conversion and on doing everything their way, as her actions during the wedding demonstrate, she in fact understood Muslim insistence to be based on a conviction of superiority to Hindus and her "lack of understanding" was an indirect rejection of their view.

In the end Mrs. R. decided and Mr. G. concurred that it would be best to make the ritual an "Indian thing"—which in this case meant, apart from doing whatever the groom's family considered proper Islamic custom, trying to remove explicitly "Hindu things" and including only those elements others believed to be Indian regardless of religious affiliation. Therefore, the house and the yard were cleaned, but no tent, wedding booth, or nuptial pole was erected, as would have been the case for a Hindu service.

The ceremony was to take place inside the house. The living room was cleared of all furniture, and the bare floor was covered with clean white sheets. It was also decided that, because all Indians "rub dye" (smear the bride's and groom's bodies with a mixture of turmeric and oil), this would be appropriate. The dyeing, which is usually part of particular components of a Hindu wedding ritual, was stripped of most of its Hindu features. On Friday night and again on Sunday morning, Mrs. R. simply seated the bride on a hasan and rubbed her body with dye. Similarly, although gifts are presented to the bride at some point in all Guyanese weddings, because gift-giving is also a feature of all Indian-style services, it was considered Indian enough to be included without contradicting Mrs. R.'s effort to emphasize Indian ethnic solidarity over religious divisiveness and in opposition to English/African/Christian subordination. She rejected, however, the formal mode of presentation characteristic of Hindu Sanatan Dharma or any other identifiable style of Guyanese wedding. Instead, she did what she considered "customary for such a mixed marriage." She passed the word that anyone who wished to show respect for the bride could give a gift to Mr. G. or to herself and it would be given to the bride.

Saturday night, "cook night" for Guyanese weddings in general, also differs in organization from one ethnic/religious setting to the next. Mrs. R. recruited men and women to assist her, as is done for Sanatan Dharma or Arya Samaj cook nights. However, instead of the gender division of labor characteristic of Hindu-style cook nights, which requires that males do the actual cooking, Mrs. R. organized tasks in such a way that females did most of the cooking. She also tried to enhance the Islamic/religious identity of the event by preparing foods for Muslim rather than Hindu tastes. That is, her helpers cooked curried beef and chicken to accompany rice and roti (bread) which, at Hindu weddings, would have been served with vegetable curries and achar (pickled fruits or vegetables). No poultry, fish, or meat, and especially no beef, is served at a Hindu ritual.

Throughout these preparations Mrs. R. complained to Mr. G. about the lackluster nature of the event. It was in her view an event of "poor quality" even for an "ordinary" Guyanese with no pretensions to middle- or upper-class status. It certainly was not what a motherless child and only daughter deserved as a send-off. Nonetheless, within the constraints she felt it necessary to observe, she could not think of any way to "brighten" the affair. She could only hope that the groom and his family would be pleased and that things would get off to a good start for the new couple.

On Sunday the groom and his party arrived very late. By the time they came, the male Hindu guests were drunk and rowdy, more rowdy, it seemed to me, than I had seen them behave at Hindu-Hindu ceremonies. I asked Mrs. R. and Mr. G. about this. They said these men had no respect for Muslim weddings and so they did not feel "shame" in behaving badly. Their assessment seemed consistent with the drunken behavior observed at two other Muslim-Hindu ceremonies. Moreover, the behavior of the male Hindu guests did not improve when the groom and his party arrived, and, with the exception of the maji, the Muslims' behavior was no better than that of the Hindu men. After about fifteen or twenty minutes most of the groom's party not directly involved in the ritual left discourteously for a local rum shop, where they stayed until all formal aspects of the wedding were over.

The rites themselves were a series of material and verbal exchanges between the bride, the groom, and a father-substitute[5] through the medium of the maji. Upon completion of these activities, the maji read several passages from the Koran, then announced that the women should prepare the bride for her departure. Mrs. R. objected, saying it was now time for the guests to "take a little something" (that is, to eat, because hospitality and conviviality are stressed features of most Guyanese social interactions); then she would ready the bride to leave.

Back inside the bedroom with the bride, Mrs. R. complained of the rudeness of the groom's party, first in arriving late and then in what she perceived as their rushing the bride. Recall that the timing of this departure has both religious and class-status implications. In this case Mrs. R. was concerned that the bride not appear eager to leave because of what this might imply about the way she, as a young girl living alone with a widowed father, might have been treated.[6] In addition, Mrs. R. and several other women argued that it would not look good if the bride hastened to leave because it would appear that Hindus were all too eager to marry off their women to Muslims, a concern that gave emphasis to interfaith, intraethnic status ranking. The women all contended that such an impression would only encourage Muslims to be even more "scornful" of Hindus.

Apart from these concerns, Mrs. R. was also troubled about how these Muslims' behavior would reflect on her as the organizer of the affair. Thus, she did not want to allow them to leave without eating well for fear they would later spread gossip about the inadequate hospitality they had received—a local reputation (face/name) issue. She delayed both the dressing of the bride and the serving of food, awaiting the return of the other members of the groom's party from the rum shop.

This delay brought complaints from the inebriated Hindu men, who were hungry and did not much care who knew it. The groom and the few members of his party who were present announced, in very poor taste, that they did not care about the food. They only wanted the women to be quick with the bride because the hour was late and they wanted to be on their way. The implied refusal of hospitality and the open interest in rushing the bride incensed Mrs. R. She and several of the other women complained under their breath about the rudeness of Muslims, especially toward Hindus. In part, they were angry because the Muslims were behaving badly despite the obvious compromise of Hinduism in the preparation of foods to suit Muslim tastes. Mrs. R. reiterated her belief that the groom's party was acting rudely as an expression of their disrespect for Hindu tradition, and that the Hindu men were making matters worse by being equally disrespectful to the Muslims.

For all this, as she dressed the bride, Mrs. R. decided she could only ignore the complaints. In the meantime, several women cleared away the sheets covering the floor, put on music, and began to dance Indian style in the center of the living room. This resulted in the last of the Muslim men moving outside to congregate on the path in front of the house near their cars. The Hindu men and women who came outside stayed in the yard. Shortly afterward, the Muslims who had been at the rum shop returned, and they, too, announced that they were ready to leave. They claimed to be surprised that the affair was not yet over. Mrs. R. did not respond. Instead, she instructed the other women to begin serving the food. Plates and spoons were distributed to all, and, apart from the music and a few drunken outbursts, there was, in Hindu terms at least, an uncharacteristic near-silence as the guests quickly ate their food.

As the guests had their meal, the bride was brought out of the bedroom and onto the front veranda. There, dressed in a Christian-style wedding gown, sewn by Mrs. R., she was seated on a chair. Mrs. R. pinned a $5 bill to the bride's gown (in this community a gesture most typical of English/African weddings). Following her lead, other women and two Hindu men did likewise. Mrs. R. then danced around the bride and was followed by the other women, as some of the Hindu men stood clapping in the yard below the veranda. Without any announcement to the groom, the bride was then led down the steps to the gate, where the groom and his father quickly rushed her into one of the waiting cars. With little further ado, within a few minutes the groom's party was gone.

What are we to make of this sequence of events? First, Mr. G.'s identity as a Portuguese Catholic had no significant impact on decisions about the symbolic content of the wedding or how it was to be conducted. As we will see, even the Christian-style wedding gown, in which the bride departed, was not specifically related to identifying her and her household as Christians. As already argued (see Chapter 6), Cockalorums do not identify Portuguese with any particular cultural inventory. In general, they hold that Portuguese have taken from, rather than contributed anything to, Guyana's cultural diversity. The inaccuracy of this assumption notwithstanding, Mr. G. did not see the problem as one of upholding Portuguese or Christian tradition, but rather as one of alleviating potential conflicts between East Indian Hindu and Muslim traditions.

For the most part, he said, his daughter had been brought up as a Sanatan Dharma until his wife's death, after which her aunt raised the girl as an Arya Samaj. He also noted that, despite his daughter's religious rearing, his own identity as Portuguese–Christian placed his household in, at best, an ambivalent status position relative to his Hindu and Muslim guests. He thought this ambivalent position helped explain the unrestrained behavior of the Hindu men, and he believed they would have behaved better had his household been a "real" Hindu household. His daughter's Doogla (Portuguese–East Indian) identity, he felt, served as a concrete reminder to the Hindu men of the Muslim charge that, for love of money, a Hindu will marry with anyone. This Muslim charge may have been particularly onerous in this case because love of money is part of the negative stereotype of the Portuguese and in a sense reduces Hindu East Indians to the lowest common denominator of a Portuguese stereotype. Here, Mr. G.'s Portuguese identity was probably also significant because it served as a concrete reminder of the stereotyped conflation of Portugese/Hindu identity.

Second, Mr. G. and Mrs. R. understood that the marriage could take place only if they tried to follow Islamic custom. They also believed this requirement was based in a status claim rather than in a theological stricture. That is, they maintained that the real reason Muslims insist on conversion and on an Islamic ritual is because they "scorn" Hindus and consider them religiously inferior. Even Mr. G. felt he had succeeded in arranging the marriage only because the groom's family could not find a more suitable Muslim bride. Although he was not wealthier than the groom's family, he believed his daughter was acceptable to them because, as an only child, she stood to inherit whatever possessions he had.

When asked why he was willing to marry her to a Muslim, convinced as he was that they scorned Hindus, he argued that she was still likely to receive better treatment from her Muslim in-laws than she would had she married into any Hindu family. Once converted to Islam, she and her children would eventually fit into her husband's household, whereas as a Doogla in a Hindu household, she and her children would always be treated as inferior outsiders. In addition, he argued that, because her rearing had been "all mixed up" (Christian, Sanatan Dharma, and Arya Samaj), she would never be able to be a good Hindu, but that her multireligious upbringing was more compatible with learning to be a good Muslim. All-in-all, Mr. G. was most concerned to get matters off to a good start by putting on a wedding that, if not praised by his daughter's in-laws, would at least not be offensive to them. Yet, dependent as he was on Mrs. R., a Sanatan Dharma, and also eager not to offend his late wife's Hindu relatives, with whom he was already on poor terms but whose future gossip could damage his reputation in the community, he also tried to avoid having the affair appear "too Muslim." It was in light of these considerations that Mrs. R. and Mr. G. decided on an "East Indian affair."

Once the activities were under way and matters began to deteriorate, Mr. G. became visibly nervous. The Hindu women assisting Mrs. R. openly expressed pity for him and his predicament. They said he could not afford to say anything to anyone for fear of aggravating his own or his daughter's situation. Mrs. R., too, pitied the father and the bride, and tried to swallow her Hindu pride, excluding Hindu features of East Indian wedding rituals.

When, several days before the event, I asked her about the Christian-style wedding gown, she said she had decided to make it for the bride because it would make her look pretty, it would show people that her father was not just "throwing her away," and, in any case, the girl wasn't a true Hindu, so it didn't matter. The gown, as Mrs. R. put it, was just the least she could do for a "motherless child." In the course of the ceremony the meaning of the Christian-style gown changed. When later I asked Mrs. R. how the gown had figured in the final sequence of events, she attributed her emphasis on the English/Christianness of the gown (by pinning on the bills and the final dancing) to her having been "made wild" (angry beyond control) by the rude, insulting actions of the groom and his party. She said she "grew weary" of the Muslims' effort to present themselves as superior to Hindus through their rude, insulting behavior and, therefore, tried to remind them that, no matter how big they might think themselves to be relative to Hindus, "dem ah still coolie"—a message she expected was transmitted through her brief emphasis on "things English."

To summarize, the actions of Mr. G. and Mrs. R. in constructing the wedding ritual and in responding to the participants' conduct are best understood against the background of Muslim-Hindu relations in Guyana. These relations, in turn, must be analyzed in conjunction with East Indians' general efforts either to struggle against or to take advantage of particular ideological linkages between material differences (class status) and cultural and intellectual capabilities (ethnic, racial, or religious status).

Case III: Sanatan Dharma and Arya Samaj in Ethnic Group Rank Presentations

In the next, and final, example we shall fracture intraethnic symbols and stereotypes one more time. Through this fractured mirror we shall see the Sanatan Dharma Hindus express their disdain for and their presumed superiority over Arya Samaj Hindus by exhibiting disrespectful demeanor and by selectively including and excluding ritual features. In this case a non-Brahman Sanatan Dharma groom was to be married to an Arya Samaj bride. As with the preceding one, neither locality nor class differences as such were stressed by either family.

Recall, however, the Arya Samaj general rejection of caste, of the manifestations of the Surpeme (deotas and dewas), and of the "born" Brahman as the sole legitimate ritual specialists: for the parties involved in fashioning the wedding, these rejections would pose several problems. First, many features of even the most abbreviated Sanatan Dharma—style ritual are linked to an acceptance of the manifestations. Second, even the most cynical anti-Brahman Sanatan Dharma is still likely to believe that a proper Hindu ceremony should be conducted by a "born" Brahman, not simply by a pious person trained to carry out the necessary activities.

Adding to the problems posed by Arya Samaj conceptions of Hindu ritual were Sanatani Hindus' contentions that becoming Arya Samaj is just another way of trying to be "big"—to put down mati. Conversion, they say, to Arya Samaj allows some Hindus to distance themselves from the lower-class Hindus without the subordination to Christians or to Muslims that a conversion to Christianity or to Islam might imply. In effect, they argue that the explicit religious sectarian distinction is really an intrareligious class distinction that permits the economically middle-class Arya Samaj to feel himself the superior of other Hindus and the equal of Christians and Muslims. It was the relation between these Sanatani convictions and Arya Samaj restrictions on ritual construction that underlay informants' comments on rumors they had heard about the negotiations between the couple's parents concerning the content of the ritual.

The bride's Arya Samaj mother refused to conduct "dig dutty," or to go "fetch lawa," features that are usually part of the wedding ritual complex among Sanatan Dharma. She also would not even allow other Sanatan Dharma "games" that did not require her direct involvement. There was to be no theft of the groom's shoes by the bride's younger sister, nor was she to demand a token fee from one of the groom's elder brothers before permitting the groom to enter the house after leaving the "marau" (wedding booth). The mother explained her rejection of these games on the ground that they were superstitions that had no place in a Vedic wedding.

The Sanatan Dharma informants who commented on her objections considered most of them to be "rude and obnoxious" but not especially serious. They, however, deemed offensive the bride's parents' objections to the practice of veiling the bride's face, to the practice requiring that the groom dye the part of the bride's hair with "sindhur" (vermilion) under cover of a sheet rather than in the open, and to the practice of circumambulating the nuptial pole as part of the final stages of the Sunday service. The informants argued that excluding the first two practices would be a serious mistake because it would make the bride appear immodest and shameless before her new in-laws—charges that could potentially damage the bride's face and her family's name in the community. The circumambulation of the nuptial pole they considered an act parallel to the Christian "I do," the exclusion of which they believed Sanatan Dharma Hindus, as well as Christians and Muslims, would interpret to mean that the couple was not really married—a charge that would make the children illegitimate and damage the reputation of the groom's family among middle-class community members.

Despite the seriousness with which others viewed the exclusion, the bride's parents stood firm on the issue of veiling the bride. They argued that the veiling was not necessary because, according to Arya Samaj teachings, the woman does not have to be ashamed and that this practice denies the equality of women as partners in marriage. On the issue of circumambulation, they recognized the difficulty and decided to compromise. Instead of seven circumambulations, which they associated with a recognition of the manifestations of the Supreme, they included one circumambulation as indicative of the unity of the Supreme. Over the objections of the bride's mother, her father agreed to have the part-dyeing take place under the cover of a sheet. Other problematic features were worked out either directly or indirectly between the families, with the bride's parents maintaining a concern for what might be offensive to the groom's parents and the groom's parents acknowledging that some ritual features would have to be omitted because the bride's family was Arya Samaj. Differences had to be accommodated if the families were to establish good relations.

It appeared by the day of the ceremony that the details had been worked out and that all would go well. It was, therefore, somewhat puzzling to me why things seemed to go so badly. Although Hindu weddings are not quiet, reverent affairs—there is usually some background noise, a few men who have had too much to drink, and children who cannot be kept still—distractions are usually held to a minimum and are not allowed to disrupt the pandit's conduct of the proceedings. In this case, however, the service was interrupted three times as the pandit tried to gain the attention of the audience and to get it to keep the noise down so that the couple could hear his instructions. Children in their zeal to get at the balloons and streamers that decorated the wedding booth wrecked one side of it before the wedding was over. As soon as the bride and the groom left the booth, the children finished the job of dismantling it, leaving only a pile of rubble around a badly leaning nuptial pole, which, in Hindu symbolism, represented disaster for the couple's future.

Later, I asked the male pandit and several of the guests why things seemed to have been so out of control. Some of the women felt Sanatan Dharma mothers had not chastized their children because they did not care that the children were being disrespectful toward an Arya Samaj. After all, it served to show "too big people" the price of "puttin' down mati." Nonetheless, it was not a simple clash between Arya Samaj as a symbol of class differentiation among East Indians and Sanatan Dharma as the symbol of a classless East Indian community of mati. The male pandit, who sought to quiet the gathering and who begged the guests to remember that they were there to witness a marriage and not simply to drink and gossip, was not the person actually performing the ceremony.

He had brought with him a young woman who, under his guidance, was training to become a pandit. It was she who carried out the rites. He watched, guided her, and tried to keep order for her, but it was clear to all that she was conducting the service. Both men and women can become pandits according to Arya Samaj beliefs; hence, it was to be expected that a woman might be retained for the service. This, Sanatani informants with whom I discussed the matter said, was not the problem. The problem was the type of female the senior pandit had chosen. She was a dark-skinned woman whom they believed to be a Madrassi, thus adding insult to injury. The Arya Samaj had not only tried to claim religious differences as a form of class superiority, but they had "gone too far" and had insulted the groom's family by employing a backward Madrassi pandit. This act, they felt, so distorted the ritual context that it had become difficult to mediate the status affront while, at the same time, taking seriously the wedding ritual, despite the earlier syncretic compromises.

Subsequent interviews with adults who had seemed most disruptive suggested that the noise and the disrespectful behavior expressed a rejection of the status implication of this particular feature—a Madrassi pandit—against the background of their general understandings about how intraethnic class differences should be symbolically represented through religious differences.

Sanatan Dharma informants contended that it was enough for them to have to tolerate a "poor" wedding that others (Africans in particular) could laugh at, but it was too much to expect them to accept a dark-skinned Madrassi pandit. Moreover, their reaction to this "insult" became a gloss on their more general reaction to what they labeled "Arya Samaj uppitiness." As for Arya Samaj informants, they asserted that the wedding was "spoiled" by jealous, mannerless Sanatan Dharma Hindus. They claimed that these Hindus would have behaved badly even if the pandit had not been Madrassi, simply because they are jealous of all Arya Samaj.

Ritualizing the Politics of Cultural Struggle in the Invention of Orthodoxy

Rituals do not provide either the sole or an especially privileged window through which to observe solutions posed to the kinds of problems confronted by subordinate ethnic groups. Neither the kinds of problems confronted by these East Indian actors nor the syncretic forms resulting from their efforts to resolve them are unique to East Indians in Guyana or to Guyana. To begin to understand the particularities of the Guyanese situation and of similar so-called plural society cases, it is necessary to focus on problems associated with relations between territorial nationalism and cultural heterogeneity, and their links to the distribution of political and economic power. Obviously, factors entailed by these problems ramify throughout all aspects of social life in any society. However, where rituals are public, and where informants place them in the center of their definition of culture and of ethnic distinctiveness, they provide an invaluable source of ethnographic data. Attention to ritual performances of the type analyzed here allows us one perspective from which to treat the particular manifestations of these general problems in carefully defined ideological fields.

What must concern us is what our understanding of the character of a particular ideological field tells us about how to analyze the play of symbols in social interactions. We may then focus on what a careful analysis of the play of symbols in social interaction reveals about the potential for change in that ideological field. We want to note how people struggle; what, in their own terms, they struggle over; and what, in these terms, impedes or facilitates possible alternative outcomes of their struggles. In treating factors that promote or hinder these alternatives, we must aim to glean from our analyses of these factors how they are manifested in symbolic domination through what Bourdieu (1977) refers to as habitus (that is, a system of durable, transposable dispositions that mediate between structures and practices), and how they are manifested in the formal coercive procedures utilized by the most powerful members of a society to develop particular structures for the distribution of economic roles and of political rights and obligations. Only by careful attention to the historical details of the interplay between informal, indirect features and formal, direct features of coercion can we begin to provide descriptions of cultural and ideological systems that suggest why people actually struggle, rather than merely hand down to them, the watchword of how they should struggle.

As Bourdieu and Boltanski note, "symbolic domination really begins when the misrecognition (*méconnaissance*), implied by recognition (*reconnaissance*), leads those who are dominated to apply the dominant criteria of evaluation to their own practices" (1975:8, trans.

Figure 9.1. The Ideological Field and Bourdieu's
Model of an Ideological Field

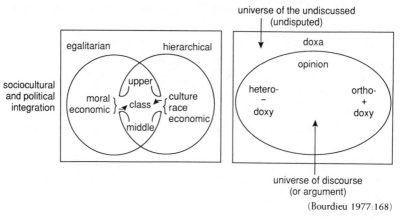

(Bourdieu 1977:168)

in Thompson 1984:46). And, speaking of linguistic markets as one
site of ideological struggle, they suggest that "the 'structure' of the
market or field is a certain state of the relation of force between the
agents or groups engaged in struggle; or, more precisely, a certain
state 'of the distribution of the specific capital which, accumulated
in the course of previous struggles, orients subsequent strategies'"
(1980:114, trans. in Thompson 1984:49). Thus, Thompson, summarizing Bourdieu's general position, concludes that

[w]hat is at stake in the struggles within particular fields is the structure of
the field itself, that is, the distribution of the capital which is specific to it.
Those who, in a given state of distribution, possess the greatest capital are
inclined towards strategies of conservation, toward preserving a state of *doxa*
in which the established structure is not questioned. Those least endowed
with capital (often the young and newly arrived) are inclined toward strategies of subversion, of heresy or *heterodoxy.* By bringing what is undiscussed
into the universe of discourse and hence criticism, heterodoxy impels the
dominant agents or groups to step out of their silence and to produce a
defensive discourse of *orthodoxy.* . . . While those engaged in struggles may
have antagonistic aims, nevertheless they generally share a basic interest in
the preservation of the market or field. By participating in the struggle they
help to reproduce the very game whose rules have become the object of
dispute. (Thompson 1984:49–50)

Bourdieu's general position is relevant to our analysis of the Guyanese situation; however, it also requires two qualifications. First, the
national pattern of ideological struggle is encapsulated and depen-

Figure 9.2. Bourdieu's Model Superimposed
on the Ideological Field

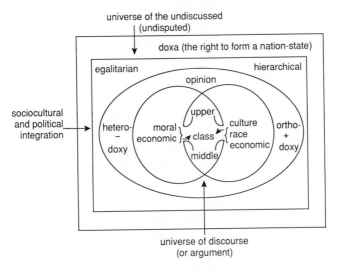

dent on relations of power and symbolic domination in the international arena. What previously dominant (hegemonic) criteria, and both orthodox and heterodox symbols generated out of them, can mean are inextricably bound to meanings associated with these criteria in the international arena. Second, the maintenance or production of doxa out of a struggle between heterodox and orthodox interpretations depends on the existence of a group sufficiently powerful to enforce the results of its defensive discourse. We have noted that, in situations where the actual distribution of political and economic power results in a transition from a determinate set of dominant criteria based on vertical racism to an indeterminate one based on horizontal racism, all criteria have a double dimension of orthodoxy and heterodoxy. That is, the only component of the ideological field that remains doxic is the legitimacy of struggling over the specific criteria that might, in combination with actual political and economic domination, allow construction of an adequate defensive discourse.

The significance of the second qualification can be made clearer by comparing Figure 7.1 with Bourdieu's diagram of an ideological field (see Figure 9.1).

By superimposing these diagrams (see Figure 9.2), we may note that the substance of the universe of the undiscussed is the internationally defined presumption of a particular kind of link between territorial nationalism and cultural heterogeneity. As the outer frame of Figure 7.1 suggests, consistent with this presumption, Guyanese ethnic groups may struggle to construct a unitary image of sociocultural and political integration. What remains doxic is the right or the necessity to engage in this struggle. The game has been reproduced in that the universe of discourse is still structured around the same sets of criteria and the same issues: the legitimation of a determinate dominant-to-subordinate linkage between ethnic/racial differentiation and class stratification. What has changed, as a direct result of trying to apply the same rules of the game under altered national and international political and economic conditions, is that the universe of opinion now subsumes the previous national doxa, pushing doxa into the international arena. In the international arena, the colony becomes the "unchic peasant state" or the "banana republic" allowed to struggle to maintain/construct its identity as a nation-state, but under political and economic conditions that reinforce the ideological power of the dominant colonial criteria—that is to say, the standards of civilized conduct.

10

Locating
and Exorcizing
the Ghost

The formation of class consciousness, and the racial and ethnic identities with which it competes, takes place in particular historically constituted ideological fields. The subordination of these competing forms of consciousness to one another, and to the homogenizing goals of territorial nationalism and cultural homogeneity, are, from the standpoint of everyday activities, spare-time projects for most citizens. On a daily basis citizens are preoccupied with the precepts and concepts that they believe allow them to formulate practical courses of action enabling them to get along with their relatives, friends, and neighbors as they make a living.

For Cockalorums, these concerns mean that they are preoccupied with the status symbolism of the spatial grid, from waterside to backdam, from estate to village, on which they move. On this grid they seek to develop means and methods for determining what the social characteristics and the material accomplishments of those with whom they move tell them about what to expect from these others. In short, they, like their counterparts in other pots of physical proximity, are caught up in the art of becoming "somebody." As they relate the apparent to the real, to identify "who is what," Cockalorums use the labels truly big men through small, small men, in addition to the shame-face, bold-faced, and doan-kay-damn designations that further distinguish persons in these categories.

Yet, as is the case for citizens of other contemporary nation-states, for Cockalorums individuals become tokens of a racial, ethnic, or class type. Their actions and capabilities are judged in terms of these types, making of such categorical identities, potential group identities. Consequently, the individuals' effort to become somebody is constrained by a group effort to claim a place in the social order that fosters such tokenism. This means that race, ethnicity, and religion become additional labels, which individuals presume allow them a reasonably accurate assessment of what to expect, in national politics, from those with whom they otherwise interact as mati.

Whereas Cockalorums expect, and in practice demand, that each person should try to make something of himself, they also expect that he will be limited in what he can make of himself by his own and others' ascription of his racial/ethnic identity. Although identities are fragmented within groups, when this expectation is contradicted, it produces an identity/status disjunction. Among those who experience the shock of this disjunction, reactions now range from fear, dismay, and indignation to a curious shrug of the shoulder. Nonetheless, even those who shrug their shoulders agree with others who are less nonchalant in claiming that such disjunctions will cease to be noted only when all Guyanese are so racially/ethnically impure as to be pure—a new nation, racially speaking, of *No Nations*.

In the heat of social and cultural interchange, the alleged distinctive characteristics of ethnic cultures, which were never absolute, become increasingly difficult to sustain. Individuals develop strategies for making life to make a living, for protecting face and name from stains, and, more generally, for living well with the people, all of which result in syncretic practices. Individuals confronted with disjunctions between their ethnic identities and the "cultural content" of their pragmatic strategies point to socialization (that is, living among the true owners of the aberrant cultural content) or to blood, appropriately enriched by the genealogical presence of ancestors of the proper cultural stripe. The outcome is an ideological war fought in the veins, the scars from which become stains on the names of individuals and ethnic groups.

As representatives of the different racial/ethnic groups, individuals debate the sociopolitical implications of the cultural interchange. Depending on the value they give cultural elements, tied as these are to assessments of contributions and to the evaluation of ethnic-group rank ordering, they aim to deny that any "borrowing" has occurred, to give the accusing group qualified recognition for previous "ownership," or to appropriate the elements. Overall, however, the cultural nationalisms formed within boundaries of ethnic pots of physical proximity, created in rural settlements that were part of a territory capped by the lid of a common political system, have not given way to a territorial nationalism capable of consistently effacing the cultural nationalisms of ethnic competition. Instead, prototypical understandings of a particular distribution of economic roles, and sociopolitical rights and obligations became dominant and subordinate stereotypes of racial groups. These stereotypes were and remain part of the process of identifying "cultures," their boundaries, and human embodiments.

Although these cultures were elements of a Guiana that political leaders, and those who had their diverse reasons for following them, sought to free from colonial domination, racial groups "owned" these cultures. In the struggle for sovereignty the concern with territorial nationalism was not at the same time a struggle to free a preexisting "nation's" culture or to return a people to its "God-given shape." Like Valetta's and Constantine's Serbs and Croats, East Indians and Africans, the major contestants, were brothers. Contrary to Valetta's conclusion about the rule of inheritance among brothers, however, though one group may have appeared to be the "older brother," the rule left "provinces" of ethnic prerogatives. It recognized no interethnic cultural patrimony and, hence, made no provision for its inheritance. Thus, in Guyana, the end of territorial colonialism set in motion the beginning of the process that might ultimately, for better or worse, create a cultural nationalism out of the current cultural nationalisms. Whether it does, however, is a matter of how political and economic power is linked to categorical identities and aspects of a system of meaning in specifications of cultural standards and their legitimation in everyday practices.

The outcome of this process depends on a change in the form of hegemony out of which these cultural nationalisms were produced and commitments to them ingrained in the collective meanings of local communities such as Cockalorum. It is not a matter of time, proximity, the permeability of ethnic boundaries, or other forms of cultural interchange per se. For nearly two decades now physical representatives of the Anglo-European elite that fostered a particular transformist hegemony have been numerically insignificant, but the constraints this kind of hegemony implied remain. These constraints continue to set the coordinates of the ideological field in which Cockalorums and other Guyanese seek to reassess previous standards of civilized conduct and to homogenize contemporary heterogeneity. They move back and forth between hierarchical and egalitarian precepts, while maintaining the centrality of contribution and place as key sources of criteria against which to evaluate elements of heterogeneity and the potential each element has to serve as a feature of a new standard of civilization.

The centrality of contribution and place highly constraints the (theoretically) infinite and arbitrary sources of criteria. The ideological naturalization of contribution, as purveyor of place, directs the focus of the homogenizing process to a struggle among the different ethnic groups to identify and to claim as their own the diverse features of the cultural amalgam. The naturalization of contribution also explains the effort to ethnically mark and, hence, to be able to claim ownership of different elements of heterogeneity. On the one hand, the emphasis on contribution encourages a quest for "purity," distinctiveness, and a glorification of the traditions they putatively symbolize. On the other hand, the structure of power relations assures the production of syncretic and, therefore, ideologically inauthentic forms and practices.

The particular interrelation of ideological precepts linking contribution, ethnic ownership, and the glorification of distinctive traditions to "place" in the social order becomes a double-edged sword in a homogenizing process devoid of any group powerful enough to enforce its valuations of non-Anglo European components of the mixture. Without a radical transformation, the Anglo-European features remain, ideologically, the superior aspects of national civil conduct and of status criteria, especially where the concern is to place the Guyanese state in the international order of nation-states.[1]

Thus, as we saw through the presentation of interpersonal and group rank claims in wedding rituals, the one edge of this sword—the indeterminacy of criteria and their valuation—cuts deep, jagged slits into any individual's public presentation of middle- to upper-class status claims as he struggles to construct these claims using, but without devaluing, ethnically marked materials that remain ambiguous with respect to their ability to symbolize anything other than lower-class status as the racial and cultural inferiority of non-Anglo-European groups and their contributions to the amalgam. Efforts to authenticate new cultural products and to find criteria suited to claiming a place for an "unchic peasant state" in the order of nation-states bring forth even deeper and more uneven cuts from the other sword edge—the external source of authentication for each group's prized cultural possessions. Moreover, the development of internal authentication can occur only by continually reopening these cuts. For, if syncretic productions/creole traditions (for instance, Kali Mai worship) are to be authenticated, this raises the questions of (1) who will select, (2) what they will select, and (3) what will be the implications of the selections for external evaluations of all Guyanese as a nation (that is to say, a people) and as a state (that is, a power in the international arena).[2]

Consequently, whether Cockalorums imaged the national culture in egalitarian or hierarchical terms, the notions of ethnic distinctiveness and contributions associated with such distinctiveness played key roles in the generation of evaluative criteria in accordance with which groups aimed to place themselves in that order. Moreover, the stereotypes and the stereotyping process that encoded this distinctiveness and spoke to the issue of ethnically differentiated persons' access to the range of cultural variation it entailed were shaped by the particular character of Anglo-European hegemonic dominance. It was around a particular intersection of the meanings of race and culture in relation to political and economic stratification that the struggle to construct a norm of homogeneity and standards of civilized conduct, rights, and obligations was ordered. During the colonial era the ideological struggle to "naturalize" a social world, centered on the contention of Anglo-European racial and cultural superiority, was buttressed by Anglo-Europeans' actual control of the political and economic institutions of the society. As a result, other social groups developed mobility strategies under conditions where the specifications of racial, ethnic, and religious contributions were the legitimate criteria for ideological interpretations of differences and similarities in the social, political, and economic rights to be accorded to individuals as members of these culturally constituted groupings. Under these conditions individuals could gain a degree of recognition for their material accomplishments by adopting Anglo-European standards for civilized conduct (that is, dress, comportment, secular and religious morality). Under the same conditions groups could attempt to increase the degree of acceptability—that is, diminish the negative consequences of adopting these Anglo-European patterns—through efforts to elevate the overall status of their racial, cultural, or religious group relative to Anglo-Europeans and other groups.

It is in terms of the precepts of this ideological field that we can make sense of Cockalorums' contention that class stratification, at least the ethnic composition of different class strata, is the product of ethnic differentiation. Ethnic cultures differ in their quality and hence in their potential to produce middle and upper-class individuals. It was only in this manner that a person claiming middle and upper-class status through the necessary display of and adherence to Anglo-European Christian standards of morality and public conduct could still be counted as a "credit" to that person's race, ethnic culture, or religion. It is also in accordance with the precepts of this ideological field that we can understand why efforts were made to revitalize and maintain distinctive traditions while at the same time reforming these traditions to eliminate elements that, in comparison with Anglo-European tradition, could too easily be deemed inferior and backward.

If in the end one had to adopt the hegemonic cultural tradition in order to display personal accomplishments in middle and upper-class terms, if one were not at the same time to be judged an inferior ape of a superior tradition as one took on these symbolic vestments, then it was necessary to be able to ideologically defend the equality and even superiority of the cultural or religious tradition with which one was otherwise identified. It is not surprising, then, that in Guyana as in other places, it was initially the more socially mobile members of these groups who called for the reevaluation or glorification of non-Anglo-European cultural traditions. Also, it should not be surprising that they attempted such a revitalization through strategies that did not call for an absolute overthrow of Anglo-European cultural traditions as the standards of civilized conduct.

Yet, without a complete reworking of the ideological field, efforts to reposition diverse cultural traditions relative to these hegemonic standards meant that variations and diversity in what was constructed as a unitary subordinated ethnic culture became more rather than less problematic. So the Hindu as Sanatan Dharma and Arya Samaj confronted one another as well as confronting Muslims in their struggle to produce criteria for cultural and interpersonal status elevation. Each grouping, in the name of the good of the whole East Indian ethnic group, proclaimed its own superiority over all comers. Although each religious grouping within the East Indian ethnic group found it worthwhile to construct a solid ethnic front for the sake of short-run material and ideological benefits to be gained from a repositioning of "Indian" culture in the sociocultural order, each also participated in this effort from behind a fence of presumed superiority. Likewise, Africans found it worthwhile to criticize the roles of Anglo-European culture and Christianity in colonial oppression as they sought to reposition themselves in the sociocultural order; however, with respect to East Indian culture and religions, they, too, did so from behind a fence of presumed superiority. The result was horizontal xenophobia without either religious groupings or racial/ethnic groups controlling both the political and economic institutions essential to enforce their claim to superiority. In this ideological jockeying to reposition the previously subordinated ethnic diversity, the ghost of Anglo-European hegemony was maintained as the standard against which criteria generated out of this jockeying were evaluated.

Guyanese are now free of the presence and direct political and economic control of this Anglo-European stratum, nonetheless, they are still citizens of an "unchic peasant state" vying for recognition and status in an international politicoeconomic arena. The ghost of Anglo-European hegemony combined with the contemporary international politicoeconomic reality continues to dictate standards of civilized conduct that no segment of the Guyanese population can ignore.[3] These factors still inform their ideological struggle to selectively reconstruct and revitalize elements of their diverse traditions.

Traditionalism, the Ghost of Hegemonic Dominance, and the Order of Nations

Despite its historical specificity, the politics of cultural struggle in Guyana has much to tell us about the relation between a general homogenizing process and the development of hegemonic dominance (especially of the transformist type) in processes of cultural production and nation building. Heterogeneity is an aspect of all human societies, and issues related to how heterogeneity will be homogenized in the construction of standards of civilization pose problems for all symbolic systems. Homogenization is always a political process. Everywhere it entails an ideological specification of how aspects of heterogeneity generated in human consociation will be valued. Everywhere it also identifies the means by which these valuations are linked to the structure and to the institutionalization of economic roles, rights, and obligations for persons differentially involved in the objective production of the material and symbolic elements that constitute social formations. Such general problems are exacerbated, but not created, by forced and voluntary population transfers or by the economic and political inequalities associated with them.

Heterogeneity, homogeneity, and the processes through which they are valuated are general aspects of all human societies. The construction of social categories and the conscious commitments to personal and group identities that develop in relation to these categories are, therefore, particular transformations of this general political process. This general process is affected by historically specific forms of colonization, colonialism, racism, and so forth. On the one hand, the relation between identity formation processes and the general homogenizing process shapes the particular ideological conceptions of territoriality that bound geographical spaces in what we refer to as the modern world system, impeding or facilitating the construction of certain kinds of personal and group identities. On the other hand, the existence of the modern world system, and the order of nation-states it implies, encourages or discourages group interest in the nationalist ideological precepts that circumscribe territories as states charged with the task of becoming putatively homogeneous nation-states, most often as they resist previous images of their heterogeneity and its implications for a place among nations and nation-states.

Audrey Wipper's (1972) examination of efforts on the part of some East and West African leaders in the early 1970s, to reevaluate their diverse precolonial traditions, illustrates well the constraints within which this kind of ideological resistance is waged. She notes that as these leaders sought to equate or claim superiority for "African" traditions over "Western European" traditions introduced during the colonial era, they publicly declared the need to revitalize these African traditions through the rejection and eradication of the corrupting, self-denigrating influences of Western European traditions. It was, they proclaimed, time to stop aping Western ways. She also notes, however, that for many of these men, wearing three-piece suits, clean-shaven, with use of the latest in Western cosmetics and shaving equipment, vying for power in the bureaucracies and parliamentary government institutions left over from the colonial era, the end to aping Western ways meant that *women* were to return to the home, lower their hemlines, remove their makeup, and stop straightening their hair, wearing wigs, and using complexion lighteners. But it also meant something even more pernicious. She argues:

Although highly critical of Western countries, African governments are also highly sensitive to their judgments. Knowing the negative image many Westerners hold of their countries—the equating of nakedness with primitiveness, for instance—and determined to change this image, they feel that they must suppress aspects of traditional life that reinforce this image. These governments are caught on the horns of a dilemma. On the one hand, they wish to preserve traditional culture, while on the other, they wish to become a modern nation. In one breath, they castigate women for changing too much and in the next, they castigate tribesmen for not changing enough. (Wipper 1972:335–36)

In such ideological struggles, "tradition" cannot be everything that anyone did in the past, nor can it necessarily center on what the precolonial elite did in the past. As in Constantine's unchic peasant state struggling for international recognition and respect, tradition is, on the one hand, that which comes closest to being the shiny thing that impresses, or, if not the shiny thing that impresses, at least not the "vulgar" thing that reinforces a negative image. On the other hand, what tradition is or can be often depends on the interests or goals of a postcolonial elite in the international arena, and competition among diversely defined strata in the national arena. For example, in the situations on which Wipper focused, it was the competitive relation between the status of men and women and between "tribesmen" and a "detribalized" urban elite.

The perniciousness of the relation between the selective reconstruction of tradition and the ghost of hegemonic dominance, reinforced by the structure of international politics, does not end with the constraints it places on revitalizing the past. It also constrains and shapes responses to cultural innovations in both the traditions targeted for revitalization and the hegemonic tradition against which such revitalizers struggle. Not surprisingly, Wipper (1972:335–36) also notes that African leaders' responses to hippie counterculture and its challenge to the cultural elements of U.S. hegemony were either to expel the hippies or insist that if they could not tidy up that they get out of the respective African states to which they had migrated in their own search for some authentic form of precapitalist culture. Without arguing that African leaders incorrectly assessed the sincerity of these hippies, as unorthodox members of the Western European and Anglo-American cultures against which these African leaders judged themselves and attempted to reevaluate their cultural traditions, these hippies, however sincere, were in no position to reevaluate that Western tradition. They were themselves vulgar outcasts and as such therefore highly suspect as the producers of worthy countertradition. Likewise, U.S. African-Americans' efforts to construct, out of an interpretation of their "African roots," new styles and traditions to positively represent themselves relative to "mainstream" U.S. American culture and its negative stereotypes of their blackness were equally summarily rejected by some of these same African leaders. Thus, as Wipper (1972:331) suggests:

> Particularly irritating to the [continental African] cultural nationalists is the Afro hairstyle that blacks in the United States have adopted as a symbol of their African heritage. To many Africans this is merely another example of Western arrogance—now black Americans have the audacity to assume they know what Africa is all about without even taking the trouble to ascertain whether Africans do, in fact, wear such a hairdo.

She goes on to quote the particulars of Kadji Konde's (an African writer) attack on this hairstyle, wherein he uses what one can hardly avoid recognizing as the ironic elements of a negative European stereotype of the African continent (that is, that place of wild, untamed bush).

> How "natural" these nests are is a mystery to me. In the United States, where this hairdo comes from, it is called an Afro style. This implies a link with Africa, although I personally fail to see how this keeping of a *wild oiled bush* on the skull has anything to do with dear mother Africa. From that land of drug-taking and draft-dodgers came another shameless importation, a mast flag of a decaying ship under the guise of a hairstyle intended to identify American Negroes with Africans. (emphasis added; Wipper 1972:331)

One wonders how Konde and others responded to U.S. African-Americans' efforts to learn African languages or to adopt styles of dress (or undress) that *could be* directly traced to African origins. The point here, however, is not to reject the continental African's right to criticize the naïveté and even corruptions and hypocrisy of hippie counterculture. Nor is the intent to reject their criticism of

U.S. African-American (mis)interpretations of aspects of continental African traditions. The point, instead, is to note the character and constraints within which this criticism was shaped. U.S. African-Americans' right to positively evaluate and innovate on a historically given link to Africa is rejected on grounds of inauthenticity. No African, past or present can, in Konde's view, be credited with the invention and use of such a hairstyle and so it cannot be genuine or "natural."

Such constraints are not simply the limits within which negative criticisms like Konde's are constructed. They also shape ostensibly positive comments like those of V. A. February, another African writer who, in praise of Negritude, comments on the same hairstyle.

Legend has it that when the first Africans from their newly independent countries arrived in America to represent their countries as diplomats, their colourful and beautiful African garments and dresses, which formed such a striking *contrast with the clothes of the whites,* set the Afro-American mind on fire. Some sources claim that it was Miriam Makeba, the South African singer, who, with her *natural African hair-do,* influenced Afro-American women into accepting fuzzy hair as aesthetically pleasing to the eye. (emphasis added; 1981:188)

Whether dressed up in White folks' clothes or African folks' clothes with an African coiffure, one can add to the complexity of the U.S. African-American "resistance" discourse similar negative responses, produced within the population, to wealthy Anglo-American hippies; the varied criticisms members of the population voiced about "nappy-head niggers," "handkerchief-head niggers," and the questions some of them raised about why the Afro-Americans (itself a problematic term for many others) in search of positive images could find no source of pride in their own struggles short of "reaching all the way back to the Africans who sold them into slavery." Moreover, even some of the most avid African-American North American pan-Africanists chided students of Swahili for learning a "trade jargon" as symbol of their interest in Africa rather than taking up a "real" African language. The point, then, is to recognize that, although there is much ideological ground to be gained through traditionalism as a process of resistance, the evaluative criteria it generates often fall far short of any fundamental reworking of the basic ideological precepts of hegemonic dominance as these relate to authenticity, legitimacy, and who has the power to construct, out of heterogeneity, a norm of homogeneity. It is a process that has tremendous practical implications for cultural innovation and creativity. It is also a process the careful analysis of which has tremendous theoretical implications for what we can mean by resistance and what we presuppose resistance tells us about the mutability of structures of domination.

Clearly, ethnic resurgence, like national efforts to purify patrimony, and other forms of traditionalism, provide subordinate groups a means to construct an alternate alignment of territorial nationalism and cultural heterogeneity whereby, from outside the realm defined as producers of the hegemonic forms, they can aim to bound and define their differential relations to the cultural heterogeneity that has been subordinated to a particular hegemonic interpretation, that is to say, to the use of a set of ideological precepts to define a norm of homogeneity and its conception of civilized conduct. The different groups who find themselves in this cultural nether realm may aim to elevate the overall status of some aspects of the cultural heterogeneity that they claim as the products of their creativity and historical experiences. They can attempt to expand the range and type of criteria relevant to evaluations of intergroup and interpersonal status claims. In turn, this direct expansion of criteria will imply an indirect expansion of standards of civilized conduct.

Traditionalism, as cultural realignment and the repositioning of culturally constructed groups, however, also raises serious problems and dilemmas. These problems center on the ways such groups can legitimate their expanded conceptions of civilized conduct in national and international arenas. First, as we have seen in the Guyanese case, traditionalism as a means of ideological resistance raises questions about what aspects of a "given" tradition are to be emphasized in this realignment. Second, it raises questions about who will control the selection and how they are to legitimate the selected aspects of tradition. And third, the locus of control and the mode of legitimation employed raises additional questions about status and power relations within the social groups this traditionalism defines or redefines. These questions are directly related to and become more or less problematic, depending on the internal diversity of the constructed category ad the nature of the goals that inspired its construction. The accomplishments of the nation-as-state, and of its political representatives who carry out the aforementioned tasks in the international order, are constrained by what they, and others as representatives/tokens of ethnic groups, do as they confront the task of homogenization within the state-as-nation.

The significance of intragroup diversity, its relation to the politics of meaning as a politic of cultural struggle, is shaped by the constraints of the ideological field on which members of such a group fashion their identity as a people sharing a common cultural tradition. As we saw in Chapters 8 and 9, any group's homogenized solutions to its problems of internal diversity are complicated by the ideological implications of these solutions for status and power relations (that is, control over shared systems of meaning in conjunction with a distribution of political and economic rights and obligations) between that group and other groups with which it shares a national territory. On the ideological field with which we have been concerned, Guyanese efforts to realign intergroup status in a national territory had to be squared with the way the ideological precepts used in that realignment were interpreted in the evaluation of interpersonal status among persons sharing a locality and economic position (that is, countrymen and mati).

Where none of the set of culturally constructed groups has the political and economic wherewithal to enforce their interpretations, criteria of cultural distinctiveness and their meanings for a realignment of territorial nationalism and cultural heterogeneity are infinitely contestable. That is to say, because no group has combined political and economic power, all groups lack the material wherewithal to enforce their claims, but equally important for a theoretical delimitation of the hegemony concept, they lack the ideological qualification to enforce their rationalizations—to make of an objective world a particular kind of subjectively "given"/"natural" world. There is no proof in the pudding even as it is hungrily gobbled up by all the "no-nation" guests. For example, in the cultural production of rituals, any particular ritual, as we have demonstrated, is syncretic, but such syncretisms are viewed as "customary practices," not "real culture."

Hence, in Guyana, even as the hegemonic status enjoyed by English culture during the colonial era is criticized, it also continues to serve as the standard against which other ethnic cultures are evaluated. The realignment of territorial nationalism and cultural heterogeneity, through traditionalism, therefore continues to take place on an ideological field that retains the basic content and structure that combines Anglo-European elite interpretation with the initial expansion of these interpretations developed by subordinates as they sought (1) to assess the meaning of contribution for place (that is, rank and the rights and obligations pertinent thereto), and (2) to assess the role of face and name (that is, egalitarian definitions of communal morality) in evaluations of interpersonal status claims in an ethnically diverse, class-stratified society.

Cultural Innovation, Homogenization, and Hegemonic Dominance

When culture is objectified as tradition, social emphasis shifts from pragmatic meaningful interpretations of human biogenetic capabilities and ecological constraints under which they are exercised to a struggle to control the way the diverse meanings generated out of such interactions are to be interrelated and what their implications are for a distribution of the material bases of human existence. Where the objectified tradition is not unitary but composed of a number of historically distinguishable traditions, these traditions are further selectively objectified as sources of criteria around which persons with different claims to these selected features can construct the coordinates of their struggle to control the total system of meanings. That is to say, at the same time a selective identification of distinctive traditions shapes personal identities and claims to different parts of the nonunitary tradition, it also shifts the interpretive focus of that tradition from the inclusive-existential construction of beings-in-the-world to the inclusive-historical construction of types-of-beings in a particular political and economic order.[4] As useful as traditionalism is as a mode of resisting hegemonic domination, these traditions within tradition make it very difficult for any of the competing groups to return to inclusive-existential interpretations of human subjectivity through an ideology of traditionalism.

Gail Landsman's (1985) analysis of an ongoing dispute between the state of New York and a group of Mohawks identifying themselves as traditional Mohawks provides a worthy example of the problematics of this kind of struggle. First, she notes that the disputants do not simply fall into two categories, but rather divide along at least four lines. The Whites are divided between upstate rural residents and downstate "liberals," while the Indians involved are the Mohawks in general and the Traditional Mohawks in particular. Then, she notes that for these varied disputants different interpretive frameworks provide a continuous background for the production of symbols and shifts in their meanings as they are used in political struggles. For the Mohawks, especially the Traditionalists, the interpretive framework is a "sovereignty" framework whereby Traditionalists maintain that the Mohawks were never conquered, their nationality never dissolved; they advocate abolishing the reservations' welfare systems, which they see as perpetuating dependency on foreign governments and alcohol, thereby destroying native lives and dignity. Traditional Mohawks have refused to participate in tribal elections and support instead the revived traditional clan-based system of chiefs. A major fear expressed by Traditional Mohawks is that the elective governments will sell the reservation lands, and without land, or territory, there is no nation. More importantly,

Sovereignty is *lived* at Ganienkeh [the community established by Traditionalists on "occupied" land]. . . . Other Indian communities may have inherent sovereignty, I was told, but true sovereignty must be created from within; if it is "given" and "accepted," it means it can also be taken away by some outside sovereignty thus formed a part of the interpretive framework held by Ganienkeh participants. (1985:832)

In opposition to this interpretive framework, Landsman (1985: 829) maintains, the White upstate residents assimilate the dispute to their own upstate-downstate interpretive framework—an important element of which was the Whites' view of Indians as a "minority group" and a "cause" taken up by "bleeding-heart downstate liberals."

Yet, it is the upstate residents' understanding of the term traditional that compounds, according to Landsman (1985:829), their view of the Indian as hypocrite and public relations manipulator. Hence, in addition to trying to demonstrate that the Indian claim to having established a self-sufficient agricultural community is a public relations lie,

[f]or local Whites, the image of the Indian is of an unchanging culture, frozen in time. If the Indians are not living as did their ancestors 200 years ago, they cannot be truly traditional, the reasoning goes. Buying groceries in the local stores, washing clothes at the laundromats, and using chain saws

and tractors rather than hand tools, all were pointed to as evidence of
Ganienkeh's hypocrisy in both Moss Lake and Altona.

The upstate participants in this dispute freeze the real Indian in
cultural time. Real Indians are part of the past; trouble-making minority radicals are part of the present. So the upstate participants know
what the peasant knows, but what the peasant knows does not
impress the "liberal dupes" downstate. Instead, by constituting themselves through this interpretive opposition, the upstate participants
help to lay the groundwork for the more powerful downstate participants to freeze them in time as either racist bigots or redneck peasants and country hicks. Quoting an upstate participant, Landsman
reports:

> You've never felt more like a piece of dirt unless you've gone to Court in
> Albany. My parents taught me respect for my elders, but there was one
> gentleman down there . . . who was an attorney for the Secretary of State's
> Office, and he wanted to know—we were just hayseed people, you know—
> what are you people doing here fighting the State of New York? He said,
> "You're making a big to-do about nothing. . . ." And then he said, "I'll bet that
> road, you claim to go on it. I'll bet if I got down and examined it I'd find
> wagon tracks?" And it was just that sneering. So with all the sarcasm I could
> muster I said, "Yes, sir, and I'll bet you're surprised I wear shoes to court!"
> (1985:832)

Thus, it would seem that the "real" culture of the powerless,
whether Indian or White, is in the past, a past that is gone forever,
leaving behind only backwardness and public relations images, the
latter constructed in the dialectic of subordinated efforts to lay claim
to a future.[5] The "authentic" culture of the present and legitimate
innovations on the traditions it implies are the prerogatives of the
powerful. Nonetheless, among the powerless, differential claims to
traditions within tradition provide the criteria around which they
may construct interpretations and attempt to assimilate diversity to
an inclusive-existential order of human subjects.

By definition, states cannot allow the formation of groupings or
the institutionalization of ways of valuating heterogeneity that contravene state control over groupings and over institutions in a single
politically defined territory. Groupings of Native Americans encapsulated by such states, regardless of the state's capitalist or socialist
economic policies, cannot be allowed to construct freely ideologies

of sovereignty that obviate the states' control over the groupings and their relation to the territory that the states also claim. As this point is approached, such groups, as Landsman aptly illustrates, are relabeled "troublesome radicals" or inauthentic "ethnics" by those allied with the state and its (homogenizing) goals. Like the term minority, the ethnic label becomes a euphemism for the political dimension of identities constructed under constraints imposed by a specific homogenizing process within a politically defined unit having the military apparatus to enforce the unit's territorial claims.

Anthropology, Identity Formation, and the Politics of Cultural Struggle

Whether we confronted ethnicity as a disengagement from a struggle over control of a state apparatus deemed illegitimate or as an insistence on having a voice in the selection and legitimation of the criteria for sociopolitical integration, this label directs our attention to a process of personal and group identity formation taking place in the intersection of territorial and cultural nationalism. Anthropological analyses of ethnicity thus become analyses of identity formation as an aspect of the homogenizing process viewed through one of its key political dimensions. Ethnicity will have features peculiar to a particular historical juncture in the development of ideologies of territorial nationalism and the distribution of power in the international politicoeconomic arena. This does not imply, however, an entirely new kind of homogenizing process common only to new states or to so-called plural societies. Instead, labeling groups ethnic in certain places and at particular times tells us that such groups, on parallel with earlier uses of the terms nationality and linguistic minority, have a subordinated position and voice with respect to the legitimation of forms of putative homogeneity in a state with particular kinds of goals, defined according to how it will achieve and maintain the status of nation-state in an international arena.

Moreover, to say that some groupings are nationalities rather than ethnic groups is to hold forth the possibility that such groupings might ultimately control a politically defined territory in which they will then confront their own heterogeneity. It also implies that when some such groups are referred to as races rather than ethnic groups, the reference serves to create additional ideological barriers restricting the role this political dimension of group identity can have in producing the heterogeneity that comes to be recognized and valued in an homogenizing process intent on melting multiple groups into a singular cultural-as-political nationality. For example, it is this latter consideration that informs the debates over the cultural nonexistence of Ecuador's noncontributing *la raza negra,* some Native American groups, or African-Americans in the United States. Similar conclusions hold for assertions claiming that real Indians do not use tractors and do not frequent laundromats. These assertions result from propositions on the part of those against whom unreal Indians struggle, that the beings now in "Indian" skin (but not wearing skins) must be something else—a fallen race, a pesty minority, or just duplicitous manipulators.

Consequently, the ideological relations among the terms nationality, minority, ethnic group, and race imply more than label switches; they are reassessments of the political implications of identity construction for the goals of the homogenizing process. In many instances these label switches imply a homogenizing process directed at ignoring as much heterogeneity as possible. So it is, at a certain historical juncture, that in the United States African-Americans become (ideologically speaking) simply biogenetic mongrels aiming to ride to the pinnacle of civilization in Anglo-European cultural wrappings, as do Afro-Guyanese in Guyana at another historical juncture. Likewise, at still another historical juncture Portuguese as Luso-Guyanese find themselves hard-pressed, first by the ideological eraser of the Anglo-European elite ideology as it removed them from the European "race," and subsequently by an Afro-Indo-Guyanese confabulation that removed them from the logbook of cultural contributions.

Where culture is believed to be determined by "blood" and transmitted through innate propensities and capabilities dichotomized as contributing and noncontributing, to be neither a race nor an ethnic group is to be judged mere politicoeconomic takers. Forever ethnic is Charlie Tuna trying to demonstrate good taste in order to be consumed by the producers of taste. Even so, Charlie Tuna is also forever the Cockalorum, for he must insist on his self-importance, because it is on that insistence that he may hope ultimately to construct his own distinction between having taste and being tasty.

The momentary materialization of ethnic groups is a product of a homogenizing process taking place in the intersection of politically defined territorialism and its implications for the valuation of aspects of the heterogeneity produced in that territory. Understanding fully the form and content of ethnic identities, as well as the manipulative strategies, the variations in self-presentation, and the general social uses to which ethnic identities are put requires that anthropological analyses consider these issues in relation to several factors. These factors are: (1) the manner in which heterogeneity is valued in accordance with nationalist ideological precepts, and (2) the articulation of those precepts in ideas about the interconnections between territorial and cultural nationalisms. Then, these two factors may be analyzed in relation to (3) the goals nationalist precepts set or imply for the nation, and (4) the economic and political consequences of those goals for social categories resulting from differential objective relations to the mode of economic production (that is, classes), as well as for categories generated out of the ideological justification of the mode of production in conjunction with standards of civilization (that is, races, ethnic groups, religious and linguistic minorities, to name but the most common).

In addition, for anthropological investigations of the politics of cultural struggles, it seems especially useful to keep in mind Sederberg's (1984:10) definition of politics as "all deliberate efforts to control systems of shared meaning"—most significantly because he goes on to suggest that

[t]hrough political action we overcome the alienation that results from seeing these collective meanings as apart from ourselves. Such is the promise of politics. Through politics one faction may impose the tyranny of their meanings upon the remainder of the community. Such is the threat of politics. Through politics we innovate collective responses more appropriate to the demands that confront us. For this reason, politics must be embraced. Through politics we weaken and dissolve patterns of life that have been organically integrated into communities of shared meaning. For this reason, politics must be feared. (1984:10–11)

Thus, any anthropological account of the politics of cultural struggle within a particular symbolic system is concerned with how heterogeneity is produced, valued, and interpreted within some unit (for instance, a politically defined territory, a culturally constructed race, a structurally defined class, or a sociopolitically constructed ethnic group). The possibilities for the production, the valuation, and the interpretation of heterogeneity are theoretically infinite. Anthropological treatments must detail how the symbolic systems produced and enclosed in any unit construct coordinates to limit the range of possibilities and are themselves limited by the coordinates they construct.

In this manner, anthropological research can contribute to an understanding of the politics of cultural struggle through its consideration of the relations between cultural struggle and the production and distribution of the material bases of social life in political units. As we analyze the interrelations of identity formation and the structural constraints under which it takes place, we will better accomplish these goals if we do not fall prey to class reductionism by assuming that ideological precepts have an absolute a priori class identity. At the same time, we should avoid the assumption that just any ideological precept and just any articulation of precepts can provide justifications for structural arrangements adequate to move such arrangements from the order of arbitrary constructions to that of naturalized givens. Contrary to Sederberg, treatments of this sort would allow us to demonstrate that sometimes and in some places we may have more to fear from politics when it does *not* "weaken and dissolve patterns of life that have been organically integrated into communities of shared meaning."

However, in providing an ethnographic account of hegemonic dominance and of the ideological struggle to dismantle it, we cannot intend such an analysis as an alternative to that of the role of force and the threat of force in society. Transformist hegemonic dominance at its most entrenched moment provides the practices and the debates about those practices that direct the energies of subordinated strata— whether based in class, race, or culture—away from a direct confrontation with the goals dictated by those in control of force and, hence, always mediates their need to use force. Beyond this hegemonic moment, the struggle to redirect those energies is a long and arduous one. At their best, anthropological treatments of the politics of cultural struggle provide assessments of what social practices suggest about the institutional and microsociological leeway a regime has between its acquisition and control of the instruments of force and its need fully to apply them. Although hegemonic dominance has not been reestablished in Guyana, and although this has created condi-

tions within which force is thinly cloaked in worn hegemonic natural-
izations, it nonetheless still makes a difference in that it provided a
frame within which a regime could steal an election, subvert a constitution, and assassinate its opponents, and expect that such
practices—more politely labeled, of course—could be justified as
revolutionary steps toward dismantling the remnants of colonialism.

Notes

Preface

1. To select a field site, I chose a community that was small enough to be studied by one ethnographer working alone but that also included a reasonably representative distribution of the ethnic diversity of the Guyana coastal strip, where approximately 90 percent of Guyana's population resides. For these reasons field work was conducted, first in the summer of 1976, and then from 1979 to 1980, in a coastal community in Demerara, the smallest but most densely populated county that has an ethnically representative sample of the population inhabiting the coastal areas of Guyana's three counties. In doing so, I also admit to having selected a coastal, regional perspective from which all other analytic movements between the stances it contains take place. In this sense, the cultural reality constructed in this treatment should be taken as an extended hypothesis on the nature of the homogenizing process, to be tested against other regional perspectives in Guyana.

1. On the Politics of Cultural Struggle

1. Cited in Epstein 1978:1; quoted in Leslie 1971:145.

2. The allusion here is to Mannoni's use of Shakespeare's *Tempest* characters, Ariel, Prospero, and Caliban, in his treatise on the psychology of colonization (see Mannoni 1964:Part II, chaps. 1 and 2). Although Ariel is generally the figure of the good native, here the intention is to suggest that in the process of decolonization Valetta and Constantine are engaged in a dialogue about what is to be the nature of the good native not yet born as they face one another, aiming for a utopian world in which Prospero, the civilized colonist, will not set the terms that define Caliban's transformation from semihuman to true human and good native. Under these conditions, the problem for them is the uncertainty about who is Prospero and who is Caliban.

3. Although they differ significantly in their approaches and conclusions, I found the following sources on nationalism most helpful in charting the varying historical relations among class, ethnicity, and race across different

political and economic contexts: Akzin, *State and Nation* (1964); B. Anderson, *Imagined Communities: Reflections on the Origin and Spread of Nationalism* (1983); Hobsbawm, "Some Reflections on 'The Break-up of Britain'" (1977); Kahin, *Nationalism and Revolution in Indonesia* (1962); Kedourie (ed.), *Nationalism in Africa and Asia* (1970); Kohn, *The Age of Nationalism* (1962); Mitchison (ed.), *The Roots of Nationalism: Studies In Northern Europe* (1980); Nairn, *The Break-Up of Britain* (1977); Roff, *The Origins of Malay Nationalism* (1967); and Seton-Watson, *Nations and States: An Enquiry into the Origins of Nations and the Politics of Nationalism* (1977).

4. The terms assimilation and acculturation derive from the same political perspective on the homogenizing process. Assimilation labels the process from the standpoint of those who dominate the selection and the legitimation of criteria in relation to the proposed cultural goals of the homogenizing process in a particular sociopolitical structure, whereas acculturation becomes the euphemistic label for the subordination of those who are not part of this politically defined dominant stratum and whose cultural products are to be appropriated or eliminated. Both terms link the homogenizing process to a form of hegemonic dominance that, following Gramsci (1971), we shall refer to as a transformist hegemony.

5. It is necessary to keep clear the distinction between precept and concept. Precepts are rules and standards, often expressed in principles, maxims, or proverbs, that declare the world to be of a certain composition and to work in a certain way. Precepts become ideological when they are linked to politically privileged interpretations of human experiences that ignore or consider irrelevant information that contradicts their logic. According to the rationalizations that come to characterize these interpretations, the precepts on which they are based are synonymous with—not images of—the world of human experiences. Such rationalizations are accomplished through the production of concepts that are the generalized ideas which objectify notions as elements of taxonomies composed of physical and social types, categories, and classes. The result is a lay philosophy of realism, a system of precepts and concepts linked by interpretations called common sense and received wisdom.

6. There is much work to be done on precolonial conceptions of race among Europeans and on how these conceptions were altered or maintained during the imperialist colonial expansion in the eighteenth and nineteenth centuries. Useful in this regard is *Social Structure* Ross 1982, the published proceedings of a Leiden University symposium on racism and colonialism. Especially instructive are the essays by Van Arkel, "Racism in Europe"; Van Den Boogaart, "Colour Prejudice and the Yardstick of Civility: The Initial Dutch Confrontation with Black Africans 1590–1635"; Betts, "The French Colonial Empire and the French World-View"; and Poliakov, "Racism from the Enlightenment to the Age of Imperialism." Also valuable is Poliakov's

(1974) extended treatment of conceptions of race and nationalism among Europeans.

7. In the past two decades scholars increasingly have compared United States and European, especially English, attitudes toward race and the cultural homogenization of immigrants. Generally, they conclude that in the United States nationality was always defined as naturalization through a process of assimilation and acculturation, whereas this view developed slowly (mainly in the twentieth century) in European countries such as England. See, for example, Banton (1967) and Sivanandan (1973). These variations might suggest the diachronic nature of the homogenizing process rather than indicate different conceptions of how heterogeneity is to be assimilated to a homogeneous core and how that core is to be ideologically justified.

8. See, e.g., Allardt, "Implications of the Ethnic Revival in Modern, Industrialized Society: A Comparative Study of the Linguistic Minorities in Western Europe" (1979); M. Anderson, "The Renaissance of Territorial Minorities in Western Europe" (1978); Beers, *The Unexpected Rebellion: Ethnic Activism in Contemporary France* (1980); Caporaso, "What is the New Nationalism or Is There a New Nationalism" (1979); Coakley, *Independence Movements and National Minorities: Some Parallels in the European Experience* (1977); Greenwood, "Continuity in Change: Spanish Basque Ethnicity as a Historical Process" and other essays in Esman (ed.), *Ethnic Conflict in the Western World* (1977); Hechter, "Ethnicity and Industrialization: On the Proliferation of the Cultural Division of Labor" (1976) and *Internal Colonialism: The Celtic Fringe in British National Development 1536–1966* (1975); Krejci, "Ethnic Problems in Europe" (1978); and Payne, *Basque Nationalism* (1975).

9. On the issue of the heterogeneous blood of the Englishman, Daniel Defoe, in *The True-Born Englishman: A Satyr,* quoted by B. Anderson (1983:10), puts forth the following scenario:

> Thus from a Mixture of all kinds began,
> That Het'rogeneous Thing, *An Englishman:*
> In eager Rapes, and furious Lust begot,
> Betwixt a Painted *Britton* and a *Scot:*
> Whose gend'ring Offspring quickly learnt to bow,
> And yoke their Heifers to the *Roman* Plough:
> From whence a Mongrel half-breed Race there came,
> With neither Name nor Nation, Speech or Fame.
> In whose hot Veins new Mixtures quickly ran,
> Infus'd betwixt a *Saxon* and a *Dane.*
> While their Rank Daughters, to their Parents just,
> Receiv'd all Nations with Promiscuous Lust.
> This Nauseous Brood directly did contain
> The well-extraced Blood of *Englishmen.* . . .

More straightforwardly, Poliakov (1982:23) maintains that "uncertainty about origins and lineages, which were thought to imply different blood-strains, was balanced by the belief in their harmonious fusion." The ideological construction of such a harmonious fusion was by no means an easy feat. In fact, Trevelyan's *A Shortened History of England* (1942) may be read as a very intricate interpretation of English history focused on the appropriation of those cultural products, influences, and contributions to the blood of Englishmen that led, in his view, to the production of a culture and a level of civilization unmatched by any other people, and which was destined to become the civilizing force in the world, while, at the same time, throughout the work he struggles to deny or to eliminate any products, influences, and contributions that might undermine such an interpretation.

10. For a discussion of some of the specific economic coordinates of this process in Ecuador, see Crespi 1975; and for a discussion of a similar ideological conflation of race and status in Peruvian national ideology, see Bourricaud 1975.

11. For useful critical summaries and theoretical essays on definitions of ethnicity and on the strategic political and economic uses of ethnic identity in plural societies, see: Aronson, "Ethnicity as a Cultural System: An Introductory Essay" (1976); Barth (ed.), *Ethnic Groups and Boundaries: The Social Organization of Culture Difference* (1969); Van den Berghe, *The Ethnic Phenomenon* (1981); Castile and Kushner (eds.), *Persistent Peoples: Cultural Enclaves in Perspective* (1981), and Spicer, "Persistent Cultural Systems: A Comparative Study of Identity Systems That Can Adapt To Contrasting Environments" (1971), which inspired the Castile and Kushner collection; Cohen, *The Symbolic Construction of Community* (1985), esp. 97–119; Epstein, *Ethos and Identity: Three Studies in Ethnicity* (1978); Keyes, "Toward a New Formulation of the Concept of Ethnicity" (1975); Gold and Paine (eds.), *Mother Country and Ethnicity* (1985); Glazer and Moynihan (eds.), *Ethnicity: Theory and Experience* (1975); Nagata, "Pluralism in Malaysia: Myth and Reality" (1975); Schermerhorn, *Comparative Ethnic Relations: A Framework for Theory and Research* (1978); Reminick, *Theory of Ethnicity: An Anthropologist's Perspective* (1983).

12. The use of ideological fields follows closely the work of S. Barnett, who defines it as a situation wherein

[A]t the same time a person is interior to an ideology, he is exterior to other ideologies (sex, class, race, kin, etc.) in the same society (all such ideologies constituting an ideological field). These exterior ideologies are at least partially understandable (sharing global symbols common to the whole society) but do not provide a direct frame for action. Placement (interior vs. exterior) is therefore critical and moves praxis to the center of the analytical stage. (1977:276)

And he goes on to state that

[S]ymbols embody, in their range of possible meanings, meanings which specify contradictions (such global symbols may, at the same time, be central to two or more ideologies in fundamental conflict). Here a stress on certain possibilities within a range of meaning (and a devaluation of other possibilities) defines a person's place (interiority) in an ideological field. The symbolic stress of groups controlling resources and use of resources defines an overall structure-in-dominance and opposition to that structure. An abstract accounting of all metaphorical possibilities of meaning without regard for stressed and unstressed aspects defines the range of options within an ideological field (but *not* the field itself since it always has dominance aspects). (1977:277)

We depart, however, from Barnett's position by insisting that the ideological field must be further sorted into the range and types of precepts from which its conceptual structures are produced by persons who, rather than being interior/exterior to the ideologies that make up this field, are instead simultaneously accountable in all situations to the variety of competing interpretations multiple ideologies make possible (see Chapter 4).

13. This comment and others on hegemony are based primarily on Gramsci's writings in *Selections from the Prison Notebooks of Antonio Gramsci* (1971). Otherwise, I follow most closely Chantal Mouffe's reading of Gramsci on the distinction between transformist and expansive hegemonies. However, as with the popularization of any concept, there are many definitions of the concept and many unfortunate applications of the term in places where domination, oppression, or simply inequality would suffice. Such generalized usage has, however, resulted in a greater concern with clarity and consistency in usage. In this regard see, e.g., Lears 1985, Katznelson 1973: esp. 467–74; Mouffe 1979, G. Williams 1960, and Sassoon 1980: esp. 109–248.

14. This absence of correspondence between producer, cultural elements, and their ideological usage in the construction and in the maintenance of political and economic structures establishes, of course, the problems with which Gramsci grappled. His concerns were (1) how to explain the means by which cultural elements are selectively assimilated to a mode of interpretation that "naturalizes" an ideology (i.e., makes conclusions that appear to be given in the nature of things rather than in the privileging of particular limits on the range of acceptable interpretations and associated practices), and (2) how consistency between this ideology and a mode of institutionalizing practices associated with it are made to serve the structural interests of a particular historical bloc (i.e., a ruling stratum and members of other strata pragmatically allied to it). In an attempt to provide a theoretical framework adequate for grappling with these problems, Laclau (1977:143–200) suggests that we treat the element through which subjects are interpellated as autonomous units that are employed by different classes and thereby come to have a class identity as these actors assimilate them to different ideological

positions. Thus, he concludes that available cultural production becomes class products and figures into the construction of ideological supports for political and economic domination in conjunction with various articulating principles used by different classes to assimilate cultural products to an ideological stance and to a set of institutional practices conducive to their own ends. Hence, the social force of these products stems from the ambiguity and multivocality generated out of contradictions and complementarities between continuities in the meanings that their producer attributes to them and the subsequent meaning they take on when articulated to the ideological projects of a dominating stratum. From this standpoint, "it is necessary to conclude that *classes exist at the ideological and political level in a process of articulation and not of reduction*" (Laclau 1977:161). Moreover, he suggests that, when the reductionist assumption is abandoned, classes defined "as the poles of antagonistic production relations . . . have no *necessary* form of existence at the ideological and political levels" (Laclau 1977:159). Further,

[i]f classes are present at the ideological and political levels—since relations of production maintain the role of determination in the last instance—and if the *contents* of ideology and of political practice cease to be the *necessary* forms of existence of classes at these levels, the only way of conceiving this presence is to say that the class character of an ideology is given by its *form* and not by its *content*. [In] what does the form of an ideology consist? . . . the answer is in the principle of articulation of its constituent interpellations. The class character of an ideological discourse is revealed in what we could call its *specific articulating principle.* (Laclau 1977:160)

Yet, as Therborn, responding to Laclau's position, asks, "if classes have no necessary form of ideological and political existence, if ideologies and political forms have no necessary class character, how can we then identify the class character of the articulating principle?" (1980:130, n. 23) To provide an answer that is consistent with the general tenor of Laclau's efforts, Therborn proposes that "the subjects of the class struggle must be conceived of as being constituted by class-specific ideologies and forms of political practice" (p. 130, n. 23). That is to say, his corrective requires a theoretical rather than a historical determination of class ideologies, but without the insistence that such ideologies are composed only of class-produced elements. A theoretical determination of specific class ideologies proceeds from an identification of a class-specific position in relation to the means of production seeking to identify the "minimum . . . interpellations of what exists, what is good, . . . what is possible . . . [and] necessary for a class of human beings to perform their economically defined roles" (Therborn 1980:55). Despite the problems raised by the introjection of a functionalist minimum, Therborn's corrective is worthwhile to the extent that it includes an analytic concern with the politicoeconomic limitation on the articulation of form and content in the construction of class ideologies and their intersection in complex ideological fields.

15. Under British colonial control the colony's name was spelled Guiana. After independence (1966) this spelling was changed to Guyana. My alternation between these two spellings indicates the political status of the territory during the period under consideration at that moment in the text. Where further clarification is needed, dates are included with both spellings and for the Guiana spelling the adjective British or colonial is affixed.

16. The linkages between practice and ideological interpretations of practice in a hegemonic process are rooted in the character of objective relations that make possible the formation of a historical bloc (i.e., pragmatically allied strata and other specific, often temporary, coalitions whose actions complement the interest of these consciously allied groupings). These objective relations create the conditions that allow this bloc to gain and to maintain control over the legitimate uses of force, political power, the levels of productivity, and the distribution of economic resources. It is, therefore, in the objective relations between what Laclau (1977) refers to as "the people" and "the power bloc" that we must seek the factors influencing variable emphasis on antagonistic articulating principles in any ideological field.

17. Premdas underscores the interrelations between ideological appropriations and material constraints in the Burnham government's efforts to nationalize its interests when he concludes that "the [economic] nationalization of foreign firms in Guyana originated from economic necessity. Socialist principles invoked post facto to justify the nationalization later became the determinative guide in government decision-making" (1978:161–62).

To the extent that socialist principles subsequently became the determining guide in government decision making, Premdas attributes the change to the ruling PNC's efforts to reach a reconciliation with the PPP, which continued to enjoy the support and loyalty of the majority of the rural East Indian population, whose cooperation was needed if any real transformation of the agricultural sector was to be achieved.

18. Attention to these political and ideological maneuvers should not lead us to ignore the development and utilization of military and other coercive forces. In addition to the harassment of any opposition and fraudulent elections, the retrenchment of the Burnham government also has been accompanied by a rapid and extensive escalation of military and paramilitary forces (see Dann 1983).

2. Cockalorum: Spatial Boundaries, Economic Limits, and Cultural Constraints

1. In order to distinguish, when necessary, differences in grammar, meaning, and usage among Guyanese English (Creolese), Standard American

English (SAE), and Standard British English (SBE), I place Creolese words and expressions in quotation marks when introducing them. Where appropriate, this introduction is followed by a definition. Thereafter, I use quotation marks whenever (1) number and tense are grammatically incorrect for SBE and SAE but are consistent with typical Creolese usage recorded during the field period, (2) similarities among SAE, SBE, and Creolese might convey meanings irrelevant to Creolese, (3) I desire to emphasize the term to clarify a point, or (4) they provide a reminder for infrequently used terms.

Hindi, Dutch, and other non-English words and phrases that are part of Creolese are treated simply as Creolese lexicon. This is consistent with the practice according to which most loan words in SBE and SAE are no longer underlined. It is important to note that to do otherwise would, especially in the case of Hindi words, result in my participation in the racist discourse that treats English elements as "standard" and "authentic," whereas other elements of the Guyanese cultural amalgam are considered inauthentic, and that makes African elements "Creole," whereas East Indian ones remain "Indian." Although this procedure, like the effort to remove sexist expressions, is not a perfect solution, it brings to the readers' attention my concern, as an American writer, to minimize my involvement in the ongoing imperialist politics of cultural oppression, euphemistically referred to as linguistic standardization.

2. The name Brooklyntown was chosen for this section because of the relationship that many residents have with persons living in Brooklyn, New York. Many have relatives living there, others have spent periods of time there themselves, and still others have plans for one day "taking a walk" to see and maybe even work in Brooklyn. A large portion of the vacant lots and houses in Brooklyntown are owned or in part controlled by these absentee relatives. It is the most frequently asked-about location in the United States, and, to the extent that one place can be accorded that role, it is the place that most influences local ideas about fashion and life among Africans in the United States. In a very real sense Brooklyn, New York, is part of the cultural universe of Brooklyntown, Guyana. East Indians in this and other sections of Cockalorum also have relations in New York City in general and Brooklyn in particular, though their kin are more likely to migrate to Canada, especially Toronto.

3. Ecological constraints made the layout of Guianese plantations fairly standard, usually 100 to 300 rods (1 rod = 12.32 feet), beginning with a depth of 750 rods. The initial size of plantations varied from 500 to 2,000 acres, increasing in size as additional land was reclaimed and smaller plantations were amalgamated. Village settlements established by emancipated slaves and by time-expired indentured laborers usually maintained this layout, which placed farmland at the rear of a nucleated residential settlement criss-crossed by drainage canals. See McLewin 1971:216–18 for a

description of a typical nineteenth-century Guianese estate, and, among others, Rodney 1981:73 for a diagram of the usual drainage system layout for the same period.

4. Proprietary villages, in which individuals bought lots, and communal villages, in which large amounts of land were purchased with the combined funds of many contributors, were distinguished from each other and from unincorporated settlements. (With reference to the implications of these distinctions for local government administration and taxation, see Young 1958.)

5. The religious affiliation of households is based on the preference given by the majority of the household members. In many homes members are affiliated with different religions or denominations of the same religion. This is likely to be the case in Christian East Indian households, where younger members are Christian at the same time older members are Hindu or Muslim, and in mixed households, where each member may be affiliated with a different religion.

6. It was not until the late 1940s for Africans and the mid-1950s for East Indians that informants reported the founding of the local retail shops by members of these groups, who eventually displaced the Portuguese and the Chinese as shopkeepers in the different sections of Cockalorum. After the disturbances of the 1960s, shopping within one's section and in shops owned by one's own racial/ethnic group took on greater importance.

7. Throughout this text, the slash (/) is used as a graphic representation of conflated variables. I present two or more terms in this manner to indicate that, with respect to the comments before or after the conflated terms, they cannot be separated because the meanings and implications of both (or several) are simultaneously and equally relevant.

I do not use a hyphen in these situations because the hyphen, as suggested by general argument of this text, indicates the assimilation of one entity to another to produce a third entity that differs from either of the entities the hyphen joins. Moreover in the politics of cultural struggle, the accomplishment of a hyphenated joining of elements of their identity is, ideologically speaking, a major task ordering the politics of cultural production among ethnic groups, in contrast to the nationalist politics of cultural production whereby ideology is directed at effacing the hyphen to make of nation-states putatively homogeneous nations or states.

8. For ordinary purposes, all Cockalorums speak an English-based creole, referred to as Guyanese English or Creolese. Standard British English (SBE) is the national language and the official language of instruction. Most community members can understand the standard forms, although they differ in both their willingness and ability to produce them in different social situations.

To date there is neither a dictionary of Creolese (i.e., Guyanese English) nor a standard orthography. Consequently, the spelling of Guyanese words used herein is consistent with the most frequent forms encountered during the field period in public documents, newspapers, and other publications. Where such examples were not available, the spelling is based on my own and on my informants' best approximations.

9. To avoid the politically unfortunate use of the masculine gender for descriptions that are equally applicable to males and females, when possible to do so without extreme redundancy, I use person, individual, and other such gender-neutral terms. At points where this procedure would result in such repetition, as an alternate I favor the standard practice over the cumbersome he/she, his/her constructions. Although I could have alternated between gender-neutral and feminine usage, I decided this would result in more confusion than clarity, given the current standard. Thus, wherever the masculine gender appears in the text, unless otherwise specified it should be understood that the issues discussed apply to both genders, and that feminine usage is reserved for those instances that have greater significance for women than for men. Where other terms such as Englishman, Scotsman, and gendered Guyanese terms, such as countrymen, are used the sexism is retained because it is either historically or ethnographically accurate.

10. The stereotypes and the need to explain away deviations are rooted in broader conceptions of the nature of ethnicity and the place of ethnic cultures in the total sociocultural order. See Part II for a discussion of the historical and ideological context of ethnic competition.

11. See Bonaparte 1969 for a discussion of the influence of culture on business practices in Trinidad and Tobago. Bonaparte argues that one set of values establishes organizational goals, while another set establishes the order of interethnic interaction that allows for the development and maintenance of particular ethnic identities. Past relationships serve as validation for the present and shape expectations of future sameness with respect to the roles of ethnically identified persons and the distribution of authority within the workplace. Moreover, Bonaparte suggests that profit maximization is frequently subordinated to the consideration of status and prestige.

12. In short, their current stereotypes of Portuguese conceptions of making life are also consistent with that expressed by Bronkhurst 1883 when he reports a Portuguese saying: "*Cobra boa firma, e deita-te a dormir,*" which he translates as, "'When your name is up, you may lie in bed till noon.'" Antonio Vieryra's *Dictionary of the Portuguese and English Languages* (1813) gives "*Cobra boa fama, e deita-te a dormir,*" which is translated as "'Get a good name, and lie down to sleep,' or '[L]ike ours, when your name is up, you may lie abed until noon'."

13. "Deh" has several meanings in Guyanese Creolese (see, e.g., McAndrew 1978:155). This sentence suggests a play on two of these: "there" (locative adverb) and "to be up to a task." Hence, the sentence translates: "Your Black heritage is much too evident and too capable of determining

your behavior for your distant Portuguese ancestry to have any influence on your actions."

3. Status Stratification and Status Signaling

1. There are real differences and financial constraints on individuals, nonetheless, the aim is to approximate what an outsider might consider to be a middle- to upper-class lifestyle. Early descriptions of rural villages often include complaints about what the writers labeled the "pretentiousness of the poorer classes." Ignoring the economic and political constraints on village development, Cropper (1912:257) complained that too much sail and not enough ballast in the education boat and the absence of a residential gentry as models had resulted in the need to "ruralise" villages, especially those on the east coast of Demerara, where he believed the "idea seems to be emphasised that every little village aspires to be a miniature Georgetown, both in its natural appearance and in the style of life of its inhabitants."

2. This notion of the government as master was heightened in 1979 during Republic Week, when the government was rumored to have announced that persons living in a housing scheme would be evicted from their homes if they did not clean their yards and their trenches as part of the effort to beautify Guyana for the holiday celebrations. Although housing-scheme residents said they received no such threat, the rumors persisted, and most people reported them as fact.

3. When East Indians in Cockalorum speak of "jat" (caste), they are referring to one of the four "varnas." Actual caste within varna is rarely known (see Klass 1961 for a similar conclusion about East Indians in a village in Trinidad). There seems to be some variation on this point in Guyana. Rauf (1974) states that his informants in a Corentyne village were able to name their caste but not the varna to which it belonged. He also argued that, although the caste system had ceased to be the basis of social stratification, it continued to exist in the reinterpreted ideas of younger East Indians, who viewed all East Indians as one caste and spoke of lower caste as a reference to personal attributes based on individual behavior in particular situations. In Cockalorum, East Indians state that all one needs to know to identify an individual's caste (varna) is his surname. Using a list of all the surnames in the community, a pandit and lay informants matched them with a particular varna. They claimed that only marriages and funerals are still influenced by considerations of caste, and they reported cases where older Sanatan pandits refused to perform the wedding ceremony for couples not of the same caste. Other informants contend that at funerals guests are not comfortable eating food served unless the deceased and those who sponsor the service are of their caste.

Yet, in many instances, the terms caste and jat are used as synonyms for "nation," which may mean either family or ethnic group. Moreover, all Guyanese tend to conflate caste and race, with Africans and East Indians being seen as two different caste groups. Caste is also associated with intraethnic religious differences, as when Muslims and Hindus are viewed as two castes within the East Indian population. These associations are also linked to conceptions of status difference and may conflate caste and class. Caste distinctions, however, do not carry with them rules of pollution, commensality, and other restrictions on social interaction generally considered part of conceptions of caste in India and in other parts of the world. Overall, most East Indian Hindus in this community argue that because their ancestors had to cross the "kali pani" (black water/ocean) to reach Guyana, they lost their purity and hence their caste identity. Thus, they say, all caste claims are false.

4. I will use the term men throughout, but the designation small or big also applies to women and across generations.

5. The term "bottom-class" also may be applied to a person who, despite economic success, is considered a moral degenerate. Likewise, "top-class" refers to those who are especially upright, regardless of their financial situation.

6. Local residents often form opinions of migrants' life abroad on the basis of how frequently they send money. Although it may not be possible to determine the type of work they do on the basis of how often they send money, informants claim that this must tell something about how the emigrants live. If remittances are infrequent, it is taken as a sign that the person is working in a low-paying position, is careless with money, or does not intend to come back to Guyana. When returning migrants describe their life abroad or attempt to claim status on the basis of it, Cockalorums consider these types of interpretations as they respond.

4. The Art of Becoming "Somebody"

1. Cockalorum small men still refer to members of this category as mati. They also continue to attribute differences among themselves to luck. However, they argue that interethnic differences are due to long-term historical conditions and to past and present racial discrimination, whereas intraethnic variations are the result of nepotism and immorality. They frequently say that those most likely to succeed in rising above the mati category are those who are also predisposed to commit immoral acts to advance themselves. This contention, despite Hindu East Indians' belief in karma and reincarnation, is consistent across ethnic/religious boundaries. Such attitudes echo a set of beliefs Hutson (1971:48) catalogued among members of an egalitarian-oriented French Alpine community, about which she concludes: "the ability to play off material and moral attributes against each

other helps to maintain equality." Thus, the seemingly higher status of the wealthy and successful is "dismissed as having been gained through cheating and the rich man is put in his place by accusation of low moral status."

2. Edwards (1978:196), distinguishing between a quarrel and a "busin' out" or "war" (also referred to in Cockalorum as "busin' down"), notes that, whereas a quarrel generally sticks to the issue that provoked the disagreement, "[i]n a *busin out* (or *war*), however, the immediate cause of the difficulty is soon ignored or allowed only minor importance and insults are made at behaviour and attributes not all involved in the immediate context." For a more detailed discussion of busin' as a speech act, see Edwards 1976.

3. Fisher's (1976) comment on the Barbadian's concern with appearance in public, where he notes that a great deal of caution is required in public interaction because all community members are acutely aware of their human surroundings, sounds a note consistent with Cockalorums' view of the public arena and its dangers. So, too, does Reisman's conclusion that "walking lost in thought is not recommended in the West Indies if one wants to keep one's friends," because "the amount of constant scanning and attention to others that most West Indians practice makes them all the rivals of some of our [American] best politicians" (1974:114). Abrahams (1968), Wilson (1973), and other scholars of Caribbean social life have also noted this attentiveness to and the ambiguity associated with moral assessments of public conduct. Such attentiveness, ambiguity, and equivocal interpretations are by no means confined to Caribbean or "face-to-face" societies. Goffman's extensive work on deference, demeanor, and self-presentation has increased our microsociological understanding of U.S. Americans' scrutiny of others' public behavior and their often highly conscious manipulations of features of interaction in the interest of impression management. Anthropologists also have been made aware of the intense attention to the public conduct of self and of others as a general feature of what Bailey (1971) calls the "small politics" of face-to-face communities—often densely populated settlements characterized by intense social interaction and multiplex relations centering on the "whole person" rather than on the separate role identities of the person. Though aspects of their arguments remain highly problematic, Frankenberg (1957), Banfield (1958), Foster (1960–61), Pitt-Rivers (1960), Jayawardena (1963, 1968), Campbell (1964), Peristiany (1966) and other scholars in the same volume, Bailey (1971) and his students, and Fleming (1979), to note but a few, have also done much to enhance our understanding of the complex relations between politicoeconomic structures, the development and persistence of egalitarian ideological precepts, and their relationship to local conceptions of morality, patterns of social interaction, and modes of status competition.

4. Broadcasting and throwing hints are similar types of behavior or speech acts. Both involve one party transmitting information about another

party without directly addressing that party. To throw hints is to emit messages to a specific third party in the presence or earshot of the party for whom the message is intended. Broadcasting differs from throwing hints because the message is not conveyed directly to a specific party. Instead, a soliloquy is performed in a location where an interested party might reasonably be expected to hear it. Both types of behavior usually occur when the party is uncertain of the facts but wishes to inform the other party that he is aware of a possible transgression and is displeased. Both are defensive maneuvers that allow the speaker to plead innocent if later charged with falsely accusing the other party.

5. In contemporary Standard American and British English, virago means a loud, ill-tempered, scolding woman—a shrew. In its archaic sense it referred to a woman of masculine strength or spirit—an Amazon. In Guyanese English (Creolese), it denotes a quick-tempered male. A woman with the same characteristics could conceivably be called a virago, though more likely she will simply be said to be "mannish" or one who "plays man." Kean Gibson, in her discussion of Guyanese slang, identifies virago and its shortened form 'rago as terms for a particularly hot-tempered thief (1976:84). In Cockalorum thievery is not a characteristic necessarily associated with a virago.

6. See, e.g., Abrahams's (1970:65ff.) description of "badman heroes" and Levine's (1977:420ff.) comments on the "moral hard man." With reference to Levine's discussion, it should be noted that the "bad-ass nigger" hero, unlike moral hard men, does not always achieve his successes within the limits of the law.

7. Mauss, in his early work (1925) on the form and the function of exchange, noted that systems of exchange are based on three obligations: giving, receiving, and repaying. He further wrote that the creation of relationships through exchange is dependent on the timing of repayment. To repay a gift immediately is to refuse the relationship established through the obligation to give and repay expressed in the initial exchange. In a more recent work, applying Mauss's conclusions, Stack (1974) has described the system of swapping among members of a U.S. Afro-American community, noting that relationships are formed not by an immediate equal exchange of goods and services, but through a recognition of the long-term obligation to give and the right to receive. See also Bloch 1971, 1973; Laughlin 1974; Riches 1981.

8. It is a typical feature of most quarrels that, as tempers flare, histories of the moral and legal transgressions of the disputants' ancestors and descendants often receive as much or more attention than the issue that instigated the quarrel. Edwards (1978:212–13), distinguishing types of busin', identifies a type of busin' in which, he states, a narrative of "the immoral history of

the ancestors of one's adversary is traced. In Jamaica one term for busin is *tracin* which takes its name from this variety of busin."

9. Consistent, however, with Jayawardena's (1968) and Weinberg's (1975) conclusions, Cockalorums complain that today people do not respect informal resolution procedures and are too quick to turn any dispute into a "court story." Disputants are quick to threaten to "carry the matter to the outpost" or to "action" (file formal charges against the other party). Between parties with equal economic and social resources, such charges are often empty threats or mere bargaining moves, whereas for others they are more serious because one party has the economic means to take the matter to court but the other does not. In the latter situation impoverished parties forced to go to court may lose face and may damage their names because they cannot afford a lawyer. Under these conditions frequently the more indigent party will seek to "settle out of court," paying the other party a demanded compensation and, therefore, accepting some damage to face to avoid involvement in a "court story." Relatives who believe their kinsperson to be wrong may, by refusing to assist with court costs, apply pressure to get them to settle out of court.

5. Ideology and the Formation of Anglo-European Hegemony

1. Rationalizations are explanations and justifications that, though consistent with some objective factors, are motivated by an interest in and an interpretation of those factors that are favorable to the person's or group's sense of responsibility for the act or situation.

2. The basic sources, many of which are cited in the text, used in the preparation of this section cover different historical periods and are uneven in quality and in the attention they devote to the treatment and to the activities of dominant and subordinate groups. Although they are fairly consistent in the sociocultural picture they present of the colonial era, there are also inconsistencies and contradictions within and across these texts. Comments in this section draw on their most consistent conclusions about the groups and the periods on which they focus. General historical references include Dalton 1855; Daly 1975; Farley 1954, 1955; Harris and de Villiers 1911; Netscher 1888 trans. Roth 1931; Rodway 1891–94, 1912; and Smith 1962. Discussion of eighteenth- and nineteenth-century British and Dutch policy toward Amerindians is primarily based on the work of Menezes (1973, 1977, 1979), with reference to Henfrey 1965 and Ridgewell 1972 for the twentieth century. The most detailed accounts of the treatment and the activities of Africans and of East Indians were found in Adamson 1972; Bronkhurst 1883, 1888; Comins 1893, 1894; Despres 1964, 1967, 1969; Farley 1954, 1955, 1956; Nath 1950; Potter 1975, 1982; Rodney 1981;

and Ruhomon 1947. Information on Chinese immigration and treatment was drawn from Clementi 1915; Fried 1956; general historical sources, and personal descriptions of colonial life such as Bronkhurst 1883; Crookall 1898; Kirke 1898; and Premium 1850. Wagner 1975, 1977 offers the most systematic analysis of the treatment and the policies affecting Portuguese activities, with Moore 1975 and Laurence 1965 offering less detailed discussions.

3. Kirke (1898:349) defines Boviander as a cross between a Dutchman and a native Indian. He suggest that the term itself derives from a creolization of "above-lander"—a geographical designation. "Cabbacula" and Boviander or Buffianda are terms still used to refer to persons of African-Aboriginal parentage; however, in daily discussions these terms are less frequently heard than Doogla with some adjective affixed to indicate the specific mixture.

4. Here the term "No Nation" refers to a local belief that, if for some reason all Guyanese were forced to leave Guyana, persons of mixed ancestry would be unable to make an unambiguous claim to historically derived rights to another nationality and would thus become people without a nation.

5. In the term "Carib-ogre," Carib suggests that the most typical union may have been between Africans and Caribs, whereas ogre suggests that Europeans' negative assessment of escaped Africans as less than human also influenced their conceptions of this mixed category.

6. The Dutch did not make Native exclusion from slavery official until 1793. Even then, they continued to encourage them to enslave one another, and nineteenth-century postholders were not infrequently accused of keeping Natives as slaves.

7. This distinction between natural and man-made Guiana not only redefined European and Native relations to the land and its productivity but also rationalized the adjustment of claims among Europeans. The "conquered" Dutch, now foreigners in the land in which they had been the first European settlers, whose technical knowledge was essential to the alteration of the coastal environment, were stereotyped by the British as dull, plodding, and lacking the vision to conquer the hostile coast. The move to the coast, although prompted by a search for the most fertile soil, in the received British rationalizations of the nineteenth and twentieth centuries, was inspired instead, to quote Pinckard (1806:323), by "the enterprise of the more adventurous planter from the British islands."

8. This was also the conclusion reported by the commission that investigated the causes of the extremely high death rate among the first Portuguese immigrants. It admitted that the Madeira emigrants had arrived in British Guiana during the wet season and at a time a yellow fever epidemic was raging. But, in its opinion, these factors were not more important than the

self-deprivation of the Portuguese, their overexertion before becoming ac-
climated, and their religiously inspired reluctance to accept medical treatment. It must, however, be kept in mind that the commission was primarily
interested in the question whether this immigration should be discontinued
on the ground that the Portuguese were physiologically unsuited to the
Guianese climate and work regimen.

9. It is also possible that by this time African villagers were not as
interested in these commercial enterprises as Europeans feared. Undoubt-
edly, Africans were concerned with economic mobility and the right to take
advantage of any opportunity available in their society. However, Hickerson's (1954) discussion of African attitudes toward shopkeeping in particular
suggests that, at least by the 1950s, they had an image of themselves and
their ancestors as persons who shunned such activities because the behavior
necessary to success was inconsistent with their communalism. It may also
be significant that anyone engaging in such enterprises at this point had to
do so without behaving in a manner that contradicted the positive features
of his own ethnic group stereotypes and without succumbing to the negative
aspects of Portuguese stereotypes (i.e., acting like a "manny," a derogatory
term for a Portuguese shopkeeper).

6. Anglo-European Hegemony and the Culture of Domination

1. As Abercrombie (1980:29) points out, those who would posit a dominant ideology and claim for it determinate effects on class relations must do
so "without lapsing into instrumentalist explanations which reduce dominant ideology to a form of indoctrination generated within the dominant
class." Moreover, subordinates' utilization (or incorporation) of ideological
content generated out of their structural relations to elite strata must, as
Gellner (1978:74) notes, have a degree of "efficacy in terms of some prior
world, a world *preceding* the one to be defined and logically dominated by the
ideology in question. So, in a curious way, ideologies tacitly and implicitly
admit that they do not dominate or fill out the world after all. They function
within a world they did not themselves make."

More to the point and consistent with the suggested transformation of
prototypical understandings into stereotypical ones and their human embodiment, Perkins argues that stereotypes "seem to be ideological phenomena" and "should therefore be capable of being accounted for by any
theory of ideology," and "as ideological phenomena of a peculiarly 'public'
and easily identifiable kind they may provide a useful means of studying the
practice of ideology" (1979:135). Taking the position that stereotypes are an
integral part of ideology, she suggests that their analysis provides a means of
studying a cross-section of ideology rather than a single stratum. Arguing
that stereotypes have the same structure as ideology, she insists that we

should not simply assert that stereotypes are rigid: we must, instead, "look at the social relationships to which they refer, and at their conceptual status" (p. 141). In this regard, she argues that "a stereotype brings to the surface and makes explicit and central what is concealed in the concept of status or role. . . . Stereotypes are selections and arrangements of particular values and their relevance to specific roles" (p. 143). Moreover, she concludes that the strength of a stereotype results from its simplicity, its recognizability, and "its implicit reference to an assumed consensus about some attribute or complex of social relationships. Stereotypes are in this respect prototypes of 'shared cultural meaning'" (p. 141).

2. See, e.g., Seymour 1970.

3. February is quoting a lecture delivered in 1971 by Wilson Harris in Aarhus, Denmark.

4. I am most grateful to John Rickford for sharing with me his transcription of this interview, recorded June 21, 1975, in an east coast Demerara village several miles west of Cockalorum.

5. The actual population demographics, for British Guiana and Cockalorum, have been provided in the preceding chapters; the size of the sections of this graphic, therefore, do not portray accurately the numerical strength of the ethnic label in the section. Pyramids and triangles are structural metaphors most frequently used in the literature to describe the Guianese social hierarchy. Thus, the segments in this graphic are simply wide enough to create a reasonable triangular representation of the layers of the stratification system. No further meaning should be attributed to their width.

The placement of the sections is to be interpreted according to the racial ideology that placed Englishmen and English culture above all other Europeans and their cultures, but situated all Europeans and their cultures above non-Europeans and their cultures. Hence, this aspect of the ideology is represented by the break between sections 1 and 2. Taken together, the two sections (labeled on the left as "Colonial era racial and cultural stratification") represent an ideological image of the colonial sociocultural order, drawn from an idealized Anglo-European perspective. Taken together, sections 3 and 4 (labeled on the left, "Future ethnic stratification of 'Givers' and 'Takers'") represent the inverted sociocultural order, drawn from an idealized East Indian perspective. The break between sections 3 and 4, as with between 1 and 2, indicates the stratification of Europeans and their separation from all non-Europeans.

7. The "Ethnic Production" of Class Stratification

1. The use of ethnic identity and ethnic culture as proof of group contributions, and, hence, as criteria for defining what ought to constitute a just distribution of power, is essentially political. In this regard, it is consis-

tent with, though somewhat different from, Verdery's conclusions about German ethnic identity in Romania. Comparing ethnicity under capitalism and under socialism in Europe, she states,

First, though the *means* of striving are similar, the ultimate *objective* of striving is not—in the one case, ethnic political competition aims to secure markets and a more certain share in self-perpetuating profits; in the other, power is sought for itself and for its patronage-generating capacities. . . . Second, because a basic achievement of socialist regimes like Romania's has been to increase *collective* mobility, rather than just individual mobility, the potentially divisive discrepancies in life chances within ethnic groups have been diminished and pose less of a hazard to the unity of ethnic movements. This may have the effect of *reinforcing* ethnic solidarities in socialist political economies, contrary to the expectations of socialist regimes. But in both socialist and capitalist systems, ethnicity still remains essentially a political struggle in which competing ethnic groups orient themselves to power, albeit for different ends. (n.d.:43)

In Cockalorum individuals of all ethnic groups can reasonably choose to pursue any available economic opportunity, despite lingering racial and ethnic discrimination. Nevertheless, ethnicity and ethnic identity continue to be linked to the *legitimation* of ethnic group rights to full participation in the social system. The features of this legitimation process provide the criteria by which ethnically identified individuals seeking particular types of opportunities are considered to be simply following their "natural tendencies" within the bounds of their rights or going against nature and being "uppity" by trying to usurp rights belonging to other contributors.

2. In the views most frequently expressed by Cockalorums, the quest for ethnic domination is too ingrained to be overcome unless the entire Guyanese population becomes biogenetically Doogla. On this latter point, Drummond (1974) reports that his Pomeroon Amerindian informants expressed the belief that the mongrelization of the population is an informal aspect of government integration policy. As proof, they point to the all-male (predominantly African) camps established in the region. They say these camps and their populations provide the means for producing "mixed persons." Yet, as Drummond also notes, cultural definitions of Amerindian identity have resulted in the addition of such mixed persons to the ranks of the Amerindian population.

3. In Figure 7.1, although it would be grammatically correct to use cultural and racial, it would be conceptually incorrect. I have used culture and race because it is the *reification* of these concepts and their conflations which serve as criteria for creating relations and evaluating entrants.

8. Religion, Class, Culture, and the Ghost of Hegemony

1. Local conceptions of "religious races" cross-cut other definitions of race based on geographical origin of ancestors or on culture generally

defined. In this sense, for example, the East Indian ethnic group is spoken of by East Indians and by others as a group composed of two major races— Hindus and Muslims. By this logic, Christians of all ethnic backgrounds are members of the same religiously, but not biologically or geographically, defined race. This possibility for "racial" integration posed, however, the same problems as those posed by the recognition and adoption of "things English."

2. Although official census statistics of national religious composition for 1980 were not available during the field period, government officials with whom I spoke estimated that Christians or persons affiliated with sects based on Christianity accounted for approximately 220,000 of the total population of 800,000. Among Christians, they estimated that Roman Catholics were the largest group, at about 120,000. Of the non-Christian religions, approximately 320,000 of the estimated 440,000 East Indians are Hindus. Muslims (mainly Sunni) number about 100,000 of that total, with the balance being at least nominal Christians. In Cockalorum 54 percent of the population of 5,000 is Christian, 36 percent Hindu, and 10 percent Muslim (see Table 2.2). The religious composition of each section of Cockalorum is given in Table 2.4, by number of households claiming affiliation with Hinduism, Islam, and Christianity.

3. I refer to Anglo-European hegemony as a ghost because its physical representatives and their direct coercive actions are now absent from the national arena; however, just as a ghost has powers that the living being does not possess, the continuing influence of this past pattern of hegemonic dominance is in many ways more powerful now than when the Anglo-Europeans lived in Guiana. When they were present, both their competencies and their incompetencies were on daily display. Now that they are absent, there is a tendency to romanticize the past; also, when one has a brass ring in hand, one can more clearly and dispassionately judge its worth than one can while struggling to attain it. Moreover, when one can only hope to gain the second rank, one is more prone to criticize the overall value of the first rank, especially when exclusion from that rank has both abstract and concrete negative consequences.

9. "Bamboo" Weddings and the Ghost of Hegemonic Dominance

1. Here I am using communal morality as a gloss for the complex use of egalitarian and hierarchical precepts in interpersonal status evaluation discussed in Chapters 3 and 4.

2. Although the name is taken from the bamboo used in the construction of the marau (Hindu wedding booth), "bamboo wedding" is employed by all Cockalorums to refer to all non-Christian East Indian wedding rituals. My

use of the expression bamboo wedding in the title of this chapter is a reference to this generalized usage. Among East Indians it is most often a neutral label, though it may also be a derogatory term, especially for the Christian or Muslim East Indian interested in denigrating "coolie ways" as lower class or Hindu. It may be derogatory in intent when used by a non-East Indian, but it is also likely to carry a tinge of "covetousness." It is, like the rituals we will discuss in this chapter, an ambivalent or ambiguous designation.

3. Some informants insist that only flour bags are truly appropriate ground cover, but others say sheets are perfectly acceptable, as flour bags were used in the past only because people had nothing else to use. These comments, like others pertaining to variation and flexibility in substituting objects and actions for one another, are part of local commentary that distinguishes what is considered to be either customary or pragmatic from what is real culture. Real cultural tradition consists of those beliefs, objects, and ways of behaving that informants say can be traced directly back to their ancestors' point of origin.

4. Pandit J.'s choice of a more expensive sari rather than a Christian-style wedding gown drew comments from the Africans in the audience of uninvited spectators. Several were heard to say later that the pandit was really keen on presenting himself as a "through-and-through" or "true" coolie. When, a week later, his son was married, he did not attend the wedding, sending his brother's son instead as a substitute so that he could remain at home for the "Second Sunday" return of his daughter. Rumors circulated soon afterward that the bride's family was so insulted that they switched the bride, substituting her less attractive sister. Although the pandit and his wife insisted that their son received the correct bride, they did acknowledge that the groom's party was treated poorly throughout the wedding. The pandit's detractors argued that it served him right for trying to be so big. Africans, on the other hand, found sweet revenge in the fact that it was his own East Indian people who "knocked him down" after he had gone to so much trouble to be a "true coolie."

5. The father-substitute was required because Mr. G., not being a Muslim, was, at least according to local interpretations of Islamic law, not a suitable participant in his own daughter's wedding. Mr. G. had agreed beforehand to allow the groom's father to select an appropriate Muslim male to play the role of the bride's father during the wedding.

6. Although Hindu women are believed to be marrying later than in previous decades, for a young girl to be much more than eighteen to twenty and unmarried may result in gossip suggesting that her father, having a sexual interest in her, is too jealous of her potential suitors to arrange a marriage. Such gossip brings shame on the family, and even where it is

viewed as a backward attitude, some concern is still maintained to avoid such gossip and shame.

10. Locating and Exorcizing the Ghost

1. Drummond (1980) argues that ethnicity in Guyana should be viewed as a continuum of interfaced systems (intersystems) in which ethnically identified individuals are considered to be familiar with the full range of cultural productions but lack the ability to control equally all parts of this range in their own behavior. The issue of individual competences cannot be ignored; however, an emphasis on relative competence is inadequate to explain the ambiguity and indeterminacy of ethnic symbolism in Guyana.

It is the ambiguity and indeterminacy in the ranking or relative prestige of cultural elements that suggests certain limitations to an analogy between creole language as a continuum and Drummond's effort to extrapolate this model to other cultural processes in Guyana. Concentrating on the similarities between creole language use and other cultural processes as a continuum, Drummond fails to consider important differences.

First, the sociological significance of the creole language continuum described by Bickerton (1975) is based on a particular assumed prestige hierarchy in which it is argued that forms of linguistic expression, however "impure," which most nearly approximate the acrolect are still most widely considered to be superior to other forms of expression in the linguistic continuum. Rickford's recent work (1983) on attitudes toward standard and nonstandard variants of the creole linguistic continuum in Guyana is relevant here. With reference to ambiguity and duality in Caribbean societies and creole communities, he concludes:

> we have some distance to go in terms of trying to specify the nature and intensity of the factors which impel speakers in these communities forward toward the acrolect and backwards toward the basilect in a seemingly endless dialectic. Social class has to be taken into account, and occasion, and relevant dimension, and undoubtedly even other factors. But it seems clear that only an approach to linguistics and cultural attitudes which is infinitely more sensitive than the "standard" view is can serve to explain the unsettled and dynamic character of creole continua. (1983:15)

Second, perhaps even more so than for the linguistic continuum, although other English cultural elements were once considered superior and the standard against which to judge other ethnically marked elements of Guyana's cultural heterogeneity, we have seen that this is no longer unambiguously accepted. Despite each ethnic group's contentions about the superiority of its cultural elements, no other "ethnic culture" has replaced

English culture as a standard for assessing the relative status of all other ethnically marked elements in the cultural continuum.

And third, a continuum model encourages a undimensional and essentially structural analysis of a relationship—the symbolic linkage of ethnicity and status—that is multidimensional and processual. It is a symbolism that has significance for expressions of who is *what* (identity) and for expressions of who is *who* (personal prestige and group-status ranking).

2. Jayawardena (1980) argues that culture in polyethnic societies should be viewed as a set of distinct or stratigraphically integrated cultures. This approach, unlike Drummond's (1980), affords us a better understanding of why, in different types of multiethnic situations, ethnically identified individual actors may be more or less able to, as Drummond (1980:468) suggests, operate without "stumbling over conflicting rules." Nonetheless, the narrow definition of political context utilized in Jayawardena's model considers only the specification of legal rights and the social and physical separation of ethnic cultures, thereby leaving out the ideological aspects of political context useful for a further determination of how concerns with distinct identity (ethnic and racial) and class position are conflated in the political context as aspects of a process of cultural production and status evaluation.

From this standpoint, the legal separation of indigenous Fijians and Fijian Indians, and the resulting spatial isolation, does not, as Jayawardena suggests, simply create "separate but equal" cultural sections left to communicate respectfully through ceremonial participation and an instrumental adoption of the medium of European modes of public conduct. Ideologically, it also establishes the ultimate priority of indigenous Fijians in the political arena and European modes of conduct in civil society. It effectively sets the conditions of political and cultural domination, conditions that, as Jayawardena notes, indigenous Fijians and Fijian Indians recognize and respond to differently.

On the one hand, indigenous Fijian politicians suggest that "blood will flow" and allude to Idi Amin's Uganda, when they feel the "privileged position" of indigenous Fijians is threatened by Indian demands for more power and greater participation in political decision making. On the other hand, Indians competing for participation in the use of power through the acquisition of positions in the political order seemed to have tacitly accepted the privileged position of Fijians when, as Jayawardena reports, they sought an indigenous Fijian to lead the government after they won the 1978 election. Moreover, Jayawardena states, "serious political conflicts can arise between Indians and Fijians, but they are largely obviated by a tacit acceptance of Fijian political hegemony" (1980:446). Thus, the current nature of the political order, viewed ideologically, and conceptions of modes of competition and cooperation within this order are firmly anchored to this tacit acceptance of political domination. For example, Jayawardena also states, "Most [Indians] have come to believe that [indigenous] Fijians have some prior rights [of dominance] and that if Indians keep a low profile and do not make any *radical demands* all will be well" (emphasis added; p. 447). Clearly, the "radical demands" to which he alludes are most likely to be those focused on a reconceptualization of the nature of the political order and a delegitimation of current modes of political and economic competition and cooperation. That reconceptualization would alter the current tacit acceptance of the Fijian Indian as an inside outsider.

3. One might ask, but what of the other world powers involved in shaping the international political arena? The argument here is not that Anglo-European hegemony now actively or subtly shapes Guyana's position in the international arena. Clearly, Great Britain, along with other world powers, does exercise influence in this arena that Guyana, like other small impoverished nations, must respond to; however, my point here is a cultural and ideological one. Guyana's cultural link to the international arena through a past of Anglo-European hegemony is a particular kind of link that differs from, but to some extent orders, its other extranational cultural ties such as those with India, countries in Africa, and Eastern bloc countries. For example, when some Cockalorums complain that their community is being "Americanized" by the "pretensions" of the returned immigrants from the United States, they evaluate the conduct they associate with this Americanization in terms of their image of conduct associated with British culture past and present. In these terms they often conclude that Americanized conduct is "vulgar" compared with the standards of conduct they associate with British Anglo-European culture as it is alleged to have existed in colonial Guiana and as it is assumed to continue to exist in Great Britain, read England. Thus, whereas culturally, Indianization or Africanization would also link them to the international arena, it would do so in terms that they often deem inferior to the links they can claim as ex-British subjects. In these terms and these terms only they are the cultural descendants of the premier "empire builders and world civilizers." That this also makes them the descendants of "Backra" is an irony visited on all and missed by few.

Yet, from an ideological standpoint, the issue of examining U.S. influence on the politics of meaning and the struggle to authenticate new standards in Guyana past and present is a complex one when one considers that although U.S. influence has been keenly felt in Guiana for more than two centuries, during much of that same period U.S. Americans were constructing their own cultural authenticity as they sought a place in the international arena. Like their Scots counterparts, they were often trying to out-English the English as they proclaimed a cultural superiority presumed to match their growing political and economic strength. During each historical juncture, their efforts were conducted within the constraints of the contemporary British Anglo-European hegemony in the international arena. That is to say, while influencing Guianese cultural production, cultural production in colonial and postcolonial U.S. America, too, was being shaped by an ideology that is generally dubbed Anglo-Saxonism and thus represented another brand of Anglo-European dominance or, perhaps to better state it, an extension or strengthening of Anglo-European hegemonic dominance in the Americas.

However, just as the relation between Scottish cultural nationalism as an opposition to English dominance in British Anglo-European domination is a complex, historically variable one that requires far more attention than it has received, the relation between patterns of cultural production in "British America" requires more attention before one can begin to usefully distinguish the relative impact of these competing forms of Anglo-European hegemonic dominance on past and contemporary Guyanese cultural production and authentication. Of course, Canada represents yet a third version because there the processes of cultural struggle operate within the constraints of its colonial linkages to Great Britain and France at the same time it grapples with the U.S. version of Anglo-European hegemony. As this struggle continues, it "exports" its own brand of Anglo-European hegemony to Guyana in the form of material goods and cultural valuations. These are most often carried to Cockalorum from Toronto by East Indians who have constructed their valuations of Canadian versus English culture out of interpretations of Canadian, British, and Indian culture provided by Indo-Canadians recently emigrated from the subcontinent.

4. I borrow these terms from Therborn (1980), who suggests that they are two of four dimensions—inclusive-existential, inclusive-historical, positional-historical, and positional-existential—which structure all ideological fields and shape the ways human subjects are constituted on an ideological field. Therborn maintains that these four dimensions make up the fundamental forms of human subjectivity, and that the universe of ideologies is exhaustively structured by the four main types of interpretations that constitute these four forms of subjectivity.

The structure of the ideological universe may be illustrated by means of the following simple fourfold table from Therborn (1980:23):

The Universe of Ideological Interpretations

	SUBJECTIVITIES OF "IN-THE-WORLD"	SUBJECTIVITIES OF "BEING"
	Existential	Historical
Inclusive	1	2
Positional	3	4

He then defines inclusive-existential ideologies as a type of ideological discourse that "provides meanings related to being a member of the world;

i.e., the meaning of life, suffering, death, the cosmos, and the natural order."
Inclusive-historical ideologies constitute human beings "as conscious mem‐
bers of historical social worlds." "These social worlds are indefinite in
number and variety, and it is only for purposes of illustration that we might
mention the forms of tribe, village, ethnicity, state, nation, church." At the
same time, positional-existential ideologies subject one to, and qualify one
for, a particular position in the world of which one is a member. He
attributes to these types of ideologies the constitution of the most significant
positions of the existential world delineated in terms of "self-others and the
two-gender distinctions and by the life-cycle of childhood, youth, maturity,
and old age." And hence, "they tell one who one is in the contrast with
others, what is good and what is possible for one." Finally, he defines
positional-historical ideologies as those that "form the members of a family
in a structure of families and lineages, the inhabitants of a particular locality
in a wider pattern of social geography, the occupants of a particular educa‐
tional status," and so on. In short, such ideologies entail "positions . . .
differentiated and linked in terms of differences only, in terms of hierarchical
grading along a single continuum of criteria, of complementarity, competi‐
tion, and frontal conflict" (1980:23–26).

He cautions that these should be taken only as analytic distinctions, not
as representations of ideologies as they "concretely appear and are labelled
in everyday language" (p. 25). Concrete ideologies may exhibit more than
one of the four dimensions at the same time or in different contexts.
Moreover, "the irreducible multidimensionality of ideologies means that a
crucial aspect of ideological struggle and of ideological relations of force is
the articulation of a given type of ideology with others. The efficacy of a
given religion, for example, will have to be understood in its articulation
explicit or implicit, with historical ideologies, positional and inclusive"
(1980:27).

In treating a particular ideological field, we must be concerned with
maintaining a focus on the multidimensionality of ideological precepts that
make up the major dimensions as well as on the multidimensionality of the
total ideological field. In this way we may hope to disclose which precepts
and which dimensions of those precepts are stressed under particular condi‐
tions. Thus, I am suggesting that when culture (as in inclusive-existential
ideology) is objectified as tradition (as an inclusive-historical ideology) in
political strategies, all ideological precepts are assimilated to this shift and,
therefore, have fundamentally different interpretive potential. Culture as
objectified tradition occurs when its members lose their ability to constitute
themselves simply as beings-in-the-world without first contesting those
precepts that define them not only as beings qualified merely for certain
positions but also as beings unqualified to assess the criteria on which that
definition is based.

5. Where the authentic culture of the powerless is not deemed to be in the past, its foundation is located in pragmatic responses, as in the case of the much heralded "working-class culture" or teen and deviant "subcultures." These pragmatic responses are transitory phenomena, not because they do not persist across generations, but because those who authenticate them have neither a past nor a future relative to "high culture" that provides them the grounds on which to legitimate their authentications. The products of working-class or other subcultures become authentic culture when they are appropriated by the producers of high culture, but then they are no longer working class—with a little ideological magic and forgetfulness, the roots soon wither and drop off.

This is still, however, a better ideological predicament than that faced by Native Americans. Their authentic culture lies not only in the past but in a peculiar past at that, in that it is unlike that of other ethnics, most of whom have not only an authentic culture in the past but a sovereign nation to which it is attached. In an international arena where the significance of cultural authenticity emanates in large measure from what it can say about positions in an international hierarchy of nations—unchic peasant states versus world powers and imperial agents of civilization—where does that leave the Native American? In Guyana it means that the Amerindian may reach back to the past for an authentic culture in ways that other ethnic groups cannot, but only with the paradoxical consequence that the further he reaches back, the more authentic the product and the lower he sinks under the weight of all that authenticity. Obviously, this sinking is not due to the inequality of cultural pasts per se, but to the power to say what any cultural past will mean. So, perhaps it is only among the Maya—those purveyors of an ancient civilization and a classic state formation—that we may find a conjuncture between Native Americans and "other ethnics" in this process of authentication.

Bibliography

Abercrombie, Nicholas, Stephen Hill, and Bryan S. Turner. 1980. *The Dominant Ideology Thesis.* London: George Allen & Unwin.

Abrahams, Roger D. 1968. "Public Drama and Common Values in Two Caribbean Islands." *Trans-Action* (July–August): 62–71.

———. 1970. *Deep Down in the Jungle . . . : Negro Narrative Folklore from the Streets of Philadelphia.* Chicago: Aldine.

Adamson, Alan H. 1972. *Sugar Without Slaves: The Political Economy of British Guiana, 1838–1904.* New Haven: Yale University Press.

Ahern, Emily M. 1981. *Chinese Ritual and Politics.* Cambridge: Cambridge University Press.

Ahmad, Aziz. 1964. *Studies in Islamic Culture in the Indian Environment.* Oxford: Clarendon.

Akzin, Benjamin. 1964. *State and Nation.* London: Hutchinson.

Allardt, Erik. 1979. "Implications of the Ethnic Revival of Modern Industrialized Society: A Comparative Study of the Linguistic Minorities in Western Europe." In *Commentationes Scientiarum Socialium* 12. Helsinki: Societas Scientiarum Fennica.

Anderson, Benedict. 1983. *Imagined Communities: Reflections on the Origin and Spread of Nationalism.* London: Verso & New Left Books.

Anderson, Malcolm. 1978. "The Renaissance of Territorial Minorities in Western Europe." *West European Politics* 1:128–43.

Armstrong, John A. 1982. *Nations before Nationalism.* Chapel Hill: University of North Carolina Press.

Aronson, Daniel R. 1976. "Ethnicity as a Cultural System: An Introductory Essay." In *Ethnicity in the Americas,* ed. Frances Henry, pp. 9–19. The Hague: Mouton.

Bailey, Frederick G., ed. 1971. *Gifts and Poison: The Politics of Reputation.* London: Basil Blackwell; New York: Shocken.

Banfield, Edward C. 1958. *The Moral Basis of a Backward Society.* Glencoe, Ill.: Free Press.

Banton, Michael P. 1967. *Race Relations.* London: Tavistock.

Barnett, Marguerite Ross. 1974. "Creating Political Identity: The Emergent South Indian Tamils." *Ethnicity* 1:237–65.

Barnett, Steve. 1977. "Identity Choice and Caste Ideology in Contemporary South India." In *Symbolic Anthropology: A Reader in the Study of Symbols and Meanings*, ed. J. Dolgin, D. Kemnitzer, and D. Schneider, pp. 270–91. Chicago: University of Chicago Press.

Barrows, Christine. 1976. "Reputation and Ranking in a Barbadian Locality." *Social and Economic Studies* 25(1): 106–21.

Bartels, Dennis. 1974. "The Influence of Folk Models upon Historical Analysis: A Case Study from Guyana." *Western Canadian Journal of Anthropology* 4(1): 73–81.

————. 1977. "Class Conflict and Racist Ideology in the Formation of Modern Guyanese Society." *Canadian Review of Sociology and Anthropology* 14(4): 396–405.

Barth, Fredrik, ed. 1969. *Ethnic Groups and Boundaries: The Social Organization of Culture Difference*. Boston: Little, Brown.

Bates, Robert. 1974. "Ethnic Competition and Modernization in Contemporary Africa." *Comparative Political Studies* 6 (Jan.): 457–84.

Beers, William R. 1980. *The Unexpected Rebellion: Ethnic Activism in Contemporary France*. New York: New York University Press.

Béteille, André. 1978. "Ideologies: Commitment and Partisanship." *L'Homme* 18(3–4): 47–67.

Bickerton, Derek. 1975. *Dynamics of a Creole System*. Cambridge: Cambridge University Press.

Bisnauth, Dwarka. 1979. *Islam Moves across the Atlantic*. Georgetown: Guyana Extension Seminary.

Bloch, Maurice. 1971. "The Moral and Tactical Meaning of Kinship Terms." *Man* 6:79–87.

————. 1973. "The Long Term and the Short Term: The Economic and Political Significance of the Morality of Kinship." In *The Character of Kinship*, ed. John R. Goody, pp. 75–88. Cambridge: Cambridge University Press.

————. 1977. "The Past and the Present in the Present." *Man* 12:278–92.

Bonaparte, Tony H. 1969. "The Influence of Culture on Business in a Pluralistic Society: A Study of Trinidad, West Indies." *American Journal of Economy and Society* 28(3): 285–300.

Bourdieu, Pierre. 1977. *Outline of a Theory of Practice*, trans. Richard Nice. Cambridge: Cambridge University Press.

————. 1980. *Questions de Sociologie*. Paris: Minuit.

Bourdieu, Pierre, and Luc Boltanski. 1975. "Le Titre et le Poste: Rapports entre le Système de Production et le Système de Reproduction." *Actes de la Recherche en Sciences Sociales* 2 (Mar.): 95–107.

Bourdieu, Pierre, and Jean-Claude Passeron. 1977. *Reproduction: In Education, Society, and Culture*, trans. Richard Nice. London: Sage.

Bourdillion, M. F. C. 1977. "Oracles and Politics in Ancient Israel." *Man* 12:124–40.

———. 1978. "Knowing the World or Hiding It: A Response to Maurice Bloch." *Man* 13(4): 591–99.

Bourricaud, François. 1975. "Indian, Mestizo, and Cholo as Symbols in the Peruvian System of Stratification." In *Ethnicity: Theory and Experience*, ed. Nathan Glazer and Daniel P. Moynihan, pp. 350–87. Cambridge: Harvard University Press.

Brass, Paul R. 1976. "Ethnicity and Nationality Formation." *Ethnicity* 3(3): 225–41.

Brathwaite, Edward. 1971. *The Development of Creole Society in Jamaica, 1770–1820.* Oxford: Clarendon.

Bronkhurst, Henry V. P. 1883. *The Colony of British Guiana and Its Labouring Population.* London: T. Woolmer.

———. 1888. *Among the Hindus and Creoles of British Guiana.* London: T. Woolmer.

Bullen-McKenzie, Maude. 1978. Some Creolese Words in Common Use. In *A Festival of Guyanese Words* (2nd ed.), ed. John R. Rickford, pp. 21–31. Georgetown: University of Guyana Press.

Campbell, John. 1964. *Honour, Family, and Patronage.* London: Oxford University Press.

Campbell, Roy H. 1980. "The Economic Case for Nationalism: Scotland." In *The Roots of Nationalism: Studies in Northern Europe*, ed. Rosalind Mitchison, pp. 143–59. Edinburgh: John Donald.

Caporaso, James. 1979. "What is the New Nationalism, or Is There a New Nationalism?" In *The New Nationalism: Implications for Transatlantic Relations*, ed. Werner Link and Werner J. Fields, pp. 6–22. New York: Pergamon.

Cassidy, Frederic G., and Robert B. Le Page. 1980. *Dictionary of Jamaican English* (2nd ed.). New York: Cambridge University Press.

Castile, George P., and Gilbert P. Kushner, eds. 1981. *Persistent Peoples: Cultural Enclaves in Perspective.* Tucson: University of Arizona Press.

Clementi, Sir Cecil. 1915. *The Chinese in British Guiana.* Georgetown: Argosy.

Coakley, Jay J. 1977. *Independence Movements and National Minorities: Some Parallels in the European Experience.* Limerick: National Institute for Higher Education.

Cohen, Anthony P. 1985. *The Symbolic Construction of Community.* Chichester: Ellis Horwood.

Comins, Dennis W. D. 1893. *Note on Emigration from India to British Guiana.* Georgetown, Demerara: Baldwin.

Coulson, Jessie, et al. eds. 1975. *The Oxford Illustrated Dictionary* (2nd ed.) Oxford: Clarendon.

Crespi, Muriel. 1975. "When *Indios* Become *Cholos*: Some Consequences of the Changing Ecuadorian Hacienda." In *The New Ethnicity: Perspectives from Ethnology*, ed. John W. Bennett, pp. 148–66. Proceedings of the American Ethnological Society. St. Paul: West Publishing.

Crookall, Reverend L. 1898. *British Guiana, or Work and Wanderings among the Creoles and Coolies, the Africans and Indians of the Wild Country.* London: T. Fisher Unwin.

Cropper, Reverend J. B. 1912. "Our Villages and Country Parts." *Timehri* 1, part 3: 255–58.

Daiches, David. 1964. *The Paradox of Scottish Culture: The Eighteenth-Century Experience.* London: Oxford University Press.

Dalton, Henry G. 1855. *History of British Guiana.* 2 vols. London: Longmans, Green.

Daly, Vere T. 1975. *A Short History of the Guyanese People.* London: Macmillan.

Dance, Charles. 1881. *Chapters from a Guyanese Log-book.* Georgetown: Royal Gazette Establishment.

Dann, George. 1983. "Decolonization and Militarization in the Caribbean: The Case of Guyana." In *The Newer Caribbean: Decolonization, Democracy, and Development*, ed. P. Henry Stone, pp. 63–93. Philadelphia: Institute for the Study of Human Issues.

Despres, Leo A. 1964. "The Implications of Nationalist Politics in British Guiana for the Development of Cultural Theory." *American Anthropologist* 66(5): 1051–77.

———. 1967. *Cultural Pluralism and Nationalist Politics in British Guiana.* Chicago: Rand McNally.

———. 1969. "Differential Adaptations and Micro-Cultural Evolution in Guyana." *Southwestern Journal of Anthropology* 25(1): 14–44.

Drummond, Lee. 1974. "The Outskirts of the Earth: A Study of Amerindian Ethnicity on the Pomeroon River, Guyana." Ph.D. diss. University of Chicago.

———. 1977. "Structure and Process in the Interpretation of South American Myth: The Arawak Dog Spirit People." *American Anthropologist* 79: 842–68.

———. 1980. "The Cultural Continuum: A Theory of Intersystems." *Man* 15(2): 352–74.

Dumont, Louis. 1970. *Religion/Politics and History in India.* Paris: Mouton.

Edwards, Walter F. 1976. "The Sociolinguistic Significance of Some Guyanese Speech Acts." Paper presented at the 1976 Conference of the Society for Caribbean Linguistics, held at the University of Guyana.

———. 1978. "Tantalisin and Busin in Guyana." *Anthropological Linguistics* 20(5): 194–213.

Epstein, A. L. 1978. *Ethos and Identity: Three Studies in Ethnicity.* London: Tavistock; Chicago: Aldine.

Esman, Milton, ed. 1977. *Ethnic Conflict in the Western World*. Ithaca, N.Y.: Cornell University Press.

Falk Moore, Sally. 1975. "Epilogue: Uncertainties in Situations, Indeterminacies in Culture." In *Communal Ideology*, ed. Sally F. Moore and Barbara G. Myerhoff, pp. 210–39. Ithaca, N.Y.: Cornell University Press.

Farley, Rawle. 1954. "The Rise of the Peasantry in British Guiana." *Social and Economic Studies* 2(4): 87–105.

————. 1955. The Shadow and the Substance. *Caribbean Quarterly* 5:132–53.

————. 1956. "Aspects of the Economic History of British Guiana, 1781–1852: A Study of Economic and Social Change on the Southern Caribbean Frontier." Ph.D. diss., University of London.

February, Vernie A. 1981. *Mind Your Colour: The "Coloured" Stereotype in South African Literature*. London: Kegan Paul.

Feuchtwang, Stephan. 1975. "Investigating Religion." In *Marxist Analyses and Social Anthropology*, ed. Maurice Bloch, pp. 61–82. London: Malaby.

Fisher, Lawrence E. 1976. "Dropping Remarks and the Barbadian Audience." *American Ethnologist* 3(2): 227–42.

Fleming, Patricia Harvey. 1979. *Villagers and Strangers: An English Proletarian Village over Four Centuries*. Cambridge, Mass.: Schenkman.

Foster, George M. 1960–61. "Interpersonal Relations in Peasant Society." *Human Organization* 19:174–79.

————. 1965. "Peasant Society and the Image of Limited Good." *American Anthropologist* 67:293–315.

Frankenberg, Ronald. 1957. *Village on the Border: A Social Study of Religion, Politics and Football in a North Wales Community*. London: Cohen & West.

Fried, Morton H. 1956. "Some Observations on the Chinese in British Guiana." *Social and Economic Studies* 5:54–73.

Gearing, Frederick O. 1958. "The Structural Poses of Nineteenth-Century Cherokee Society." *American Anthropologist* 60:1148–57.

Geddie, William, ed. 1965. *Chambers's Twentieth-Century Dictionary*. London: W. & R. Chambers.

Geertz, Clifford. 1972. "Deep Play: Notes on the Balinese Cockfight." In *Myth, Symbol, and Culture*, ed. Clifford Geertz, pp. 1–38. New York: W. W. Norton; Toronto: George J. McLeod.

————. 1973. "Thick Description: Toward an Interpretive Theory of Culture." In *The Interpretation of Cultures: Selected Essays by Clifford Geertz*, pp. 3–32. New York: Basic Books.

————. 1976. "From the Native's Point of View: On the Nature of Anthropological Understanding." In *Meaning in Anthropology*, ed. Keith H. Basso and Henry A. Selby, pp. 221–37. Albuquerque: University of New Mexico Press.

Gellner, Ernest. 1978. "Notes toward a Theory of Ideology." *L'Homme* 18(3–4): 69–82.

Gibson, Kean. 1976. "Guyanese Slang." In *A Festival of Guyanese Words* (2nd ed.), ed. John R. Rickford, pp. 75–88. Georgetown: University of Guyana Press.

Gilsenan, Michael. 1970. "Lying, Honor, and Contradiction." In *Transaction and Meaning: Directions in the Anthropology of Exchange and Symbolic Behavior*, ed. Bruce Kapferer, pp. 191–219. Philadelphia: Institute for the Study of Human Issues.

———. 1983. *Recognizing Islam: Religion and Society in the Modern Arab World.* New York: Pantheon.

Glasgow, Roy A. 1970. *Guyana: Race and Politics among Africans and East Indians.* The Hague: Martinus Nijhoff.

Glazer, Nathan, and Daniel P. Moynihan, eds. 1975. *Ethnicity: Theory and Experience.* Cambridge: Harvard University Press.

Godelier, Maurice. 1977. *Perspectives in Marxist Anthropology.* Cambridge: Cambridge University Press.

Goffman, Erving. 1959. *The Presentation of Self in Everyday Life.* Garden City, N.Y.: Doubleday.

———. 1961. *Encounters: Two Studies in the Sociology of Interaction.* Indianapolis: Bobbs-Merrill.

———. 1963. *Behavior in Public Places: Notes on the Social Organization of Gatherings.* New York: Free Press; London: Collier Macmillan.

———. 1967. *Interaction Ritual: Essays on Face-to-Face Behavior.* Garden City, N.Y.: Doubleday.

———. 1969. *Strategic Interaction.* Philadelphia: University of Pennsylvania Press.

———. 1971. *Relations in Public: Microstudies of the Public Order.* New York: Basic Books.

———. 1974. *Frame Analysis: An Essay on the Organization of Experience.* New York: Harper & Row.

Gold, George, and Robert Paine, eds. 1985. *Mother Country and Ethnicity.* St. John's: Institute of Social and Economic Research.

Goveia, Elsa V. 1965. *Slave Society in the British Leeward Islands at the End of the Eighteenth Century.* New Haven: Yale University Press.

Graham, Sheila, and David Gordon. 1977. *The Stratification System and Occupational Mobility in Guyana.* Mona, Jamaica: University of the West Indies Institute of Social and Economic Research.

Gramsci, Antonio. 1971. *Selections from the Prison Notebooks of Antonio Gramsci*, trans. and ed. Quintin Hoare and Geoffrey N. Smith. New York: International Publishers.

Grasmuck, Sherri. 1980. "Ideology of Ethnoregionalism: The Case of Scotland." *Politics and Society* 9:471–94.

Greenwood, Davydd. 1977. "Continuity in Change: Spanish Basque Ethnicity as a Historical Process." In *Ethnic Conflict in the Western World*, ed. Milton Esman, pp. 81–103. Ithaca, N.Y.: Cornell University Press.

Halliday, Sir Andrew. 1837. *The West Indies: The Natural and Physical History of the Windward and Leeward Colonies; With Some Account of the Moral, Social, and Political Condition of the Inhabitants, Immediately Before and After the Abolition of Negro Slavery.* London: J. W. Parker.

Harris, Sir Charles Alexander, and J. A. J. de Villiers, eds. 1911. *Storm van's Gravesande: The Rise of British Guiana, Compiled from His Despatches.* 2 vols. London: The Hakluyt Society.

Harris, C. L. G. N.d. "The Maroons of Jamaica: A Colonel Speaks." Unpublished manuscript.

Hechter, Michael. 1975. *Internal Colonialism: The Celtic Fringe in British National Development, 1536–1966.* London: Routledge & Kegan Paul; Berkeley: University of California Press.

———. 1976. "Ethnicity and Industrialization: On the Proliferation of the Cultural Division of Labor." *Ethnicity* 3(3): 214–24.

Henfrey, Colin. 1965. *Through Indian Eyes: A Journey among the Indian Tribes of Guiana.* New York: Holt, Rinehart & Winston.

Hewick, J. E. 1911. "Our People." *Timehri* 1, part 3: 231–37.

Hickerson, Harold. 1954. "Social and Economic Organization of a Guiana Village." Ph.D. diss., University of Indiana.

Hobsbawm, Eric J. 1977. "Some Reflections on the '*Break-up of Britain.*'" *New Left Review* 105:3–23.

Horowitz, Donald L. 1985. *Ethnic Groups in Conflict.* Berkeley: University of California Press.

Hunt, Eva. 1977. "Ceremonies of Confrontation and Submission: The Symbolic Dimension of Indian-Mexican Political Interaction." In *Secular Ritual*, ed. Sally F. Moore and Barbara G. Myerhoff, pp. 124–47. Assen: Van Gorcum.

Hutson, Susan. 1971. "Social Ranking in a French Alpine Community." In *Gifts and Poison: The Politics of Reputation*, ed. Frederick G. Bailey, pp. 41–68. London: Basil Blackwell; New York: Shocken.

Jamieson, John. 1887. *A Complete Dictionary of the Scottish Language.* 13 vols. New York: AMS.

Jayawardena, Chandra. 1960. "Marital Stability in Two Guianese Sugar Estate Communities." *Social and Economic Studies* 9(1): 76–100.

———. 1962. "Family Organisation in Plantations in British Guiana." *International Journal of Comparative Sociology* 3(1): 43–64.

———. 1963. *Conflict and Solidarity on a Guianese Plantation.* London School of Economics Monographs on Social Anthropology 25. London: Athlone.

———. 1968. "Ideology and Conflict in Lower Class Communities." *Comparative Studies in Society and History* 10(4): 413–46.

————. 1980. "Culture and Ethnicity in Guyana and Fiji." *Man* 15(3): 430–50

Kahin, George McTurnan. 1962. *Nationalism and Revolution in Indonesia.* Ithaca, N.Y.: Cornell University Press.

Katznelson, Ira. 1973. "Participation and Political Buffers in Urban America." *Race* 14(4): 465–80.

Kedourie, Elie, ed. 1970. *Nationalism in Africa and Asia.* New York: Meridian.

Keesing, Roger M. N.d. "Racial and Ethnic Categories in Colonial and Post-Colonial States: Sociological and Linguistic Perspectives on Ideology." Unpublished manuscript.

Kelly, Raymond. 1977. *Etoro Social Structure: A Study in Structural Contradiction.* Ann Arbor: University of Michigan Press.

Keyes, Charles F. 1975. "Towards a New Formulation of the Concept of Ethnic Group." *Ethnicity* 3(3): 202–13.

Kirke, Henry. 1898. *Twenty-five Years in British Guiana.* London: Sampson, Low, Harston.

Klass, Morton. 1961. *East Indians in Trinidad: A Study of Cultural Persistence.* Prospect Heights, Ill.: Waveland.

Knight, Franklin. 1978. *The Caribbean, the Genesis of a Fragmented Nationalism.* New York: Oxford University Press.

Kohn, Hans. 1946. *The Idea of Nationalism: A Study in its Origins and Background.* New York: Macmillan.

————. 1955. *Nationalism: Its Meaning and History.* 1965 reprint. Princeton, N.J.: D. Van Nostrand.

————. 1962. *The Age of Nationalism: The First Era of Global History.* New York: Harper & Row.

Krejci, Jaroslav. 1978. "Ethnic Problems in Europe." In *Contemporary Europe: Social Structures and Cultural Patterns,* ed. Salvador Giner and Margaret Scotford Archer, pp. 124–71. London: Routledge & Kegan Paul.

Laclau, Ernesto. 1977. *Politics and Ideology in Marxist Theory: Capitalism-Facism-Populism.* London: Verso; Atlantic Highlands: Humanities Press.

Landsman, Gail. 1985. "Ganienkeh: Symbol and Politics in an Indian/White Conflict." *American Anthropologist* 87:826–39.

Laughlin, Charles D. 1974. "Deprivation and Reciprocity." *Man* 9(3): 380–96.

Laurence, K. O. 1965. "The Establishment of the Portuguese Community in British Guiana." *Jamaican Historical Review* 5:50–74.

Leach, Edmund R. 1954. *Political Systems of Highland Burma: A Study of Kachin Social Structure.* London: London School of Economics and Political Science.

Lears, T. J. Jackson. 1985. "The Concept of Cultural Hegemony: Problems and Possibilities." *American Historical Review* 90(3): 567–93.

Leslie, S. C. 1971. *The Rift in Israel*. London: Routledge & Kegan Paul.

Levine, Lawrence W. 1977. *Black Culture and Black Consciousness: Afro-American Folk Thought from Slavery to Freedom*. New York: Oxford University Press.

Little, W., ed. 1975. *The Oxford Universal Dictionary*. Oxford: Clarendon.

Luxemburg, Rosa. 1971. *Selected Political Writings of Rosa Luxemburg*, ed. Dick Howard. New York: Monthly Review Press.

McAndrew, Wordsworth. 1978. "Guyanese Folksongs." In *A Festival of Guyanese Words* (2nd ed.), ed. John R. Rickford, pp. 237–40. Georgetown: University of Guyana Press.

McLewin, Peter. 1971. "Power and Economic Change: The Response to Emancipation in Jamaica and British Guiana." Ph.D. diss., Cornell University.

McNeill, James, and Chimman Lal. 1915. *Report to the Government of India on the Conditions of Indian Immigrants in Four British Colonies and Surinam*. Part 1. London: His Majesty's Stationary Office.

McNeill, William H. 1985. *Polyethnicity and National Unity in World History*. Toronto: University of Toronto Press.

Malinowski, Bronislaw. 1922. *Argonauts of the Western Pacific: An Account of Native Enterprise and Adventure in the Archipelagoes of Melanesian New Guinea*. 1961 reprint. New York: E. P. Dutton.

Mandle, Jay R. 1973. *The Plantation Economy: Population and Economic Change in Guyana, 1838–1960*. Philadelphia: Temple University Press.

———. 1982. "The Post-Colonial Mode of Production in Guyana." In *Patterns of Caribbean Development: An Interpretive Essay on Economic Change*, pp. 110–25. New York and London: Gordon & Breach.

Mannoni, Oscar. 1964. *Prospero and Caliban: The Psychology of Colonization*, trans. Pamela Powesland. New York: Frederick A. Praeger.

Mason, Phillip. 1970. *Patterns of Dominance*. London: Oxford University Press.

Mauss, Marcel. 1925. *The Gift: Forms and Functions of Exchange in Archaic Societies*, trans. Ian Cunnison. 1967 reprint. New York: W. W. Norton.

Menezes, Sister Mary N. 1973. "The Dutch and British Policy of Indian Subsidy: A System of Annual and Triennial Presents." *Caribbean Studies* 13:64–88.

———. 1977. *British Policy Towards the Amerindians in British Guiana*. Oxford: Clarendon.

Menezes, Sister Mary N., ed. 1979. *The Amerindians in Guyana, 1803–73: A Documentary History*. London: Frank Cass; Totowa, N.J.: Biblio Distribution Centre.

Mitchison, Rosalind. 1980. "Nineteenth-Century Scottish Nationalism: The Cultural Background." In *The Roots of Nationalism: Studies in Northern Europe*, ed. Rosalind Mitchison, pp. 131–42. Edinburgh: John Donald.

Mitchison, Rosalind, ed. 1980. *The Roots of Nationalism: Studies in Northern Europe.* Edinburgh: John Donald.

Monar, Rooplall. 1980. "Indo-Guyanese Death Rites: Ceremonies Too Extravagant." Georgetown *Sunday Chronicle,* October 19, 1980, p. 10.

Moore, Brian L. 1975. "The Social Impact of Portuguese Immigration into British Guiana after Emancipation." *Boletin de Estudios Latinoamericanos y del Caribe* 19 (Dec.): 3–15.

Mouffe, Chantal. 1979. "Hegemony and Ideology in Gramsci." In *Gramsci and Marxist Theory,* ed. Chantal Mouffe, pp. 168–204. London: Routledge & Kegan Paul.

Nagata, Judith A., ed. 1975. "Pluralism in Malaysia: Myth and Reality." *Contributions to Asian Studies* 7. Leiden: Brill.

Nairn, Tom. 1977. *The Break-Up of Britain.* London: New Left Books.

Nath, Dwarka. 1950. *A History of the East Indian in Guyana.* London: published by the author.

Netscher, Pieter M. 1888. *History of the Colonies Essequibo, Demerary, and Berbice from the Dutch Establishment to the Year 1888,* trans. V. Roth. 1931 reprint. The Hague: Provincial Utrecht Society for the Arts and Sciences.

Norton, Robert. 1984. "Ethnicity and Class: A Conceptual Note with Reference to the Politics of Post-Colonial Societies." *Ethnic and Racial Studies* 7(3): 426–34.

Patterson, Orlando. 1967. *The Sociology of Slavery: An Analysis of the Origins, Development and Structure of Negro Slave Society in Jamaica.* London: MacGibbon & Kee.

Payne, Stanley G. 1975. *Basque Nationalism.* Reno: University of Nevada Press.

Peacock, James. 1968. *Rites of Modernization: Symbolic and Social Aspects of Indonesian Proletarian Drama.* Chicago: University of Chicago Press.

Peristiany, Jean G., ed. 1966. *Honor and Shame.* Chicago: University of Chicago Press.

Perkins, Teresa E. 1979. "Rethinking Stereotypes." In *Ideology and Cultural Production,* ed. Michèle Barrett, P. Corrigan, A. Kuhn, and J. Wolff, pp. 135–59. London: Croom Helm.

Pierronet, Thomas. 1798. *Remarks Made during a Residence at Starbroek, Rio Demerary.* Vol. 6. Boston: Massachusetts Historical Society.

Pinckard, George. 1806. *Notes on the West Indies.* 3 vols. 1970 reprint. Westport, Conn.: Negro University Press.

Pitt-Rivers, Julian. 1960. *The People of Sierra.* Chicago: University of Chicago Press.

Poliakov, Léon. 1974. *The Aryan Myth: A History of Racist and Nationalist Ideas in Europe,* trans. Edmund Howard. London: Chatto & Windus for Sussex University Press; New York: Basic Books.

————. 1982. "Racism from the Enlightenment to the Age of Imperialism." In *Racism and Colonialism: Essays on Ideology and Social Structure*, ed. Robert J. Ross. Norwell, Mass.: Kluwer Academic.

Potter, Leslie. 1975. "Internal Migration and Resettlement of East Indians in Guyana, 1870–1920." Ph.D. diss., McGill University.

————. 1982. "The Post-Indenture Experience of East Indians in Guyana, 1873–1921." In *East Indians in the Caribbean: Colonialism and the Struggle for Identity*, ed. Bridget Brereton and R. Dookaran, pp. 71–92. Millwood, N.Y.: Kraus.

Premdas, Ralph R. 1978. "Guyana: Socialist Reconstruction or Political Opportunism." *Journal of Interamerican Studies and World Affairs* 20(2): 133–64.

Premium, Barton. 1850. *Eight Years in British Guiana: Being the Journal of a Resident in the Province of British Guiana from 1840–1848*. London: Longman, Brown, Green & Longmans.

Rauf, Mohammad A. 1974. *Indian Village in Guiana: A Study of Cultural Change and Ethnic Identity*. Leiden: Brill.

Reisman, Karl. 1974. "Contrapuntal Conversations in an Antiguan Village." In *Explorations in the Ethnography of Speaking*, ed. Richard Baumann and Joel Sherzer, pp. 110–24. London: Cambridge University Press.

Reminick, Ronald. 1983. *Theory of Ethnicity: An Anthropologist's Perspective*. Lanham, Md.: University Press of America.

Riches, David. 1981. "The Obligation to Give: An Interactional Sketch." In *The Structure of Folk Models*, ed. Ladislav Holý and Milan Stuchlik, pp. 209–32. New York: Academic Press.

Rickford, John R. 1983. "Standard and Non-Standard Language Attitudes in a Creole Continuum." *Society for Caribbean Linguistics*, Occasional Paper 16. Mona, Jamaica: School of Education, University of the West Indies.

Ridgewell, W. M. 1972. *The Forgotten Tribes of Guyana*. London: Tom Stacey.

Robinson, Pat. 1970. "The Social Structure of Guyana." In *The Cooperative Republic of Guyana*, ed. L. Searwar, pp. 51–76. Georgetown: Government of Guyana.

Rodney, Walter. 1981. *A History of the Guyanese Working People, 1881–1905*. Baltimore: Johns Hopkins University Press.

Rodway, James. 1891–94. *History of British Guiana from the Year 1668*. 3 vols. Georgetown: J. Thompson.

————. 1893. *Hand-book of British Guiana*. Georgetown: Columbian Exposition Literary Committee of the Royal Agricultural and Commercial Society.

————. 1912. *Guiana: British, Dutch and French*. London: T. Fisher Unwin.

Roff, William R. 1967. *The Origins of Malay Nationalism*. New Haven: Yale University Press.

Ross, Robert, J., ed. 1982. *Racism and Colonialism: Essays on Ideology and Social Structure*. Norwell, Mass.: Kluwer Academic.

Rubenstein, Hymie. 1976. "Incest, Effigy Hanging, and Biculturation in a West Indian Village." *American Ethnologist* 3(4): 765–81.

Ruhomon, Peter. 1947. *A Centenary History of the East Indians in British Guiana, 1838–1938*. Georgetown: Daily Chronicle, Guiana, Edition 10.

Sahlins, Marshall. 1965. "On the Sociology of Primitive Exchange." In *The Relevance of Models for Social Anthropology*, ed. Michael P. Banton, pp. 139–236. London: Tavistock.

Salzman, Philip C. 1981. "Culture as Enhabilmentis." In *The Structure of Folk Models*, ed. Ladislav Holý and Milan Stuchlik, pp. 233–56. New York: Academic Press.

Sassoon, Ann Showstack. 1980. *Gramsci's Politics*. New York: St. Martin's Press.

Saul, John. 1976. "The Dialectic of Class and Tribe." *Race and Class* 20(4): 347–72.

Schermerhorn, Richard A. 1970. *Comparative Ethnic Relations: A Framework for Theory and Research*. 1978 reprint. Chicago: University of Chicago Press.

Scoles, Ignatius. 1885. *Sketches of African and Indian Life in British Guiana*. Georgetown: Argosy.

Sederberg, Peter C. 1984. *The Politics of Meaning: Power and Explanation in the Construction of Social Reality*. Tucson: University of Arizona Press.

Seton-Watson, Hugh. 1977. *Nations and States: An Enquiry into the Origins of Nations and the Politics of Nationalism*. Boulder, Colo.: Westview.

Seymour, Arthur J. 1970. "Cultural Values in the Republic of Guyana." In *The Cooperative Republic of Guyana*, ed. L. Searwar, pp. 79–92. Georgetown: Government of Guyana.

Silverman, Martin. 1977. "Making Sense: A Study of a Banaban Meeting." In *Symbolic Anthropology: A Reader in the Study of Symbols and Meanings*, ed. J. Dolgin, D. Kemnitzer, and D. Schneider, pp. 451–79. Chicago: University of Chicago Press.

Sivanandan, Ambalavaner. 1973. "Race, Class, and Power: An Outline for Study." *Race* 14(4): 383–91.

Skinner, Elliott P. 1955. "Group Dynamics in British Guiana." *Annals of the New York Academy of Sciences*, no. 83.

Smith, Raymond T. 1955. "Land Tenure in Three Negro Villages in British Guiana." *Social and Economic Studies* 4(1): 64–82.

———. 1956. *The Negro Family in British Guiana: Family Structure and Social Status in the Villages*. London: Routledge & Kegan Paul; Mona, Jamaica: University of the West Indies Institute for Social and Economic Research.

———. 1962. *British Guiana*. London: Oxford University Press.

———. 1963. "Culture and Social Structure in the Caribbean: Some Recent

Work on Family and Kinship Studies." *Comparative Studies in Society and History* 6(1): 24–45.

————. 1966. "People and Change." In *New World* (2) *Guyana Independence Issue,* ed. G. Lamming, pp. 49–54. Georgetown.

————. 1970. "Social Stratification in the Caribbean." In *Essays in Comparative Social Stratification,* ed. Leonard Plotnicov and Arthur Tuden, pp. 43–76. Pittsburgh: University of Pittsburgh Press.

Smith, Raymond T., and Chandra Jayawardena. 1959. "Marriage and the Family amongst East Indians in British Guiana." *Social and Economic Studies* 8(4): 321–76.

Spicer, Edward H. 1971. "Persistent Cultural Systems: A Comparative Study of Identity Systems That Can Adapt to Contrasting Environments." *Science* 174 (4011): 795–800.

Stack, Carol B. 1974. *All Our Kin: Strategies for Survival in a Black Community.* New York: Harper & Row.

Stein, Howard F. and Robert F. Hill. 1977. *The Ethnic Imperative: Examining the New White Ethnic Movement.* University Park: Pennsylvania State University Press.

Strauss, Anselm L. 1959. *Mirrors and Masks: The Search for Identity.* Glencoe: Ill.: Free Press.

Stutzman, Ronald. 1981. "*El Mestizaje:* An All-Inclusive Ideology of Exclusion." In *Cultural Transformations and Ethnicity in Modern Ecuador,* ed. Norman E. Whitten, Jr., pp. 45–93. Urbana: University of Illinois Press.

Swan, Michael. 1957. *British Guiana: The Land of Six Peoples.* London: Her Majesty's Stationary Office.

Szwed, John. 1975. "Race and the Embodiment of Culture." *Ethnicity* 2(1): 19–33.

Therborn, Göran. 1980. *The Ideology of Power and the Power of Ideology.* London: Verso & New Left Books.

Thomas, Clive. 1984. *Plantations, Peasants, and State: A Study of the Mode of Sugar Production in Guyana.* CAAS Monograph Series 5. Los Angeles: Center for Afro-American Studies and University of California Press.

Thompson, John B. 1984. *Studies in the Theory of Ideology.* Berkeley: University of California Press.

Tinker, Hugh. 1982. "British Policy toward a Separate Indian Identity in the Caribbean, 1920–1950." In *East Indians in the Caribbean: Colonialism and the Struggle for Identity,* ed. Bridget Brereton and R. Dookaran, pp. 33–48. Millwood, N.Y.: Kraus.

Trevelyan, George M. 1942. *A Shortened History of England.* London: Longmans, Green.

Trouillot, Michel-Rolph. 1984. *Nation, State, and Society in Haiti, 1804–1984.* Washington, D.C.: The Wilson Center, Smithsonian.

Valentine, Charles A. 1965. "Voluntary Ethnicity and Social Change: Classism, Racism, Marginality, Mobility, and Revolution with Special Reference to Afro-Americans and Other Third World Peoples." *Journal of Ethnic Studies* 3(1): 1–27.

Van den Berghe, Pierre L. 1981. *The Ethnic Phenomenon*. New York: Elsevier.

Verdery, Katherine. n.d. "The Decline of Corporate German Ethnicity in Romania." Unpublished manuscript.

Vieryra, Antonio. 1813. *Dictionary of the Portuguese and English Languages*. London: N.p.

Wagner, Michael J. 1975. "Structural Pluralism and the Portuguese in Nineteenth Century British Guiana: A Study in Historical Geography." Ph.D. diss., McGill University.

———. 1977. "Rum, Policy, and the Portuguese: Or, the Maintenance of Elite Supremacy in Post-Emancipation British Guiana." *Canadian Review of Sociology and Anthropology* 14(4): 406–16.

Wallerstein, Immanuel. 1972. "Social Conflict in Post-Independence Black Africa: The Concepts of Race and Status-Group Reconsidered." In *Racial Tensions and National Integration*, ed. Ernest Q. Campbell, pp. 207–26. Nashville: Vanderbilt University Press.

Warren, Kay. 1978. *The Symbolism of Subordination: Indians in Guatemala*. Austin: University of Texas Press.

Weber, Max. 1946. *From Max Weber: Essays in Sociology*, trans. and ed. H. H. Gerth and C. Wright Mills. 1958 reprint. New York: Oxford University Press.

Weinberg, Daniela. 1975. *Peasant Wisdom: Cultural Adaptation in a Swiss Town*. Berkeley: University of California Press.

West, Rebecca. 1940. *Black Lamb and Grey Falcon*. New York: Viking Penguin.

Whitten, Norman E., Jr., ed. 1981. *Cultural Transformations and Ethnicity in Modern Ecuador*. New York: Harper & Row.

Wilkinson, Bertram, and Rooplall Monar. 1980a. "800 Million Are Followers of Christianity." *Guyana Chronicle*, June 19, p. 7. Georgetown.

———. 1980b. Islam: Achievements and Problems. *Guyana Chronicle*, June 21, 1980, p. 7. Georgetown.

———. 1980c. "Final Part." *Guyana Chronicle*, June 28, p. 7. Georgetown.

Williams, B. F. 1983. "Cockalorums in Search of Cockaigne: Status Competition, Ritual and Social Interaction in a Rural Guyanese Community." Ph.D. diss., Johns Hopkins University.

Williams, Gwyn. 1960. "The Concept of Hegemonia in the Thought of Antonio Gramsci." *Journal of the History of Ideas* 21(4): 586–99.

Wilson, Peter J. 1973. *Crab Antics: The Social Anthropology of English-Speaking Negro Societies of the Caribbean*. New Haven: Yale University Press.

Wipper, Audrey. 1972. "African Women, Fashion, and Scapegoating." *Canadian Journal of African Studies* 6(2): 329–49.

Woodson, Drexel G. 1978. "Tradition and Change: A Caribbean View with Special Reference to Haiti, 1760–1843." M.A. thesis, Department of Anthropology, University of Chicago.

Young, J. A. E. 1958. *Approaches to Local Self-Government in British Guiana.* London: Longmans, Green.

Index

A History of the East Indian in Guyana (Nath), 190
Homogenizing process as hegemonic process, 33
Houses as status symbols, 85–91

Identity, political, 16
Identity formation: cultural struggle and, 267–71; ethnicity and, 29; homogenization and, 258; nationalism and, xvi, 29; racial, British, 23–24; Scottish, 25
Identity production, xiv
Identity/status disjunction, 252
Ideological field, the, 276 n.12
Ideological rationalization: East Indian success in agriculture and, 149; Portuguese commercial success and, 143–44
Ideological structures of domination, 33
Indentured labor: introduction of, 129; reasons for use of, 138
Innate tendencies, presumed, 175–76
Intraethnic status, religious diversity and, 215–18

Jagan, Cheddi, 35
Jayawardena, C.: on egalitarianism, 94–95, 97, 99; on egalitarian precepts, 93; on Negro Muslims, 206; on religious differences, 201–3

Kali Mai worship, 211–14
Knight, F., 55
Kohn, H., 16–17

Landsman, G., 264–66
Laurence, K. O., 144
Levine, L. W., 175
Living well, 94–101
Locality types, 71–73

McClintock, W. C. F., 136, 137
"Making a living" vs. "making a life," 56–69
Making life, 54–69

Mandle, J. R., 33, 35–38
Manners: definition of, 107–8; giving of compliments and, 112–13; granting of favors, and, 111–12; greetings and, 108–9; reciprocity and, 110; sense and, 106; socioeconomic standing and, 110; status competition and, 108
Marginalized groups, 30–31
Marx, K., 3
Mason, P., on work activities, 49
Mati, definition of, 94–95
Mauss, M., on manners and conflict, 111
Menezes, M. N.: on Aboriginal ethnic diversity, 128; on use of Aborigines, 133, 134, 135; on control of native population, 136–37
Mikulski, Barbara, cultural differences and, 10
Mitchison, R., 25
Monar, R., 219, 222
Moore, B. L., 142
Mulattoes: definition of, 129; use of, as buffer population, 141–42

"Name" as a cultural construct, 93–94
Nath, D., 190
Nationalism: British colonial rule and, 8; European, and the norm of heterogeneity, 18–19; identity formation and, 29; marginalized groups and, 30; nationalist ideologies and cultural homogenization, 30; territorial and cultural, 15–16
Nationalities, nonhomogenized, European, 18–25
National origin myths, European, 20
National versus ethnic groups, 267
"No Nations," definition of, 129
Norton, R., on ethnicity, 28

"Ownership," social mobility and, 184–92

The Paradox of Scottish Cultures: The Eighteenth-Century Experience (Daiches), 22

Patterson, O., 55
People's National Congress. *See* PNC
People's Progressive Party. *See* PPP
Personal and group identity linkages, 12–15
Physical proximity, effects of, 15–25
Pierronet, T., 129
Pinckard, G., on poldering, 140
PNC, 35; influence on employment opportunities, 66
Poldering, effect of, on plantation economy, 140
Poliakov, L., 19, 20, 23–24; on race and class, 26
Portuguese immigrants, 142–46
Potter, L., 148
PPP, 35

Race, class, ethnicity interrelation, 33
Race/culture/class conflation, 152–54
Racial: class superiority, European, 20; cultural stereotypes, subordinate group adoption of, 158–59; differentiation, European, 20; ethnic groups, 267–68; ethnic identity, 252; identity and work attitudes, 55; rationalization of Portuguese commercial success, 143–44; self-identification, British, development of, 23–24; stereotypes, status and, 73
Rauf, M. A., 131; on religious differences, 203–4
Religion, legacy of hegemonic dominance and, 219–24
Religious differences, Anglo-European hegemonic dominance and, 201–15
Religious diversity, 215–18
Renan, E., 155
Representation, protection against stains and, 118–21
Robinson, P., on European dominance, 151
Rodney, W., 35; on contribution of African slaves, 163; on creole stereotyping, 147; on East Indians, 148; on

egalitarianism, 97; on ethnically determined work limitations, 56
Rodway, J.: on Aborigines, 138–39; on Chinese immigrants, 146; on Dutch-Aborigine intermarriage, 137
Ross, R. J., 19

Sahlins, M., 110
Schermerhorn, R. A., 17–18; on racist ideologies, 152–53
Scottish Nationalist Party, ideology of, 21–23, 25
Sederberg, P. C., on political action, 269–70
"Sense," definition of, 106
"Shame," definition of, 103, 106
Short History of the Guyanese People (Daly), 160
Slavery, introduction of, 129
"Small" as status category, 78–83
Smith, R. T., 33; on Chinese societal rank, 161; on creole elite, 161; on cultural exclusion of Portuguese, 142; on East Indian defensive organizations, 167; on East Indians, 149; on egalitarianism, 97; on European dominance, 151; on status symbols, 205; on work attitudes, 55
SNP. *See* Scottish Nationalist Party
Social and cultural interchanges, 25–28
Social geography, status and, 71–78
Social mobility, 184–92
Sociocultural and political order, egalitarian and hierarchical images of, 68–74
Socioeconomic standing, manners and, 110
"Stains": definition of, 103–4, 116; protection against, 118–21; surname and, 118
Status: achievement of, 92–124; categories, 78–83; claims, cultural syncretisms and, 226–46; Cockalorum-defined categories of, 123–24; competition, egalitarianism and, 94–101; competition, hierarchical ideology

About the Author

Brackette F. Williams is an
Associate Professor of Anthropology
at Queens College, New York.

Library of Congress Cataloging-in-Publication Data
Williams, Brackette F.
Stains on my name, war in my veins: Guyana and the politics of
struggle / Brackette F. Williams.
p.   cm.
Includes bibliographical references (p.   ) and index.
ISBN 0-8223-1114-3 (cloth). — ISBN 0-8223-1119-4 (paper)
Guyana—Civilization—20th century.   2. Pluralism (Social
ces)—Guyana—History—20th century.   3. Ethnicity—
—History—20th century.   4. Guyana—Ethnic relations.
nalism—Guyana—History—20th century.   I. Title.
F2384.W55   1991
90-47529
CIP